CONVOY!

CONVOY!
DRAMA IN ARCTIC WATERS

PAUL KEMP

CASTLE BOOKS

This edition published in 2004 by
CASTLE BOOKS ®
A division of BOOK SALES, INC.
114 Northfield Avenue
Edison, NJ 08837

This book is reprinted by arrangement with
Orion Publishing Group Ltd.
Orion House, 5 Upper St. Martin's Lane, London WC2H 9EA

First published by Arms & Armour 1993
Cassell Military Paperbacks edition 2000
Reprinted 2000, 2001

British Library Cataloguing-in-Publication Data
A catalog record for this book is available from the British Library

ISBN 0-7858-1603-8

Printed in the United States of America

Contents

Acknowledgements

I would like to express my thanks to the many people who have helped in the writing of this book: J. D. Brown of the Naval Historical Branch at the Ministry of Defence; Allison Duffield of the Department of Printed Books at the Imperial War Museum; Simon Robbins and Nigel Steel of the Department of Documents at the Imperial War Museum; Charles Stirling of the Fleet Air Arm Museum; Bob Todd of the National Maritime Museum; and the staffs of the Public Record Office and Kent County Library.

I am also deeply grateful to those people who have allowed to me to use, or quote from, their papers and interviews: Commander E. E. Barringer RNVR, James Caradus, David Chance, A. J. Clark, Surgeon Lieutenant J. C. H. Dunlop, Donald McKinnon, A. D. Newman, the late Admiral Sir Frederick Parham, Edward Reynolds, Commander R. F. C. Struben, Commander Stanley Walker and R. J. Wood. I am also grateful to the Controller of HM Stationery Office for permission to quote from official documents in the Public Record Office; to the Archivist at Churchill College, Cambridge, for permission to quote from the papers of the late Captain Stephen Roskill; to the Custodian of Manuscripts at the National Maritime Museum, for permission to quote from the papers of Rear-Admiral L. H. K. Hamilton; and to the Trustees of the Imperial War Museum for permission to use many of the photographs which appear in this book.

Particular thanks are due to Arnold Hague, who has generously shared with me the results of his own research into Arctic convoys and who also read the manuscript; to Roger Chesneau, for editing a very messy typescript; to David Gibbons and Tony Evans of DAG Publications, for producing the book; to Peter Burton at Arms & Armour Press, whose patience goes above and beyond the call of duty; and to my wife, Kitty, who has tolerated our house's being turned into an annexe of the Public Record Office without complaint.

Finally, this book is dedicated to my father James Kemp (1923–1991), a Merchant Seaman of the 1939–1945 War.

Paul Kemp

7

Chapter 1

Allies of a Kind

These people have shown themselves worth backing.
—Winston Churchill

When the German Army invaded the USSR on 21 June 1941, the Soviet authorities were taken completely by surprise. At a stroke the European diplomatic situation was transformed, and Britain, hitherto standing alone against Hitler, found herself with an ally of huge potential. However, the wartime alliance between Britain and the Soviet Union was not one of two like-minded states engaged through common ideology to common purpose. It was instead a joining of two states who at best distrusted each other deeply and were united by no more than the aim of defeating Germany. Yet during the Second World War, despite the gulf in ideology which separated the two countries, Britain strove to send as much aid to the Soviet Union as could be spared, even at the cost of her own requirements.

The communist government of the USSR was the pariah of Europe during the inter-war period. For the most part Britain and France, the dominant powers in Europe, viewed the Bolshevik government as little more than a bunch of regicides. The German Government took a more pragmatic view and from 1922 began the process of Russo-German *rapprochement* that was to culminate in the Treaties of Rapallo (1922) and Berlin (1926). There was little amity in these agreements between the two states, only self-interest. Diplomatic relations between the two countries were placed on a proper footing, the Soviets agreed to abandon their claims to a war indemnity from Germany and both parties agreed to remain neutral in the event of an attack by any third power. There were other, secret clauses which permitted the *Reichswehr* to train in the vast and hidden spaces of the USSR and which allowed the Red Army access to German training and equipment. Most important of all, the two treaties gave Germany security in that she would not be engaged on two fronts in the event of another European war. From the Soviet Union's point of view, the German alliance meant that there would be no grand anti-Bolshevik campaign against her.

The election of the Nazi party to power in Germany in 1933 caused a re-alignment of European alliances. An alliance with the Bolshevik government of the USSR was something the Hitler government regarded as doctrinally unsound and thus the Russo-German *rapprochement* was allowed to lapse. The gradual dis-engagement of Germany and the USSR did not pass unnoticed. The French Government, which spent most of the inter-war period trying to cobble together various alliance systems designed to place a *cordon sanitaire* around Germany, saw the chance to enrol a new member. The French had already concluded a Treaty of

9

Arbitration and a Non-Aggression Pact with the USSR in 1932; now, with German-Soviet relations in retreat, the French seized their chance and in 1934 concluded a full-scale Franco-Russian Treaty of Mutual Assistance.

Thus things remained until the summer of 1939, when Germany, having incorporated the Rhineland, devoured the Sudetenland and swiftly swallowed up the remainder of the Czech state, turned her attention to Poland with a series of demands relating to East Prussia and the free city of Danzig. At the same time the Germans unilaterally abrogated the German-Polish Non-Aggression Pact and the Anglo-German Naval Agreement. In a belated effort to contain the German demands, the British Government responded by offering unilateral and unconditional security guarantees to Poland, Rumania, Greece, Turkey and Belgium. These guarantees, though noble in intention, were valueless since there was no practical way in which Britain could aid any of these countries (except Belgium) in the face of German aggression without the co-operation of the USSR. Accordingly, the Chamberlain government sought to extricate itself from the difficulty it had created by asking the Soviet Union to guarantee the security of these countries. The Soviet Union had already proposed a Four-Power Pact (involving the USSR, France, Britain and Poland) which had been rejected by the Poles. Now the British enquired if the Soviet Union would protect any of her neighbouring states should they be attacked.

This was not enough for the Soviet Union, which wanted a binding military alliance. Both sides wanted an agreement—but not the same agreement. Stalin wanted an alliance which would offer the Soviet Union security in the face of a German attack and which would ensure that the Soviet Union did not fight Germany alone; Britain wanted the help of the Soviet Union in protecting Poland and the Baltic States. However, Britain wished to keep a certain distance from the Soviet Union since Whitehall feared that a grand Anglo-French-Soviet alliance would lead to the Soviet Union's exercising disproportionate influence in Eastern Europe. The talks dragged on throughout the summer of 1939 with each side becoming increasingly suspicious of the other.

As German pressure on Poland mounted, the Soviets' position became acute. They wanted an alliance—any alliance—which would guarantee their security. The Anglo-French proposals seemed at first to offer the best hope. Yet it became clear to the Soviets that the British at best were not interested in a Soviet alliance and at worst were deliberately drawing out the negotiations. British proposals were given almost instant replies by the Soviet Union, but it took weeks to elicit answers to Soviet questions from Whitehall.[1]

To a certain extent the Soviets' desperation played into the Germans' hands. Hitler was determined on military action to solve the 'Polish Question', but the position of the USSR in the event of a German invasion of Poland was a matter of concern. We know now that the prospect of a hostile Soviet Union would not have deterred Hitler from invading, but to have the country quiescent was an advantage.

The Germans' plans for the invasion of Poland were governed by the weather. The assault had to go in prior to the middle of September 1939, before the rains rendered the roads unsuitable for tanks and motor transport. It was at this juncture that Ribbentrop flew to Moscow to offer the Soviet Union an alliance—an oppor-

10

tunity which the Russians seized with both hands. Although the Soviet Government incurred universal odium for the signing of the Hitler-Stalin pact, the agreement at least satisfied its own criterion that the Soviets should not have'to fight Hitler on their own.

While the Germans won victory after victory in the west, the Soviet Union watched from the sidelines. In the meantime the Soviets had further damaged their reputation by taking a share of Polish territory and by their invasion of Finland. But by the summer of 1941 Hitler's strategic aims had focused on the Soviet Union and German forces were transferred from the west to holding positions in Poland. This vast movement of men and equipment did not pass undetected. The British were aware of the German Army's move to the east because of their interception and deciphering of German wireless signals, a capability which gave them a priceless window on German policy. Throughout the spring of 1941 the Churchill government, in a very generous gesture, warned the Soviet Government of likely German intentions—though naturally without revealing the source of the information. The Soviets did not treat the British warnings seriously, and Stalin chose to place his confidence in the alliance with Hitler. As one Soviet writer put it,

> Molotov had come back from Berlin thoroughly frightened: agents reported that Hitler was transferring his forces eastward; Hess flew to England and Churchill warned Stalin of an attack. Every jackdaw in the woods of Byelorussia and on the poplars of Galicia had shrieked war. Every peasant woman in every market-place in Russia had prophesied war day in, day out.[2]

Stalin's confidence was rudely shattered in the morning of 21 June 1941 when the German Army poured across the border.

Churchill was informed of the German invasion at 0800 on 22 June. His first move was to arrange to broadcast to the nation on the BBC that evening. As he prepared his broadcast throughout the day, he consulted with ministers and service chiefs and canvassed their opinions as to how the Soviets would fare. There was a widespread feeling that the Red Army would quickly be defeated. General Sir John Dill, Chief of the Imperial General Staff, believed that Russia would last no more than six weeks; others, including the Foreign Secretary, Anthony Eden, were of the same pessimistic opinion. Churchill dismissed their fears: 'I will bet you a monkey to a mousetrap that the Russians are still fighting, and fighting victoriously, two years from now'.[3]

Churchill had no doubts about the response that Britain should make to the German attack. In his broadcast that evening he was at his best:

> No one has been a more consistent opponent of communism for the last twenty-five years. I will unsay no word that I have spoken about it, but all this fades away before the spectacle which is now unfolding. The past, with its crimes, its follies, its tragedies, flashes away. The Russian danger is therefore our danger, and the danger of the United States, just as the cause of any Russian fighting for his hearth and home is the cause of free men and free peoples in every corner of the globe . . . we shall give whatever help we can to Russia.[4]

Churchill was true to his word. On 27 June the cryptographers at Bletchley Park had broken the 'Enigma' key being used by the German Army on the Eastern Front. Within twenty-four hours Churchill ordered that the fruits of this success be passed to the Soviet High Command—though in a form designed to conceal its origin. This was priceless military intelligence, and it enabled Stalin's commanders then and in the coming months to anticipate the Germans' advances.

On 10 July Churchill proposed the dispatch of a Royal Navy task force to work alongside the Soviet Navy in the Arctic. In recommending the scheme to his colleagues, he said:

> The advantage we should reap if the Russians could keep in the field and go on with the war, at any rate until the winter closes in, is measureless. A premature peace by Russia would be a terrible disappointment to great masses of people in our country. As long as they go on it does not matter so much where the front lies. These people have shown themselves worth backing and we must make sacrifices and take risks, even at inconvenience, which I realise, to maintain their morale.[5]

Two days later, in Moscow, an Anglo-Soviet agreement was signed pledging mutual assistance against Germany and no separate peace.

To investigate the practicality of sending a naval force to the Arctic, Rear-Admiral Philip Vian, commanding officer of the destroyer HMS *Cossack* and hero of the *Altmark* incident, was urgently ordered to leave his command on 12 July and report to London. There he was told that he was to go to the Soviet Union for discussions with Admiral Kuznetsov, Chief of Staff for the Soviet Navy, on the deployment of British naval forces to the White Sea or Murmansk. Vian, together with Rear-Admiral George Miles, who was joining the British military mission in Moscow, endured a twenty-two hour flight in a Catalina to Archangel, followed by another eight-hour flight to Moscow—a city which

> . . . presented a scene of drabness and squalor which bombed London never approached; everywhere women were digging trenches; every ear was deafened by the blare of propaganda loudspeakers.[6]

Discussions in Moscow were followed by visits to Polyarnoe and Archangel, where Vian met Admiral Arsenii Golovko, Commander-in-Chief of the Northern Fleet, who was to be the Soviet senior officer with whom the British had the most dealings concerning the Arctic. There was then the long flight back to London, where Vian was to brief Admiral of the Fleet Sir Dudley Pound, the First Sea Lord, and the other service chiefs.

Vian was never an officer to mince his words, and his recommendations were delivered in a characteristically forthright fashion. He did not consider the sending of a task force to the Arctic to be a realistic proposition:

> It seemed to me that there could be no future in sending a surface force to operate from the Kola Inlet in the summer months when there was twenty-four hours of daylight and the Germans were operating submarines and had airfields within thirty miles. Further,

it seemed questionable policy to use cruisers and destroyers, which I understood had been the intention, to operate against an occasional convoy in which German surface forces were not present. I suggested that we should send a submarine or two.[7]

This view was accepted by the Chiefs of Staff, but at a meeting of the War Cabinet the next day, the politicians threw up their hands in horror. Eden had already given Ivan Maisky, the Soviet Ambassador in London, an undertaking that a naval force would be sent. As a compromise solution, the Chiefs of Staff agreed to send the submarines to Polyarnoe and also to deploy naval forces in the Arctic so long as sufficient fuel were available for them to operate for useful periods of time.

On 19 July Stalin asked the British to help ease the pressure on the Red Army by distracting the Germans by means of landings in northern Norway and France. This was the first in a series of demands for the 'Second Front' which, as Churchill recorded, would 'recur throughout our subsequent relations with monotonous disregard, except in the Far North, for physical facts'.[8] Churchill felt duty-bound to put the proposals to the Chiefs of Staff, but they rejected them as too risky, given the lack of British resources. Churchill replied on 20 July 1941 that

... [the result] would be to encounter a bloody repulse while petty raids would only lead to fiascos doing more harm than good to both of us. It would be all over without their having to move, or before they could move, a single unit from your front. You must remember that we have been fighting alone for more than a year and that, though our resources are growing and will grow fast from now on, we are at the utmost limits of our resources both at home and in the Middle East.[9]

What could be done was already being done. As a start, the Admiralty had decided that the island of Spitzbergen should be investigated in order to discover whether it would serve as an alternative base to the Kola Inlet. There were two coal-mining settlements on Spitzbergen, one at Longyearby in Adeventfjord which was Norwegian and the other at Barentsburg in Granfjord which was under Soviet administration. There was no communication by land between the two settlements. It was feared that the first might have fallen under German control, while the second was obviously threatened.

Vian was ordered to hoist his flag in the cruiser HMS *Nigeria* and, in company with the cruiser *Aurora* and the destroyers *Punjabi* and *Tartar*, sailed from Scapa Flow on 27 July, arriving off Spitzbergen on the 31st. Both settlements were found to be free from German occupation, although both the Norwegian governor and the Soviet commissar had expressed doubts as to how long this position would remain. After clearing Spitzbergen, Vian proceeded to Bear Island—lying midway between Spitzbergen and the North Cape—where there was a meteorological station whose reports were of great value to the Germans. The station was destroyed and the Norwegian personnel were evacuated to England.

Back in London, Vian reported that, although the Spitzbergen archipelago undoubtedly possessed many fine natural harbours, there were absolutely no facilities on any of the islands and it would have taken an immense effort to establish an operational base there. Accordingly, it was decided to evacuate the mining communities and destroy the installations. It was accepted that Iceland would provide the most suitable alternative forward operating base, and thus Hvalfjord and Seidisfjord were established as defended anchorages for the Home Fleet. As it happened, the Admiralty's rejection of Spitzbergen as a base was somewhat premature: later in the war the islands proved useful as a fuelling rendezvous for convoy escorts, and at one time both Allied and German meteorological parties were operating there unknown to each other.

Although the reconnaissance of Spitzbergen had not led to the establishment of a base there, on 6 July the Admiralty had informed Admiral Sir John Tovey, Commander-in-Chief Home Fleet, that everything should be done to aid the Soviets. In particular, the latter had asked that attacks be mounted on German seaplane bases and transports in Kirkenes, Petsamo and Varangerfjord in northern Norway. Tovey pointed out the dangers involved in a daylight attack—there was no night in such high latitudes at that time of year—on ships in enemy harbours 1,300 miles away, with airfields close at hand. However, not for the first time in the story of the Arctic convoys, military rationale was overridden by political necessity.

Two aircraft carriers, HMS *Furious* and HMS *Victorious*, were available, but the latter had only just arrived at Scapa to begin working up with three new squadrons, 809, 827 and 828, and would require at least a fortnight before she would be ready for operations. On 23 July the two carriers, escorted by the 1st Cruiser Squadron and destroyers, left Scapa to carry out Operation 'EF'. The minelayer HMS *Adventure* accompanied the carriers to a position north of the Finnish coast, where she parted company and proceeded independently to Archangel, arriving on 1 August with her cargo of parachute magnetic mines.

Arrangements had been made for the whole force to fuel at Seidisfjord in Iceland on 25 July. Early that day the destroyer HMS *Achates* struck a mine near the south-east coast of Iceland and lost her bows and 65 members of her crew. She had to be towed back to Iceland by HMS *Anthony*, and the incident put back the operation by twenty-four hours.

By 30 July the carriers were in position to launch their aircraft and, thanks to bad weather, had remained undetected. But in the morning of 30 July, just as the aircraft were about to take off, the clouds thinned and the ships were spotted by a German reconnaissance aircraft. The vital element of surprise had now been lost, but it was too late to cancel the operation. Twenty Albacores and twelve Fulmars were flown off by *Victorious* to attack Kirkenes. They found few targets but encountered fierce opposition, and eleven Albacores and two Fulmars were shot down. Two merchant ships were sunk and another two damaged. *Furious* launched eighteen Albacores and six Fulmars against Petsamo. They encountered less opposition but found the harbour empty. Instead they attacked jetties, oil tanks and a repair yard, and two Fulmars and an Albacore were shot down. Despite the gallantry of the air crews, who had flown knowing that they had lost the element of surprise, the losses represented a serious setback.

Other assistance for the Soviet Union was being arranged. Two British submarines were sent to Murmansk, *Tigris* sailing from Scapa Flow on 26 July and *Trident* on 1 August. Both boats were based at Polyarnoe, where quarters had been arranged, including accommodation for spare crews, and the fullest co-operation was received from the Soviet authorities. However, in December 1941 the submarines—or rather their replacements, *Sealion* and *Seawolf*—were withdrawn on the grounds that there were insufficient targets to justify their continued maintenance in the theatre. The Senior British Naval Officer at Polyarnoe believed that there was a certain amount of jealousy of the British submariners by their Soviet counterparts, in spite of the bonds which unite submariners the world over.[10]

All these initiatives were encouraging and morale-boosting, but they did little to aid the USSR where it mattered. What the country really needed was supplies—*matériel* to make good the savage losses suffered by the Red Army in the initial thrust of the German attack until such time as the Soviet industrial machine, then in the midst of a colossal evacuation to sites east of the Urals, recovered.

In August 1941 Churchill met with President Roosevelt at Placentia Bay on board the battleship HMS *Prince of Wales*. After listening to Harry Hopkins, who had just returned from Moscow as Roosevelt's personal emissary to Stalin, they pledged aid to Russia on a 'gigantic scale'. In order to assess what was required by the Soviet Union, an Anglo-American military mission was dispatched to Moscow. The importance of the mission was underlined by the status of its two chiefs, Lord Beaverbrook for Britain and Averell Harriman for the United States. Both were masters of production. At their meeting with Stalin on 29 September the full Soviet 'shopping list' was handed over. It included anti-aircraft guns, automatic small arms and aluminium for aircraft manufacture.

On 1 October the Moscow Protocol was signed whereby Britain and America undertook to supply tanks, aircraft, oil, petrol, trucks, strategic metals and a host of other items. The Protocol was renewable annually[11] and was the cause of much haggling. However, it mentioned nothing about cargo losses as a result of enemy action. The Soviets, punctilious to the *n*th degree, regarded such losses as failures or sabotage by their allies rather than the hazards of war.

The Soviets could be very poker-faced about the aid supplied to them. One British naval historian, commenting on British aid to Malta and the USSR, wrote that 'the reception accorded to the material and those responsible for delivering it matched the respective climes'.[12] In addition to the aid agreed under the Moscow Protocol, on 30 October Roosevelt granted a $1 billion credit to purchase material under Lend-Lease and in February 1942 authorized a similar credit. On 7 November 1941 he declared that the defence of the USSR was vital to the national interests of the United States. This declaration formally brought the Soviet Union into the Lend-Lease programme and allowed it access to the vast resources of the USA.

Beaverbrook returned from the Soviet Union undismayed by the somewhat chilly reception which had been accorded him in Moscow and began to enlist the support of fellow ministers for his 'Aid to Russia' programme. Despite their rough treatment of him, the Soviets had a good friend in Beaverbrook for he began to urge the dispatch of as much *matériel* as could be spared, even at the cost of equipment required for Britain's own forces. He certainly convinced Churchill, who informed Stalin on 6 October that 'We intend to run a continuous cycle of convoys leaving every ten days'.

There were three ways in which supplies could be sent to the USSR: by sea around the north of Norway to the Soviet ports of Murmansk and Archangel; by sea from the United States and Canada across the Bering Sea to Siberia, thence overland via the Trans-Siberian Railway; and by sea to Persia (Iran) and thence by rail up through the Caucasus. The last two routes were comparatively unaffected by enemy action, yet their capacity was limited by the ability of Soviet railways to handle goods and by the immense distance the goods had to travel in order to reach the front. The sea route around the north of Norway was the shortest; it also delivered the goods near to the front—where they were most required—and there was, theoretically, no limit to the number of ships which could be included in a convoy. The only constraining factors were the port facilities at Murmansk and Archangel and the proximity of German bases in Norway and the Murman peninsula, which would mean the convoys' having to fight their way through. All three routes would be used throughout the war, but it was the Arctic route that was to become the most important in Anglo-Soviet relations.

Churchill's decision to aid the Soviet Union had been a magnificent, impulsive gesture, typical of the man. However, it added another burden to the Royal Navy, which was already overstretched in meeting worldwide commitments. Admiral Tovey calculated that a minimum of four cruisers and eight destroyers would have to be allocated to escort the convoys in addition to smaller units. This took no account of ships damaged by the weather—a frequent occurrence in those waters—nor of ships requiring refit or damaged by enemy action. He needed more cruisers and destroyers to screen his battleships should any German capital ships try to break out in the Atlantic, and he was constantly required to provide ships at short notice for other theatres. Although the Soviet Union undertook to ease the burden by providing escorts east of Bear Island, their assistance could not be counted on; thus the British force had to be large enough to take the convoy the whole way. The British commitment to the Soviet Union was a generous one and was a demonstration of a determination to aid anyone in the fight against Hitler. However, the decision to use the Arctic route to send supplies to the Soviet Union was a triumph of political expediency over military reality.

The decision to assist the Soviet Union proved to be very popular in Britain. On 22 September 1941 'Tanks for Russia' week began in British factories. Workers were told that anything they produced until the 29th of the month would be dispatched to the USSR. Beaverbrook, the Minister for Aircraft Production, launched an appeal:

Come then, in the foundries and forges of Britain, in the engine works and the assembly lines, to the task and duty of helping Russia to repel the savage invaders, who bring torment and torture to mankind.[13]

At a Midlands tank factory, on 22 September, the wife of the Soviet Ambassador in London named the first tank to leave the assembly line 'Stalin'. Other tanks further down the line bore the names 'Lenin' and 'Another for Joe'. Such patriotic sentiments were not above manipulation by management for the benefit of Britain's own war effort. In factories where labour relations were unusually bad, the labelling of an order with 'Goods for Russia' would guarantee speedy completion. A railway works at Ashford in Kent finished an order for 1,000 railway wagons for Russia in ten days, despite 76 air raid warnings. Thus there was a certain starry-eyed idealism about aid to the Soviet Union among the British public.

The story of the Arctic convoys exerts a particular fascination for the historian. It is not because the convoys suffered huge losses or were the cause of great actions: for example, though sinkings of merchant ships were high and there were a number of engagements, the losses suffered on the Arctic route came nowhere near those suffered by convoys going to Malta, where, on one occasion, they amounted to 50 per cent of the convoy's strength. Of the 41 convoys which went out to Russia, 30 made the passage without loss due to enemy action, while of the 34 homeward-bound convoys, 24 returned without loss. It is the adverse climatic conditions which have given these convoys a character of their own and earned them a distinct place in the history of the Second World War. The weather pushed officers and men to levels bordering on the limits on human endurance, where the cold was so sharp that no amount of clothing would keep a man warm.

After assembling in a Scottish loch or in the grim surroundings of Reykjavik in Iceland, the convoys sailed through the Norwegian and Barents Seas to the Soviet port of Murmansk at the head of the Kola Inlet, which was the only ice-free anchorage along the Soviet Union's northern coast. During the summer months the convoys would also use the ports of Archangel and Molotovsk on the White Sea.[14] The latitudes through which the convoys sailed are notorious for gales and blizzards of great intensity. The high latitudes also produce abnormal daily rhythms: in winter there is little or no daylight, while in the summer it is almost perpetual. These conditions would have a serious effect on the scheduling of the convoys—as would the seasonal movements of the polar ice-field, which in summer would recede, allowing the convoys to make a more northerly passage, but in winter would force the ships south, nearer to the German bases in northern Norway. Furthermore, the warm waters of the Gulf Stream, which run in a north-easterly direction along the Norwegian coast, create both fog and a very poor asdic environment.

As if the climatic horrors were not enough, the convoys faced considerable opposition from German naval and air forces stationed in Norway. The rugged and indented Norwegian coast provided the *Kriegsmarine* with superb deep-water anchorages, while the *Luftwaffe* was able to make use of airfields in the north of the country, particularly Banak. Once east of the Greenwich meridian, the convoys could not avoid coming within range of German aircraft for the rest of the journey; even while at anchor at Murmansk or Archangel, the merchant ships were subject to air attack. In the words of one historian, by sending supplies to the Soviet Union via the Arctic

> . . . we were undertaking the impossible task of passing convoys along hundreds of miles of enemy-held territory, where the air was completely dominated by the *Luftwaffe*, [and] the sea patrolled by most of the surviving enemy surface fleet and as many U-boats as Hitler cared to spare.[15]

To one British flag officer charged with escorting a convoy to the Soviet Union in the summer of 1942, the system was an 'unsound operation of war'[16] and to an ordinary seaman on board the sloop HMS *Lapwing* they were 'just hell on earth'.[17]

The first convoy, code-named Operation 'Dervish', had sailed from Liverpool on 12 August 1941. It consisted of six merchant ships carrying stores and aircraft, and an RFA oiler. The cargo of one of the ships, the *Trehata*, may be considered fairly typical of the types of cargoes carried: boots, 725 tons; cobalt, 4 tons; rubber, 3,990 tons; 'A' type mines, 20; depth charges, 750; crated fighter aircraft, 20; ethyl fluid, 150 tons; ground communications facility consisting of three trailers, 1.[18] At the same time as the 'Dervish' convoy, another operation, code-named 'Strength', was arranged to convey 48 Hurricanes aboard HMS *Argus*. It was necessary for the ships of the 'Dervish' convoy to arrive at Archangel four days before *Argus* since they carried the ground staff and necessary stores.

The convoy proceeded via Iceland, where the ships fuelled, escorted by three destroyers and three minesweepers. The covering forces consisted of the cruisers *Devonshire* and *Suffolk*, the aircraft carrier *Victorious* and three destroyers. This force left Scapa Flow on 23 August and met the convoy west of Bear Island on 26 August. On 30 August, off the entrance to the White Sea, the escorts parted company. The covering force turned back to escort *Argus*, which had left Scapa on 30 August escorted by the cruiser HMS *Shropshire* and three destroyers.

The 'Dervish' convoy arrived at Archangel on 31 August. The covering force successfully intercepted *Argus*, which, after a certain amount of manoeuvring to avoid the prying eyes of German air reconnaissance, successfully flew off her Hurricanes on 7 September. All the aircraft arrived safely at Murmansk.

In August the decision was taken that the mining communities on Spitzbergen should be evacuated. In Operation 'Gauntlet', Vian was sent back to complete the task following his reconnaissance in July. Flying his flag in HMS *Nigeria* and with *Aurora*, *Icarus*, *Anthony* and *Antelope*, together with the liner *Empress of Canada* carrying Canadian troops detailed for the demolition of the mines, Vian sailed from Scapa on 19 AugustThe Russian settlement at Barentsburg was the first to be visited. The mine was successfully destroyed and the 2,000-strong mining comm- unity embarked in *Empress of Canada*. However, the embarkation was not without problems, for in the process of the demolition and destruction of the settlement the community's vodka stocks were broached and there was mass drunkenness among the Russians. The Soviet Consul was in a particularly bad way, having

> . . . finished a further two bottles of champagne and half a bottle of Caucasian brandy and passed out. The consul was carried on board on a stretcher covered by a sheet so that his own people should not know what had happened to him.[19]

The Soviet authorities later complained that some of their people had been roughly treated and manhandled by the British, but, according to British documents,

> No man-handling was used at any time except where it was necessary to get the drunks aboard. A guard then had to be placed over the eau de cologne store because it was being looted by the Russians and they were drinking it.[20]

Nigeria and *Empress of Canada* then sailed for Archangel to land the Russians, after which they returned to Longyearby to evacuate the Norwegian community.

On the return journey to England Vian received a message informing him that a German convoy was expected to reach Hammerfjord at the northern end of the Norwegian Leads. The information had, of course, come from the deciphering of German naval signals. This was an ideal operation for the destroyers in Vian's force, but he felt that he could not leave the *Empress of Canada*, packed with Norwegian civilians, to make the remainder of the passage back to Britain unescorted. Accordingly, he left the destroyers to look after the liner and took the two cruisers to search for the convoy.

The appalling weather meant that the two cruisers could approach the coast unmolested by air reconnaissance. However, the poor conditions meant that fixing the ships' position accurately was extremely difficult, and Vian was probing his way inshore using radar.

At 0123 on 7 September *Nigeria*'s radar picked up contacts ahead, which were interpreted as being the land. Accordingly Vian brought the ships around to starboard to clear the land, but, as he did so, look-outs sighted ships off the port bow. The poor weather and the high rate of change of bearing had made conditions very difficult for the fire control team in the director, but it was clear that the radar contact interpreted as land was, in fact, a number of ships. This was the convoy that Vian had been ordered to intercept. It consisted of two transports carrying 1,500 troops of the 15th Mountain Division with their equipment and was escorted by the former gunnery training vessel *Bremse* (*Korvettenkapitän* von Brosy-Stein) and a number of smaller escorts. The action that followed was, because of the bad weather, brief and extremely confused.

Nigeria, with *Aurora* following astern, checked her starboard turn when the contacts were confirmed as hostile. She opened fire at 0129. She then sighted a two-funnelled vessel with the pennant number A03 (which was *Bremse*) off her port bow and crossing close across her bows. *Nigeria*'s director was trying to acquire the target which had been first sighted, a trawler, and in the confusion the order to switch target to the larger vessel was not heard. *Aurora* had originally thought to engage the trawler with torpedoes, but when *Bremse* was sighted Capt Agnew ordered the cruiser's 6in armament to engage that ship instead.

At the start of the action *Bremse* was steaming at 18kts and sighted the cruisers off her starboard bow at a range of about 2,000m. Because of her zigzag pattern, she found herself in the uncomfortable position of having the British cruisers between her and the convoy she was supposed to be protecting. She therefore increased speed to 24kts and made smoke while altering course to run parallel with them. Meanwhile the convoy and the close escort had made a quick turn to starboard to seek the shelter of the fjords as *Bremse* got off a sighting report.

The German vessel now received the full attentions of the British cruisers. With only three 15.9cm guns she was hopelessly outclassed; nevertheless, her crew put up a gallant resistance. By 0144 she was listing badly, with all her guns out of action and considerable damage on the upper deck. Brosy-Steinberg had no alternative but to order his crew to abandon ship. Thirty-seven men were later picked up.

The British cruisers had withdrawn just before daybreak and had set course for Scapa, where they arrived on 10 August. It had been a successful action, but the British ships had not escaped without damage. During the action, *Nigeria* had been violently shaken by a shock at 0137 which at the time was thought to have resulted from a collision with the wreck of *Bremse*. The damage extended from the forefoot up to the main deck and aft to the hawseholes. However, post-war analysis showed that *Bremse* was still afloat at this time and the true cause of the damage is a mystery which is likely to remain unsolved. The most likely explanation is that *Nigeria* struck a drifting mine, possibly one laid by a Soviet submarine. Alternative explanations which have been aired are that the cruiser struck a Soviet submarine and that she struck an uncharted rock.

These early operations were the prelude to a series of 41 outward-bound and 35[21] homeward-bound convoys to and from north Russia. After the war, the Soviet Ambassador to Britain, Ivan Maisky, described the convoys as

> . . . [a] northern saga of bravery, heroism and endurance. This saga will live for ever, not only in the hearts of your people, but also in the hearts of the Soviet people, who rightly see in it one of the most striking expressions of collaboration between Allied governments, without which our common victory would have been impossible.[22]

Such sentiments were all very well, but for the men of the Royal and Merchant Navies the convoys were a brutal ordeal fought out against a cruel climate and a dangerous enemy.

NOTES TO CHAPTER 1

1. Taylor, A. J. P., *Europe: Grandeur and Decline*, Penguin Books, 1974, p.126.
2. Solzhenitsen, Alexander, *The First Circle*, Collins/Fontana Books, 1970, p.133.
3. Gilbert, Martin, *Churchill—A Life*, Heinemann, London, 1991, p.701. Churchill was offering odds of 500-1 using racing parlance.
4. *ibid.*, pp.701–2.
5. *ibid.*, p.703.
6. Vian, Admiral of the Fleet Sir Philip, *Action This Day*, Frederick Muller, London, 1960, p.65.
7. *ibid.*, p.67.
8. Churchill, Winston, *The Second World War*, Cassell & Co, 1948–53, p.343.
9. Gilbert, *op. cit.*, pp.703–4.
10. SBNO Polyarnoe War Diary, January 1942.
11. The dates of the respective Protocols were: First Protocol—1 October 1941 to 30 June 1942; Second Protocol—1 July 1942 to 30 June 1943; Third Protocol—1 July 1943 to 30 June 1944; and Fourth Protocol—1 July 1944 to 12 May 1943. Thereafter aid was supplied under 'Pipeline' Agreements whereby the USSR contracted to purchase materials which had been assigned to it.
12. Brown, J. D., 'North Russia and the Navy', unpublished NHB paper S10505.
13. Calder, Angus, *The People's War*, Panther Books, 1971, p.302.
14. See Appendix 4 for a fuller description of these ports and their facilities.

15. Lewis, Michael, *The History of the British Navy*, George Allen & Unwin, 1957, p.233.
16. Hamilton Papers, National Maritime Museum.
17. Donald McKinnon to author, 19 February 1992.
18. Admiralty, 'The War at Sea—Preliminary Narrative', 1944, para 390.
19. PRO ADM.199/730, 'Reports of Proceedings, Operation Gauntlet'.
20. *ibid.*
21. The figures include the 'Dervish' convoy but not convoy JW.61A, which sailed in unique circumstances.
22. Schofield, Vice-Admiral B. B., *The Arctic Convoys*, Macdonald & Janes, 1977, p.137.

Chapter 2

All Aid to Russia—Now!

A wonderful chance, which may achieve most valuable results. God be with you.—Admiral Sir John Tovey to *Victorious*'s air crews before their attack on *Tirpitz*

Every Allied convoy during the Second World War was identified by a letter/number group which indicated its route and destination. For the new series of convoys running to the Soviet Union, the Admiralty chose the letters 'PQ' for the outbound convoys and 'QP' for those returning to the United Kingdom. The letters were chosen completely at random—they were, in fact, the initials of an officer in the Operations Division of the Admiralty, Commander P. Q. Roberts—but they would soon acquire a grim significance.

The first convoy in the series was in fact the homeward-bound QP.1, which consisted of the six merchant ships from the 'Dervish' convoy together with eight Soviet ships sailing in ballast to collect cargo in the west. The convoy sailed from Archangel on 28 September escorted by the cruiser *London*, which was relieved by *Shropshire* on 2 October. Other escorts included the destroyers *Electra* (28 September–9 October), *Active* (28 September–5 October) and *Anthony* (4–5 October). The trawlers *Macbeth* and *Hamlet* escorted from 28 September to 9 October, with *Ophelia* from 28 September to 5 October. During the early stage of the voyage the minesweepers *Halcyon*, *Harrier* and *Salamander* provided the local escort, but these vessels turned back on 30 September: they were now based in Murmansk and would be used for minesweeping ahead of convoys and for escorting merchant ships on passage to and from Murmansk, Archangel and other Soviet ports in the area. There was no enemy activity, and the convoy arrived safely at the Orkneys on 10 October. Two of the Soviet merchant ships, *Mossovet* and *Sukhona*, straggled from the convoy but arrived safely.

From 29 September, when convoy PQ.1 sailed from Hvalfjord, until the end of the year there were seven outward-bound and four homeward-bound convoys. Fifty-three ships were escorted to northern Russia and 34 returned. With the exception of PQ.6, all the convoys made their voyage unmolested by the Germans, and no merchant ships were lost. German destroyers sent out to look for PQ.6 encountered the minesweepers *Speedy* (Lt-Cdr J. G. Brooks DSC) and *Hazard* (Lt-Cdr J. R. A. Seymour) instead. The destroyers—*Z23*, *Z24*, *Z25* and *Z27*— mistook the British ships for much larger Soviet destroyers and so did not press home their attack. The only result was four hits on *Speedy*, which was quickly replaced by HMS *Leda* (Cdr H. A. Wynne-Edwards).

The only problem lay in the choice of Archangel as the reception port for the convoys. Archangel was selected because it was further away from the German air bases in Norway and therefore less vulnerable. However, it was not ice-free. Soviet icebreakers worked hard to keep the Gourlo (the entrance to the White Sea) open until 12 December for the arrival of PQ.5. The next convoy, PQ.6, had to go to Murmansk, where the port facilities were inadequate for dealing with so many vessels at once. As a result, five of the seven merchantmen in the convoy had to winter in Murmansk until the spring. One of these ships, the tanker *El Oceano*, operated for a period under Soviet control. While returning to Murmansk in February 1942 for a homeward-bound convoy, she broke away from her escort at night and made an independent passage to Iceland, where she arrived safely on 18 February—having caused a good deal of anxiety when she failed turn up at Murmansk as arranged.

With Archangel obviously unsuited as a reception port during the winter months, the convoys would have to go to Murmansk. In his diary for 10 December, Admiral Golovko wrote that 'Matters are evidently moving in favour of Murmansk becoming the reception port for the convoys' and went on to say that he had raised the matter with the Naval Staff in Moscow but to no avail. On Christmas Day, five days after the arrival of PQ.6 and with the port of Murmansk completely clogged up with shipping, he noted that 'The signs are that cargo vessels will sail into Murmansk. Now there is no end to our troubles.'[1] Nevertheless, by the end of 1941 a considerable amount of supplies had been delivered to the USSR by the Arctic convoy route—750 tanks, 800 fighter aircraft, 1,400 vehicles and more than 100,000 tons of general stores.

There had been no attempt to interdict the passage of the convoys by the Germans. However, in truth, the German Navy was in no position to launch such attacks since its strength was still depleted after the losses incurred during the Norwegian Campaign. The only German naval forces in Norway were five 'T' class torpedo boats,[2] which were not particularly suitable for operations in the heavy Arctic seas, together with a number of smaller craft.

German naval forces in Norway were under the command of Naval *Gruppe Nord*, Admiral Friedrich Boehm, based at Kiel. Boehm exercised general command through two Flag Officers based in Norway, Flag Officer Northern Waters (responsible for shore defences, minelaying etc) at Narvik and Naval Commander Norway (responsible for Fleet units through the Flag Officer Battle Group) at Oslo. This top-heavy and cumbersome organization existed until May 1943, when the appointment of Flag Officer Northern Waters was abolished, his duties being taken over by *Gruppe Nord*.

Despite the losses suffered during the Norwegian Campaign, the *Kriegsmarine* still possessed the capability to send a substantial battle group to Norway if desired: the new battleship *Tirpitz* was working up in the Baltic; the battlecruisers *Scharnhorst* and *Gneisenau* were, together with the cruiser *Prinz Eugen*, at Brest; and the pocket-battleship *Lützow* was completing repairs in the Baltic, where also were the cruisers *Hipper, Emden, Nürnberg, Leipzig* and *Köln* and all remaining destroyers and torpedo boats. In addition to naval forces there were also the 230 aircraft of *Fliegerkorps V* which were based at Petsamo, Tromsø, Banak, Bardufoss and Narvik. Although the air crews had not been trained in naval co-operation, the

24

port of Murmansk and the Kola Inlet were well within range and they were able to attack shipping anchored there.

Grand Admiral Erich Raeder, Commander-in-Chief of the *Kriegsmarine*, had stressed to Hitler the importance of capturing the port of Murmansk ever since the invasion of the Soviet Union began. However, his urgings went unheeded while Hitler's attention was wholly focused on the drive to Moscow. When the German offensive ground to a halt in the winter of 1941, Raeder was able to press his arguments afresh, particularly as evidence showed that the British were making increasing use of Murmansk as the destination for their convoys. At a conference with Hitler on 17 September 1941 he informed him that

> The British realise the vital importance of the sea route off the Arctic coast for supplies for the Soviet armed forces and they are operating in the Northern Area with several cruisers, destroyers, one or two carriers and submarines.[3]

He renewed his arguments on 13 November when he told Hitler that British activity had been less than expected but that the bad weather and long hours of winter darkness hampered air reconnaissance to a considerable degree. Raeder wanted to move *Tirpitz* to Trondheim once she had completed her work-up and been modified for the Arctic to counter the convoys, and he also wanted to send the pocket-battleship *Admiral Scheer* into the Atlantic on a commerce-raiding mission. He got an unenthusiastic response from Hitler, who was still smarting over the loss of *Bismarck* in May. The most Raeder could secure was the transfer of *Scheer* to Trondheim and the relief of the five 'T' class torpedo boats by five *Leberecht Maass* class destroyers,[4] which were much more suited to Arctic operations. It was these ships which had engaged the two minesweepers sent out to meet PQ.6.

In December 1941 the situation changed completely with the entry of the United States into the war. Now that this country was a belligerent rather than a very benevolent neutral, the flow of supplies to the Soviet Union increased dramatically. The Germans were slow to appreciate the impact that American entry into the war would have on the Arctic front:

> In 1941 the German High Command paid little attention to the shipping of war material to Soviet harbours. Hitler was convinced that the Soviets would not resist for long. . . After the failure of the attack on Moscow, as the war in the Soviet Union took on a new and unexpected character, a determined effort was made to stop the passage of the convoys, with the deployment of German naval forces, U-boats and air units.[5]

Raeder renewed his request for *Tirpitz* to be moved to Norway on 29 December. His arguments were supported by the fact that, only a few days previously, British commandos had raided Vestfjord and Vaagso Island. These operations, minor in themselves, had thrown the question of the defence of the Norway into sharp relief for the German High Command. Hitler, in particular, felt that Norway was the potential Achilles' heel of *Festung Europa* and was prepared to reconsider his earlier opposition to moving *Tirpitz*. Raeder used the situation to maximum effect. He argued that moving the battleship to Norway would strengthen the German position in the area and would lessen the risk of enemy operations designed to establish a bridgehead on Norwegian territory. *Tirpitz's* move to Norway would also provide opportunities for attacks on the convoys: the ship would be able to deal with the escorts while other units, such as destroyers, got in amongst the merchant ships. Lastly, the presence of *Tirpitz* in northern waters would impair the Royal Navy's ability to use the Home Fleet as a strategic reserve for other theatres, dispatching forces as and when necessary for specific operations, since a sufficient margin of superiority in home waters would have to be retained in order to deal with her should she venture forth. However, in a sense Raeder was bluffing, for the *Kriegsmarine* did not possess sufficient stocks of fuel oil for *Tirpitz* to carry out all these tasks. Nevertheless, his arguments were ultimately successful, for on 12 January 1942 Hitler gave in to Raeder's request.

Raeder wasted no time in implementing Hitler's order. *Tirpitz* (*Kapitän zur See* Richard Topp) had already been moved to Wilhelmshaven in anticipation of her being sent to Norway and successfully made the passage to Trondheim during the night of 14/15 January. The British did not notice her absence until 17 January, and, it being feared that she was on her way into the Atlantic on a commerce-raiding sortie, the sailing of PQ.9 was postponed. It was not until 23 January that *Tirpitz* was finally located in Asafjord, 15 miles east of Trondheim. The news of her discovery prompted Churchill to demand of the Chiefs of Staff that she be destroyed:

> The destruction, or even the crippling, of this ship is the greatest event at sea at the present time. The whole strategy of the war turns at this period on this ship, which is holding four times the number of British capital ships paralysed, to say nothing of two new American battleships retained in the Atlantic.[6]

Now that Hitler had been persuaded to send substantial naval forces to Norway, there was, seemingly, no stopping him. On 22 January, at another conference with Raeder, Hitler declared that the Norwegian theatre was the decisive one of the war and that all available ships and U-boats be sent there regardless of any other operational commitments. The battlecruisers *Scharnhorst* and *Gneisenau*, with the cruiser *Prinz Eugen*, were brought back from Brest via the English Channel. Both battlecruisers were seriously damaged by mines, which delayed them in German ports for repairs, but *Prinz Eugen* and *Admiral Scheer* proceeded to Trondheim between 20 and 23 February 1942. While en route for Trondheim, *Prinz Eugen* had her stern blown off by the British submarine *Trident* in an attack on 23 February and as a result had to spend nine months in dockyard hands. Nevertheless, these moves left *Tirpitz* and *Admiral Scheer* at the centre of a powerful battle group in Norwegian waters.

Hitler also ordered that the entire U-boat fleet to be sent to Norway. However, this directive was countermanded forty-eight hours later after the Naval Staff had pointed out that repair facilities in Norway were insufficient for such a large concentration of submarines. Even so, Raeder ordered that the number based there should be increased form six to eight. This met with some opposition from Rear-

Admiral Karl Dönitz, the head of the U-boat arm, who protested (unsuccessfully) that all his boats were urgently needed in the Atlantic.

From Britain's point of view, the Germans could not have chosen a worse time to open what was, in effect, another theatre of operations. Almost everywhere, the spring of 1942 marked the low point of Allied fortunes during the war. In the Far East, the Japanese seemed unstoppable: Singapore had fallen on 15 February, Java capitulated on 9 March, Rangoon was under Japanese occupation and the fate of India lay in the balance. The Japanese had also landed in New Guinea, posing a threat to Australia. In the Western Desert the *Afrika Korps* had pushed the British and Commonwealth forces back 300 miles toward Cairo in the first week of February. The Royal Navy had suffered huge losses in the Mediterranean and was now hard pressed to escort convoys to Malta against increasing air and naval opposition. The Battle of the Atlantic had entered its grimmest phase: U-boats sank a higher tonnage of merchant shipping in the quarter ending March 1942 than in any previous period and the slaughter showed no signs of diminishing. Only in the Soviet Union had Hitler's forces been checked. The German Army, having failed to deliver a decisive blow against the Red Army in the autumn, was forced to endure, unprepared, the rigours of the Russian winter and had suffered heavily as a result. The Royal Navy was stretched to the utmost. Serious casualties had been suffered,[7] while at the same time there was a need to find a new fleet for operations in the Far East.

By the time the Germans had taken the decision to oppose the sailing of the convoys to Russia, the first losses had already occurred. On 2 January 1942 the freighter *Waziristan*, one of two ships in convoy PQ.7A which had left Iceland on 26 December, having been separated from her consort during bad weather, found herself stranded on the edge of the polar ice-pack. She was attacked by aircraft and later given the *coup de grâce* by *U134* (*Kapitänleutnant* Rudolf Schendel).

PQ.8, the first convoy of 1942, had sailed from Hvalfjord in Iceland on 8 January with eight ships escorted by the minesweepers *Harrier* and *Speedwell*, joined on 11 January by the cruiser *Trinidad* and the destroyers *Matabele* and *Somali*. The Eastern Local Escort, consisting of the minesweepers *Hazard* and *Sharpshooter*, joined on 16 January and took the convoy into Murmansk the next day. Facilities for cargo reception in Murmansk were chaotic, and would remain so for some time. The tankers *British Pride* and *British Workman*, both carrying aviation spirit, discharged their cargoes directly into railway wagons on the jetty since there were no facilities for the bulk storage of petroleum products.[8]

However, PQ.8's passage had not been without incident. The convoy had been spotted by the Germans, and on 17 January *U454* (Kapitänleutnant Burckhard Hacklander) torpedoed the Commodore's ship *Harmatris* practically at the entrance to the Kola Inlet. *Harmatris*, though damaged, was able to proceed under her own power escorted by *Matabele* (Cdr A. C. Stanford DSC). However, the counter-attack was ineffectual, frustrated by poor asdic conditions, and Hacklander was able to stay with the convoy. Shortly afterwards he fired at *Matabele*, which sank within two minutes leaving only two survivors out of a ship's company of 200 officers and men. A large number of bodies wearing lifejackets were seen in the water where the destroyer had been sunk, and this rapid succumbing to exposure was a grim foretaste of things to come.

Up to the end of February there were a further two outward convoys (PQ.9/10, a combination of two sailings comprising ten ships; and PQ.11, of thirteen ships) and three homeward-bound convoys (QP.5, of four ships; QP.6, of six ships; and QP.7, of eight ships). All sailed and arrived safely without loss, although the freighter *Empire Redshank* of QP.6 had been damaged during an air attack on 31 January.

Convoys PQ.12 and QP.8 were the first to encounter a significant attempt by the Germans to interdict a passage. Each consisted of fifteen ships, and both were to sail on 1 March, from Hvalfjord and Murmansk respectively. The admiral responsible for the safe passage of the convoys was Admiral Sir John Tovey, Commander-in-Chief of the Home Fleet.

Tovey, born in 1885, was a destroyer specialist who had distinguished himself at the Battle of Jutland while in command of the destroyer *Onslow*. Rapid promotion followed in the inter-war period, culminating in his being appointed to command the destroyers and light forces in the Mediterranean Fleet—in which capacity he was second in command to the redoubtable Admiral Andrew Cunningham, by co-incidence another destroyer officer. In 1940 Tovey was appointed Commander-in-Chief of the Home Fleet and oversaw the destruction of the German battleship *Bismarck* in May 1941, for which he received the KBE. He was an officer of utter integrity who had established a great fighting reputation for himself. He was not afraid to make his opinions known, and it was this trait which brought him into conflict with Churchill. Tovey was much concerned about the Navy's lack of air support and never ceased to make the point. The Prime Minister, whose interest in naval affairs was considerable, considered Tovey to be 'stubborn and obstinate'. Whatever Churchill's opinion of Tovey, however, the latter's courage and integrity inspired a confidence throughout the Fleet which was to stand it in good stead throughout some difficult times.

In connection with the combined sailing of PQ.12 and QP.8, Tovey was aware that his prime concern was the safe passage of the convoys. However, he was also aware that *Tirpitz* might leave her Norwegian lair to attack the convoys, and therein lay the hope of bringing her to action. Accordingly he proposed dividing his forces. Vice-Admiral A. T. B. Curteis would take the battleship *Duke of York*, the battle-cruiser *Renown* and a screen of destroyers and cruise between 5°W and 14°E during their passage, while he remained at Scapa with *King George V*, the aircraft carrier *Victorious* and another cruiser. In this fashion Tovey would be free either to reinforce Admiral Curteis should the need arise or, alternatively, to deal with a possible break-out into the Atlantic by ships of the German squadron in Norway. Tovey felt that *Tirpitz* would not engage with Curteis's force but that his dispositions might allow him to cut off the German ship's retreat should she venture out. Moreover, Tovey had in the back of his mind the need to husband his strength for the summer, when he feared that, once their repairs were complete, *Scharnhorst* and *Gneisenau* would move to northern waters.

The Admiralty disapproved. Tovey was ordered to keep his ships together to ensure total superiority over *Tirpitz* should she sail, and to ensure the presence of fighter protection provided by *Victorious*'s aircraft. In view of Tovey's concern about a possible German break-out into the Atlantic, he was informed on 3 March 1942 that the Admiralty took 'full responsibility for for any break out of German ships which may occur while you are covering PQ and QP convoys'.[9]

Tovey therefore ordered Curteis, who was at Hvalfjord with his ships, to rendezvous with him at 71°N 3°E on 6 March, which was when PQ.12 was expected to be passing to the north of this position. Curteis sailed on 3 March and joined Tovey—who had departed from Scapa on 4 March—at 1200 on 6 March. The combined force comprised the battleships *King George V* and *Duke of York*, the battlecruiser *Renown*, the aircraft carrier *Victorious*, the cruiser *Berwick* and nine destroyers.

PQ.12 had sailed from Reykjavik on 1 March under the command of Commodore H. T. Hudson RNR with a Local Escort of trawlers. The minesweeper HMS *Gossamer* and five minesweeping whalers were to have joined the convoy on the 4th, but, in the event, only two of the whalers—one of which, *Shera*, later capsized in the Barents Sea owing to the weight of ice on the upper deck—made the rendezvous; the others passed the convoy without sighting it.[10] Early on the 5th the escort was augmented by the destroyers *Offa* and *Oribi* (Cdr J. E. H. McBeath, Senior Officer), which relieved the Local Escort 100 miles south of Jan Mayen Island, and later in the day the cruiser *Kenya* (Capt M. M. Denny) joined, having been detached by Admiral Curteis. Shortly afterwards the convoy was located and shadowed by a German reconnaissance aircraft, and that same evening came the news that *Tirpitz* and one 8in-gun cruiser had sailed from Trondheim and were steering to the north up the Norwegian coast.

The report came from the submarine HMS *Seawolf* (Lt R. F. Raikes RN), which was on a routine patrol off the northern approaches to Trondheim together with HMS *Trident* (Lt-Cdr G. M. Sladen RN). Air reconnaissance of the area on 5 and 6 March had failed to reveal that *Tirpitz* had sailed (she had, in fact, sailed at 1100 on 6 March), so it was left to the submarines to warn of her departure. *Trident* sighted a group of ships at 1700 on the 6th but was too far off to distinguish them. About half an hour later *Seawolf* sighted flying boats wave-hopping towards her and then faint smoke to the southward, followed by the emergence of the foretop and funnel of a large warship steaming fast up the coast about ten miles offshore. Two hours later Raikes brought *Seawolf* to the surface to send his sighting report, bitterly disappointed that he had not been able to launch an attack.

Before *Tirpitz* could menace PQ.12, the convoy had other problems to contend with. In the evening of 6 March considerable quantities of loose pack-ice were encountered, forcing the convoy on to a south-easterly course. During the night more ice was encountered and the destroyer *Oribi* was badly damaged. Next morning, however, the ice cleared and the convoy was able to resume its proper course, and there began a curious game of hide-and-seek in varying visibility and arctic squalls, with Tirpitz searching for the convoys, particularly PQ.12 (but luckily south of its track), and the Home Fleet hunting *Tirpitz* (but always to the south-east of her area of operations). The various groups were within 100 miles of each other during most of the day, and both *Tirpitz* and the convoy had narrow escapes, but the only contact which occurred was that between the German destroyer *Friedrich Ihn* and the merchant ship *Ijora*, a straggler from QP.8.

QP.8, consisting of fifteen ships escorted by the minesweepers *Hazard* and *Salamander* with the corvettes *Oxlip* and *Sweetbriar*, had sailed from Murmansk on 1 March. Local Escort was provided by the minesweepers *Harrier* and *Sharpshooter* until 3 March and by the Soviet destroyers *Gremyashchi* and *Gromki* as far west as 30°E. The cruiser HMS *Nigeria*, repaired after her action with *Bremse* and flying the flag of Rear-Admiral H. M. Burrough, Flag Officer Commanding 10th Cruiser Squadron, sailed the next day to provide close cover but failed to find the convoy in the bad weather and poor visibility and proceeded to Scapa independently. On 4 March the convoy was scattered by a heavy gale, but by noon on 5 March the ships, except for *Ijora* and *Larranga*, had re-formed. Another gale dispersed the convoy on the 6th, but by the 7th the ships had once again re-formed with the exception of the first two stragglers. These two gales had the combined effect of putting the convoy about 100 miles to the east of its scheduled position.

At noon on 7 March the two convoys passed each other in a snowstorm at 72°09′N 10°34′E, approximately 200 miles south of Bear Island. Some two hours later *Kenya* sighted smoke to the north, so she left PQ.12 to investigate and stood out from the convoy at high speed for about half an hour. The strange ship was steaming at about 7kts to the south-west; Capt Denny thought her to be a straggler from the homeward-bound convoy and therefore turned back to his own convoy.

At 1600 Denny received a signal from the Admiralty indicating that enemy surface forces might be near his convoy, a possibility arising from *Seawolf*'s sighting report of the previous evening, and that he should steer 360° until ordered to do otherwise. Accordingly, at 1640 the convoy obediently wheeled to the north. No sooner had the manoeuvre been carried out than Denny was informed that a distress message had been read, through the ship's company wireless set on the mess deck, from Ijora that she was being 'gunned' by a warship in position 72°35′N 10°50′E. Denny thought it more than likely that this was the vessel whose funnel smoke he had observed two hours earlier. She would now be 30 or 40 miles to the west of PQ.12, whose northerly course might lead the convoy straight into the path of the raider.

Denny assumed that neither the Admiralty nor Admiral Tovey was aware of PQ.12's alteration of course the previous evening to avoid the icefield and its consequent loss of distance: they probably supposed that the convoy was to the west of the enemy. He was also concerned that his northerly course would again lead him into the ice, against which he would be trapped should he encounter the enemy. Consequently he decided to turn away to 060° at 1800, but without signal for fear of giving away his position. Meanwhile *Kenya*'s Walrus was sent up at 1720 to search between the bearings of 210° and 270°. The Walrus returned shortly after 1800, having found nothing out to a range of 45 miles.

The Germans were prepared for the sailing of PQ.12 and QP.8. On 1 March air reconnaissance of Murmansk showed that the port was empty, while on 5 March PQ.12 was discovered. Measures to intercept this convoy were put in hand at once. Four U-boats at sea to the west of Bear Island were ordered to form a patrol line across the convoy's estimated track, and at the same time preliminary orders were issued to *Tirpitz*. This final decision required the assent of the *Führer*, who gave his approval on 6 March, and at 1100 *Tirpitz*, flying the flag of Vice-Admiral Otto Ciliax (who had recently distinguished himself by bringing *Scharnhorst* and *Gneisenau* home through the English Channel) and escorted by the destroyers *Hermann Schoemann*, *Friedrich Ihn* and *Z25*, left Trondheim and set course for the north. Ciliax's intentions were to avoid action with the British fleet if possible but to engage equal forces if his main objective—the destruction of the convoy—required that he do so.

Ciliax was ill-served by the U-boats and the *Luftwaffe* in terms of their providing further information about the whereabouts of PQ.12. No further reports were provided after Ciliax left Trondheim, so at 0850 on 7 March he detached the three destroyers to sweep to the NNW towards the estimated position of PQ.12. An hour later *Tirpitz* altered course to port in order to search further to the north-westward. The Germans were unaware that PQ.12 lay only 95 miles ahead of the destroyers, while Tovey's ships were 100 miles to the west of *Tirpitz* and steering a converging course.

On receiving *Seawolf*'s signal reporting *Tirpitz* at sea, Tovey had concluded that her target was PQ.12 since, as far as was known, QP.8 had not been sighted since leaving the Kola Inlet. He also considered the possibility that *Tirpitz*'s sortie was based on a false premise by the Germans that the convoy might be an invasion fleet bound for Norway. Accordingly, he continued to steer 060° throughout the night of 6/7 March while ordering *Victorious* to carry out an air search to a range of 120 miles in sector 065° to 115°. However, severe icing was experienced and no flying was possible all day. This was a great misfortune, for, had the search been flown, then *Tirpitz* would undoubtedly have been discovered.

At 0930 on 7 March Tovey turned to the north in the hope of escaping the fog, but conditions did not improve and at 1130 he steered away to the south-west in the hope of finding clearer weather and being in a central position to cover both convoys. Meanwhile Admiral Ciliax was continuing to head north-west and was gradually closing the British fleet. Ciliax had ordered *Tirpitz*'s two Ar 196 seaplanes to fly a reconnaissance mission on the morning of the 7th but, like Tovey's reconnaissance, this operation was frustrated by bad weather. Had the floatplanes been able to fly, then they would certainly have encountered the British ships—which would have come as a considerable surprise to Ciliax, who had no idea that substantial enemy forces were at sea, let alone so near. In the event *Tirpitz* passed some 60 miles to the east of Tovey's ships at 1300. At the same time Ciliax altered course to the north so that the distance between the two forces opened rapidly.

The two convoys had passed each other an hour previously. This was the most dangerous time for them, since, although PQ.12 was heading out of danger to the north-east, PQ.8, on a WSW course, was only 50 miles to the north-east of *Tirpitz* and much nearer to the German destroyers which were sweeping to the NNW, spread out five miles apart in line abreast. The two forces were tantalizing close to one another, for the right-hand ship, *Z25*, must have passed only 10 miles ahead of the convoy shortly before 1400 but no contact occurred. However, at 1545 the destroyer *Friedrich Ihn* sighted smoke to the north-east, which turned out to be from *Ijora*, a straggler from QP.8 which had been sighted by *Kenya* earlier in the afternoon. *Ijora* was swiftly disposed of, and, as she sank, *Tirpitz* hove into sight, Ciliax having closed the position on receiving *Ihn*'s report in the hope that the remainder of the convoy would be nearby. The sinking hull of *Ijora* would be the only enemy vessel sighted by the German battleship in the course of her career.

The three destroyers rejoined *Tirpitz* at 1728 and Ciliax decided to head east in the hope that the convoy had been diverted or turned back on receiving *Ijora*'s distress call. But the destroyers were running short of fuel. Ciliax had hoped that they could take fuel from *Tirpitz* during the night, but the weather made it impossible. At 2035 *Friedrich Ihn* was detached to return to Tromsø and the other two were sent back at 0400 on the 8th, leaving *Tirpitz* to continue alone.

Meanwhile the Home Fleet had been steering south-east all afternoon in the hope of finding clearer weather. At 1632 *Ijora*'s distress signal was received, followed shortly afterwards by a DF bearing on an enemy transmission which was plotted as being 200 miles north-east of the fleet. Tovey considered that the signal came from *Tirpitz*, which he thought was returning to port, and, acting on this assumption, he altered course to ESE at 1750. However, in the chance that the signal might not be *Tirpitz*'s, he ordered Capt H. T. Armstrong (D17) in HMS *Onslow* to take the destroyers *Punjabi*, *Fury*, *Ashanti*, *Echo* and *Eclipse* and head south-east and intercept *Tirpitz* should she be coming south, while he took the remainder of the fleet toward Bear Island in case the German were remaining in the north. However, before the destroyers had left, several signals were received from the Admiralty as a result of 'Ultra' decrypts which indicated that *Tirpitz* was prepared to remain at sea for some time and operate well to the east of Bear Island—and, more importantly, that the Germans were unaware that the Home Fleet was at sea. In these circumstances Tovey kept the destroyers with him and stood on towards Bear Island to cover PQ.12.

At 1940 another DF bearing was received from the same unit which indicated that the German battleship was moving south at high speed, so Armstrong was detached with his destroyers at 2009. They searched to the north until 0600 the next morning but found nothing. Armstrong then proceeded to Iceland to fuel. At midnight on the 7th/8th Tovey turned back to the south to be in a position to launch an air strike should the destroyers encounter *Tirpitz*, but by 0400 he knew that the latter had eluded him. He gave orders to head for Iceland to pick up some destroyers, for, since the departure of Armstrong's ships, he did not wish to remain long without a screen.

In the morning of the 8 March the general situation was as follows. PQ.12 was 90 miles to the south of Bear Island and was steering 40°. Ninety miles to the south-east, *Tirpitz* was on an easterly course but would (at 0700) swing round to the north to search the waters around Bear Island. About 250 miles to the south-west of *Tirpitz*, the Home Fleet was just about to head for Iceland since Tovey was under the impression that the Germans had abandoned the operation. QP.8 was out of danger, being nearly 300 miles WSW of *Tirpitz* and steadily opening the range.

Throughout 8 March *Tirpitz* and PQ.12 manoeuvred within 120 miles of each other around Bear Island. Around noon *Tirpitz* came within 80 miles of the convoy and the Admiralty, who were plotting her position from intercepts, ordered it to go north around Bear Island. This signal was ignored by Capt Denny in view of the masses of ice lying around the island and the damage already sustained by *Oribi*. Instead he continued to follow the southern edge of the ice.

At 1120 Ciliax received a signal from *Gruppe Nord* which indicated other areas to the west of his current position where the convoy might be found. However, at 1820 he received a further signal from *Gruppe Nord* informing him that the convoy had possibly turned back after being sighted on the 5th and leaving the decision to him as to whether or not he remained at sea. Ciliax decided that he had had enough and at 2025 signalled his intention to return, asking for destroyers to meet him west of Vestfjord. Ten minutes later *Tirpitz* swung round to 191° and headed for the Norwegian coast.

Ciliax's signals acknowledging the 1830 message from *Gruppe Nord* and his request for destroyers had presented the Home Fleet with excellent bearings indicating that a German unit was moving south. Moreover, by a stroke of luck the code-breakers at Bletchley Park had broken Ciliax's signal of 2025 (which had been repeated back to him by *Gruppe Nord* at 2232) with a delay of only three hours. Tovey received the news that *Tirpitz* was heading south at 0240 on 9 March. Up to that time he had been heading for Iceland, but at 1830 on 8 March he had been obliged to break wireless silence to ask the Admiralty to operate his cruisers and destroyers for him owing to his great difficulties of communication. He also hoped that his signal would be intercepted by the Germans, who would then recall *Tirpitz*. This would not only ensure the safety of the convoy but would bring the German battleship within range of *Victorious*'s aircraft. The Admiralty acted swiftly. The cruisers *Kent, London, Trinidad* and *Liverpool* were stationed off Jan Mayen Island to provide fuel for Tovey's destroyers, while every available destroyer in Iceland, Scapa Flow, Rosyth and Loch Ewe was ordered to prepare for sea.

Now, with the news that he might still catch *Tirpitz*, and regardless of the fact that he had no destroyer screen, Tovey swung his ships round to head for the Lofoten Islands while working up to 26kts. *Tirpitz* was then 200 miles to the east and it was just possible to reach a position near enough for a dawn air strike, so a searching force of six Albacores from 817 and 832 Squadrons was flown off at 0640, followed by a striking force of twelve, seven from 832 and five from 817, armed with torpedoes and led by Lt-Cdr W. J. Lucas of 832 Squadron at 0730. The Fairey Albacore was a torpedo-bomber-reconnaissance aircraft which had entered into service in the summer of 1940 and represented an improvement on the earlier Swordfish. It was powered by the 1,010hp Bristol Taurus engine, which gave a maximum level speed of 155kts, or 130kts when the aircraft was carrying a torpedo. Considerable attention had been paid to aerodynamics: the pilot had an excellent view from the cockpit, which was fully enclosed, as was the cockpit for the observer and telegraphist/air-gunner (TAG). It was intended to fit the Albacore with air-to-surface-vessel (ASV) radar, but great difficulty was experienced in so doing, and only six of the aircraft on board *Victorious* were radar-equipped.

When the aircraft were launched, *Tirpitz* had been 115 miles to the east, heading straight for Trondheim. At 0650 she was joined by *Friedrich Ihn*. At 0800, when only 70 miles from the Home Fleet, she was sighted by Albacore '4F' and a brief sighting report was transmitted at 0803. This initial report was amplified by messages from '4L' while two other aircraft, 'H' of 832 and 'F' of 817, took up shadowing positions. Albacore '4F' had been sighted at 0815, and Ciliax knew that it was but a matter of time before the main strike force arrived. He therefore sent up a single Ar 196A to drive off the shadower while altering course to head directly for Vestfjord and Narvik—only 50 miles away.

Meanwhile the strike aircraft were heading in at 500ft and had received the initial sighting reports and the report of *Tirpitz*'s alteration of course. At 0845 Lt-Cdr Lucas began the climb up to 3,500ft. The Albacores were now closing *Tirpitz* in the cloud and were using ASV radar to track her movements. Cloud and radar were the aircraft's only assets. Since the quarry was heading at 26kts into a 35kt wind, and because the aircraft were approaching at their best cruising speed of 90kts, the closing rate was one mile every two minutes. At the same time *Tirpitz*'s Ar 196 was doing its best to drive off the persistent '4F'. The Arado made several unsuccessful passes, but on each occasion the Albacore took refuge in the cloud. However the German aircraft was more succesful against '5K', whose observer, Sub-Lt(A) G. Dunworth RNVR, was wounded.

At 0917, when *Tirpitz* was less than a mile away, the strike aircraft reached a break in the clouds. Alas, the aircraft were poorly placed for attack. Lucas's flight of three aircraft was on *Tirpitz*'s port beam, but the remaining aircraft were all to starboard of the target. If *Tirpitz* should turn to port to avoid Lucas's torpedoes, then the other aircraft would not be in a suitable position for an attack. Lucas decided to attack immediately, fearing that if he waited until his aircraft had attained a better position, *Tirpitz*'s guns' crews would be alert and waiting. He led the first three aircraft into the attack at 0920, but all the torpedoes missed astern. The next group of aircraft to attack, the second sub-flight of 817 Squadron, crossed over to *Tirpitz*'s port side to cover evading action in that direction, leaving the other six aircraft to attack from the battleship's starboard side. However, once again, all three torpedoes missed astern.

During the two attacks, *Kapitän zur See* Karl Topp had handled his ship with consummate skill. He first turned her to port, then brought her back to starboard, thus completing an 'S' turn. The remaining six Albacores came in at 0925 but once again all missed astern. Two of the aircraft of this group were shot down and others sustained minor damage. The surviving aircraft returned to *Victorious* and landed-on at about 1100:

> Never again was the opportunity to occur for carrier aircraft to slow *Tirpitz* in the open sea so that the Home Fleet could bring her to action and destroy her like her sister ship.[11]

Capt H. C. Bovell of HMS *Victorious* was not happy with the results of the attack and blamed the unfortunate Lucas who, he felt, had initiated the attack too early with his aircraft unfavourably disposed. Bovell also considered that the torpedoes were released at too great a range. The criticism was somewhat strong, and the air crews cannot be wholly blamed. Lucas was new to the squadron and had not had the opportunity to fly with them. Moreover, air-launched torpedo attacks were a skilled business requiring intensive training and constant practice. The far-flung requirements of the Home Fleet meant that no capital ships could be made available solely for air crew training.

Tirpitz gained the security of Narvik during the afternoon of 9 March and, after a brief respite, sailed for Trondheim, where she arrived in the evening of the 13th. Her wanderings around the Barents Sea, and those of her destroyers, had cost the *Kriegsmarine* 8,100 tons of fuel with nothing other than the sinking of the unfortunate *Ijora* to show for it. The following day Tovey brought the Home Fleet back to Scapa. Of the convoys, which had been the cause of all the action, PQ.12 arrived on 12 March at Murmansk and QP.8 arrived at Hvalfjord on 11 March with some ships going on to Akureyi.

The whole episode gave Tovey much food for thought. *Tirpitz*'s aimless meanderings in the Arctic convinced him that the Germans would not place any of their capital ships at risk by engaging the British Fleet. On 14 March he signalled this new appreciation to the Admiralty:

> The *Tirpitz*, by her existence, contains very large British and United States forces and prevents their transfer to the Far East or the Mediterranean. She is so valuable an asset to all the Axis powers that I am convinced that the enemy will not expose this unique and irreplaceable asset to any unnecessary risk. The promptitude with which she entered the nearest harbour when attacked by aircraft from the *Victorious* . . . supports my conviction.[12]

On this assumption, Tovey argued that he preferred the disposition of his forces which he had suggested in early March. He considered that taking the whole of the Home Fleet into submarine-ridden waters was a 'risky proceeding'[13] since he was often without a destroyer screen as these ships were of limited endurance and as refuelling techniques at sea were primitive in the extreme. Tovey did not mince his words and told the Admiralty (though in reality his remarks were addressed directly at Admiral Pound) that he was 'seriously embarrassed' by the Admiralty's detailed instructions on how he should handle his ships. He argued that the destruction of *Tirpitz* was his main priority and that it was worth risking a convoy to achieve it.

Some of the Admiralty's 'interference' was justified since Their Lordships had access to the priceless 'Ultra' signals. But Tovey did have a point: Pound had an unwelcome tendency to intervene in the most trifling operational matters. The Admiralty did take some of Tovey's comments to heart. They felt that Tovey's proposals for dividing his force would not leave a sufficient margin of superiority over *Tirpitz*—particularly in view of the experience with *Hood* and *Prince of Wales* against *Bismarck*—but did agree that Tovey should not go beyond 14°E without a destroyer escort. They also accepted that the destruction of *Tirpitz* was his first priority, though they considered that the best way of achieving this was to provide a strong escort to the convoys.[14]

If the British were dissatisfied with their operational performance, then it had an even more profound effect on the Germans. The attack by the Albacores had been particularly impressive. Of the bravery shown by the air crews, Admiral Ciliax had written that they 'had displayed the fanaticism of which every Briton is capable'.[15] *Tirpitz* had escaped unharmed, but the *Seekriegsleitung* (SKL) were shocked at how easily she might have been sunk. The German Naval Staff considered that

> The *Tirpitz* operation had not resulted in any great success. Only sheer good fortune had saved the ship from damage by enemy ships, torpedo bombers and submarines. But the operation clearly revealed the weakness of the German Navy's position in the north. Vice-Admiral Ciliax pointed out that operations by single ships without adequate air cover in an area patrolled by the British fleet offered slight prospects and were not worth a great risk. Grand Admiral Raeder stressed the risk involved in such operations in view of the lack of aircraft carriers and the weakness of the *Luftwaffe*. He queried whether the use of capital ships in this way was consistent with their main task of defence against invasion . . . The lesson derived from the *Tirpitz* operation appeared to be that caution must be used in the employment of warships, if they were to be kept in a fit state to repel an invasion.[16]

Thus Hitler ordered that, in future, *Tirpitz* was not to be used unless the position of British aircraft carriers was accurately known—a restriction which was to limit the *Kriegsmarine*'s options considerably, so much so that the ships's intervention in future operations was highly unlikely. *Tirpitz* was to be preserved as a deterrent to a British invasion of Norway, and even a whole convoy was not worth her loss.

Raeder rightly complained, though, that the lack of accurate air reconnaissance had been a main factor in both *Tirpitz*'s failure to achieve anything and her nearly being sunk. To balance British superiority in naval air power, Raeder persuaded Hitler to sanction the resumption of work on the unfinished aircraft carrier *Graf Zeppelin* and the conversion of the cruiser *Seydlitz* and of the liner *Potsdam* for this role. However, the jealously of *Reichsführer* Hermann Göring would ensure that the *Kriegsmarine* never received the air arm it needed. Raeder was more successful in having the *Luftwaffe* forces in Norway reinforced. *KG 26* and *KG 30*, specially trained torpedo-bomber units, were transferred to Norway together with *I/KG 40* with its long-range FW 200 reconnaissance aircraft. Moreover, on 19 March the cruiser *Admiral Hipper* joined *Tirpitz* and *Scheer* at Trondheim. Thus the *Kriegsmarine* was now committed to two tasks in Arctic waters—the destruction of the convoys and the defence against invasion. As a compromise, the SKL decided to keep *Tirpitz* as a deterrent against invasion while employing light forces, particularly destroyers, against the convoys.

The first assault on an Arctic convoy had not been successful for the German Navy. Nevertheless, the build-up of its forces in Norway indicated that its determination to stop the convoys was increasing.

NOTES TO CHAPTER 2

1. Golovko, Admiral Aresnii, *With the Red Fleet*, Putnam & Co, London, 1965, p.86.
2. 'T' class torpedo boats: displacement 844 tons (*T5–T12* 839 tons); dimensions 269ft 8in (wl) x 28ft 3in x 9ft 8in (max); armament one 105mm, one 37mm and five to eight 20mm

guns, plus six 533mm torpedo tubes and 30 mines (optional); speed 35.5kts; complement 119 officers and men.

3. *Führer's* Conferences on Naval Affairs.

4. *Leberecht Maass* class destroyers: displacement 2,200 tons; dimensions 374ft x 37ft x 9ft 6in; armament five 12.7cm, four 37mm and six to eight 20mm guns, plus eight 533mm torpedo tubes; speed 30kts; complement 315 officers and men.

5. Von Tippleskirch, *Geschichte des Zweiten Welt-Krieges*, Athenaum Verlag, 1951, p.552.

6. Churchill, Winston, *The Second World War*, Vol IV, Cassell & Co, 1948–53, p.98.

7. *Ark Royal* and *Barham* had been sunk in the Mediterranean and *Prince of Wales* and *Repulse* off Malaya, while *Valiant* and *Queen Elizabeth* had been badly damaged by Italian 'human torpedoes'.

8. John Eyre to author, 10 February 1993. John Eyre was a cadet on board *British Pride*.

9. PRO ADM.234/369: 'Battle Summary No 22: Arctic Convoys 1941–45', 1954, p.7.

10. *Gossamer* and one whaler proceeded independently to Murmansk; two of the whalers put back to Iceland.

11. Barnett, Corelli, *Engage the Enemy More Closely*, Hodder & Stoughton, 1991, p.701.

12. PRO ADM.234/369, p.21.

13. *ibid.*

14. It is unclear whether these views were conveyed to Tovey, for no reply to the latter's letter of 14 March 1942 can be found in the PRO files.

15. Brown, D. J., *Tirpitz: The Floating Fortress*, Arms & Armour Press, 1977, p.21.

16. Admiralty, 'German Surface Ships, Policy and Operations', p.105.

11-1-07 's
Tim Horton's
Fenton

Chapter 3

The Political Imperative

If they [the convoys] *must continue for political reasons, very serious and heavy losses must be expected. The force of German attacks will increase not diminish. We in the Navy are paid to do this sort of job but it is beginning to ask too much of the men of the Merchant Navy.*—Rear-Admiral Stuart Bonham-Carter

The next pair of convoys, PQ.13 and QP.9, sailed on 20 and 21 March respectively, while the lessons resulting from *Tirpitz*'s sortie were still being digested by both sides. As a result, the disposition of the British covering forces remained unaltered. Admiral Tovey sailed with the battleships *King George V* and *Duke of York*, the battlecruiser *Renown*, the aircraft carrier *Victorious*, the cruisers *Kent* and *Edinburgh* and eleven destroyers. The Close Escorts for the convoys were, however, rather meagre. PQ.13 was escorted by the destroyers *Eclipse* and *Fury*, the trawlers *Blackfly* and *Paynter* and the whalers *Sulla*, *Simba* and *Silja*. The Eastern Escort consisted of the destroyers *Oribi*, *Gremyashchi* and *Sokrushitelny* with the minesweepers *Gossamer*, *Hussar* and *Speedwell*. QP.9 had an Eastern Escort of the minesweepers *Gossamer*, *Hussar*, *Harrier*, *Niger* and *Speedwell* with the Soviet destroyer *Gremyashchi*. The Ocean Escort consisted of the destroyer *Offa* and the minesweepers *Britomart* and *Sharpshooter*. The cruiser HMS *Trinidad* (Capt L. S. Saunders) provided close cover to PQ.13, while *Kenya*, carrying ten tons of bullion, was due to cover QP.9 but did not make the rendezvous. HMS *Nigeria* cruised to the west of Bear Island in support.

The Admiralty feared another sortie by German heavy surface ships, particularly as *Admiral Hipper* was going north to Trondheim, but they were unaware that any operations were limited to destroyers owing to insufficient fuel stocks. Before the convoys sailed, Tovey issued the following instructions:

> I wish it to be clearly understood that in the event of a Russian convoy being attacked by a force overwhelmingly superior to the escort, the primary object of the escort is to ensure the enemy being shadowed to enable them to be brought to action by our heavier forces or submarines, or to be attacked after dark, or under more suitable conditions by the escort itself. Any delaying action is to be taken with this primary object in view.[1]

QP.9 had a relatively uneventful passage. During a snow squall on 24 March the minesweeper *Sharpshooter* sighted a U-boat, *U655* (*Kapitänleutnant* Otto Dumrese), on the surface and immediately turned in to ram. The U-boat rolled over and disappeared. There were no survivors. *Sharpshooter* sustained the inevitable damage to her bows as a result of this encounter but was able to continue with the convoy, which arrived at Reykjavik without loss on 3 April. PQ.13, however, endured the full Arctic repertory of foul weather and attacks by enemy ships, submarines and aircraft. Four days after leaving Reykjavik the convoy was struck by a fierce north-easterly gale which lasted for four days and scattered the escorts and merchant ships over an area of 150 miles. By 27 March the gale had abated to a certain extent and the cruisers *Trinidad* and *Nigeria* joined in the task of rounding up the scattered merchant ships. While engaged in this work on 28 March there came the unwelcome sight of the three-engine BV 138B reconnaissance aircraft. Powered by 880hp Junkers Jumos, the BV 138 had a range of 2,670 miles and was to become horribly familiar to men on the Arctic convoys as the warning of imminent air attack. Even when, from PQ.18 onwards, the convoys were given their own air cover, the brutes were so heavily armoured that they could often fend off the fighter attacks.

Air attacks did soon follow: an hour later Ju 88s of *III/KG 30* arrived, and these aircraft made intermittent attacks throughout the day which resulted in the stragglers *Raceland* and *Empire Ranger* being sunk. The trawler *Blackfly* was sent to look for survivors but failed to find any. Meanwhile the destroyers *Z24*, *Z25* and *Z26*, under the command of *Kapitän zur See* Pönitz in *Z26*, had sailed from Kirkenes on receipt of the BV 138's sighting report. On reaching the convoy's estimated line of advance, he spread his ships at intervals of three miles and commenced a sweep to the north-west. That evening he sighted a boat-load of survivors from the *Empire Ranger* and rescued them. It is possible that some useful intelligence was obtained from these survivors, for on 29 March *Fregattenkapitän* Fritz von Berger's *Z26* found the freighter *Bateau* and sank her with gunfire and torpedo after taking off the seven-man crew. Pönitz was now building up an accurate picture of the convoy's strength and whereabouts from his prisoners and, deciding that he should should be sweeping to the south, ordered his ships to alter course at 0140 on the 29th. This move in fact took the German ships too far to the south, so at 0530, when he had sighted nothing, he turned and ran north for three hours before resuming the westerly sweep, heading into deteriorating weather all the while.

In fact, the convoy was now in two groups which were about 80 miles apart, with four ships whose whereabouts were unknown. The westerly group of eight ships was being escorted by HMS *Eclipse* (Lt-Cdr E. Mack) and the trawler *Paynter* (Lt R. H. Nossiter DSC RANVR). At 0645 on the 29th they were reinforced by HMS *Oribi* and the Soviet destroyers *Gremyashchi* and *Sokrushitelny*. At 0843 the cruiser *Trinidad*, with *Fury* in company, was steaming east to collect the easterly group of four ships and bring them back to the other group when *Trinidad*'s radar picked up a contact bearing 079° at a range of 6½ miles. Six minutes later the German destroyer *Z26* came in sight almost right ahead. *Trinidad* immediately turned to starboard to open her 'A' arcs and opened fire at a range of 2,900yds. *Z26* took violent avoiding action and, although being hit, managed to seek the safety of the mist. *Trinidad* manoeuvred to avoid any torpedoes which the destroyer might have fired, and at 0922 she fired one at *Z26* which had reappeared and was seen to be alight. The torpedo appeared to be running true, but two others failed to leave their tubes because of icing. Meanwhile *Trinidad* was still pounding the unfortunate *Z26* with 6in shell and all was going well, when at 0923 a torpedo broke surface 200yds off

Trinidad's port bow. Although the wheel was put hard over to port, it was too late and the torpedo struck on the port side. The ship assumed a 17-degree list and her speed fell to 8kts. *Z26* made the most of this opportunity and sped off, hotly pursued by *Fury*, which had been astern of *Trinidad* during the action.

The three German destroyers were now on a course which took them towards the westerly group of merchant ships and their escorts. In the poor visibility there was a mêlée in which it was difficult to tell friend from foe. *Eclipse* sighted a warship (in fact *Z26*) bearing 020° but refrained from opening fire, mistaking her for *Trinidad*. One of the Soviet destroyers was less discriminating and opened fire immediately. At this moment, when matters were becoming very confused, *Fury* suddenly appeared out of a squall dead ahead of *Eclipse* and fired several salvos at the latter before recognition was assured. *Fury* then turned back to the damaged *Trinidad*. *U585* attempted to attack *Trinidad* but was driven off by *Fury*; the U-boat was later mined in the German 'Bantos' field. Lt-Cdr Mack, in command of *Eclipse*, hauled round to the west 'as there seemed altogether too many destroyers around the convoy'[2] to follow *Z26* with dogged determination.

Spray breaking over the destroyer's bows froze immediately as it landed on 'A' and 'B' mountings and the bridge. The use of binoculars by bridge or director personnel was well-nigh impossible. Conditions could not have been worse. Nevertheless, at 0950 Mack was rewarded by the sight of *Z26* through the snow and opened fire. *Eclipse* inflicted further damage on *Z26* until the latter was lying dead in the water with her stern awash and heavily on fire. Mack decided to sink the cripple by torpedo and was on the point of firing when the other two German destroyers appeared about two miles off, on *Eclipse*'s starboard beam. The odds were now reversed and *Eclipse* made off to the north-west at high speed, but matters were not helped by the visibility, which now began to improve. *Eclipse* managed to take cover in a snow squall at 1025, but not before she had been hit aft by two shells and holed above the waterline forward by two others. Her main aerials were also shot away. After surveying the damage, Mack decided to make an independent passage to Kola: his ship was badly damaged, he was short of fuel and he had nine men on board who urgently required medical attention. He arrived at Murmansk the next day with only 40 tons of fuel remaining in the bunkers. Commenting later on Lt-Cdr Mack's actions, Tovey wrote that

> HMS *Eclipse* was most gallantly handled by Lieut-Commander Mack and she was gallantly fought under the most severe conditions . . . I consider that Lieut-Commander Mack was entirely correct in retiring in the face of this superior force and handled his ship cleverly to avoid more serious damage.[3]

Fortunately for *Eclipse*, the German destroyers made no attempt to pursue her but instead stood by the sinking *Z26*, which eventually capsized at 1057. After rescuing 96 survivors, the remaining two destroyers returned to Kirkenes.

Meanwhile the various groups and stragglers from the convoy were making their way eastward and turned south on reaching the 37th meridian. Fortunately low cloud and poor visibility gave protection from air attack, and they were not yet in the area patrolled by U-boats. One of the four stragglers, the *Induna*, which had the whaler *Silja* in tow (the latter having run out of fuel), had been caught in the ice and finally freed herself in the afternoon of 29 March and set course for Murmansk. Five hours later the tow parted and the *Silja* disappeared in a squall. The *Induna* continued alone, but at 0720 on 30 March she was caught by *U376* (*Kapitänleutnant* Friedrich-Karl Marks); her survivors were not rescued until 2 April, by which time many had died of exposure. An hour later *U435* (*Kapitänleutnant* Siedfried Strelow) torpedoed the freighter *Effingham*, one of the eastern group, 45 miles to the south-west. That afternoon the convoy commodore's ship, *River Afton*, which was proceeding independently, was chased by a U-boat for some hours.

The Eastern Local Escort, consisting of the minesweepers *Harrier*, *Gossamer*, *Hussar* and *Speedwell*, had left Kola on 28 March to bring the convoy in and look for survivors and stragglers. An interesting sidelight on their operations is that they were specifically directed to look out for the merchant ships *Empire Cowper* and *River Afton*, from which two officers and a rating were to be removed to avoid their being incarcerated by the Soviet authorities on arrival at Murmansk.[4] *Harrier* was detached to look for survivors from *Empire Ranger*, but when she heard that *Trinidad* had been torpedoed, she altered course to for the cruiser's position. In doing so she found the whaler *Silja* on 30 March, helplessly adrift after parting company with *Induna*, and took her in tow.

No further enemy interference was encountered, except for an air attack on the eight ships of the western group off the Kola Inlet, during which the *Tobruk* claimed to have shot down two aircraft. By nightfall on 30 March thirteen of the survivors had reached Murmansk, one straggler arriving on 1 April. Nineteen ships had left Reykjavik with PQ.13 and five had been lost. Even allowing for the dispersal of the convoy because of the gale and the scale of enemy attacks, these losses might not be considered excessive. However, they were greater than 25 per cent and had to be viewed with concern, given that the lengthening hours of daylight and the shifting position of the ice increasingly favoured the enemy.

But what of HMS *Trinidad*? After being struck by the torpedo, the cruiser had turned to the south-east and was steering 130° at 6kts when she was rejoined by HMS *Fury*. Speed was cautiously increased, and at 1100 the western group of merchant ships was overhauled. Capt Saunders ordered *Oribi* to join his screen, and early in the afternoon HMS *Harrier* joined too. By this time good damage control had succeeded in reducing the list so that the ship now lay on an even keel and was making between 12 and 14kts. Late that night, however, salt-water contamination of the boiler feed-water forced the ship to reduce speed to 2kts and threatened to stop her altogether. A signal was sent to SBNO North Russia requesting tugs and air cover, but by 0200 on 30 March her speed had increased to 7kts. By early morning the wind had risen and was blowing hard from the north with a considerable sea. Once the ship broached to and had to go astern in order to bring her stern into the wind and head to the proper course. Tugs were met, but their assistance was not required and at 1230 *Trinidad* and *Fury* anchored at Rosta.

The story of *Trinidad*'s torpedoing had a curious sequel. On 7 May, while the cruiser was still under repair at Murmansk, a stoker discovered part of a torpedo pistol while clearing wreckage from 'A' boiler room. The item was speedily identified, by its markings and shape, as having come from the torpedo fired by *Trinidad* during the engagement with *Z26*. *Trinidad* had undoubtedly been struck by her own torpedo. A Board of Enquiry subsequently convened at Plymouth found that the torpedo had not been prepared for cold-water running since the necessary oils had not been available. A number of technical possibilities for the torpedo's malfunction were examined, but it the end it seemed likely that the intense cold had caused the engine and gyro oil to freeze. No blame was attributed to *Trinidad*. As Tovey put it in his report, it was 'cruel, hard luck'.[5] Unfortunately for *Trinidad*, there was more such luck in store.

Reviewing these operations, the German Naval Staff felt that the loss of *Z26* for the sinking of the *Bateau* was not an acceptable rate of exchange. They recommended that destroyers needed cover by heavy units if they were to continue to attack the convoys. Admiral Hubert Schmundt, Flag Officer Northern Waters, disagreed and urged greater caution in their operation. Whatever the merits of either argument, German naval planning in the Arctic was dominated by a lack of fuel. Nevertheless, despite these problems and disagreements, time and the weather was on the Germans' side. As the days lengthened, opportunities for attack, particularly air attack, would multiply.

From the British side, the prospect of running further convoys into the summer was viewed with gloom. Tovey wrote that

> The enemy was determined to do everything in his power to stop this traffic. The U-boat and air forces in Northern Norway had been heavily reinforced, the three remaining destroyers were disposed offensively at Kirkenes and the heavy forces at Trondheim remained a constant, if reluctant, threat.[6]

In representing his position to the Admiralty, Tovey requested that the escorts be considerably augmented. However, there were no ships which could be spared for this duty without depleting another command. The only other command which employed a large number of escorts was the Western Approaches Command at Liverpool, and taking ships from there would mean depleting the already overstretched Atlantic escort forces. Moreover, ships from Western Approaches had minimal anti-aircraft armament since the air threat was of less importance in the Atlantic. Nevertheless, sufficient escorts were wrung from Western Approaches to bring the close escort of an Arctic convoy up to ten ships.

Admiral Sir Dudley Pound, the First Sea Lord, was aware of the problems facing Tovey. He warned the Defence Committee of the War Cabinet that, with the increasing hours of summer daylight, losses were inevitable and that the maintenance of the Arctic route might not become worthwhile. Political factors, however, overruled operational ones, and the convoys had to continue since both Churchill and Roosevelt were determined to honour their obligations to the USSR under the Moscow Protocol.

So the convoys continued, facing increased opposition. PQ.14, of 24 ships, left Iceland on 8 April and two days later the homeward-bound QP.10, of sixteen ships, left the Kola Inlet. PQ.14 was escorted by the minesweepers *Hebe* and *Speedy* and four trawlers, which were augmented SSW of Jan Mayen Island by the cruiser *Edinburgh* (which was carrying steel plating for the repair of HMS *Trinidad*) and the destroyers *Bulldog, Beagle, Amazon* and *Newmarket* (the last in fact did not join the escort owing to condenser trouble) with the corvettes *Campanula, Oxlip, Saxifrage* and *Snowflake*.

On the night of 10/11 April the convoy encountered heavy ice which was further south than usual. The convoy was delayed and scattered and sixteen of the merchant ships, together with the minesweepers *Hebe* and *Speedy*, failed to regain contact and had to put back to Iceland. The remaining eight pressed on with their escort and were found by the *Luftwaffe* on 15 April. Intermittent air attacks followed for two days, though none of the ships was hit. The U-boat forces were more successful. On the 16th *U403* (*Kapitänleutnant* Heinz-Ehlert Clausen) torpedoed the commodore's ship, *Empire Howard*, which subsequently exploded. Early on the 17th two Soviet destroyers joined the escort, as did the minesweepers *Niger, Hussar, Gossamer* and *Harrier* on the 18th. The convoy was spared further attentions by a strong gale which came from the north-west, and the seven survivors struggled into the Kola Inlet on 19 April. Rear-Admiral Bonham-Carter's report on the passage of PQ.14 was not encouraging:

> Under present conditions, with no hours of darkness, continually under air observation for the last four days, submarines concentrating in the bottle-necks, torpedo attack to be expected, our destroyers unable to carry out a proper hunt or search owing to the oil situation, serious losses must be expected in every convoy.[7]

The homeward-bound convoy, QP.10, consisting of sixteen ships escorted by the destroyers *Oribi, Punjabi, Fury, Eclipse* and *Marne*, with a minesweeper and two trawlers and with the cruiser *Liverpool* providing distant cover, sailed from Kola on 10 April. Two Soviet destroyers went as far as 30°E together with the minesweepers *Harrier, Gossamer* and *Hussar*. In the three-day passage between the Kola Inlet and Bear Island the convoy was heavily attacked by aircraft. Several ships were damaged and four were lost. On 11 April the *Empire Cowper* was bombed and sunk, while the *Kiev* and the *El Occidente* were both torpedoed by *U435* on the 12th. The *Harpalion*, having lost her rudder during an air attack on the 13th, had to be sunk the escort.

Enemy activities were frustrated by dense fog followed by a gale, so although the convoy was relocated by air reconnaissance on the 14th, no further attacks materialized. QP.10 reached Reykjavik on 21 April augmented by six of the stragglers from PQ.14. Neither convoy was molested by the Kirkenes-based destroyers. The three destroyers had, in fact, put to sea on two occasions to intercept the convoys but each time the operation had been cancelled on account of bad weather.

Reviewing these operations, Tovey requested that the next pair of convoys be postponed until the icefield had receded. If this were not possible, then the convoys ought be reduced in size. These demands were sympathetically considered by Pound, but the political imperative governing the Russian convoys dictated that the maximum amount of aid be delivered. The next pair of convoys, PQ.15 and QP.11, contained 26 and thirteen ships respectively.

PQ.15 sailed from Reykjavik on 26 April. This was the first convoy to be afforded the protection of a CAM (Catapult Aircraft Merchant) ship, the *Empire Morn*. The CAM ship was a standard merchant ship fitted with a catapult on which was mounted a Hurricane fighter. Its purpose was to provide some means of dealing with the ubiquitous BV 138 and FW 200 reconnaissance aircraft. It was, however, literally a one-shot weapon: once launched, the aircraft could not be recovered, and the pilot had to ditch alongside a friendly ship—in the Arctic, not a particularly appealing prospect. Also included in the convoy were two icebreakers, the Soviet *Krassin* and *Montcalm*.

From 26 April to 5 May the trawlers *Cape Palliser*, *Chiltern*, *Northern Pride* and *Vizalma* escorted the convoy; the destroyer *Ledbury* joined, escorting the oiler *Grey Ranger*, but detached to return to Lerwick where she arrived on 8 May. The minesweepers *Bramble*, *Leda* and *Seagull* were present for the whole voyage. On 28 April the convoy was joined by the destroyer escort, which consisted of *Badsworth*, *Boadicea*, *Matchless*, *Somali*, *Venomous* and the Norwegian *St Albans* together with the AA ship *Ulster Queen*. The submarine HMS *Sturgeon* accompanied the convoy from 28 April to 1 May before departing to carry out a patrol off the Norwegian coast. The cruiser HMS *London* covered the convoy from 30 April to 1 May and was relieved by *Nigeria* from 28 April to 2 May.

The Home Fleet covering forces comprised the battleships *King George V* (later relieved by HMS *Duke of York*), the aircraft carrier *Victorious*, the cruiser *Kenya* and the destroyers *Belvoir*, *Escapade*, *Faulknor*, *Hursley*, *Inglefield*, *Lamerton*, *Marne*, *Martin*, *Middleton*, *Oribi* and *Punjabi*. Since the strength of the Home Fleet had been depleted in order to find ships for the forthcoming invasion of Madagascar, for the first time the United States Navy provided elements of the covering force. This was appropriate, for fifteen of PQ.15's merchant ships were American. The US Navy force, under the command of Rear-Admiral R. C. Giffen USN, consisted of the battleship *Washington*, the cruisers *Tuscaloosa* and *Wichita* and the destroyers *Madison*, *Plunkett*, *Wainwright* and *Wilson*. Covering submarine patrols off the Norwegian coast were provided by *Sturgeon*, *Truant*, *Unison*, *Uredd* (Norwegian), *Minerve* (Free French) and *Jastrzab* (Polish).

PQ.15 and QP.11 were fortunate in their passages. Despite unfavourable ice conditions, air and surface attack and a heavy concentration of U-boats in the Barents Sea, only four of the 39 ships in both convoys were lost. The same cannot be said for the escort forces, which lost one cruiser, one destroyer and a submarine and had a further three destroyers damaged.

The Home Fleet was cruising to the south of the convoy routes when, on 1 May, there was a collision in fog between the battleship *King George V* (Capt W. R. Patterson CB CVO) and the destroyer *Punjabi* (Cdr The Hon J. M. G. Waldegrave DSC). The day had been calm but with frequent snow showers and patches of dense fog. The destroyer screen was stationed eight cables[8] from the capital ships, but, if the visibility worsened, the destroyers were permitted to close to four cables' distance so as not to lose touch with the flagship. *Punjabi* was the second ship in the starboard column, with *Martin* and *Marne* astern of her. It was just before 1600 when the visibility suddenly worsened and the starboard leader closed in toward the battleships. *Punjabi* turned to follow the leader's fog buoy, lost it, but continued towards the line of advance of the fleet at an angle of 80 degrees. Suddenly *King George V*, travelling at 25kts, loomed out of the fog and crashed into *Punjabi*'s port side just aft of the engine room, slicing straight through her hull. *Punjabi*'s stern sank almost immediately, and as it did so the ready-use depth charges on the stern went off, causing severe internal bruising to those of the ship's crew who were in the water. Both *King George V* and *Washington* sustained shock damage as a result of the explosions. The two destroyers astern of *Punjabi*—*Marne* and *Martin*—had to go hurriedly astern and were nearly run down by *Victorious* and *Wichita*.

Punjabi's forward section sank more slowly, so that 169 officers and men, including Cdr Waldegrave, were rescued. Many men were picked out of the water unconscious due to the intense cold and could not be revived, but one survivor owed his life to the cold water. The rating in question had been thrown against a bulkhead by the force of the collision and was then severely scalded when a tea urn overturned on top of him. The pain and blisters were considerably reduced by his near-immediate immersion in the freezing water. Another rating, displaying considerable *sang froid* in adverse circumstances,

> . . . had time to change into his best suit, collect his valuables, put on an immersion suit and gently lower himself into the sea. He came on board HMS *Martin*, emptied out his shoes, took off the immersion suit, donned dry socks and, save for a damp patch on his collar, looked ready for Sunday Divisions in barracks.[9]

HMS *Duke of York* (Capt C. H. J. Harcourt CBE) was hastily summoned from Hvalfjord to relieve *King George V*, which proceeded to Scapa and then to Liverpool for permanent repairs.

The Germans found PQ.15 250 miles south-west of Bear Island shortly before midnight on 30 April, but it was not until 1 May that the first attacks occurred, when six Ju 88s performed what Admiral Burrough, flying his flag in HMS *Nigeria*, described as a 'ragged and poorly executed'[10] attack, losing one of their number in doing so.

By 1000 on 2 May the *Grey Ranger*, with her escort HMS *Ledbury*, had left the convoy together with the cruisers *London* and *Nigeria*, which had been ordered not to proceed into U-boat-infested waters east of Bear Island unless the convoy were definitely being threatened by German cruisers or larger vessels.

Capt J. Crombie RN in HMS *Bramble* was now the Senior Officer of the escort. Shortly before midday on 2 May the westbound QP.11 came in sight. Crombie detached the destroyer *Somali* to make contact, but she returned with the news that QP.11 had endured air, submarine and destroyer attack and had to contend with the awkward position of the ice-pack. When, half an hour later, the convoy was relocated by the *Luftwaffe*, the prospects looked very bleak. From then until it reached longitude 36°E, the convoy was under continuous surveillance from aircraft or U-boats.

At 2009 on 2 May the destroyer *St Albans* and the minesweeper *Seagull* obtained an asdic contact at 7°31′N 17°32′E. An attack with depth charges was carried out and the submarine was forced to the surface, where she was identified as the unfortunate *Jastrzab* and found to be so badly damaged that she had to be sunk by gunfire after her crew had been taken off. A subsequent enquiry found that the submarine was nearly 100 miles out of position and in waters where U-boats were known to be operating. No blame, therefore, could be attributed to *St Albans* or to *Seagull*.

Five hours later, at 0127 on 3 May, the convoy was attacked from the air. Six aircraft from *I/KG 26* came in low on the convoy's starboard bow and as a result were not picked up on radar. The half-light of the Arctic night, combined with haze, made the planes very difficult to spot. Although two of the attackers were shot down and a third later crashed, the remaining three all found targets. The merchant ships *Botavon*, *Cape Corso* and *Jutland* were hit and sunk, the derelict hulk of the last being dispatched by *U251* (*Korvettenkapitän* Heinrich Timm).the next day.

A further air attack took place on 3 May when the trawler *Cape Palliser* was badly shaken by a near-miss and one aircraft was shot down, but otherwise the escorts kept both the shadowers and the U-boats at bay. The *Ulster Queen* had been particularly successful in driving off the air attacks, and eloquent testimony to the effectiveness of her gunnery was paid by the negro steward of an American freighter visited by *Ulster Queen*'s officers while the ship was at Kola: 'Gee! You come from that little white ship? Oh boy! Can she throw up the shit!'[11] Visibility deteriorated from the evening of the 4th when a south-easterly gale sprang up, accompanied by strong snow squalls. These effectively hid the convoy for the rest of the passage and the ships entered the Kola Inlet at 2100 on 5 May.

The aerial torpedo strike had been a new development. The *Luftwaffe* had been slow to take up this form of attack, but doubtless the British attack on Taranto (11 November 1940), that by the Japanese on Pearl Harbor (7 December 1941) and the increase in merchant ships' defensive armament (which made bombing more difficult) acted as a spur towards its adoption. After considerable inter-service friction with the *Kriegsmarine*, which considered the torpedo its own preserve, the *Luftwaffe* obtained permission in December 1941 to develop its own torpedo aircraft. The Ju 88 and He 111 were found to be the most suitable types, and by April 1942 twelve crews had been trained. These were sent quickly to Bardufoss to commence operations.

The outward-bound convoy had enjoyed an eventful though unspectacular passage. On the other hand, QP.11, which sailed from Murmansk on 28 April, had a terrible journey, being constantly attacked and suffering from the weather. The disposition of the escort was as follows. From 28 to 29 April the Eastern Local Escort consisted of the Soviet cruiser *Kuibyshev* and destroyer *Sokrushitelny* and the minesweepers *Niger*, *Gossamer*, *Harrier* and *Hussar*. The Ocean Escort from 28 April to 7 May consisted of the destroyers *Bulldog* (Cdr M. Richmond DSO RN, Senior Officer), *Amazon*, *Beagle* and *Beverley* with the corvettes *Campanula*, *Oxlip*, *Saxifrage* and *Snowflake* and the trawler *Lord Middleton*. From 28 and 30 April the escort was augmented by the destroyers *Foresight* and *Forester*, and the cruiser *Edinburgh* joined on 30 April, flying the flag of Rear-Admiral Bonham-Carter. *Edinburgh* was carrying five tons of Soviet gold—payment for Allied war material.

The gold was stored in the cruiser's bomb room and was supposed to have been loaded in conditions of some secrecy. However, the traditional ingenuity of the British sailor triumphed and the working party succeeded in dropping one of the unmarked wooden crates the thirty or so feet down the hatch from the boat deck to the lobby outside the bomb room so that the crate smashed, revealing its contents.

Bonham-Carter decided to take *Edinburgh* out to a distance of fifteen miles ahead of the convoy in order to be in a good position to head off any attacks by destroyers. It was while *Edinburgh* was in this exposed position that she was struck by two torpedoes fired by *U456* (*Kapitänleutnant* Max Martin Teichert). Petty Officer L. D. Newman was in 'B' turret when the torpedo struck:

> I was leaning over the centre gun tray watching the card-playing when suddenly the whole ship shook, accompanied by a terrific explosion, throwing me about two feet up into the air, and no sooner had I come down again when another similar explosion [came], sending me up into the air. At the second explosion all the lights went out.[12]

The first torpedo had struck on the starboard side forward and had caused considerable flooding. The second virtually blew the stern off, although the port shafts remained intact. The force of the explosion blew the quarterdeck back over the guns of 'Y' turret. The explosion was seen from the convoy and the destroyers *Foresight* (Cdr J. S. Salter) and *Forester* (Lt-Cdr C. P. Huddart) were sent to *Edinburgh*'s assistance, followed shortly afterwards by two Russian destroyers. With the four destroyers providing a screen, the crippled cruiser slowly began the 250-mile passage back to Murmansk.

The vigilance of the destroyers prevented Teichert from sinking *Edinburgh*, but he remained in contact and reported her movements. This information prompted Flag Officer Northern Waters to send the three destroyers based at Kirkenes to attack the convoy and its depleted escort, and at 0100 on 1 May *Z24* (*Korvettenkapitän* Martin Salzwedel), *Z25* (*Korvettenkapitän* Heinz Peters) and *Hermann Schoemann* (*Korvettenkapitän* Heinrich Wittig) put to sea, the whole force under the command of *Kapitän zur See* Alfred Schulze-Hinrichs flying his broad pennant in *Schoemann*.

Meanwhile the convoy continued on its way. At 0540 on 1 May, when in a position roughly 150 miles ESE of Bear Island, it was unsuccessfully attacked by four torpedo-carrying aircraft. At the same time a U-boat was sighted but was put down by HMS *Amazon* (Lt-Cdr The Lord Teynham). However, frequent HF/DF bearings indicated that at least four other U-boats were shadowing the convoy, and consequently course was altered 40 degrees to starboard to shake them off. Then ice was sighted ahead in considerable quantities and was found to extend for twenty miles to the south of the convoy's track, so course was again altered to the westward.

At 1345 the convoy was on a westerly course, with heavy drift ice to starboard, when the corvette *Snowflake* reported three radar contacts astern of her. At the same moment the destroyer *Beverley*, stationed on the convoy's port bow, reported three ships in sight bearing 210°. The contacts proved to be the three destroyers from Kirkenes. Cdr Richmond immediately ordered the destroyers in the escort to join him and moved over to the threatened side of the convoy. Meanwhile the convoy, still escorted by the corvettes, made a 40-degree turn to starboard under cover of a smokescreen. At 1400 *Bulldog* turned towards the enemy on a south-westerly course with the destroyers in line ahead in the order *Beagle*, *Amazon* and *Beverley*. The three German ships were about 10,000yds away, heading towards the convoy, and at 1407 both sides opened fire, the Germans turning to starboard to open their 'A' arcs and the British turning to port. Both sides fired torpedoes, but to no effect. During the brief engagement before the Germans turned away at 1410, *Amazon* was hit, her steering gear and one gun being rendered useless. However, she managed to keep going and was stationed at the rear of the line.

Between 1433 and 1742 the Germans made four more attempts to attack the convoy. On each occasion they were frustrated by the very aggressive tactics adopted by Cdr Richmond, who constantly kept his ships between the threat and the convoy, using smokescreens to hide the convoy's precise whereabouts as appropriate. During the action the convoy entered the icefield, and Richmond was faced with the tricky problem of maintaining touch with the merchant ships while retaining sufficient sea room to manoeuvre should the German destroyers reappear. By this time the convoy was spread out over seven miles and was in single-line formation, with merchant ships leading the thin-hulled destroyers through lanes of open water.

At 1742 Schulze-Hinrichs abandoned the attack on the convoy and sought easier prey in the shape of the damaged *Edinburgh*. Richmond, of course, was unaware of how successful his tactics had been, and for the next three hours the four destroyers cruised between the estimated location of the enemy and the convoy. By 2155 on the 1st the convoy was clear of the ice and the destroyers resumed their screening positions. The rest of the journey was uneventful for QP.11, and the convoy duly arrived at Reykjavik on 7 May. The only loss sustained had been that of the Soviet merchant ship *Tsiolkovsky*, which was hit by one of the torpedoes fired by the German destroyers.

Meanwhile *Edinburgh* had been making slow progress towards Murmansk. At 0600 the two Soviet destroyers had to go ahead to Murmansk to fuel, so HMS *Foresight*, which had been secured astern of the cruiser acting as a drogue, cast off to resume screening duties which, since *U456* was still in the area, was of greater importance. Without the balancing weight of *Foresight* astern of her, *Edinburgh* now began to yaw from side to side. All that could be done to correct this was to go astern on one engine periodically, but this reduced the cruiser's speed to about 2kts. In the afternoon of the 1st Admiral Bonham-Carter received the news of the destroyer attack on QP.11 and ordered that, in the very likely event that the destroyers came looking for *Edinburgh*,

> *Foresight* and *Forester* are to act independently, taking every opportunity to defeat the enemy without taking undue risks to themselves in defending *Edinburgh*. *Edinburgh* is to proceed wherever the wind permits, probably straight into the wind.[13]

At 1800 on the 1st the screen was reinforced by the Soviet tug *Rubin*, which unfortunately had insufficient power to tow *Edinburgh*, and later by the four minesweepers *Harrier, Gossamer, Niger* and *Hussar. Rubin* secured to *Edinburgh*'s port bow and, with *Gossamer* acting as a drogue aft, a speed of 3kts was attained. The weather remained stable and there was every indication that the stricken cruiser would make the Kola Inlet.

However, this was not to be, for, at 0627 on the 2nd, *Hussar*, on *Edinburgh*'s starboard quarter, came under fire from Schulze-Hinrich's three destroyers, which could just be seen through the fog. The destroyers tried to close *Edinburgh*, but once again aggressive tactics were displayed by the destroyers and minesweepers, which Admiral Bonham-Carter later said 'were like three young terriers, going in and firing when they could'.[14] *Edinburgh* herself was not going to give up without a fight. On sighting the destroyers, Capt Faulkner ordered the tug and *Gossamer* to cast off. Although the cruiser was slowly circling, totally out of control, the crew of 'B' turret brought their guns into action, firing by local control.

Edinburgh's second salvo hit *Hermann Schoemann*, causing considerable damage to the German vessel, which took no further part in the action. Two of the 112lb, 6in shells exploded in *Schoemann*'s engine room and the destroyer lost all steam and electric power. As her commanding officer, *Korvettenkapitän* Heinrich Wittig, remarked, 'That the cruiser with her second salvo managed to hit two such vital parts of our ship was the worst luck that could have possibly overtaken us.'[15]

Meanwhile *Foresight* and *Forester* were engaged in a running fight in and out of the smokescreens and snow flurries with *Z24* and *Z25*. Just after 0650 *Forester* fired three torpedoes at the destroyers but was herself hit by three shells which killed her commanding officer, Lt-Cdr G. P. Huddart RN, and wrecked No 1 boiler room and 'B' and 'Y' mountings. Three minutes later *Z24* fired four torpedoes at *Forester*, all of which missed but sped on towards *Edinburgh*. The cruiser could not take avoiding action and was struck on the port side almost exactly opposite the point at which the first of *U456*'s torpedoes had hit.

Capt Faulkner ordered an inspection of the damage, and his engineer officer reported that the ship was completely open to the sea amidships on both sides and that at any moment her back might break. Bonham-Carter ordered *Gossamer* alongside to take off the wounded and the Merchant Navy personnel embarked in *Edinburgh* for the passage. The transfer was not without incident:

A particular man was paralysed from the hips downwards from exposure when his ship was sunk. He was on a stretcher and the bearers had got as far as the side of the *Edinburgh* in preparation to handing him over to the men on the *Gossamer*. The movement of the two ships was very much like that of a concertina: one moment they would be close together and the next some distance apart, so the bearers had to wait for a favourable moment. That moment seemed a long time in coming and it must have tried the patience of the cot case, for as the two ships came together, he scrambled from one ship to the other, where he collapsed on the deck.[16]

Four hundred and forty officers and men were transferred to *Gossamer*, and, while the transfer went on, 'B' turret continued to fire and in so doing prevented *Z24* and *Z25* from going to the aid of *Hermann Schoemann*. However, when the list reached 17 degrees the guns would no longer bear and the turret had to cease firing.

Bonham-Carter gave Captain Faulkner the order to abandon ship and the 350 remaining officers and men were taken off by HMS *Harrier*.

Z24 and *Z25* were concentrating their fire on *Forester*, which was being repeatedly straddled. Cdr Jocelyn Salter in HMS *Foresight* took his ship boldly between *Forester* and the enemy, firing torpedoes at the crippled *Hermann Schoemann*, which missed, and drawing the enemy's fire. However, he found himself in the same predicament as *Forester*, for *Foresight* was engaged at a range of less than 4,000yds and was hit four times, which brought her to a stop with only one gun remaining in action. It is hard to understand why Schulze-Hinrichs did not press home his advantage, since he had two undamaged destroyers against two damaged British vessels and four minesweepers. It is thought that he mistook the minesweepers for fleet destroyers, making him over-cautious. *Z24* went alongside the latter and took off 200 of her crew but left 60 on a raft which were later picked up by *U88* (*Kapitänleutnant* Heino Bohmann). The two German vessels then returned to Kirkenes at high speed.

Since there was no hope of saving *Edinburgh*, Bonham-Carter ordered Cdr Salter to sink her with his last torpedo:

> Slowly and what seemed like leisurely the *Edinburgh* sank beneath the waves. But suddenly her bows reappeared, shooting up almost vertically and then gradually slid beneath the waves again. We turned away sadly, never realising till then what a good and stout ship we had had beneath us.[17]

NOTES TO CHAPTER 3

1. PRO ADM.234/369, 'Battle Summary No 22: Arctic Convoys 1941–45', 1954, p.23.
2. 'Report of Proceedings of the Commanding Officer HMS *Eclipse*', quoted in PRO ADM.234/369, *op. cit.*
3. PRO ADM.234/369, *op. cit.*, p.30.
4. The author has been unable to ascertain why these men were wanted by the Soviet authorities.
5. PRO ADM.234/369, *op. cit.*, p.33.
6. *ibid.*, p.34.
7. PRO ADM.234/369, *op. cit.*, p.35.
8. A cable is equal to 100 fathoms, 200 yards or 183 metres.
9. Brice, Martin, *The Tribals*, Ian Allan, 1975, p.217.
10. Letter of Proceedings of the Rear-Admiral Commanding the 10th Cruiser Squadron, quoted in PRO ADM.234/369.
11. Papers of Cdr R. F. C. Struben RN, IWM Department of Documents.
12. TS account of the loss of HMS *Edinburgh* by L. D. Newman, IWM Department of Documents, p.431.
13. PRO ADM.234/369, *op. cit.*, p.40.
14. *ibid.*
15. Bekker, Cajus, *Hitler's Naval War*. Macdonald & Janes, 1974, p.269.
16. Newman, *op. cit.*, p.431.
17. *ibid.*

Chapter 4

A Matter of Duty

*The Russians are in heavy action and will expect us to run the risk
and pay the price.*—Winston Churchill

The loss of HMS *Edinburgh* marked the start of a period of increasing German
opposition to the Arctic convoys which was to culminate in the disaster which befell
PQ.17 in July 1942.

HMS *Trinidad*, which had been under repair at Kola since March, had been
patched up and made sufficiently seaworthy for the voyage back to Iceland, from
where she would proceed to the United States for permanent repairs. Wearing the
flag of Rear-Admiral Bonham-Carter, she sailed from Murmansk in the evening of
13 May—an inauspicious day, as events were to show. She was escorted by the
destroyers *Somali* (under the command of Capt J. W. Eaton, Captain (D) 6),
Matchless, *Foresight* and *Forester*. Virtually the whole of the Home Fleet was
mobilized to cover her passage. A force of four cruisers, *Nigeria*, *Kent*, *Norfolk* and
Liverpool, under the command of Rear-Admiral Burrough, was steaming to the west
of Bear Island, while the battle fleet—consisting of *Duke of York* (flagship of the
Commander-in-Chief), *Victorious*, *London*, USS *Washington*, USS *Tuscaloosa* and
eleven destroyers—provided further cover to the south west.

The *Luftwaffe* found the cruiser the next morning at 0730. Weather conditions
were poor at first, which gave the ship some degree of cover, but during the
afternoon the visibility began to clear. An air escort of Hurricanes and Pe-3 fighters
of the Red Air Force which was supposed to cover the cruiser for the first 200 miles
of her passage failed to appear, although three Hurricane fighters were present for a
period of 45 minutes. There were also a number of U-boat alarms while the icefield
restricted movement to the north. By 1852 on 14 May there were four aircraft
shadowing the ships and from then on homing signals were virtually continuous.

The first air strikes materialized after 2200 that evening when Ju 88s started a
series of dive-bombing attacks on *Trinidad* and her escort. After about twenty-five
of these had taken place—unsuccessfully, although some ships had some very near
misses—a force of ten torpedo bombers was detected coming in fairly low. While
attention was focused on this attack, a lone Ju 88 dived out of the cloud and released
its stick of bombs on *Trinidad*'s starboard quarter from a height of 400ft. One bomb
struck the starboard side of the bridge and burst on the lower deck, starting a fire
which rapidly spread between decks and over the bridge. The second bomb, which
was either a hit or a very near miss, flooded the magazine for 'B' turret and adjacent
compartments and blew in a temporary patch in the ship's side abreast the Marine's
mess deck. Despite a 14-degree list to starboard, *Trinidad* was still steaming at

20kts, and Capt Saunders was able to avoid the torpedoes. The torpedoes from another attack made fifteen minutes later were also avoided.

However, at 2315 Capt Saunders had to stop the ship to reduce the draught which was fanning the flames. By midnight it was accepted that the fire was out of control. In view of the fact that *Trinidad* lay only 170 miles from the enemy-held coast, the presence of U-boats and the certainty of further air attack, it was decided to abandon the ship and scuttle her. The wounded were taken off by HMS *Forester* and the remainder by the other destroyers. Admiral Bonham-Carter, who had transferred his flag to the destroyer *Somali*, found himself in the unenviable position of having to order his flagship to be scuttled for the second time in less than a fortnight. The *coup de grâce* was administered by HMS *Matchless*, and *Trinidad* finally sank at 0120 on 15 May.

The destroyers then joined Rear-Admiral Burrough's cruisers and headed for Iceland. At 2000 on 15 May they were bombed by a force of about twenty-five Ju 88s. This attack was unsuccessful, but the fact that it took place over 350 miles from the nearest airfield showed the range and power which the *Luftwaffe* now enjoyed. It meant that, in future, convoys could expect air attack for the majority of their passage.

Bonham-Carter's experiences in QP.11 and the subsequent loss of *Trinidad* left him in no doubt of the dangers to which the convoys were now exposed. On his return to Britain he wrote:

> I am convinced that until the aerodromes in North Norway are neutralised and there are some hours of darkness . . . the continuation of these convoys should be stopped. If they must continue for political reasons, very serious and heavy losses must be expected. The force of German attacks will increase not diminish. We in the Navy are paid to do this sort of job but it is beginning to ask too much of the men of the Merchant Navy. We may be able to avoid bombs and torpedoes with our speed, [but] a six or eight knot ship has not this advantage.[1]

Bonham-Carter's views were endorsed by Admiral Tovey, who had repeatedly made representations that the size of the convoys should be reduced. Tovey's views were supported by Pound who, as early as 18 April, had written to Admiral King in Washington that

> The Russian Convoys are becoming a regular millstone around our necks and cause a steady attrition in both cruisers and destroyers . . . the whole thing is a most unsound operation with the dice loaded against us in every direction . . . but I do . . . recognise the necessity of helping the Russians all we can at the present time.[2]

The convoys to Russia had already been the subject of discussions at the highest levels of the Allied command. Churchill was sympathetic to Tovey's representations, which had been conveyed to him via Admiral Sir Dudley Pound, the First Sea Lord. On 26 April 1942 Churchill had telegraphed to Harry Hopkins, Roosevelt's Special Emissary to Britain, warning him of the 'serious convoy situation' and a growing quantity of supplies which could not be convoyed to the Soviet Union.[3]

If Churchill was dropping hints that he would like Roosevelt's support in suggesting to Stalin that the convoys be suspended for the summer, then he was to be disappointed. Roosevelt's reply came one day later, informing Churchill that the President was 'greatly disturbed' about supplies not reaching the USSR quickly enough and in sufficient quantities. To abandon deliveries 'except for the most compelling reasons' seemed to Roosevelt to be 'a serious mistake'.[4] Churchill replied that he was unable to run more than two convoys every three months. PQ.15 had just sailed, but he promised that future convoys would be increased in size to 35 ships. However, Roosevelt had to realise that a Russian convoy was, in fact, nothing less than a major fleet operation.

Roosevelt, however, was emphatic. Britain had to recognize 'the urgent necessity of getting off one more convoy in May in order to break the log-jam of ships already loaded or being loaded for Russia. Any further delays would leave [an] impossible and very disquieting impression in Russia.'[5] Churchill was likewise adamant: 'With very great respect, what you suggest is beyond our power to fulfil.' After recapitulating the problems suffered by the recent PQ/QP convoys, Churchill added:

I beg you not to push us beyond our judgement in this operation, which we have studied most intently and of which we have not yet been able to measure the full strain. I assure you, Mr President, that we are absolutely extended, and I could not press the Admiralty further.[6]

Roosevelt agreed that the matter be put to naval professionals on both sides of the Atlantic, Admiral Pound in London and the redoubtable Admiral 'Ernie' King in Washington. After reading their exchange of telegrams, Roosevelt was forced to accept Churchill's view. Roosevelt suggested that Stalin be requested to reduce his munitions requirements to the bare minimum and that he be told that Britain and the United States needed to build up stocks of munitions for Operation 'Bolero',[7] which had just begun.

Churchill was to be pressed by Stalin as well. On 7 May the latter had asked him to take all possible measures to ensure that the ships bottled up in Iceland sailed in May. On the 9th Churchill replied in typically generous fashion. Though he pointed out to Stalin some ways in which the Soviet forces could help escort the convoys, notably in the provision of long-range air cover, he promised that 'We are resolved to fight our way through to you with the maximum amount of war materials . . . we shall continue to do our utmost.'[8]

By now the political pressure to continue the convoys was overpowering, and it was compounded by bad news from the Eastern Front, where the Red Army's spring offensive had become bogged down. On 18 May, the very day that Pound described the convoys to King as a 'millstone', the German Army launched a massive counter-attack in the Ukraine which forced the Red Army to retreat. All the while, through 'Ultra', the British could see the build-up of German Army formations in the Soviet Union and knew that a summer offensive of incomparable ferocity was planned. As the Red Army would endure, so would the convoys have to sail. In a minute addressed to the War Cabinet on 17 May 1942, Churchill noted that

Not only Premier Stalin but President Roosevelt will object very much to our desisting from running the convoys now. The Russians are in heavy action and will expect us to run the risk and pay the price entailed by our contribution . . . I share your misgivings but I feel it is a matter of duty.[9]

Thus it was that, on 21 May, in the most unfavourable season of the year with near-perpetual daylight, convoy PQ.16 left Hvalfjord. It consisted of 35 ships and was the largest convoy to sail to Russia to date. The Local Escort consisted of the minesweeper *Hazard* (which remained until 31 May), the trawlers *St Elstan* and *Lady Madeleine* from 21 to 24 May and the trawlers *Retriever* (Free French) and *Northern Spray* from 21 to 25 May. On 23 May the convoy was joined by the Ocean Escort, consisting of the AA ship *Alynbank*, the destroyers *Ashanti* (Cdr R. G. Onslow RN, Senior Officer), *Achates*, *Martin*, *Volunteer* and *Garland* (Polish) and the corvettes *Honeysuckle*, *Hyderabad*, *Starwort* and *Roselys* (Free French) together with the destroyer *Ledbury* escorting the oiler *Black Ranger*. The Ocean Escort remained with the convoy until 30 May, and 31 May in the case of *Alynbank*.

The presence of ORP *Garland* exemplified the topsy-turvy origins of the Anglo-Soviet alliance. To most of *Garland*'s Polish crew, the Soviet Union was not much worse than Nazi Germany for having participated in the carve-up of Polish territory after the Hitler-Stalin Pact. Some of the men had been captives of the NKVD[10] before being allowed to join Polish forces in the West; now they found themselves escorting merchant ships loaded with supplies being sent to their former oppressor, who was now their ally only out of military necessity. The shortage of escorts meant that the sensitivities of *Garland*'s crew were of little account to the Admiralty planners—every ship was needed—and, despite their scruples, the Polish sailors would acquit themselves magnificently.[11]

The cruiser force consisted of *Kent, Liverpool, Nigeria* and *Norfolk* and its movements were synchronized to coincide with those of the homeward-bound QP.12. The Home Fleet provided distant cover with the battleships *Duke of York* and USS *Washington*, the aircraft carrier *Victorious*, the cruisers *London* and USS *Wichita* and the destroyers *Blankney, Eclipse, Faulknor, Fury, Icarus, Intrepid, Lamerton, Middleton, Wheatland, Mayrant, Rhind, Rowan* and *Wainwright* (the last four all USN). From 28 to 30 May the Local Eastern Escort consisted of the Soviet destroyers *Grozni, Kubyshev* and *Sokrushitelny* and the minesweepers *Bramble, Gossamer* and *Seagull* from 28 to 30 May, with *Leda* joining on 30 May.

After sailing, PQ.16 had encountered dense fog and the destroyers of the Ocean Escort had difficulty in locating it. It was not until after midnight on 24/25 May that the convoy was reassembled with its escorts. At 0535 on the 25th the cruisers joined and took station in pairs between the fourth, fifth and sixth columns. This formation was intended to provide the best defence against air attack.

Soon after the cruisers arrived, an FW 200 appeared and began to circle the convoy. No attacks immediately materialized, and the destroyers were able to fuel from *Black Ranger*. However, at 2035 came the first attacks by aircraft of *III/KG 26* and *III/KG 30* which were to persist for the next five days. Seven He 111s and eight Ju 88s circled the front of the convoy and then attacked out of the sun, evidently heading for the cruisers in the centre of the formation. According to the war correspondent Alexander Werth, who was en route to the Soviet Union in the *Empire Baffin*,

> The tracer bullets from our Oerlikons were rushing at the yellow belly of the Ju 88 as he swooped over us. A loud squeal, growing louder and louder, and then the explosion, as a stick of bombs landed between us and the destroyer on the port side.[12]

This time though, the convoy had some response other than anti-aircraft fire. The CAM ship *Empire Lawrence* flew off her Hurricane, which shot down one He 111 and damaged another. Unfortunately, the fighter was shot down by gunners on the US freighter *Carlton*, whose enthusiasm was evidently greater than their aircraft recognition, though the pilot, P Off A. J. Hay RAF, survived and was picked up by HMS *Volunteer. Carlton* was then herself immobilized by a fractured steam pipe and had to be towed back to Iceland by the trawler *Northern Spray*. The next attack, which was equally unsuccessful, came in at 2315. Then heavy grey clouds began to gather, putting a halt to any further air operations.

The U-boats had not been idle. One had already been sighted on the starboard beam of the convoy and had been put down by HMS *Martin*. But at 0305 on the 26th *U703* (*Kapitänleutnant* Hans Bielfeld), lurking to the south of the convoy, managed to penetrate the screen and torpedo the *Syros* on the starboard side of the convoy. Twenty-eight of her crew of 37 were rescued by *Hazard* and *Lady Madeleine* before she sank.

PQ.16 had passed the homeward-bound QP.12 at 1345 on the 25th and Burrough was supposed to have detached his cruisers to cover it at this point. However, wishing to cover PQ.16 for as long as possible, he stayed with this convoy until 0400 on the 26th, when it was 240 miles south-west of Bear Island. Fortunately, the low cloud which lasted throughout most of 26th protected the convoy from further air strikes, but shortly after 1800 eight He 111s and three Ju 88s made an unsuccessful attack.

So far, the *Luftwaffe* had been frustrated in its attempts to attack the convoy. However, on the 27th the weather improved and the Germans launched an all-out effort. The first attack came in at 0320, shortly after which the convoy had to alter course to the south-east for two hours because of heavy pack-ice. At 1115 came the first of a series of attacks from over 100 Ju 88s which would last for the next ten hours. Conditions were good from the bombers' point of view, the 3,000ft cloud base allowing them to approach the convoy almost unseen.

At 1310 the *Alamar* was hit and set on fire; five minutes later the *Mormacsul* was badly damaged by two near-misses. Both ships had be sunk later by the escorts. In the afternoon the CAM ship *Empire Lawrence* was hit and set on fire. As the trawler *Lady Madeleine* closed to render assistance, the CAM ship was attacked and hit again. Lt-Cdr Graeme Ogden of the trawler recalled that

> The next thing I remember was that the sky was full of strange shapes. We were covered with falling wreckage and enveloped in suffocating brown smoke. I thought

we must have been hit. When, minutes later, the smoke had cleared away, there was no sign of the 12,000-ton *Empire Lawrence*.[13]

Alexander Werth, watching from the *Empire Baffin* (which was immediately to starboard of the stricken CAM ship) remembered

A flash which in the sun was not very bright and, like a vomiting volcano, a huge pillar of fire, smoke and wreckage shot two hundred feet into the air—and then slowly, terribly slowly, it went down to the sea.[14]

Empire Lawrence was loaded with ammunition, like most of the ships in the convoy, and the explosion had, to quote one author, 'a profound effect'[15] on the crews of the other ships.

The Soviet tanker *Stari Bolshevik* had also been hit during this attack and was forced to drop out of her position in the convoy's eighth column. During a lull in the attacks the destroyer HMS *Martin* went back for her to transfer her surgeon and found the crew, which included a significant number of women, making strenuous efforts to save their ship. Three of the worst casualties were transferred to *Martin* for treatment. The French corvette *Roselys* came alongside and began to pump water into the *Stari Bolshevik*'s forward tanks and slowly the tanker got under way again. For their determination in saving their ship the *Stari Bolshevik*'s Master and First Officer were made Heroes of the Soviet Union, while the ship received a unit citation of the Order of Lenin. The crew also received a letter of congratulation from the Board of Admiralty.

Other casualties in PQ.16 from the midday attacks included the *Empire Baffin*, which was badly damaged together with the *City of Joliet* and had to be sunk later. The destroyer *Garland* was badly damaged by a group of four bombs which fell about 20ft abreast of the bridge. Lt B. Pawlowicz was an official war correspondent embarked in *Garland* for the voyage:

Then I heard a long, shrill and, as it seemed to me, everlasting whistle of falling bombs. Against the background of previous explosions I saw, as in a nightmare, the dark spear-like shapes of four bombs. I instinctively huddled against the wall of the range-finder. My eyes seemed filled with dust, my open mouth had an unpleasant metallic taste. A huge pall of smoke covered the ship, the convoy and the whole world . . . I heard the moans of wounded men and I ran round the range-finder to the battle deck. The officers and signallers, shocked by the explosion, had momentarily been brought to a standstill. Blood was streaming from every face, not one [of which] had escaped some scratch or another from flying splinters of bombs and particles of broken glass.[16]

From the *Alynbank* the crew saw

. . . terrific mountains of water and smoke obliterate the destroyer. When it subsided we saw the *Garland* with smoke pouring from her. 'That's the end of her,' I remember saying. Just at that moment the *Garland*'s guns and machine guns began firing. It was incredible.[17]

Garland was riddled from stem to stern with splinter holes. 'A' and 'B' mountings were put out of action, as was the Oerlikon gun on the starboard side of the bridge. No 1 boiler room had to be shut down and a fire was started in the forecastle. Casualties amounted to 25 killed and 43 wounded, many of the latter seriously. It was later thought that this extensive and unusual splinter damage was brought about by the first bomb exploding on hitting the water, its detonation causing the other three to explode in the air. *Garland*'s damage was so extensive and the plight of her wounded so serious that the destroyer was detached that evening to proceed independently to Murmansk.

Shortly after these attacks, the convoy was able to swing back to the north as the ice cleared. Cdr Onslow thought that there appeared to be more cloud in that direction and that the northerly course would take the convoy away from the German bases in Norway and thus lessen the weight and frequency of air attacks. The afternoon passed fairly peacefully, with only an ineffective attack by eight Ju 88s, until 1945, when another combined dive-bombing and torpedo attack developed. The *Empire Purcell* was bombed and blew up and the *Lowther Castle* was torpedoed. The commodore's ship, *Ocean Voice*, was also torpedoed, the explosion tearing away 20ft of plating abreast No 1 hold, only two feet above the waterline. Fort- unately the sea remained calm, but Cdr Onslow was sanguine about her prospects of survival:

> I had little hope of her survival but this gallant ship maintained her station, fought her fire and with God's help arrived at her destination.[18]

That was the last attack for the day, although two BV 138s remained in contact. The situation appeared very grim. Five ships had been lost—the *City of Joilet* would be scuttled on the 28th—and there were roughly three more days to go before reaching Murmansk. Wrote Cdr Onslow:

> I felt far from optimistic . . . The question of ammunition began to worry me badly. I ordered all ships to exercise strict economy and restricted controlled fire in *Ashanti* to one mounting at a time. We were all inspired, however, by the parade ground rigidity of the convoy's station-keeping, including *Ocean Voice* and *Stari Bolshevik*, who were both billowing smoke from their foreholds.[19]

However, the worst was over. There were to be no further losses, and during the morning of the 28th the convoy was reinforced by three Soviet destroyers, *Grozni*, *Sokrushitelny* and *Kubyshev*—welcome additions with their considerable AA firepower. There was only one attack on the 28th—a high-level bombing raid by four Ju 88s which was not pressed home with any degree of determination.

There was another unsuccessful attack on the morning of the 29th, but in the evening the escort was reinforced by six minesweepers of the Eastern Local Escort under Capt Crombie in HMS *Bramble*. At this stage the convoy divided. In order to ease the load on Murmansk's bomb-devastated port facilities, six of the surviving merchant ships, escorted by the minesweepers with *Martin* and *Alynbank*, would proceed to Archangel. Just after the convoy divided, and while both sections were still in sight of each other, 32 Ju 88s attacked both sections, but to no effect. The ships arrived at Archangel on 1 June without loss, although, sadly, the *Steel Worker* was sunk during a subsequent air raid.

The departure of the Archangel section only increased Cdr Onslow's anxieties. *Alynbank*'s departure left him with no long-range radar cover—the only other ship so fitted had been the ill-fated *Empire Lawrence*—and U-boats were known to be gathering off the Kola Inlet, and he therefore had to deploy his escorts to meet this latter threat as well as the continued threat from the air. Fortune was now evidently smiling on PQ.16, however, for although there were three attacks during the 30th, there were no further losses and the submarine threat did not materialize. From midday on the 30th air cover was provided by Hurricanes of the Red Air Force, and just after 1600 the convoy entered the Kola Inlet, 'reduced in numbers, battered and tired, but still keeping perfect station'.[20]

By way of contrast, QP.12, the homeward-bound convoy, had a singularly uneventful passage. Consisting of seventeen ships, it sailed from the Kola Inlet on 21 May. The Eastern Local Escort accompanied the convoy until 23 May and consisted of the Soviet destroyers *Grozni* and *Sokrushitelny* with the minesweepers *Bramble*, *Gossamer*, *Leda* and *Seagull*. The Ocean Escort consisted of the destroyers *Inglefield* (Capt P. Todd RN, Senior Officer), *Escapade*, *Venomous*, *St Albans*, *Boadicea* and *Badsworth*, the AA ship *Ulster Queen*, the trawlers *Northern Pride*, *Northern Wave* and *Vizalma* and the minesweeper *Harrier*. Admiral Burrough's cruisers joined on 26 May while the Home Fleet provided distant cover for both convoys.

QP.12 was completely unmolested, the enemy being totally engaged with PQ.16. The CAM ship *Empire Morn* launched her Hurricane on 25 May against a shadower. The intruder, a Ju 88 which was sending out homing signals, was shot down, but the Hurricane pilot, P Off J. B. Kendall RAF, lost his life after baling out from his aircraft when his parachute failed to open. That was the only action seen by QP.12. The freighters *Kuzbass* and *Hegira* turned back, but otherwise all fifteen ships arrived at Reykjavik on 29 May.

The passage of PQ.16 was quite successful, given the scale of attacks launched against it, although much of the success was due to Cdr Onslow's skilful and resolute defence. In his review of the operation, Tovey wrote that the success

> . . . was due to the gallantry, efficiency and tireless zeal of the officers and men of the escorts and to the remarkable courage and determination of those of the merchant ships. No praise too high for either.[21]

Onslow made a number of recommendations, most of which would eventually, when resources permitted, be adopted. Defence against air attack was his greatest recommendation. All ships should carry sufficient stocks of ammunition, and there should be reserve stocks both at Kola and with the convoy. An auxiliary carrier or a large number of CAM ships should accompany every convoy, together with additional AA ships. The firepower of the *Alynbank* had been most impressive. A Polish officer on board *Garland* had noted that

The ceaseless fire from the destroyers and auxiliary cruiser rumbled like tropical thunder. The auxiliary cruiser *Alynbank*'s fire seemed to be the heaviest of all of us. I noticed that the Germans preferred to keep out of her range. She must have had an unlimited store of ammunition.[22]

The provision of radar was equally important. There could never be too many long-range warning sets; in PQ.16 only two ships, *Alynbank* and *Empire Lawrence*, had been so fitted. Other recommendations by Onslow included the provision of a salvage tug with a fire-fighting capability: such a ship, he believed, would have saved the *Empire Purcell*. He also recommended that rescue ships accompany the convoy as the escorts were often overcrowded with survivors.

Despite the fact that they had sunk 20 per cent of the ships in PQ.16, the Germans had not had things all their own way. In particular, the U-boat arm was despondent since, apart from the sinking of the *Syros* by Bielefeld's *U703*, its boats had been little more than a latent threat. Moreover, *U703* and *U436* had received severe depth-charge damage which resulted in diving restrictions being placed on them, thereby greatly affecting their operational effectiveness, while several other boats had received depth-charge damage which would require them to spend some time in dockyard hands. The very factors which had proved crucial in the success of the *Luftwaffe* against PQ.16 hampered submarine operations considerably. The long hours of daylight robbed the U-boats of their greatest asset, darkness, and forced them to operate in near-continuous daylight—not their usual *modus operandi*. Coupled with the very aggressive stance taken by the escort, this brought about the poor results described. Dönitz was forced to conclude that 'The German Air Force would seem a better means of attacking the convoys in the north in the summer'.[23]

On the other hand, the *Luftwaffe* had done well against PQ.16, although its claims to have scattered the convoy after the attack during the evening of the 25th represented a hopeless over-estimation of its success. *Reichsmarschall* Hermann Göring, who had shown no enthusiasm for the development of torpedo-bombing squadrons, now revelled in the glow of his success and rewarded his air crews with liberal showers of decorations.

On a more serious note, the Germans had appreciated that the co-ordination of torpedo attacks with high-level bombing could weaken a convoy's anti-aircraft defences. In future the torpedo bombers would attack in line abreast and drop their torpedoes simultaneously from a height of about 300ft; this method became known as the 'Golden Comb' and would prove very successful, particularly against PQ.18. It was also decided to launch the torpedo attacks at twilight, with the ships silhouetted against the lighter sky. New methods were matched by reinforcements of aircraft. At the beginning of June the *Luftwaffe* had available in this theatre 103 Ju 88 bombers, 42 He 111 torpedo bombers, fifteen He 115 torpedo bombers, 30 Ju 87 dive-bombers and eight FW 200, 22 Ju 88 and 44 BV 138 reconnaissance aircraft, the BV 138s being operated by the *Kriegsmarine*. This formidable force began an intensive training programme before the next convoy, PQ.17, sailed.

As the cycle of convoys to and from northern Russia became established, it became inevitable that some merchant ships had to wait in Soviet ports until a return convoy formed, either because of delays in the unloading of the ship concerned or arising from the need to repair damage. Generally such ships were transferred to Archangel if at all possible, since that port lay outside the reach of the *Luftwaffe*. Occasionally the ships would trade between Murmansk and Archangel, timber being the principle cargo. However, the voyage of the British tanker *Hopemount* from the time of her arrival in Soviet waters with PQ.14 on 8 April to her departure for the United Kingdom in December 1942 with RA.51 is something of an epic and worthy of description.

From April to June *Hopemount* lay in the river at Murmansk, her crew constantly being called to defend their ship against air attacks, 132 of which were recorded for this period alone. However, on 29 June she was moved to Archangel, escorted by HMS *Hazard* and HMS *Leda*, where she was to support operations by the Soviet Fleet in the White Sea. On 29 July she sailed for Port Dickson with a heavy escort consisting of two Soviet icebreakers and three destroyers, with HM ships *Bramble*, *Hazard*, *Seagull*, *Dianella*, *La Malouine* and *Lotus* in attendance also. At the edge of the ice-pack the escorts, save for the icebreakers, turned back, leaving the tanker and her two companions to proceed into the frozen wastes.

Hopemount's role in this unusual voyage was to support the annual transfer of ships between the Arctic and Pacific theatres by the 'north-about' route. This route was the only practical means for the Soviets to move ships from Vladivostok to the Arctic and *vice versa*, although the seasonal movement of the ice-pack meant that the route was only open in summer. *Hopemount* would proceed with the eastbound convoy as far as Tiksi, fuelling the escorts and merchant ships as required. At Tiksi she would meet the westbound convoy and return to Archangel with them.

By 18 August *Hopemount* had reached Cape Chelyshin, and she arrived at Hansen Island on the 25th. Here her Master and crew received the alarming news that a German raider was loose in the Kara Sea and was following the convoy. On 26 August a ship was sighted astern of the convoy: this was first assumed to be the raider but it later turned out to be a Soviet ship sailing independently. The raider, which was in fact *Admiral Scheer* (see Chapter 7), never came north of the ice-edge and was never a threat. On 31 August *Hopemount* arrived at Tiksi, position 134°E 83°N, where she took on a further 3,000 tons of oil and some badly needed fresh water. On 16 September three Soviet destroyers, *Baku*, *Razumny* and *Razyarenny*, arrived, en route to reinforce the Northern Fleet; a fourth destroyer, *Revnostny*, had been damaged in a collision and forced to return.

On 18 September *Hopemount* started the return journey, but she had damaged her propeller by hitting the ice and, her speed reduced, she was left behind by the faster Soviet ships. She eventually reached Port Dickson on 26 September, where she fuelled the Soviet destroyers. By this time supplies of food on board the *Hopemount* were running low and the crew were living on a diet of tinned corned beef, dried peas, flour and tea. She sailed west again on 6 October and reached Yugorski Shar on the 11th. She remained there until 19 October, when the minesweepers *Halcyon*, *Hazard* and *Leda* arrived to sweep the area. By now winter had come, and *Hopemount* needed the assistance of two Soviet icebreakers to reach clear water on 20 November. Her damaged propeller meant that she could not keep up with the convoy, so she proceeded independently, being collected at Iokanka by British minesweepers on 29 November.

The surgeon on board HMS *Harrier* found the whole crew of *Hopemount* to be suffering from scurvy on account of their appalling diet. Fortunately, however, their ordeal was nearly at an end. On 8 December they received their first mail from the United Kingdom since March. The ship sailed for home with RA.51 and arrived at Methil on 16 January 1943, marking the end of her voyage by colliding with another ship. In his report of the voyage, *Hopemount*'s Master, Capt W. D. Shields, praised his crew, saying that 'Nobody was outstanding—it was a case of all pulling together'.[24]

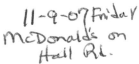

NOTES TO CHAPTER 4

1. PRO ADM.234/369, 'Battle Summary No 22: Arctic Convoys 1941–45', 1954, p.46.
2. PRO ADM.205/19.
3. Prime Minister's Personal Telegram, T.634/2, 'Personal and Secret', 26 April 1942, Churchill Papers, 20/74.
4. President to Prime Minister, No 141, 'Priority', 27 April 1942, Churchill Papers, 20/74.
5. President to Prime Minister, No 143, 30 April 1942, Churchill Papers, *op. cit.*
6. Prime Minister's Personal Telegram, T.670/2, 'Personal and Secret', 2 May 1942. Churchill Papers, 20/74.
7. The build-up of Anglo-American forces in Britain prior to the opening of the Second Front.
8. Prime Minister's Personal Telegram, T.707/2, 'Personal and Most Secret', 9 May 1942, Churchill Papers, 20/75.
9. Churchill, Winston, *The Second World War*, Vol IV, Cassell & Co, 1948–53, pp.233–4.
10. The much-feared Soviet security service.
11. The booklet *ORP Garland in Convoy to Russia* (Surrey Press, 1943) provides an excellent account of *Garland*'s ordeal.
12. Werth, Alexander, *The Year of Stalingrad*, Hamish Hamilton, 1946, p.31.
13. Ogden, Graeme, *My Sea Lady*, Hutchinson, 1963, p.121.
14. Werth, *op. cit.*, p.35.
15. Scholfield, Vice-Admiral B., *The Arctic Convoys*, Macdonald & Janes, 1977, p.44.
16. Pawlowicz, B., *ORP Garland in Convoy to Russia*, Surrey Press, 1943, pp.38–9.
17. *ibid.*, p.78.
18. PRO ADM.234/369, *op. cit.*, p.49.
19. *ibid.*, p.50.
20. *ibid.*
21. PRO ADM.234/369, *op. cit.*, p.51.
22. Pawlowicz, B., *op. cit.*, p.37.
23. BdU's War Diary, 3 June 1942, quoted in Admiralty, Naval Staff History of the Second World War, 'Battle Summary No 22: Arctic Convoys 1941–45', London, 1954, p.52, note 1.
24. Hage, Arnold, and Ruegg, Bob, *Convoys to Russia*, World Ship Society, 1992, p.19.

Chapter 5

'Convoy is to Scatter'

The Commodore's Chief Yeoman has made a proper balzup this time: that signal means 'Convoy is to scatter' —Yeoman of Signals on board HMS *Ledbury*

Nearly a month passed between the arrival of PQ.16 and the sailing of the next Russian convoy. The delay was because of the diversion of units of the Home Fleet to the Mediterranean for Operation 'Harpoon', an eastbound Malta convoy. It was not until the middle of June 1942 that sufficient forces became available in home waters to form the escort for PQ.17.

Admiral Tovey wished to suspend the running of the next convoy, already coded PQ.17, until such time as sufficient escorts—particularly an aircraft carrier—could be provided to fight the ships through. However sound Tovey's tactical recommendations might have been, he was overridden by political imperatives. At the time, the Red Army was reeling under the onslaught of the renewed German offensive in the Caucasus and the Soviets were desperate for aid. Moreover, vast amounts of *matériel* from the United States and destined for the Soviet Union was piling up in ports on the American East Coast and political pressure from that direction added to Whitehall's problems. Tovey's alternative suggestion for more, smaller, less vulnerable convoys was also rejected. Hitherto the defence of the convoys had just managed to cope with the level of attack. However, those concerned with the running of the Russian convoys felt that the *Kriegsmarine* would not be content solely to use aircraft and U-boats coupled with the occasional destroyer sortie to attack the convoys and that it would not be long before *Tirpitz* ventured out again.

This supposition was correct. The *Luftwaffe* had performed well against PQ.16 and were jubilant at their success. U-boats had been less successful, partly on account of the combative tactics employed by the escort but also because the long hours of summer daylight militated against submarine operations. Only the capital ships, swinging idly round their buoys in their Norwegian lairs, had been inactive. Now that the fuel stocks in Norway were sufficient to permit operations, plans were drawn up to employ a powerful task force comprising *Tirpitz*, *Scheer*, *Lützow* and *Hipper* in an all-out attack on the next convoy. Plans for such a move, code-named *'Rösselsprung'*, were drawn up by the Naval Staff and presented to Hitler on 1 June 1942.

'*Rösselsprung*' called for the four ships to sortie from their Norwegian bases on receiving reports of the convoy's whereabouts from the *Luftwaffe* or U-boats. The force would then proceed to attack the convoy in the Barents Sea between longitudes 20° and 30°E. In theory this seemed an acceptable operational proposal. However, the Naval Staff had not reckoned with Hitler's temerity in maritime affairs. Despite an assurance from Raeder that the operation would not be given the go-ahead unless air cover were available and there were no superior British units within striking distance, Hitler insisted that the whereabouts of the British aircraft carrier be determined before the ships sailed so that the *Luftwaffe* could destroy her. This was clearly asking too much, so Raeder managed to persuade Hitler to permit the splitting of '*Rösselsprung*' into two parts. The first, which could be ordered by the Naval Staff without obtaining Hitler's approval, would involve moving *Tirpitz* and *Hipper* from Trondheim to Vestfjord and *Scheer* and *Lützow* from Narvik to Altenfjord close to the North Cape. There the ships would await news that the British carrier had either been sunk or was so far away as to be no threat before sailing. They would rendezvous at a point 100 miles north of the North Cape before proceeding as planned.

Through 'Ultra' and other intelligence, it was clear to Admiral Tovey that the Germans intended using their surface ships in a full-scale assault, and he regarded the prospect bleakly:

> The strategic situation was wholly favourable to the enemy. His heavy ships would be operating close to their own coast with the support of powerful shore-based air reconnaissance and striking forces and protected, if he so desired, by a screen of U-boats in the Channels between Spitzbergen and Norway. Our covering forces, on the other hand, if they entered these waters, would be without shore-based air support, one thousand miles from their base, with their destroyers too short of fuel to escort a damaged ship to harbour.[1]

Tovey wished to deal with this unpromising situation by means of a series of deceptive manoeuvres designed to confuse the Germans, rather than simply try to fight the convoy through against what he regarded as near-impossible odds. He also recommended that, once PQ.17 reached 10°E, it should be turned and ordered to reverse course for a period of between twelve and eighteen hours. Should the Germans have taken the bait and put to sea, it was hoped that they would proceed further to the west than they intended and go beyond the range of their air cover and be easier to destroy. Only if the German ships were known to be in harbour, or if the weather was bad enough to prevent shadowing by aircraft, was the convoy to go straight through.

Tovey was therefore somewhat startled and perturbed to receive instructions on 27 June which

> . . . envisaged the possibility, under certain circumstances, of the convoy being temporarily turned back by the Admiralty, but not of this turn being timed to achieve the object the Commander-in-Chief had in view.[2]

Instead, the Admiralty laid down that British forces were to defend the convoy only as far as Bear Island but not beyond, where the task was to be left entirely to submarines. The Admiralty emphasized that the cruiser force was not to proceed east of Bear Island unless the convoy were directly threatened by surface forces which the cruisers were capable of tackling without battleship support—and even then the cruisers were on no account to proceed beyond 25°E.

The Admiralty in London was definitely concerned about the threat posed by the German ships. This was amply demonstrated to Tovey in a telephone conversation with Pound in which the latter said that under certain circumstances he would order PQ.17 to scatter if it were menaced by the German ships. This flew in the face of all accepted convoy practice and experience. Once a convoy lost cohesion, the individual ships were easy prey for whatever enemy found them. Pound's decision to adopt this course, strongly condemned by Tovey at the time, was an ominous portent of how he would react when PQ.17 was threatened.

The covering forces for the convoy were comprehensive and resembled very much those used for PQ.16. The immediate escort consisted of the minesweepers *Halcyon*, *Britomart* and *Salamander*, with four trawlers. The Close Escort, under the command of Cdr J. E. Broome in HMS *Keppel*, consisted of the destroyers *Leamington*, *Wilton*, *Ledbury*, *Fury* and *Offa*, the corvettes *Lotus*, *Dianella*, *Poppy* and *La Malouine* (Free French) and the submarines *P614* and *P615*. Broome was one of the most colourful characters in the Royal Navy:

> . . . an able and witty cartoonist, a man with a sense of humour buoyant even in the most hazardous of circumstances; a skilled and resolute fighting sailor in the best tradition of convoy escorts.[3]

Two anti-aircraft ships, *Pozarica* and *Palomares*, were also attached to the convoy, with three rescue ships, *Rathlin*, *Zaafaran* and *Zamalek*. Force 'Q' consisted of the oiler *Grey Ranger*, with the destroyer HMS *Douglas* as escort. The latter was to transfer to the homeward-bound QP.13 after refuelling PQ.17's escorts and eventually rendezvous with the battle fleet to fuel its destroyers.

Cruising just out of sight of the convoy, but forbidden to go beyond Bear Island, were four cruisers under the command of Rear-Admiral Louis 'Turtle' Hamilton flying his flag in HMS *London*. Accompanying him were HMS *Norfolk* and the American cruisers *Wichita* and *Tuscaloosa*—the first time that the Americans had participated directly in the running of an Arctic convoy—and the destroyers HMS *Somali*, USS *Wainwright* and USS *Rowan*. Finally, prowling to the north-east of Jan Mayen Island was the battle fleet consisting of HMS *Duke of York* (Admiral Sir John Tovey), USS *Washington*, HMS *Victorious*, HMS *Nigeria*, HMS *Cumberland* and fourteen destroyers.

Meanwhile the convoy was assembling in the unwelcoming surroundings of Hvalfjord in Iceland. PQ.17 consisted of 35 merchant ships, including the CAM ship *Empire Tide*, their holds and decks packed with supplies for the Red Army. In command was Commodore Jack Dowding DSO RNR in the *River Afton*. The Masters had attended the usual pre-sailing conference, where Rear-Admiral Hamilton had assured them that, although the convoy would be 'no joyride', the merchantmen would be well protected by the covering Anglo-American fleet: 'You may not see a lot of these vessels. But they will be in close support throughout.'[4] These remarks were enthusiastically received by the assembled Masters, and when taken with Hamilton's prediction that he saw no reason why PQ.17 should not reach Archangel unscathed, they only made what was to happen seem more cruel.

On 27 June the merchant ships left Hvalfjord with their escorting minesweeper and trawlers. On the 30 June Cdr Broome's close escort of destroyer, corvettes and submarines joined and the whole force steamed eastwards. Since the ice had receded further north than usual, the convoy was routed to go north of Bear Island, which would place it further away from the German airfields in northern Norway. Its destination was Archangel rather than Murmansk since the latter had virtually ceased to exist after protracted bombing by the *Luftwaffe*.

The deception plan advocated by Admiral Tovey involved the five ships of the 1st Minelaying Squadron, four colliers and some destroyers and trawlers, escorted by the cruisers *Sirius* and *Curacao*, making feints to the eastward as far as 1°E. Two advances were made on 30 June and 1 July but, unfortunately, the ships went unseen by the Germans. A diversionary bombing raid on targets in southern Norway also had no effect.

Although the Germans were aware of the convoy's progress through their *B-Dienst* service, the first contact with the convoy occurred on 1 July when the escorts attacked *U255* (*Kapitänleutnant* Reinhard Reche) and *U408* (*Kapitänleutnant* Reinhard von Hymmen), which had been sighted on the surface, several miles from the convoy. However, once the U-boats had been beaten off and forced to dive, the attack was not pursued. Cdr Broome commented in his report on this difference in policy with regard to U-boats between the Atlantic and North Russia convoys:

> In the Atlantic, with one main threat, sighting a U-boat is a clear lower-deck affair, followed by determined and prolonged hunting, whereas [in the Arctic] with air attack as probably the greater threat, all one can do is throw something at the U-boats as they appear.[5]

U334 (*Kapitänleutnant* Wilmar Siemon) and *U456* (*Kapitänleutnant* Max-Martin Teichert) were directed on to the convoy while the boats of the '*Eisteufel*' group (*U251, U335, U657, U457, U88* and *U376*) were ordered to take up a patrol line across the convoy's line of advance further to the east.

At noon on the same day the first shadowing aircraft came on the scene. From then on, apart from small intervals when the vessels were hidden by fog, one or more shadowers was constantly with the convoy. Meanwhile the westbound convoy, QP.13, had sailed from Archangel and the Kola Inlet with 12 and 23 ships respectively. This convoy, too, was detected by air reconnaissance, but since the Germans had relatively little interest in empty ships in ballast when there were bigger fish to fry, it was left unmolested. The two convoys passed each other on 1 July in position 73°N 3°E. The oiler *Grey Ranger* was now detached from PQ.17 and joined the homeward-bound convoy.

Early in the evening of 1 July PQ.17 received its first air attack when seven He 115s of *I/KüFlGr 906*, having been vectored on to the merchantmen by *U456* (Teichert) and a circling BV 138 shadowing aircraft, made an unsuccessful low-level torpedo attack. One of the aircraft was shot down by HMS *Fury*, although *Zaafaran* and USS *Rowan* also claimed the honour of scoring PQ.17's first success. As the crew abandoned their sinking aircraft, Broome told the destroyer *Wilton* to pick them up. However, as *Wilton* approached the site of the crash, one of the other He 115s swooped down alongside the men in the water, took them on board and then struggled to get airborne again through a hail of anti-aircraft fire. This was a tremendous feat of airmanship in any circumstances—but first blood had, nevertheless, gone to the convoy.

By this time Hamilton's cruisers had overhauled the convoy and were standing away to the northward. Hamilton had decided to steer a parallel course to the convoy some 40 miles away, out of sight of the shadowers, in order to keep the enemy guessing his whereabouts. He considered that *Tirpitz* might go for QP.13 in order to draw the British battle group south while *Lützow* and *Scheer* made for PQ.17. Accordingly, the longer he stayed out of sight, the greater were his chances of bringing the two pocket-battleships to action.

However, during the evening of 1 July Hamilton decided that he was on the wrong side of the convoy since *Lützow* and *Scheer* might attack in the fog and escape unscathed. He therefore closed the convoy and, thinking (wrongly) that he had been sighted, opened out again to his former distance. He closed the convoy again at 2215 when it was 30 miles north-west of Bear Island. This time the shadowers did sight the cruisers and report their presence, which pleased Hamilton enormously since he had heard from London that the German ships were on the move.

Although Tovey's battle fleet had been sighted by an FW 200 long-range reconnaissance aircraft, there was no reason why stage one of '*Rösselsprung*', the move of the fleet to northern Norway, should not go ahead. Accordingly, after a staff meeting on 2 July, Raeder authorized *Gruppe Nord* in Kiel to issue the appropriate orders. However, the strong hand of central control was never far away, for Raeder also had to ensure that Admiral Theodore Krancke, the *Kriegsmarine*'s representative at the *Führer*'s headquarters, was kept fully informed of all developments—including all operational orders issued to the Fleet.

The operation got off to a shaky start. As *Tirpitz* and *Hipper* left Trondheim, three of their escorting destroyers ran aground and had to be left behind, so that the group arrived at Gimsøystrammen in the Lofoten Islands with only one. Misfortune also attended the Narvik group: *Lützow* ran aground in Tjelsund and sustained severe damage, and she was unable to take part in the operation. Hitler's strictures about no further movement until the British aircraft carrier had been located and disabled held good, so Raeder's hands were tied. However, he was able to concentrate his forces by moving *Tirpitz*, *Hipper* and their one destroyer to join *Scheer* in Altenfjord during the night of 4 July. And there the ships stayed.

Early on 4 July the convoy suffered its first loss when a single He 115, diving through a gap in the cloud, dropped a torpedo which struck the US freighter *Christopher Newport* amidships. The crew were picked up by *Zaafaran*, and Broome sent the minesweeper HMS *Britomart* to investigate whether the ship was worth salving. At 0520 *Britomart* reported:

Master of *Christopher Newport* reports that engine room and stokehold flooded. Might float if bulkheads hold. Steering gear out of action.[6]

Broome took the painful but necessary decision that precious escorts could not be diverted to help the cripple. The corvette *Dianella* was ordered to escort the submarine *P614* over to the stricken freighter and sink her. However, two or three torpedoes had no effect, so *Dianella* tried dropping a couple of depth charges under her counter. Again there was no result. By this time the convoy had disappeared over the horizon and only *Zamalek* remained in sight. Reluctantly, the two ships left the *Christopher Newport* afloat, eventually to be sunk by *U457*.

Meanwhile the dual nature of command being exercised by Admiral Pound in Whitehall and Admiral Tovey at sea was resulting in a series of at best puzzling and at worst contradictory orders being issued to Hamilton. From various intelligence sources open to them, the Admiralty deduced that the German ships would attack PQ.17 when it had reached a position between 15° and 30°E, which would occur some time on 4 July, and informed Tovey, whose ships were disposed 100 miles south-west of Spitzbergen, of this. At 1230 the Admiralty informed Hamilton that he could, after all, take his cruisers east of 25°E in support of the convoy unless Tovey ordered him otherwise.

Tovey regarded this order as a change of policy which he had previously agreed with Pound. There was clearly an edginess between the two men over the conduct of the operation, and Tovey obviously disliked having his assets ordered around:

At 1345 I received [a signal] giving CS One permission to proceed beyond 25 degrees East. This was a reversal of the policy agreed between their Lordships and myself in your 0157B/27. No information in my possession justified this change.[7]

Accordingly he ordered Hamilton, at 1512, to leave the Barents Sea, unless he could be assured by the Admiralty that *Tirpitz* was not at large, once the convoy had passed 25°E, or earlier if he felt it safe to do so. This signal crossed one sent by Hamilton at 1520 stating that he intended to remain with the convoy until the position regarding the movements of the German ships had been clarified, but certainly not later than 1400 on 5 July. However, at 1809 he amended this and expressed his intention of withdrawing at 2200 on 4 July once his destroyers had fuelled. Even then the long arm of Admiralty control intervened across the chain of command, for at 1858 Pound ordered Hamilton to stay with the convoy pending further instructions, adding that 'further information may be available shortly'.

Meanwhile the convoy was ploughing steadily along. The fog which had been very thick earlier in the day had cleared and visibility was excellent. Despite the fog, the convoy had maintained a good, tight formation, as Cdr Broome recalled:

Fog may have its protective angle, I wrote later, but it can play hell with a convoy's figure. The bold stand on, the cautious edge outwards, the timid drop back, formation goes to blazes. I wish I had an aerial photograph of what I saw then [as the convoy emerged from the fog]. Column leaders had kept their distance, ships in column their station. They seemed to be saying as I went by, 'Look, no radar.' It was a splendid sight.

That morning stands out in my memory; in bright sunshine, a glass calm sea and, except for the whining Blohm and Voss duet, peaceful. The air was crisp and brand new, the visibility back to phenomenal. Across the northern horizon was strung a weird-shaped lumpy line of vivid emerald green icebergs like chunky jewellery.[8]

At 1645, in order to increase the distance between the convoy and the German air base at Banak, Hamilton suggested to Broome that the convoy alter course to the north-east. However, it was not long before the *Luftwaffe* took advantage of the good conditions and at 1930 a single Ju 88 led a group of He 111 torpedo bombers from *I/KG 26*, under the command of *Hauptmann* Eicke, into an attack from the convoy's starboard bow. This attack was frustrated by the very aggressive tactics of the American destroyer *Wainwright* (Cdr D. Moon USN).

Wainwright was part of the screen for Hamilton's cruisers but had come over to the convoy to fuel. As the aircraft were sighted, Moon cast off from the oiler and stood out from the convoy at 32kts until he was some 4,000yds away. He then swung his ship to port and unleashed a barrage of fire which so discomforted the German pilots that they dropped their torpedoes hopelessly out of range. As Broome wrote later in his report,

> This ship [*Wainwright*] lent valuable support with accurate long-range AA fire. I was most impressed for the way she sped round the convoy worrying the circling aircraft and it was largely due to her 4 July enthusiasm that the attack completely failed. One torpedo exploded harmlessly outside the convoy and two bombs fell through the clouds ahead of the convoy between *Wainwright* and *Keppel*.[9]

One German aircraft, flown by *Leutnant* Kaumaeyer, was lost during the attack. Kaumeyer and his crew were picked up by *Ledbury*, whose commanding officer, Lt-Cdr Roger Hill RN, informed Broome that the German pilot had said that the German air crew had been told that the convoy was in thick fog and that the merchant ships would put up little resistance.

However, no sooner had this attack been broken up than a second group of He 111 torpedo bombers approached from the convoy's starboard quarter. This time there was no gallant *Wainwright* to break up the attacking formation, and the aircraft were able to approach to within 6,000yds before dropping their torpedoes. The *William Hooper* was hit and began to settle in the water. Another Heinkel, flown by *Leutnant* Henneman, ploughed through the convoy despite a hail of AA fire—'a very brave action', as Cdr Moon later said—before dropping its torpedoes aimed at the *Bellingham* and *Navarino*. That intended for the *Bellingham* missed by a matter of feet, but the other struck the *Navarino* under her bridge and she suddenly took a large list to starboard. She was then hit by a second torpedo. *Bellingham*, astern of her, had to haul out of line to avoid a collision. As she swept by, one of *Navarino*'s survivors, swimming in the icy water, raised his fist and yelled, 'On to Moscow—see you in Russia!' The rescue ships were quickly on the scene. *Zaafaran* picked up 30 survivors from the *Navarino* and eleven from the *William Hooper*, while Rathlin picked up another 44 from *William Hooper* and nineteen from *Navarino*.

The third casualty of the raid was the Soviet tanker *Azerbaijan*. When she was hit she was engulfed by a cloud of smoke, and all feared the worst. However, she emerged 'holed but happy and capable of nine knots', according to Cdr Broome. The presence of women on board the *Azerbaijan* was a never-ending source of wonder to the British and American merchant seamen. It was rumoured that *Azerbaijan*'s boatswain was a woman and was delivered of a healthy child on arrival at Murmansk.

Four German aircraft had been shot down during the raid, in return for three ships damaged. *Azerbaijan*'s engine room department had got the tanker going again, but *William Hooper* and *Navarino* were beyond redemption. Broome ordered *Britomart* and *Halcyon* to sink both of them with gunfire. However, after twenty rounds of 4in SAP both ships were still afloat, although blazing merrily. The two minesweepers could not loiter in U-boat-infested waters and so sped off after the convoy, passing as they did so a raft containing ten of *Navarino*'s survivors in the water:

The horizon emptied and we were on a raft in the middle of the Arctic Ocean, and we began to fear that the others had reported that we had gone down with the ship. We saw one ship approaching, but it turned out to be a minesweeper hastening to catch up with the convoy. We knew they wouldn't stop for us, but we jokingly stood up and tried to 'thumb a lift'; the men in the minesweeper, which passed less than 200 yards away from us, crowded the rails and cheered us, but their ship did not pause. It had been an act of bravado on our part but we would have liked it better had they stopped . . .[10]

Eventually the rescue ship *Zamalek*, which had remained in the area long enough to ensure than none were left behind, saw the raft and picked up the ten men.

Admiral Hamilton, who had been a distant observer of the attack from his flagship HMS *London*, was impressed by the courage and determination shown by the merchantmen. He was also amazed that the *Luftwaffe* had left his squadron alone, despite their proximity to the convoy: clearly, the pilots had been ordered to concentrate on the merchant ships.

Morale in PQ.17 was now at an all-time high. During the evening Broome turned *Keppel* round and steamed through the ranks of merchant ships. The air attacks had been launched from the point where the convoy was nearest to Banak, and every mile steamed now opened the range. The merchant ships had shown that they could beat off a concerted air attack and, although fire discipline left something to be desired, Broome was filled with confidence about the convoy's prospects:

All this was summed up by what I saw from my bridge. It looked as if nothing had happened. The two gaps had been filled, a place left for the Russian. The Commodore was dead right when he called it hardly a successful attack.[11]

That night Broome felt confident enough to write in his diary:

My impression on seeing the resolution displayed by the convoy and its escort was that, providing the ammunition lasted, PQ.17 could get anywhere.[12]

It was at this moment, when all seemed to be going so well, that disaster struck. Although part one of *'Rösselsprung'* had been executed, the ships were still swinging round their buoys in Altenfjord, waiting for clarification of the whereabouts of the British aircraft carrier. There they remained until the afternoon of 5 July. As Capt Stephen Roskill, the official British historian, pointed out, 'So much for the enemy's actual dispositions. Let us now see how they appeared to the Admiralty at the time.'

Air reconnaissance of the north Norwegian coast had been undertaken by Catalina flying boats of No 210 Squadron RAF based in northern Russia, and these were supplemented by regular patrols from UK-based aircraft. However, between 1100 and 1700 on 4 July there was a gap in the coverage owing to one aircraft having become unserviceable. It is therefore likely that the uncertainty produced by this gap was of critical importance in influencing the Admiralty's judgement. As well as the failure of air reconnaissance, there was a delay in deciphering the German naval codes from midday on 3 July to midday on the 4th.

In the evening of 4 July Pound convened a staff conference to discuss the situation. He visited Cdr Norman Denning in the Operational Intelligence Centre (OIC) to study the plot, accompanied by Rear-Admiral E. J. P. Brind (ACNS), Capt John Eccles (Director of Operations—Home) and Vice-Admiral Henry Moore (VCNS). Rear-Admiral Clay- ton, the Director of OIC, recalled that

> Pound sat down on a stool in front of the main plotting table. The plot showed the planned convoy route, the position of the convoy, our own forces and, as far as was known or estimated, the position of U-boats and German surface forces.
>
> Bletchley had not yet broken the new keys.
>
> *Luftwaffe* reconnaissance had still not relocated Tovey's force and had not yet located Hamilton's cruiser force.
>
> Almost immediately Pound asked what would be the furthest position of *Tirpitz* assuming she had sailed direct from Trondheim Fjord to attack the convoy . . . someone—I think it was Brind—plotted a rough course and estimated that she could then be within striking distance of the convoy.
>
> I interjected that it was unlikely in any event that she would have taken a direct course from Trondheim Fjord as she would have certainly made as much use as she could of the Inner Leads and proceeded via Vest Fjord. I also consider that she would put into Narvik or Tromsø to refuel her escorting destroyers before setting out on a sortie.[13]

Denning then told Pound that Bletchley Park would have deciphered the latest German naval traffic within a few hours, and this evidently prompted Pound's signal to Hamilton ordering him to remain with the convoy 'until further instructions'.

At 1900 the first new decrypts came through from Bletchley Park. A *Luftwaffe* message timed at 0400 that morning reported the sighting of a force of three cruisers and a battleship. From the position given in the report, this was correctly interpreted as being Hamilton's force. The second decrypt was from Raeder to Admiral Commanding Cruisers at Narvik. This read:

> Immediate. Arriving Alta [Altenfjord] 0900. You are to allocate anchorage to *Tirpitz* . . . Newly arrived destroyers and torpedo boats are to complete with fuel at once.[14]

Denning was in the middle of drafting a signal to convey this information to Tovey and Hamilton when Pound returned to OIC, followed by several members of the Naval Staff and then shortly by Moore and the ACNS (Trade), Vice-Admiral E. L. S. King. Pound asked Denning

> . . . what I was proposing to say. I gave the gist of the two intercepts and a proposed comment that all indications pointed to *Tirpitz* and accompanying ships still being in harbour at Alta. Pound apparently considered the comment premature and my proposed 'Ultra' was whittled down to the bald facts that *Tirpitz* had arrived at Alta at 0900 that morning and that *Admiral Scheer* was already there.[15]

What followed depended on whether or not *Tirpitz* was at sea heading for the convoy.

> Pound resumed the seat at the head of the plotting table and enquired how long it would take for the destroyers to top up with fuel. I had mentally calculated this at about three hours. Then he asked what was likely to be the speed of the *Tirpitz*. I replied probably 25 or 26 knots provided the weather was favourable for the destroyers but probably 2 or 3 knots less if the pocket-battleships were in company.
>
> Taking up the dividers and using a smaller chart of the area for plotting, Pound remarked that if *Tirpitz* had sailed from Alta that morning she could be up with the convoy at about midnight. He then asked why I thought *Tirpitz* had not yet left Alta?[16]

Denning recalled the experience gained of noting the Germans' *modus operandi* during *Tirpitz*'s sortie against PQ.12. He told Pound that no order telling U-boats to clear the operational area—for fear of their attacking *Tirpitz* in error—had been received, and the HF/DF readings were showing numerous U-boats trailing the convoy. Moreover, there had been none of the usual radio chatter usually associated with German capital ship movements. Finally, there had been no sightings by any of the submarines deployed off the North Cape. Denning also told Pound that the signal erroneously reporting Hamilton's squadron as including a battleship so near the convoy would only increase the German Naval Staff's apprehension. The *Luftwaffe* had also sighted an aircraft near the convoy (which was *London*'s Walrus, flown off on ice reconnaissance), which raised the grim prospect of the British carrier stalking somewhere to the north of the convoy. After a brief discussion,

> Pound got up to proceed to the U-boat tracking room but, before leaving, he turned to me and asked, 'Can you assure me that *Tirpitz* is still in Altenfjord?'
>
> My reply was to the effect that although I was confident that she was, I could not give absolute assurance but fully expected to receive confirmation in the fairly near future when Bletchley had unbuttoned the new traffic.[17]

Denning's beliefs were confirmed when at 2031 a new decrypt arrived from Admiral Commanding *Gruppe Nord* to all U-boats pursuing PQ.17, advising them that no friendly surface units were in the area. Denning showed the signal to Clayton, who took it along to Pound. To Denning it appeared wholly unlikely that *Tirpitz* was at sea. The Germans had not relocated Tovey's fleet and now there was this second report of a battleship, and possibly a second carrier, near the convoy. To any German admiral, a sortie at this juncture would involve an unacceptable risk. Accordingly, the Germans were urging their U-boats and aircraft to carry on the attack while confirming, for the benefit of the U-boats, that there were no 'friendly' ships in the area. This appreciation dovetailed entirely with Tovey's letter to the Admiralty of 14 March in which he claimed that the Germans would never risk *Tirpitz* in any operation unless the chances of success were absolute.

Denning now began to draft a signal to Tovey and Hamilton based on his conclusions. According to his later recollection, it stated that

. . . it was considered that *Tirpitz* and accompanying ships were still in Altenfjord at 1200/4. Indications strongly pointed to them not having yet sailed. It was unlikely that they would sail until Germans have established location and strength of the forces in support of the convoy.[18]

Denning did have the authority to send this signal of his own volition but felt it ought to await Clayton's return from a meeting with the First Sea Lord. His fears were aroused in a conversation with Cdr Roger Winn, of the U-boat Tracking Room, who understood from the discussion going on in his department that Pound believed *Tirpitz* to be at sea and was considering dispersing the convoy. When Clayton returned he was shown Denning's draft signal and agreed to take it to Pound. Almost immediately he was back and told Denning that 'Father's made his decision and he's not going to change it now'.[19]

Pound had made the decisions to order Hamilton's ships to withdraw to the westward at high speed and to disperse the convoy based wholly on negative evidence. He had never held operational command during the present war and his thoughts and opinions had been conditioned by the artificiality of peacetime exercises. Moreover, instead of showing Tovey the available intelligence and letting him deal with the situation accordingly. Pound could never resist the temptation to assert direct control of an operation over the head of the relevant commander-in-chief.

The first of three fateful signals was dispatched at 2111:

Most Immediate. Cruiser force withdraw westward at high speed.

This was followed at 2123 and 2136 respectively by

Immediate. Owing to threat from surface ships, convoy is to disperse and proceed to Russian ports.

and

Most immediate. My 2123/4. Convoy is to scatter.

The order to scatter was purely a technicality issued to correct the term 'disperse' used in the signal sent at 2123. In the context of convoy instructions, 'disperse' meant merely to spread out, while 'scatter' meant literally that. The use of a more urgent priority on the 2136 signal undoubtedly gave it greater importance.

Three factors have to be taken into account when discussing Pound's directive. First, the decision to scatter was based on the German's anticipated intentions rather than on evidence that *Tirpitz* was at sea. To scatter the convoy was taking a gamble in that the risks to the merchant ships from air and submarine attack were less than the risk from attack by the German surface ships—although the latter threat had not arisen and might not do so. Second, the order to scatter was categorical in tone and gave those at sea no indication of the intelligence which underlay it. The official historian observes that 'it is hard to justify such an intervention made in such a way.'[20]. The language used in the three signals, which almost conveys a note of panic, does Pound no credit as a leader in a crisis. Third, the manner in which the signals were sent to the convoy gave the impression that *Tirpitz* and her consorts were just over the horizon. To Hamilton and Broome, the three signals, taken as a whole, would constitute the 'further information' promised to them earlier and indicate that a moment of extreme urgency had arisen demanding immediate action.

Pound's leadership and judgement during these critical hours raise a number of questions. Why had he not left matters to the Commander-in-Chief at sea to decide? Why did he find it easier to believe that *Tirpitz* was at sea rather than in Altenfjord? And why, having assumed that *Tirpitz* was at sea, did he order Hamilton's cruisers to withdraw, which was contrary to Tovey's own directive issued in March that in the face of attack by surface ships the escorts should remain with the convoy. Why, also, did he order the convoy to disperse and then scatter at all? This order flew in the face of Admiralty policy, derived from bitter experience gained at sea, which stated that a convoy was better off staying together. Why did Pound concentrate overwhelmingly on the threat posed by *Tirpitz* and ignore the more immediate threat posed by U-boats and aircraft? As one eminent historian has concluded,

> It is not unjust to see in all of this a combination of Pound's old-fashioned naval authoritarianism and his well-known stubborn close-mindedness— coupled with that lack of imaginative talent which is the mark of great commanders.[21]

The signal was received on *Keppel*'s bridge with incredulity followed by anger. Broome later described his feelings as akin to having received an electric shock. A signalman on *Keppel*'s bridge, Leading Signalman Elliot, later described Broome as 'a very angry man'. Broome subsequently wrote:

> I was angry at being forced to break up, disintegrate such a formation and to tear up the protective fence we had wrapped around it, to order each of these splendid merchantmen to sail on by her naked defenceless self; for once that signal reached the masthead it triggered off an irrevocable measure. Convoy PQ.17 would cease to exist.[22]

Even so, Broome never questioned the Admiralty's judgement:

I wish to make my appreciation at this moment quite clear. An order to scatter—especially when made most immediate by signal, following an order to disperse, thereby giving the impression of a situation developing rapidly—is, in my impression, given when the threat is imminent, from surface forces more powerful than the escort. By imminent I mean that surface forces are in sight. We were all expecting, therefore, to see either the cruisers open fire, or to see enemy masts appearing over the horizon.[23]

Rear-Admiral Hamilton, in his flagship HMS *London*, steaming some five miles ahead of the convoy, entertained similar sentiments:

Up to the receipt of the Admiralty's 2111, 2123 and 2136, according to the information available to me, the *Tirpitz* could not arrive in the vicinity of the convoy until 2am/5July, assuming the *Admiral Scheer* was with her, or midnight if alone. The Admiralty's signals referred to therefore led me to believe that not only were they in possession of later information but that *Tirpitz* was at sea and in the near vicinity of the convoy.[24]

The order had been given, so the white pennant with the red cross of St George fluttered up to *Keppel*'s yardarm to execute the order to scatter. However, the signal was received in the convoy with disbelief, and most ships hoisted the same flag but kept it at the dip, indicating that the signal had not been understood. To Broome it was imperative that the convoy be scattered before *Tirpitz* appeared over the horizon. Accordingly, he took *Keppel* into the convoy and wove in and out of the ships, repeating the signal by searchlight and R/T. He closed the *River Afton*, Commodore Dowding's ship, and Broome later recalled:

We were not strangers. We had sailed together before, we respected one another. My visit and conversation were brief, for time was not for wasting. Naturally I put him in the picture as I saw it, [and] told him outright that I had faith in this order from Admiralty. When I sheered *Keppel* away from *River Afton* I left an angry and, I still believe, unconvinced Commodore.[25]

Broome also had to consider the dispersal of the escort. The trawlers, minesweepers, corvettes and AA ships would be of no use against *Tirpitz* but could not be left to meander around the Barents Sea, so Broome ordered them to proceed to Archangel while at the same time ordering the destroyers to join him. The two submarines, *P614* and *P615*, were ordered to act independently, and there then occurred one of the classic signal exchanges which rose above the tragedy of the situation. Lt Beckley in *P614* signalled to Broome, in all seriousness, that in the event of *Tirpitz* appearing he intended to remain on the surface, presumably in the hope that the sight of a submarine would scare the *Tirpitz* off. To this signal Broome replied with grim humour, 'So do I'.

Broome felt that his destroyers—all of which except for the two 'Hunts', *Ledbury* and *Wilton*, carried a sizeable torpedo armament—would be of more use supporting Hamilton's cruisers, which were now streaking across the bows of the convoy. From their mounting bow waves and stern wakes, it was clear that they were going flat out. At 2230 he signalled 'Propose Close Escort destroyers join you' and received the affirmative. In his report, Hamilton considered that

> My reason for attaching the destroyers to my force was that I assumed that *Tirpitz* was at sea and approaching the vicinity. Had this in fact been so, the addition of six destroyers to my force would have been invaluable, whereas the possibility of their being any protection to the scattering convoy was negligible in comparison.[26]

So the four cruisers and six destroyers tore away to the westward, expecting to go into action at any minute. The Commanding Officer of HMS *Ledbury*, Lt-Cdr Roger Hill, remembered that

> We sent down most of the anti-aircraft shells and got up armour piercing. I told my Number One that when the destroyers which carried torpedoes went into attack . . . we would go with them to make another target and give fire support. We would turn as if firing torpedoes and throw some big metal bins over the side. Privately, I decided that, if we ever got that far, we would go on and try to ram the *Tirpitz*.[27]

Broome and his fellow destroyer Commanding Officers were not running away. They were prepared to bring *Tirpitz* to action and sell their lives dearly in the defence of the convoy and the best traditions of the Service. But as time wore on and nothing happened, anger and anticipation gave way to puzzlement and a sense of shame. The change from exhilaration and a feeling of success following the beating-off of the air attack was so great that many officers and men felt numb. Hill wrote in his report that

> It was now realised that we were abandoning the convoy and running away and the whole ship's company was cast into bitter despondency.[28]

The feeling was more bluntly expressed by Vice-Admiral W. D. O'Brien, who at the time was serving in HMS *Offa* as First Lieutenant:

> I have never been able to rejoice with my American friends on Independence Day, because July 4 is, to me, a day to hang my head in grief for all the men who lost their lives on Convoy PQ.17 and in shame at one of the bleakest episodes in Royal Navy history, when the warships deserted the merchant ships and left them to their fate. For that in simple terms was what we were obliged to do.[29]

As time went on, Hamilton and Broome became more and more puzzled as to what could have led the Admiralty to have ordered the convoy to scatter. Broome thought that Hamilton was acting on more comprehensive information than he possessed and expected to be sent back to aid the merchant ships as soon as Hamilton felt the situation allowed. The ships ran into thick fog, which lasted until early on the morning of 5 July; when the fog cleared, Broome informed Hamilton of his last orders to the convoy and requested that they should be amended if necessary.

Hamilton, however, was as much in ignorance of the situation as was Broome. Correctly as it turned out, he believed that, once air reconnaissance had told the Germans that the convoy had scattered, they would leave the merchant ships to the *Luftwaffe* and U-boats. Hamilton gave the Germans more credit than they deserved, for he also believed that *Tirpitz* and her consorts would transfer their attentions to his ships. He felt that, with Broome's destroyers under his command, he could fight a delaying action and lure the Germans to within range of *Victorious*'s aircraft and possibly the big guns of the Home Fleet. He therefore decided to keep Broome's ships under his command. A secondary consideration was that

> . . . they could do little except screen individual ships, if they could find them. In view of their fuel situation and the difficulties they would have in finding an oiler, I considered that, with the possibility of offensive action by the battlefleet and *Victorious* against the enemy ships, the most useful service the destroyers could perform would be with the battlefleet.[30]

Accordingly, Hamilton continued to head west until 1740, when the force was spotted by an FW 200. Having been discovered, Hamilton felt that he could break radio silence without compromising himself and reported the position, course and composition of his force to Tovey. This was the first news Tovey had had that the destroyers were not with the convoy.

At this time Tovey's ships were heading back toward Scapa. After receiving news that the German ships had, in fact left port (see next chapter), Tovey was reluctant to reverse course to the eastward since he felt that he would not be able to close the area sufficiently for *Victorious* to launch a strike. Although he had reports that *Tirpitz* had been damaged by the Soviet submarine *K21* (Capt 2nd Rank N. A. Lunin), Tovey still considered that the battleship would be protected by such a huge air umbrella that an air strike would be suicidal.

Hamilton's ships joined the fleet at 1040 on 6 July but were detached to proceed to Seidisfjord at 1240 while the battle fleet headed for Scapa. All ships reached harbour on the 8 July. Behind them in the icy wastes of the Barents Sea, the merchant ships, alone and defenceless, were at the mercy of the *Luftwaffe* and U-boats.

11-11-07

NOTES TO CHAPTER 5

1. Dispatch of Admiral of the Fleet Sir John Tovey, *The London Gazette*, 17 October 1950.

2. PRO ADM.234/369, 'Battle Summary No 22: Arctic Convoys 1941–45', 1954, p.55.

3. Barnett, Corelli, *Engage the Enemy More Closely*, Hodder & Stoughton, London, 1992, p.712.

4. Irving, D., *The Destruction of Convoy PQ.17*, William Kimber, 1980, p.57.

5. PRO ADM.234/369, *op. cit.*, p.57.

6. Irving, D., *op. cit.*, p.96.

7. Commander-in-Chief Home Fleet's Dispatch, quoted in Broome, Capt J., *Convoy is to Scatter*, William Kimber, 1972, p.151.

8. Broome, *op. cit.*, p.149.

9. *ibid.*, p.150.

10. Account of Capt John Evans, Second Officer of the Navarino, in Irving, *op. cit.*, p.119.

11. Broome, *op. cit.*, p.167.

12. *ibid.*

13. ROSK5/72: Photocopy of an unpublished memoir by Vice-Admiral Sir Norman Denning, the OIC officer responsible for the evaluation of German fleet movements.

14. *ibid.*

15. *ibid.*

16. *ibid.*

17. *ibid.*

18. *ibid*

19. *ibid.*

20. Roskill, Capt S. W., *The War at Sea 1939–45*, Vol 2, HMSO, London, 1956, p.140.

21. Barnett, *op. cit.*, p.719.

22. Broome, *op. cit.*, p.187.

23. PRO ADM.199/757, 'Report of Proceedings of the Commanding Officer of HMS *Keppel*'.

24. PRO ADM.199/757, 'Report of Proceedings of Flag Officer Commanding the First Cruiser Squadron'.

25. Broome, *op. cit.*, p.193.

26. PRO ADM.199/757, 'Report of Proceedings of Flag Officer Commanding the First Cruiser Squadron'.

27. Hill, Roger, *Destroyer Captain*,William Kimber, p.45.

28. PRO ADM.199/757, 'Report of Proceedings of the Commanding Officer of HMS *Ledbury*'.

29. Quoted in Lund and Ludlam's *PQ.17: Convoy to Hell. The Survivors' Story*. W. Foulsham & Co, 1968.

30. PRO ADM., 'Report of Proceedings of Flag Officer Commanding the First Cruiser Squadron'.

Chapter 6

A Bloody Business

Sorry to leave you like this. Goodbye and good luck. It looks like a bloody business.—Signal from Commander Jack Broome, Senior Officer of PQ.17's escort, to Commodore Jack Dowding following the order for the convoy to scatter

The procedure for scattering a convoy was quite simple. The ships in the centre column (or that to the right of centre in the case of convoys with an even number of columns) continued their course; ships in the columns either side of the centre turned 10 degrees away from the centre column; ships in the next further out on each side turned 20 degrees away from the centre column; and this procedure was continued, with the ships of each column turning 10 degrees more than those of their adjacent inner column. The effect was that the ships started to diverge as though along the spokes of a fan. Additionally, each ship was to increase to full speed and to maintain a constant W/T watch. Subsequent action was left to the discretion of the individual ships' Masters.

This, therefore, was the scene on the night of 4 July 1942 as the ships of PQ.17 scattered. The remaining ships of the escort needed no urging to get going and clear the area as quickly as possible. The AA ship *Palomares* ordered the corvettes *Lotus*, *Poppy* and *La Malouine* to join her to provide anti-submarine screening; she in return was able to provide the corvettes with AA defence, and headed north-east toward the ice barrier, where she was joined by *Rathlin* with over 60 survivors on board. Her sister-ship *Pozarica* gathered up *Dianella*, *Salamander* and *Britomart* and headed south-east. The trawlers *Lord Middleton*, *Lord Austin* and *Northern Gem* also headed north-east, as did the trawler *Ayrshire* (to whose proceedings we shall return later). The remaining ships in the convoy all steered eastward at best speed. As the two groups of escorts made their way east, many of the merchant ships tried to keep up with them for protection. However, the escorts were going too fast:

We'd actually gone into a deep bight in the ice which took us much further northwards than we needed to go. So we had to turn round and come back down again. By this time the merchant ships were strung out over ten or fifteen miles behind us. No way could we give them the necessary protection.[1]

Although it made sense for the corvettes and AA ships to provide each other with mutual protection, the spectre of the warships clinging together for mutual protection while the merchant ships were later picked off one by one is less than edifying.

It did not take the Germans long to realize that the convoy was now defenceless. The Germans' first reaction, however, was puzzlement at what had happened to the convoy. Air reconnaissance reported at 0100 on 5 July that the convoy was spread over 25 miles. Teichert in *U456* had meanwhile reported that the cruiser squadron was heading south-west while the merchant ships were steaming northwards past him. These reports were confirmed by *Kapitänleutnant* Hilmar Simeon in *U334*, who had previously diposed of the *William Hooper* and *Navarino* damaged in the earlier air attack.

Shortly after 0200 Teichert, who had lost the convoy in fog, sighted scattered groups of merchant ships, as did *Korvettenkapitän* Brandenburg in *U457*. At 0315 Admiral Hubert Schmundt received a signal from North East Air Command which confirmed what he was already hearing from his U-boat commanders. The *Luftwaffe* reported that the convoy had split into two loose groups, one steering north and consisting of nineteen freighters, three 'destroyers' and two corvettes; and a southern group consisting of twelve freighters and a light cruiser—which was certainly one of the AA ships wrongly identified. The aircraft confirmed that there were no heavy forces at all in the area. Further such signals throughout the night confirmed the position, and so Schmundt ordered the *'Eisteufel'* U-boats to concentrate on the merchant ships.

It was not long before the U-boats found their first victim. *U703 (Kapitänleutnant* Hans Bielefeld) was rapidly overhauling the *Empire Byron* while *U88 (Kapitänleutnant* Heino Bohmann) was manoeuvring for a firing position against the *Carlton*. At 0715 Bielefeld fired two torpedoes to sink the *Empire Byron*. However, he gravely overestimated her speed, and it was not until he fired his fifth torpedo that he scored a hit. Twenty minutes after the attack *Empire Byron* rolled over and sank, leaving 42 survivors in lifeboats, eighteen of her company having lost their lives. Bielefeld surfaced and moved over to the two lifeboats. He ordered an English-speaking officer down on to the casing to see if the *Empire Byron*'s Master was among the survivors. However, Capt John Wharton had prudently removed his uniform jacket and told the other officers to do the same. But Capt John Rimington, an REME[2] officer going to Russia to advise the Red Army about their British-built Churchill tanks, neglected to remove his jacket, and after a brief argument he was taken aboard the U-boat and hustled below. At the same time the submarine's crew handed over tins of biscuits, sausage and apple juice before she submerged. Bielefeld broke radio silence to report to Schmundt:

Ten thousand ton *Empire Byron* sunk, pinpoint, AC.2629. Cargo: tanks. Destination: Archangel. Captain John Rimington taken aboard as prisoner . . . Convoy in rout. Heading 120 degrees. I am following hard.[3]

An hour and a half after Bielefeld had disposed of the *Empire Byron*, Bohmann's *U88* was stalking the *Carlton*. At 1015 he fired two torpedoes and scored one hit. The explosion smashed two of the three lifeboats so the crew would have to cram into the one surviving boat and four rafts. Three of the *Carlton*'s crew died in the explosion, but the remaining forty got away from the sinking ship although some were badly burned. Bohmann brought his boat to the surface to have a look at his handiwork and to send a victory signal to Schmundt announcing the sinking of a

10,000-ton ship, but he did not approach the survivors and instead sped off to the east, leaving the lifeboat and two rafts on a glassy, calm sea, alone except for chilling glimpses of grey icebergs. Later that afternoon German seaplanes took off 23 of the survivors, leaving the remainder gathered in one boat.

Meanwhile four of the merchant ships, *Fairfield City, Daniel Morgan, Benjamin Harrison* and *John Witherspoon*, had caught up with the AA ship *Pozarica* and the minesweepers *Britomart* and *Halcyon*—four merchant ships clinging to the remains of the escort in a mute appeal for protection. This little group did not escape the eagle eye of a BV 138, which shadowed them all night, evidently broadcasting homing signals for a U-boat. However, *Pozarica* (Capt J. H. Jauncey RN) did not reduce speed to accommodate the merchant ships, which were running at maximum revolutions in order to keep up with her, but at 1300 on 6 July altered course, telling the merchant ships not to follow her, and sped off with the two minesweepers at superior speed.

The four merchant ships then headed for the safety of a nearby fogbank, with the BV 138 relentlessly overhead. Just before she disappeared into the fog the *Daniel Morgan* reversed course and fired off a barrage of 3in gunfire to prevent the aircraft from determining the course of the other three ships as they entered the bank. However, her lone, gallant stand had separated her from the other three ships, so *Daniel Morgan* headed off towards Novaya Zemlya.

At about 1500 in the afternoon *Daniel Morgan* joined up with the *Fairfield City*, but as the two ships headed east they were attacked by a flight of Ju 88s from *KG 30*. While the *Daniel Morgan* put up another barrage of AA fire, the aircraft concentrated on the *Fairfield City*, hitting her with three sticks of bombs. Three lifeboats got away before the burning ship sank, taking her cargo of tanks to the bottom. *Daniel Morgan* sped off towards the east, leaving the lifeboats to follow as best they could.

The *Luftwaffe* had not given up on the *Daniel Morgan*, and over the next few hours she was on the receiving end of numerous air attacks, all of which were avoided by the skilful action of her Master, Capt Sullivan. However, his luck could not last for ever, and eventually a stick of bombs exploded alongside the ship's starboard quarter, rupturing the plates between Nos 4 and 5 holds. She immediately assumed a list to starboard and, with her steering gear out of action, began to meander about aimlessly.

Observing all of this was Bohmann in *U88*, who had been stalking the *Daniel Morgan* all day. He could hear machinery noises from the stopped merchant ship on his hydrophones and concluded that a party of men was still aboard the merchantman, trying to restore her shattered machinery. A single torpedo fired into the *Daniel Morgan*'s port side, followed by another into the engine room, put paid to any attempts at repair, and the freighter was soon on her way to the bottom, leaving her survivors in three lifeboats on the surface.

The 6,977grt *Honomu* was the next to go. She was being followed by Siemon's *U334*, which was finally able to fire at 1536 on 5 July. An explosion was noted ahead after what was assumed to be the correct running time, but shortly afterwards the U-boat's hydrophone operator reported that he could still hear the torpedo running. *Honomu* had been torpedoed by another U-boat—Lt-Cdr Max Martin Teichert's *U456*. Nineteen of *Honomu*'s crew were killed in the attack, leaving 34 survivors in the water.

By this time SOS messages from merchant ships under attack were coming in thick and fast. The commanding officer of HMS *Lotus*, Lt Henry Hall RN, suggested to Capt Lawford of *Pozarica* that the escorts go back and render assistance to some of the merchant ships. Lawford diagreed:

> I have been giving full consideration to this matter for half an hour and have come to the conclusion that the order to scatter was to avoid vessels falling into traps and unless you feel strongly to the contrary in the matter I think we ought to stick to our original arrangment.[4]

The strain of the incessant air attacks, and the loneliness now that they were without escort, rapidly told on the crews of some of the merchant ships. On 5 July the crew of the *Samuel Chase* abandoned their ship on sighting a U-boat. The U-boat did not attack, and the *Chase*'s crew were left, somewhat sheepishly, to reboard their vessel; ironically, she would be one of the merchant ships to survive the débâcle. The crew of the *Alcoa Ranger* hoisted the international signal flags for unconditional surrender and struck the Stars and Stripes when they were sighted by a prowling aircraft. Some members of the crew tried to abandon ship, but the Second Officer, evidently made of sterner stuff, confined the Master to his cabin and got the ship under way again. When the Master realized that his ship was not about to be sunk he re-assumed command. The British freighter *Earlston*, on the other hand, was being chased by a U-boat, but the merchantman spiritedly fought the submarine off with her 4in gun and eventually forced it to dive. The *Earlston*'s Master knew that as long as the U-boat remained dived his ship was safe, so he pressed on to the east at his best speed.

The evening of 5 July saw the massacre culminate in six merchant ships together with an auxiliary oiler being sunk in a matter of hours. The *Peter Kerr* was the first to go, being overwhelmed by four Ju 88s from *V/KG 30*. She was hit by three bombs which caused fires but was also immobilized by a large number of near-misses. The *Bolton Castle*, *Paulus Potter* and *Washington* had all clung together and were heading north-east at their best speed, hoping to put as much distance between them and the German airfields as possible. Eventually they found that their way was barred by the ice and were forced to turn back. After being sighted by a lone German aircraft, the ships were attacked by a force of eight Ju 88s from *Hauptmann* Hajo Hermann's *III/KG 30*. *Bolton Castle* and *Washington* were sunk outright, while *Paulus Potter* was left afloat as a derelict, eventually to be sunk on 13 July by *U255*. *Kapitänleutnant* Reche ordered the wreck to be boarded in the hope finding something useful from an intelligence point of view as well as any supplies. The boarding officer was delighted to find that, in the general haste to abandon ship, the *Paulus Potter*'s Master had neglected to throw overboard his sailing orders, signal codes and other useful information. This intelligence haul was to pay useful dividends for the Germans.

The *Olopana*, which had been following the three ships, slowed to rescue their survivors, who were all in open boats. To Capt Mervyn Stone's surprise, none of the men wished to set foot on the unescorted *Olopana* but preferred instead to take their chances in the open boats. Those from *Paulus Potter* and *Washington* were heading to Novaya Zemlya, an island chain separating the Barents Sea from the White Sea, but Capt John Pascoe of the *Bolton Castle* preferred to head for north Russia, 400 miles away, claiming that the much shorter voyage to Novaya Zemlya would take the lifeboats into regions of intense cold.

One hundred miles or so to the south of where the *Bolton Castle* and her consorts had been sunk, the *Luftwaffe* turned its attention to a small group of vessels consisting of the rescue ship *Zamalek*, the freighter *Ocean Freedom*, the oiler *Aldersdale* and the minesweeper HMS *Salamander*. This little group possessed considerable AA firepower, so when four Ju 88s roared over shortly after 1730, it was not surprising that the first three aircraft were discomforted by the barrage put up and dropped their bombs short. It was the fourth plane which pressed on, despite the AA fire, and did the damage. Its stick of bombs exploded obliquely under *Aldersdale*'s stern, completely wrecking her machinery. When her Chief Engineer reported that there was no hope of restarting it, she too had to be abandoned.

At around the same time the other rescue ship, *Zaafaran*, was sunk. She had moved on ahead of her sister-ship and other consorts since her Master, Capt Charles McGowan, reckoned that his faster vessel was better off making for Novaya Zemlya on her own. In this belief he was cruelly mistaken, for his ship was found by the Ju 88s and sunk. Her crew and their 'passengers' were picked up by *Zamalek*. Joined by the anti-aircraft ship *Pozarica* and the minesweepers *Britomart* and *Halcyon*, the little group headed off for Novaya Zemlya.

To the north-west, *Earlston* was not so fortunate when she was attacked by a lone Ju 88 which bombed her and brought her to a halt. Now the U-boats had their chance, for no fewer than three had been shadowing this gallant ship. Siemon's *U334* and Teichert's *U456* surfaced on her starboard bow, followed shortly afterwards by a third boat. Capt Stenwick lost no time in abandoning the *Earlston*, which was dispatched by one torpedo from *U334*. In accordance with usual procedures, Siemon took Stenwick prisoner.

Capt Stenwick's ordeal was not over. As if in revenge, shortly afterwards *U334* was attacked from the air and badly damaged by a prowling Ju 88. Evidently, in the confused tactical situation in the Barents Sea the *Luftwaffe* were sinking anything on sight. Siemon radioed that he could no longer continue on patrol and that he required an escort back to Kirkenes—which was eventually supplied by Teichert's *U456*.

The attacks on these merchant ships had meant a further outbreak of distress signals on the ether. It was galling for some of the officers and men in the escorts, who felt that they were running away. Lt James Caradus in the corvette *La Malouine* expressed the mood perfectly:

Enemy torpedo planes were having a piece of cake on the scattered ships which were being attacked about 100 miles away. Complete destruction of the convoy is the German intention and we in *La Malouine* might have been able to help the odd merchant vessel but were too occupied protecting a well-armed anti-aircraft ship. A sore point with us all.[5]

Following *Pozarica* and her escorts was the merchant ship *Bellingham* trying to keep up. Behind her was the *Olopana*, which came across the wreck of the *Pankraft* which had been bombed and set on fire. Stone stopped to look for survivors but found none; they had in fact been collected by HMS *Lotus*, which had eventually secured permission to return and search for any men adrift in boats or on rafts. Petty Officer Edward Reynolds was the Yeoman of Signals on board *Pozarica* and remembers his feelings when *Lotus* signalled her intention to return to look for survivors:

> . . . the *Lotus* said to our skipper, 'Can I return to pick up survivors?' And at the time I remember thinking how brave that skipper was to go back into waters which were obviously infested by the enemy, when we were in sight of a haven which would have been safe from them . . . we didn't expect to see any more of the *Lotus*.[6]

Lotus picked up 29 men from *Pankraft*'s boats and while returning to rejoin *Pozarica* came across boats bearing the survivors from the Commodore's ship *River Afton*. This ship had been torpedoed by Bielefeld's *U703* at around midday on 5 July by *U703*. The survivors, who included Commodore Jack Dowding, had spent nearly four hours on rafts before being found by *Lotus* just as their smoke flares were burning out. In the first twenty-four hours following the order to scatter, thirteen merchant ships and a rescue ship had been sunk.

On 6 July the first of PQ.17's ships—*Palomares* in company with three minesweepers and the rescue ship *Zamalek*, and with the *Ocean Freedom* grimly keeping up—reached the haven of the Matochkin Strait seaprating the two halves of Novaya Zemlya. Later in the day they were joined by *Pozarica* with *La Malouine* and *Poppy*. After recognition signals had been exchanged and the warships moored so that they provided mutual cover, *La Malouine* was sent out into the Barents Sea in a belated attempt to see if any merchant ships could be found and led to safety. In a short time she rounded up *Hoosier*, *Samuel Chase*, *El Capitan* and *Benjamin Harrison* and, despite difficulties caused by attrocious weather, succeeded in bringing the ships back to Matochkin Strait. In the hours that followed, the trawlers *Lord Austin*, *Lord Middleton* and *Northern Gem* arrived, followed shortly afterwards by the gallant *Lotus*, her decks crammed with over sixty survivors from the *Pankraft* and *River Afton*. It seemed to all who had reached this desolate spot that they were the sole survivors of the convoy.

The next day saw the slaughter continue. At least seven of the ships were strung out in an ungainly gaggle in the northern Barents Sea. All were hugging the ice and making for Novaya Zemlya at their best speed. At their head was the US Liberty ship *John Witherspoon* and behind her were *Alcoa Ranger*, *Empire Tide*, *Bellingham*, *Hartlebury*, *Olopana* and *Winston Salem*. To the west of these ships was the lone *Pan Atlantic*, making a dash for the White Sea. She was being followed by two U-boats, Bielefeld's *U703* and Bohmann's *U88*, but in the evening of 6 July, as the latter was just about to fire, a single Ju 88 bombed the ship. Both bombs struck the hold containing a vast quantity of cordite, and in the resulting expolsion the *Pan Atlantic*'s bows were blown off and she sank within three minutes. Bohmann was furious at being cheated of his prey, as was Bielefeld, who had also been about to fire at the hapless merchantman.

Although the merchant ships had put nearly 400 miles between themselves and the German air base at Banak, they were not wholly beyond the long reach of the *Luftwaffe*. Air reconnaissance also indicated that a loose gaggle of merchant ships was headed towards Novaya Zemlya. Accordingly, Schmundt ordered the available boats—*U255*, *U703*, *U88*, *U251*, *U376* and *U408*—to concentrate in this area. *U255* sank the *John Witherspoon* on 6 July and the *Alcoa Ranger* the following day. The *Empire Tide*, still carrying her Hurricane fighter, had observed the sinking of the *Alcoa Ranger*. Her Master, Capt John Harvey, saw three U-boats watch the American vessel sink and then one of them detach itself and head towards him. Harvey immediately reversed course to the north and sought safety in Moller Bay, placing his bulky ship behind an island and resolving to lie low.

Also on 7 July, *U355* (*Kapitänleutnant* Günther la Baume) sank the *Hartlebury*, while *U457* disposed of the derelict hulk of the *Aldersdale*. On 8 July the *Olopana*, which had reached the desolate shores of Novaya Zemlya and was heading south for the White Sea, was caught by Reche's *U255*, which, after torpedoing her, surfaced and finished her off with gunfire. The Master of the *Winston Salem*, having received the distress signal from *Olopana* only a few miles ahead of him, had had enough. He swung his ship into Obsiedya Bay and ran her aground. He and his crew then abandoned ship and set up camp in a disused lighthouse nearby. The intact hull of the *Winston Salem* was later found by a boat-load of *Hartlebury*'s survivors.

Meanwhile, what of *Tirpitz*? Hitler's approval for stage two of *'Rösselsprung'* was secured in the morning of 5 July and at 1137 Admiral Otto Schniewind, the Fleet Commander, was ordered to proceed. Off Ingøy the Soviet submarine *K21* (Capt 2nd Rank A. N. Lunin) sighted the force and made an attack without success but claiming to have damaged *Tirpitz*. The force was sighted by a Catalina of No 201 Squadron and by the British submarine *Unshaken* (Lt C. E. Oxborrow RN).

Unshaken made contact at 1922/5 in position 71°40´N 28°19´E. She first sighted smoke and increased speed to close the range but was put down by an aircraft. By 2013 the unmistakable superstructure of *Tirpitz* was in view, with *Hipper* astern of her. The battleship was steering a course of 080°, bearing 200°, and Oxborrow would only get a chance if *Tirpitz* altered course to the north. By 2020 the range had opened and Oxborrow reluctantly broke off his attack. His next duty was to report his sighting. He surfaced at 2118 but was immediately put down again by an aircraft. Finally, at 2157 he was able to surface and transmit unmolested. HMS *Trident*, also in the area, received the Catalina's sighting report (timed at 1816/5) and went south-east beyond her patrol area until 0005/6 when she reached 32°25´E but saw nothing, though visibility was excellent.

The reports of the presence of enemy submarines, together with the sighting of the Catalina, caused the German naval staff some anxiety. When they also considered that the *Luftwaffe* and U-boats were decimating the convoy quite satisfactorily without assistance from the surface ships, the order was given to return to Altenfjord at 2132—much to Admiral Schniewind's disappointment. *Tirpitz*'s part in the operation was over: she had succeeded in her objective without hardly having had to move from her anchorage.

Back in the bleak surroundings of Matochkin Strait, Capt J. H. Jauncey RN of *Pozarica* was the Senior Officer and at a meeting of Commanding Officers and Masters decided that the ships should remain in the exposed anchorage not a minute longer than was necessary. An attempt was made to reconnoitre a way through into the Kara Sea so that the ships could proceed down the eastern side of Novaya Zemlya, and *Norfolk*'s Walrus seaplane[7] was sent up to see if a passage through the ice was clear. The passage, however, was blocked, and there was no alternative but to break out.

Thus, in the evening of 7 July, the seventeen ships left the anchorage and headed south for the entrance to the White Sea. On leaving Matochkin Strait they ran into thick fog: the *Benjamin Harrison* lost touch with the main group and, rather than press on alone, her Master decided to return to the anchorage. During 8 July the fog thickened, but, hugging the coastline and hoping to pass east of Kolguev Island, the ships pressed on. Suddenly and without warning, the leading ships ran into ice and for a minute all was confusion as vessels hurriedly went full astern and manoeuvred to avoid collision. Only the *Ocean Freedom* sustained damage to her bows by hitting the ice.

Jauncey ordered the ships on to a westerly course in the hope of finding clear water, and it was not until the morning of 9 July that they were able to turn south again. Ominously, the weather cleared, revealing two boat-loads of survivors from the *Pan Atlantic*, which were picked up. All eyes scanned the horizon for a sight of the Soviet aircraft which had been promised, the ships being now less than 60 miles from the mainland; instead, the unwelcome sight of a BV 138 appeared, and it was evident that it would not be long before the *Luftwaffe* returned.

During the pseudo-night of 9/10 July forty Ju 88s of *II/KG 30* carried out a series of attacks lasting over four hours, during which *Hoosier* and *El Capitan* were badly damaged by near-misses and had to be abandoned. Their crews were picked by the *Poppy* and *Lord Austin* as the *Zamalek* had over 240 survivors on board and could not accommodate any more. The two derelicts were later sunk by *U376 (Kapitän-leutnant* Friedrich-Karl Marks) and *U251 (Korvettenkapitän* Heinrich Timm) respectively.

Zamalek became the *Luftwaffe*'s main target during one attack and at one stage was completely hidden by the splashes from exploding bombs: 'One stick of bombs actually took the *Zamalek* right out of the water so that you could see daylight between the keel and the water.'[8] She sustained shock damage to her engines and had to stop while repairs were made. Fortunately, with so many survivors on board, there was no shortage of experienced engine room personnel to help in the work. She was given up for lost by the other ships, and when she rejoined the convoy she was loudly cheered by her consorts. The *Samuel Chase* was also damaged during this series of air attacks but was sufficiently seaworthy to be taken in tow by the *Halcyon*. Finally, on 11 July, Commodore Dowding led his ships through the White

Sea and into the port of Archangel. There he found the Soviet tanker *Donbass* and the US freighter *Bellingham*, which had arrived on 9 July together with the rescue ship *Rathlin* and the corvette *Dianella*. 'Not a successful convoy. Three ships brought into port out of 37,'[9] wrote Dowding pithily in his report.

Dowding is one of only two people to emerge with any sort of credit from the PQ.17 disaster. After having had his ship sunk under him and having spent nearly four hours on a raft in the Arctic, he had led the ships which had taken shelter in Matochkin Strait to safety at Archangel. Now, hearing that a second group of five ships had reached the Strait, he prepared to go back out into the Arctic and bring them back to Archangel. That these ships had survived was solely due to the initiative of Lt J. A. Gradwell RNVR, commander of the trawler HMS *Ayrshire*. Gradwell and his First Lieutenant were both lawyers in civilian life, and of their actions it was later said, 'The more law that comes to sea the better and let litigation look after itself.'[10]

When the order to scatter was given, Gradwell headed north towards the ice-pack with the freighters *Troubador*, *Ironclad* and *Silver Sword*. Using the *Troubador* with her stiffened bows an an icebreaker, he took his charges some 20 miles into the ice, and when they could make no further progress they hove-to. Immediately all hands turned-to and began to paint all south-facing surfaces on the ships white, using a large stock of paint conveniently found on board the *Troubador*. Fires were banked so that smoke trails would not give away the position, and for two days the ships lay in the ice, during which they listened to the distress calls as their consorts were attacked and sunk by aircraft and submarines. Finally Gradwell decided that it was safe to break out, and after a high-speed dash along the edge of the ice-pack his ships reached the north island of Novaya Zemlya on 10 July. After spending twenty-four hours at anchor in a fjord, they steamed south and reached the Matochkin Strait the next day. There they found the *Benjamin Harrison*, which had been joined by the Soviet tanker *Azerbaijan* and icebreaker *Murman*. The Soviet trawler *Kirov* completed this little gathering. Gradwell went ashore, and after some communication problems he persuaded a Soviet signal station to send the following report to Archangel:

> The situation at present is that there are four ships here in Matochkin Strait. My asdic is out of action, and the Masters of the ships are showing unmistakable signs of strain. I much doubt if I could persuade them to make a dash for Archangel without a considerably increased escort and a promise of fighter protection in the entrance to the White Sea. Indeed, there has already been talk of scuttling ships while near shore rather than go to what they, with their present escort, consider certain sinking.
>
> In these circumstances, I submit that increased escort might be provided and that I may be informed as to how to obtain air protection. I shall remain in the Matochkin Strait until I receive a reply.[11]

After everything he had endured, Commodore Dowding could be excused for leaving the rescue of these six ships to another officer. But, on hearing that they were in Matochkin Strait, he at once set out, taking the corvettes *Lotus*, *La Malouine* and *Poppy*. After a stormy passage he reached Byelusha Bay in southern Novaya

Zemlya, where he found twelve frozen and exhausted survivors from the *Olopana*. A little further up the coast he found the *Winston Salem* aground south-east of North Guisini Nos. Although deserted by her own ship's company, she provided a welcome home for survivors from the *Hartlebury* and *Washington*. Dowding pressed on north, leaving her behind since she was hard aground and would need tugs to salvage her. The corvette *La Malouine* was sent to look for any other ships in Moller Bay, where she found the CAM ship *Empire Tide*. Capt Harvey was doubtless incredibly relieved to see the corvette. His ship had become the home for 129 survivors who were rapidly exhausting his ship's meagre supplies. Morale was low because most of the survivors felt that to remain on board the merchantman was to invite another sinking, and, after acrimonious dispute, 46 of them voted to abandon the ship and set up camp ashore. They were given a proportion of the *Winston Salem*'s supplies together with some of *Empire Tide*'s, but, before they left, Capt Harvey warned them that he was not accepting any liability for their future safety. Harvey's anxieties were not eased by the appearance of a Ju 88 overhead. The Hurricane fighter, which so far had sat inactive on the catapult, was prepared for flying-off, and evidently the sight of the aircraft warming up was sufficient to scare the intruder away. On the arrival of the corvette, the 'campers' came back aboard and Capt Harvey was told to have his ship ready to sail that evening when Dowding came back with the ships from Matochkin Strait.

Dowding arrived at Matochkin Strait on 20 July. He transferred to the Soviet *Murman*, which would lead the convoy back because of her strengthened bows. The little convoy left in the evening of the same day and did so just in time: a day later a U-boat appeared in the Matochkin Strait and, finding it empty, shelled the signal station at Guisini Nos. On the way back Dowding collected the *Empire Tide* but had to leave the *Winston Salem* where she was. The behaviour of the latter's ship's company was less than creditable. A Soviet Catalina which had collected some severely frost-bitten seamen from *Empire Tide* on 17 July took a message from the *Salem*'s Master to the US Naval Attaché, Capt S. B. Frankel USN, that he wanted a US destroyer sent to take them back to the USA. Frankel's response was, 'Let them stew in their own juice.' *Salem*'s Master further claimed that, since his ship now lay in a Russian 'harbour', his responsibilities were at an end. Commenting on this incident, Admiral Arsenii Golovko, Commander-in-Chief of the Soviet Northern Fleet, was moved to write:

> By harbour, this shameless entrepreneur meant a desolate bay on an Arctic island, thousands of miles from the nearest railway line. And these are our allies.[12]

On 22 July the convoy's escort was augmented by the AA ship *Pozarica*, the corvette *Dianella* and the minesweepers *Leda*, *Bramble* and *Hazard*, together with two Soviet destroyers, *Gremyashchi* and *Grozny*. All ships reached Archangel safely in the evening of 24 July. Four days later the *Winston Salem* was refloated by two Soviet tugs under the watchful eye of Capt Frankel—who had been flown up to Novaya Zemlya by a Soviet Catalina—and taken into Archangel, bringing the total number of PQ.17's ships to escape destruction to eleven.

A matter of continuing concern for the naval authorities at Murmansk was the fear that a large number of seamen might still be adrift in the Arctic since there was a great discrepancy between the number of boats seen to get away from sinking ships and survivors recovered. Slowly, however, the gap began to close. The covette *Dianella*, which had sailed to search for survivors only hours after arriving at Archangel on 9 July, returned on the 16th with 61 of the crew of *Empire Byron*. *Dianella*'s captain reported seeing much wreckage in the Barents Sea, including a bell marked with the name 'SS *Edmore*'. A quick check in Lloyds' Register indicated that this was a former name of the *Honomu*, thus confirming that she had been sunk.

Two of *Alcoa Ranger*'s lifeboats had reached Novaya Zemlya while a third reached the mainland at Cape Kanin Nos. Twenty-one crewmen from the *Honomu* had drifted for thirteen days in an open boat before being rescued by the Royal Navy minesweepers *Halcyon* and *Salamander* hundreds of miles off Murmansk. The *Honomu*'s survivors were incredibly lucky, for the two warships were on the point of turning back when the merchantman's lifeboat was spotted. Peter Kerr's survivors also landed near Murmansk after rowing over 360 miles from the position where their ship was sunk. The two lifeboats from the *Bolton Castle* had eventually reached the north Russian coast after a dreadful journey marked by fights between Arab and white seamen. Had they not come across an abandoned lifeboat from the *El Capitan*, packed with provisions, they probably would not have survived. Of the *Earlston*'s survivors, one boat had been picked up by a British escort seven days after the freighter had been sunk but the other, containing 26 men, endured ten days and nights on the open sea before coming ashore in German-occupied Norway, where its occupants became prisoners of war. Finally, on 24 July, the lifeboat containing the remaining seventeen survivors from the *Carlton* also came ashore in Norway.

Of the thirty-seven ships which had sailed from Iceland, two had turned back and eight had been sunk by air attack, nine by U-boats and seven by U-boats having first been damaged by air attack. The stores and equipment lost with PQ.17 amounted to 430 tanks, 210 crated aircraft, 3,350 vehicles and 99,316 tons of general cargo. One hundred and fifty-three merchant seamen lost their lives. The losses in *matériel* were all the more serious because on 18 June 1942 the Germans had launched their summer offensive on the southern half of the Eastern Front, which completely destroyed the Red Army's defences within two weeks. The Germans had achieved this for the loss of five aircraft.

On 11 July, just as the *Zamalek* was arriving in Archangel, Rear-Admiral Sir Geoffrey Miles, head of the British Naval Mission in Moscow, was beginning an uncomfortable interview with Admiral V. I. Kuznetsov, Chief of the Soviet Naval Staff, about PQ.17. Miles had already had a stormy interview with Vice-Admiral Alafusov, the Vice-Chief of Staff, who had read the signal ordering PQ.17 to scatter and was furious, demanding explanations and hurling accusations of cowardice about. That with Kuznetsov was more polite, but the Russians were still angry at what had happened. In London Ivan Maisky, the Soviet Ambassador, demanded, with more nerve than tact, to know when the next PQ convoy would sail. The Foreign Secretary, Anthony Eden, replied that to send more ships to be sunk in the

Barents Sea at this stage would be futile. The Russians were not pleased. On 28 July a joint Anglo-Soviet enquiry met in London to consider the affair. Present were Eden, A. V. Alexander, the First Lord of the Admiralty and Admiral Pound. On the Russian side were Maisky, Admiral H. G. Harlamov (head of the Soviet military mission in London) and his assistant. If the meeting was intended to explain the rationale behind the Admiralty's decision to scatter the convoy, then it was a failure, for it soon degenerated into a slanging match, with Pound roaring at Harlamov that if he, Harlamov, knew all the answers, then he, Pound, would ask the Prime Minister to make the Soviet officer First Sea Lord in his place.

On 1 August Pound fully briefed the Cabinet on what had happened. He told the assembled ministers that he had given the fateful order on the strength of the information which was available to him and claimed that he had intelligence that *Tirpitz* was at sea and that she had evaded the submarine patrols off the North Cape—an assertion which an examination of post-war records fails to confirm. However, Churchill, who was present at Pound's briefing, wanted to put as much distance as possible between himself and the affair. In his memoirs he lied blatantly, claiming that

> . . . so strictly was the secret of these orders being sent on the First Sea Lord's authority guarded by the Admiralty that it was not until after the war that I learned the facts.[13]

At the same time as distancing himself from the affair, Churchill was quickly at pains to find a scapegoat. Loyalty to his own friend Pound deprived him of the obvious candidate. Instead, the full weight of Churchillian opprobrium fell on Admiral Hamilton:

> I was not aware until this morning that it was the Admiral of the cruisers, Hamilton, who ordered the destroyers to quit the convoy. What did you think of this decision at the time? What do you think of it now?[14]

This, of course, was nonsense. Broome had taken the destroyers with him on his own authority and his decision was endorsed by Hamilton. Churchill later thundered that the decision to withdraw the destroyers was a 'mistake' and that 'All risks should have been taken in defence of the merchant ships.'[15] It was all very well being wise after the event, and it was disgraceful that Hamilton should have been made the scapegoat for what had happened.

Inside the Navy, opinion as to what had happened generally disapproved of Pound's decision. Admiral Tovey's view of the affair was that

> The order to scatter the convoy had, in my opinion, been premature; its results were disastrous. The convoy had so far covered more than half its route with the loss of only three ships. Now its ships, spread over a wide area, were exposed without defence to the powerful enemy U-boat and air forces. The enemy took prompt advantage of this situation, operating both weapons to their full capacity.[16]

The key to the disaster lay in the dogmatic and authoritative personality of Admiral Sir Dudley Pound. Early studies of Arctic convoy operations (i.e., those made before the declassification of 'Ultra' intercepts) argued that Pound was correct to scatter the convoy on the basis of the information available to him. Now that 'Ultra' material is available, we know that sufficient information existed to present a convincing case that *Tirpitz* was not at sea. However, Pound proved intractable, and unwilling to listen to contrary arguments. The cost of 'Father''s failing to change his mind was the annihilation of PQ.17. But it is too easy merely to assign the blame to Pound as an individual. He, after all, was a product of the system which allowed the concentration of administrative and operational authority in one office-holder. Pound had many admirable qualities which will give him a place in history as one of the Royal Navy's better First Sea Lords. However, operational command of a sea-going fleet was not his forte, and it can be argued that the twin burdens of administrative and operational command were too much for one man to bear.

The role of the intelligence officers in the PQ.17 affair must also be considered. That 'Ultra' provided useful information is undeniable; however, there was often so much of it and of such quality that it must have seemed as if the Admiralty had representatives at the various German headquarters taking notes on what was happening! It must also have been difficult for commanders of long standing like Pound to accept the veracity of this intelligence—which, moreover, was frequently presented in a fashion which emphasized negative factors rather than positive ones, as in the case of PQ.17.

Another aspect of the PQ.17 affair was the deterioration in relations between the Royal Navy and the Merchant Navy. The latter felt themselves to have been deserted. There was a sense of shame in the Royal Navy at what had happened, and, in an effort to set the record straight, Admiral Hamilton took the unprecedented step of clearing lower deck in his flagship *London* and giving the ship's company the full facts of PQ.17 as available to him. This, however, did not stop *London*'s being dubbed the 'Wop Flagship'. The author's father was on the Clyde at this time, waiting for the formation of the 'Pedestal' convoy to Malta, and remembers that PQ.17 was the cause of innumerable pub brawls between Royal and Merchant Navy sailors.

Hamilton himself was bitterly disillusioned by the affair. After being briefed by Admiral Tovey on the full story of what had happened to the merchant ships, he wrote to Tovey formally, recording that

> It would have been a great assistance to me had I known that the Admiralty possessed no further information on the movements of the enemy's heavy units other than I had already received.[17]

After his interview with Tovey, Hamilton went ashore with his Flag Captain, Capt R .M. Servaes. Hamilton remarked, 'Well, I suppose I ought to have been a Nelson. I ought to have disregarded the Admiralty's signals.'

The Germans, on the other hand, were naturally elated by their success. 'I beg to report the destruction of convoy PQ.17,' crowed *Generaloberst* Hans-Jurgen Stumpff to Göring, while the War Diary of the *Seekriegsleitung* reported that

This is biggest success ever achieved against the enemy with one blow—a blow executed with exemplary collaboration between air force and submarine units. A heavily laden convoy of ships, some of which have been under way for several months from America, has been virutally wiped out, despite the most powerful escort, just before reaching its destination.

A wicked blow has been struck at Soviet war production, and a deep breach torn in the enemy's shipping capacity. The effect of this battle is not unlike a battle lost by the enemy in its military, material and morale aspects. In a three-day battle, fought under the most favourable conditions, the submarines and aircraft have achieved what had been the intention of the operation 'Knight's Move' [i.e., '*Rösselsprung*'], the attack of our surface units on the convoy's merchant ships.[18]

However, the feeling of jubilation was not shared among the officers and men of the surface battle group, who felt that they had been cheated of their prey. *Kapitän zur See* Heinz Reinicke wrote that

. . . they should have let us make one little attack! Heaven knows, they could have always recalled us after we had bagged three or four of the merchantmen.[19]

Fregattenkapitän Günther Schulze was equally pessimistic:

Here the mood is bitter enough. Soon one will feel ashamed to be on the active list if one has to go on watching other parts of the armed forces fighting while we, 'the core of the Fleet', just sit in harbour.[20]

Admiral Schniewind was more forthright. He complained that

It was a pity that that *Luftwaffe* had not devoted the same effort to keeping the enemy heavy forces shadowed [which was vitally important for getting Hitler's approval for '*Rösselsprung*'] as it had to destroying the enemy off its own bat.[21]

The disaster which befell PQ.17 has tended to obscure the equally unpleasant passage of the westbound convoy QP.13. This convoy of 35 ships had sailed in two parts from Murmansk and Archangel and had joined up at sea on 28 June under Commodore N. H. Gale. The escort consisted of five destroyers, *Inglefield* (Cdr A. G. West, Senior Officer), *Achates, Volunteer, Intrepid* and *Garland* (Polish), the AA ship *Alynbank*, the corvettes *Starwort, Honeysuckle, Hyderabad* and *Roselys* (Free French), the minesweepers *Niger* and *Hussar* and two trawlers.

The convoy had an uneventful passage. Although it was reported by the *Luftwaffe* on 30 June and 2 July while east of Bear Island, it was left unmolested, the Germans concentrating instead on PQ.17. On 4 July the convoy divided off Iceland, sixteen ships under Commodore Gale turning south for Loch Ewe while the remaining nineteen headed around the north coast of Iceland to Reykjavik with Capt J. Hiss, Master of the US freighter *American Robin*, as Commodore. At 1900 on 5 July the convoy was approaching the north-west corner of Iceland in five columns, escorted by *Niger* (Cdr A. J. Cubison, Senior Officer), *Hussar, Roselys* and two trawlers. The weather was bad, with visibility down to less than one mile, rough seas and the wind coming from the north-east at Force 8. The bad weather had meant that it had not been possible to take star sights since 2 July, and the convoy's position had been calculated by dead reckoning and therefore was considerably in doubt.

At 1910 Cubison suggested to Hiss that the convoy's front be reduced to two columns in order to pass between the Straumnes and the minefield to the north-west of Iceland. Soon afterwards he gave his estimated position at 2000 as being 66°45′N 22°22′W and suggested altering course to 222° to clear Straumnes Point. This was done. Two hours later *Niger*, which had gone ahead to make a landfall leaving *Hussar* as a visual link with the convoy, sighted what she took to be the North Cape bearing 150°, one mile, and ordered course to be altered to 270°.

What *Niger* had actually sighted was an iceberg, and the alteration of course to the north had the effect of taking the convoy directly into the minefield. At 2240 *Niger* blew up and sank with heavy loss of life, Cubison being among the casualties. At that very moment a signal from *Niger* was being handed to Hiss, recommending a return to 222° and explaining the mistake. It was too late. As Hiss looked around him, explosions were occurring all over the convoy as ships ran into mines. In the reduced visibility six ships came to grief, *Exterminator*, *Heffron*, *Hybert*, *Massmar* and *Rodina* sinking and *John Randolph* being damaged. The escorts displayed conspicuous gallantry in entering, or remaining in, the minefield to rescue the survivors. The action of the French corvette *Roselys*, commanded by *Lieutenant de Vaisseau* A. Bergeret, was particularly noteworthy. Although Bergeret appreciated that the convoy had blundered into a minefield, he kept his ship in the highly dangerous waters for six and a half hours, during which time he rescued 179 survivors. Finally, a definite shore fix was obtained by *Hussar* and the remaining merchant ships re-formed and reached Reykjavik on 7 July without further misfortune.

Flag Officer Iceland (Rear-Admiral Dalrymple-Hamilton) conducted an enquiry into the affair and concluded that the main cause had been *Niger*'s navigational error, which had been compounded by bad weather, preventing sights from being taken for three days before landfall. He also commented on the fact that Capt Hiss, who had taken over as Commodore after QP.13 had split up, had not been provided with full information about the defences north-east of Iceland—Hiss was unaware that a minefield existed here. Hamilton also recommended that a DF beacon be installed to help ships make a landfall in these treacherous waters.

NOTES TO CHAPTER 6

1. Reynolds, Edward John, Department of Sound Records, Imperial War Museum 10779/6.
2. Royal Electrical and Mechanical Engineers.
3. Irving, D., *The Destruction of Convoy PQ.17*, William Kimber, London, 1980, p.148.
4. Irving, *op. cit.*, pp.159–60.
5. Diary of Lt James Caradus RNVR, 5 July 1942.
6. Reynolds, *op. cit.*

7. The Walrus seaplane from HMS *Norfolk* had been airborne when the convoy had scattered and there had been no time to recover the aircraft. She was eventually picked up by *Palomares*. After a series of adventures worthy of a novel, aircraft and crew were reunited with *Norfolk* at Rosyth, where lower deck was cleared to cheer them aboard.

8. Reynolds, *op. cit.*

9. PRO ADM., 'Report of Proceedings of Commodore Jack Dowding DSO RNR'.

10. PRO ADM.199/1104, 'Letter of Proceedings of the Senior British Naval Officer, North Russia', 16 July 1942.

11. PRO ADM., 'HMS *Ayrshire*, Report of Proceedings', 13 July 1942.

12. Golovko, Admiral A. G., *Vmetse s'Flotom*, Moscow, 1960, p.101. An abridged edition of this book has been published in English under the title *With the Red Fleet* (Putnam, 1965).

13. Churchill, Winston, *The Second World War*, Vol IV, p.236.

14. Churchill, *op. cit.*, pp.237–8.

15. *ibid.*, p.238

16. PRO ADM.234/369, 'Battle Summary No 22: Arctic Convoys 1941–45', London, 1954, p.69.

17. PRO ADM., 'Flag Officer Commanding First Cruiser Squadron to Commander-in-Chief Home Fleet', 9 July 1942.

18. German Naval War Staff Diary, 6 July 1942. The Commanding Officer of *U334* might not agree with the success of the 'exemplary co-operation' mentioned in the report.

19. Cdr H. Reinicke quoted in Bekker, Cajus, *Hitler's Naval War*, London, 1974, p.278.

20. Bekker, *op. cit.*, p.278.

21. *ibid.*, p.276.

ALLIES OF A KIND

Top: Convoy JW.53 heads towards the Soviet ports of Murmansk and Archangel in February 1943, passing light pancake ice. (IWM A.15359)

Above: The signing of the Moscow Protocol on 1 October 1941 by the USSR and a joint UK/US delegation led by Averell Harriman (shown seated at the desk). (US National Archives)

Right: Rear-Admiral Philip Vian, who headed the first British mission to the USSR and subsequently undertook the reconnaissance and evacuation of Spitzbergen.

Above: The bleak surroundings of Hvalfjord in Iceland, the starting place for many of the early convoys. (IWM A.20427)

Left: The entrance to Polyarnoe from the Kola Inlet—hardly the most inviting destination for the mariner!

ALL AID TO RUSSIA— NOW!

Below left: All Aid to Russia—Now! The desire to help the Soviet Union was widespread in Britain. (IWM P.233)

Right: Admiral Sir John Tovey, Commander-in-Chief of the Home Fleet, was responsible for the safe passage of the convoys from 1941 until April 1943. (IWM A.14840)

Opposite top left: Grand Admiral Erich Raeder, Commander-in-Chief of the *Kriegsmarine*. He pressed Hitler to take action against the convoys. (IWM A.14906)

Opposite top right: Vice-Admiral Otto Ciliax, Commander of the German surface force consisting of *Tirpitz* and three destroyers which sailed on 6 March 1942 to attack PQ.12.

Opposite centre: The destroyer HMS *Matabele* was torpedoed and sunk with heavy loss of life on 8 January 1942—the first of 22 Allied warships to be lost in support of these convoys. (IWM A.6647)

Opposite bottom: A superb view of the German battleship *Tirpitz*—known as 'The Lone Queen of the North' or 'The Beast', depending on whose side you were on—on trials in the Baltic in 1941. Her presence in Norway from January 1942 dominated convoy operations until she was sunk on 11 November 1944.

Above: HMS *Duke of York* ploughs through rough seas in March 1942, providing distant cover for PQ.12 and QP.8. (IWM A.8143)

Below: An Albacore torpedo bomber taking off from HMS *Victorious*. On 9 March twelve of these aircraft made an attack on *Tirpitz* which, though unsuccessful, was delivered with great bravery.

Above: Stores, clearly of American origin, lie on the quayside at Murmansk. The entry of the United States into the war turned the trickle of supplies into a flood.

THE POLITICAL IMPERATIVE

Below: A BV 138 long-range reconnaissance aircraft used by the *Luftwaffe*. As spring turned into summer, the lengthening hours of daylight favoured the operation of such aircraft. (IWM GER.255W)

Right, top: The Soviet merchant ship *Kiev* was torpedoed on 13 April 1942 by *U455* while bound for Iceland with QP.10. (IWM A.8040)

Right, centre: The cruiser HMS *Trinidad* was damaged by her own torpedo during the destroyer attack on PQ.13. (IWM A.8087)

Right, bottom: HMS *Eclipse*, whose pursuit and sinking of the German destroyer *Z26* on 29 March 1942 is one of the epic stories of the Arctic convoys. (IWM A.11551)

Left: Lt-Cdr E. Mack RN
(centre of photograph),
Commanding Officer of HMS
Eclipse.

Below: The cruiser HMS
Edinburgh was torpedoed on 30
April 1942 by *U456* while
screening ahead of QP.11.

Right, top: *Edinburgh* after
being torpedoed by *U456*. The
first torpedo struck the starboard
side amidships; the second blew
off the cruiser's stern. (IWM
HU.43866)

Far right, top: HMS *Harrier*
alongside *Edinburgh*, taking off
the survivors. Note the large
Battle Ensign flying from the
mainmast: it remained there
until the cruiser sank. (IWM
MH.23857)

Right, centre: *Edinburgh* was
finally scuttled by a torpedo
fired by HMS *Foresight*. The
photograph shows the impact of
the torpedo.

Right, bottom: Damage to the
bows of HMS *King George V.*
The photograph was taken in
Hvalfjord. (IWM A.9946)

A MATTER OF DUTY

Left, top: Rear-Admiral Stuart Bonham-Carter, who became more and more pessimistic about Arctic convoy operations. (IWM A.9241)

Left, bottom: The cruiser HMS *Trinidad* after being bombed on 14 May 1942. She was eventually scuttled by the destroyer HMS *Matchless*. (IWM HU.43937)

Above: Survivors from HMS *Trinidad* at Greenock on their return to the United Kingdom.

Below: The CAM ship *Empire Lawrence*, which accompanied PQ.16. The Hurricane fighter on the catapult shot down one He 111 and damaged another before falling victim to the convoy's AA fire. (IWM A.9292)

Above: The Soviet destroyer *Razyarenny* lying in the Kola Inlet in March 1944. She was one of the four destroyers from the Pacific Fleet transferred to the Arctic in 1942 and fuelled by the tanker *Hopemount*.

CONVOY IS TO SCATTER

Left: Cdr J. Broome, who commanded the Close Escort for PQ.17. (IWM A.21926)

Above: Escorts and merchant ships assembling in Iceland in June 1942 for the passage of PQ.17. Behind the destroyer *Icarus* (I03) is the Soviet tanker *Azerbaijan*. (IWM A.8953)

Right: Rear-Admiral Louis 'Turtle' Hamilton, who commanded PQ.17's Anglo-American cruiser screen.

Above: The first attack on PQ.17 was successfully broken up by the USS *Wainwright*, which celebrated American Independence Day by steaming out from the convoy to put up a very effective barrage. (IWM A.10693)

Below: The German battle group in Altenfjord, seen from Tirpitz: *Lützow* is to the left and *Hipper* to the right. The move from Trondheim had been detected by RAF air

reconnaissance but not the ships' subsequent arrival at Altenfjord. This was to have the most fundamental and far-reaching consequences for PQ.17.

Right, top: An He 111 over the convoy during the second attack on 4 July. On this occasion the attack was not broken up and two merchant ships, *Navarino* and *William Hooper*, were sunk and a third, the Soviet tanker *Azerbaijan*, damaged.

Right, centre: A pillar of smoke rising from the damaged *Azerbaijan*. Almost unbelievably, she emerged from the smoke with all guns blazing.

Right, bottom: The rescue ship *Zamalek* closes the *Azerbaijan* to render assistance. In the centre is a boat containing a number of the tanker's crew who had abandoned ship precipitately.

Left: *Kapitän zur See* Karl Topp (centre) on the bridge of *Tirpitz* while the battleship was on her the voyage north from Trondheim to Altenfjord during the first stage of '*Rösselsprung*'. Note the splendid clothing supplied by *Kriegsmarine* personnel, in contrast to the inadequate attire worn by officers and men of the Royal Navy shown throughout this book.

Below: Admiral of the Fleet Sir Dudley Pound, who took the fateful decision to 'scatter' PQ.17 in the evening of 4 July 1942. (IWM A.16722)

Chapter 7

Fighting Back

You British are afraid of fighting. You should not think the
Germans are supermen. You will have to fight sooner or later. You
cannot win a war without fighting,—Marshal Josef Stalin

Following the PQ.17 débâcle, the Defence Committee of the War Cabinet met on 13 July and decided, after hearing the recommendations of the Chiefs of Staff, that the July convoy to Russia be cancelled together with those scheduled for August and September. Churchill justified the decision to Roosevelt by explaining that the arrival of only a quarter of PQ.17's ships was not satisfactory and that the loss of 500 out of the 600 tanks carried in the convoy was only helping the enemy.

The decision was communicated to Ivan Maisky, the Soviet Ambassador in London, on 14 July; Maisky, in turn, reported the very grave position that the Red Army was in as the German offensive swept east and down towards the Caucasus. Maisky's description of the efforts and sacrifices of the Red Army evidently struck a chord with Churchill, for the next day the Prime Minister sent one of his famous 'Action This Day' personal minutes to Admiral Pound and A. V. Alexander, the First Lord. Churchill's proposal was typically rumbustious. 'In defeat, defiance,' he oft maintained, and this proposal was no exception:

> Suspend the sailing of PQ.18 as now proposed from 18th inst. See what happens to our Malta operation. If all goes well bring the carriers *Indomitable*, *Victorious*, *Argus* and *Eagle* north to Scapa Flow and collect with them at least five auxiliary aircraft carriers together with all available *Dido*s and at least twenty-five destroyers. Let two 16" battleships go right through under this umbrella and destroyer screen, keeping southward, not hugging the ice but seeking the clearest weather, and thus fight it out with the enemy. If we can move our armada in convoy under an air umbrella of at least 100 fighter aircraft we ought to be able to fight our way through and out again, and if a fleet action results, so much the better.[1]

In theory there was much to be said for this plan; however, the Admiralty could not accept the risk of losing an aircraft carrier. Accordingly, Churchill had to steel himself for an icy exchange of signals with the Soviets when he informed Marshal Stalin on 17 July that PQ.18 would not sail as planned. The Anglo-American decision to suspend the convoys for the summer could not have come at a worse time, for on 14 July Churchill had told Stalin that there would be no Second Front in Europe in 1942 but that the first major Anglo-American military operation would be in North Africa. Stalin's reply was to level a sly accusation of cowardice at the Royal Navy over PQ.17:

Our experts found it also difficult to understand and to explain the order given by the Admiralty that the escorting vessels of PQ.17 should return whereas the cargo boats should disperse and try to reach the Soviet ports one by one without any protection at all.

The telegram ended on an incredulous and accusatory note:

I never expected that the British Government will stop dispatch of war materials to us just at the very time when the Soviet Union, in view of the serious situation on the Soviet-German front, requires materials more than ever.[2]

And there the matter rested. However, in August 1942, during Churchill's visit to Moscow, Stalin once again lashed out over the PQ.17 convoy:

This is the first time in history that the British Navy has ever turned tail and fled from the battle. You British are afraid of fighting. You should not think the Germans are supermen. You will have to fight sooner or later. You cannot win a war without fighting.[3]

No wonder Churchill pressed Attlee, his representative in the UK during his absence, for some good news to tell Stalin.

Stalin's remarks were unjustified and tactless, but beneath them the disappointment was understandable. The Soviets were facing a deteriorating military situation on the Eastern Front following the Red Army's failure to regain the offensive at Kharkov in May. Sevastopol in the Crimea had just surrendered after an epic nine-month siege which the Soviets were not slow to compare with the speedy collapse of Tobruk in the Western Desert in June 1942. The Soviets needed help—in the form either of a Second Front or increased aid—and were being deprived of both for reasons which they could not understand. All the Soviets could see was that British and American boasts about the amount of material being produced for and allocated to the USSR were not being matched in actual deliveries. It mattered little that so many hundred tanks were promised if only half that number arrived.

Nevertheless, Stalin and the Soviet Government did the British an injustice. Preoccupied with their immediate crisis in July 1942, they chose to ignore what they had freely acknowledged only four months earlier when Stalin informed the British Ambassador of his gratitude at the

. . . promptitude and regularity with which supplies were arriving from Great Britain, which he confessed had taken him and his people by surprise.[4]

The Arctic, however, did not remain quiet throughout the summer. To begin with, there was an urgent need to resupply the escorts and merchant ships from PQ.17 which were now in Soviet ports with stores and ammunition. Such supplies had to come from Britain, and on 20 July the destroyers *Marne, Martin, Middleton* and *Blankney* were dispatched from Scapa Flow for Murmansk via Seidisfjord. Although the force was sighted by German air reconnaissance off Jan Mayen Island, there was no enemy reaction and on 24 July it arrived safely in the Kola Inlet having fuelled en route from RFA *Black Ranger*, which latter was being escorted by the destroyer *Wilton*. Two Soviet merchant ships, *Friedrich Engels* and *Belomorcanal*, which were lying loaded at Iceland, sailed independently for Archangel at the request of the Soviet Government. They left Iceland on 11 and 12 August respectively and both arrived safely at their destination.

As part of British aid to the Soviet Union, it had been agreed that a proportion of RAF Coastal Command's strike and search aircraft should be transferred to northern Russia. This move had been advocated for some time by Air Chief Marshal Sir Philip Joubert de la Ferte, who believed that the PQ.17 disaster might have been averted had proper air cover been available. The aircraft involved consisted of four photo-reconnaissance Spitfires, Hampden torpedo bombers of Nos 144 and 455 Squadrons RAF[5] and Catalina reconnaissance and anti-submarine aircraft of No 210 Squadron. The whole force was under the command of Gp Capt F. L. Hopps RAF. Before the aircraft could be flown in, an advance party of technicians and ground crew with 300 tons of stores were embarked in the US cruiser *Tuscaloosa* and the destroyers USS *Rodman* and *Emmons* with HMS *Onslaught*. The ships sailed from Greenock on 13 August. Eight hundred miles from Archangel, they were met by HMS *Marne* and HMS *Martin* and escorted into harbour.

The aircraft began to arrive in northern Russia at the beginning of September. Five of the Hampdens were lost in transit, one crashing near Vadsø in Norway on 5 September. Unfortunately the crew neglected to destroy the aircraft, and *Luftwaffe* wreck investigators recovered a wealth of intelligence concerning the composition of the escort for future convoys.

Also embarked in *Tuscaloosa* were the personnel of a medical unit who were to set up a hospital at Murmansk for wounded merchant seamen. On arrival at Archangel the British Senior Naval Oficer ws astounded when the Soviets refused permission for the unit to land. This incident is often cited as example of the general Soviet bloodymindedness which pervaded all aspects of Anglo-Soviet relations. The reality is a little different. The Russians were annoyed at the high-handed attitude taken by the British, who assumed that the medical personnel would be allowed to land and set up their hospital without so much as a by-your-leave from the Soviet authorities. No permission had been sought from the Soviet authorities for the establishment of the hospital, and the British had not attended to routine formalities such as passports, visas or customs clearance. The result was the application of the full rigour of Soviet officialdom.

The *Kriegsmarine* had not been inactive during this period. Admiral Klüber, who had relieved Schmundt as Flag Officer Northern Waters, assumed that another convoy would follow PQ.17 fairly shortly, but when nothing materialized he released *Admiral Scheer* for '*Wunderland*', an operation which had been planned for some time against Soviet shipping in the Kara Sea. After air reconnaissance showed that that the route north of Novaya Zemlya was free of ice, *Scheer* left Narvik on 16 August accompanied by *U251* (*Kapitänleutnant* Heinrich Timm) and *U601* (*Kapitänleutnant* Peter Grau). Rounding Cape Zhelania three days later, she entered the Kara Sea. However, the German ship found little in the way of pickings. The

Soviet icebreaker *Sibiryakov* was sunk on 25 August after stout resistance from her crew. *Scheer* bombarded Port Dickson for two hours on 27 August, sinking the patrol vessel *SKR10/Deznev* and damaging the freighter *Revolutsioner* before returning to Narvik by the same route, arriving there on 30 August. She was unmolested by the Soviet Navy, since *Glasevmorput*, the authority responsible for shipping control in the Kara Sea, did not tell the Northern Fleet command that a raider was in the area until thirty-six hours had elapsed.

Unaware of *Scheer's* activities, *Tuscaloosa* and the destroyers USS *Rodman* and *Emmons* and HMS *Martin*, *Marne* and *Onslaught* had sailed from Archangel on 24 August. During the passage back to the United Kingdom the three British destroyers were detached, as a result of an 'Ultra' intercept, for a sweep to the south, where the German minelayer *Ulm* (*Korvettenkapitän* Biet) was on her way to lay a minefield off Cape Zhelania as soon as *Scheer* had cleared the area. The Germans had seen how ships from PQ.17 had hugged the coast of Novaya Zemlya, and *Ulm's* minefields were to bar Allied ships from these waters. The interception was made on 25 August and, despite gallant resistance by her crew, *Ulm* was sunk. However, the incident proved traumatic for many of the survivors from PQ.17 who were travelling back to Britain in the destroyers, particularly for those embarked in *Marne* and *Martin*, where the Sick Bay lay directly under 'X' turret.

By September the forces from the Home Fleet which had been deployed to the Mediterranean for the August convoy to Malta, Operation 'Pedestal', had returned, and planning for the next Russian convoy, PQ.18, could go ahead. With the PQ.17 débâcle fresh in his mind, Tovey realized that a radical revision of the methods used to escort the convoys was required. He was convinced that a convoy could withstand air and submarine attacks, albeit with heavy loss. However, if the Germans used their surface forces with skill and imagination, then there was every possibility that the PQ.17 disaster would repeat itself. Clearly, the cruiser screen and the distant battleship cover were not sufficient to protect the convoy from surface attack, since they could only give such cover for part of the voyage—the risks of their operating in the Barents Sea without air cover were too great.

Tovey was convinced that, in future, the convoy's escort must be sufficient to deter the surface threat. He and his staff developed the concept of the 'Fighting Destroyer Escort', a force of twelve to sixteen destroyers which would remain with the convoy throughout the whole of its passage, augmenting the anti-air and anti-submarine escort but detached to act independently in the face of any attack by surface ships. Tovey considered that such a force would be sufficient to deter any aggressor. If, on the other hand, the enemy peristed, then the force would be strong enough to defeat him.

Accordingly, the 39 merchant ships gathering in Loch Ewe (six more would join from Hvalfjord) were protected by a mighty escort. The battleships *Anson* and *Duke of York*, escorted by four destroyers and the cruiser *Jamaica*, were prowling north-west of Jan Mayen Island. Additional cover in the shape of the cruisers *Norfolk*, *Suffolk* and *London* were operating west of Spitzbergen in support of the homebound QP.14 and also in support of the cruisers *Cumberland* and *Sheffield*, which, with the destroyer *Eclipse*, were engaged in Operation 'Gearbox', the routine rotation of the garrison at Spitzbergen. For the first time, however, Admiral Tovey chose not to exercise his command at sea: instead, he directed operations from Scapa Flow, where he could more easily communicate with the Admiralty in London, leaving operations at sea in the capable hands of his second-in-command, Vice-Admiral Sir Bruce Fraser. Other covering forces included eight submarines deployed off Norway to intercept any movement of German warships north from Narvik and to form a shifting patrol line to cover the convoy's flank once east of Bear Island. The boats involved were *Shakespeare*, *Unique*, *Unrivalled*, *Tribune*, *Tigris*, *Sturgeon*, *Unshaken* and the Norwegian *Uredd*.

The convoy sailed from Loch Ewe on 2 September 1942, and from there until the ships had reached the Iceland meeting point they would be escorted by ships from Western Approaches Command. The escort consisted of the destroyers *Campbell*, *Eskdale*, *Farndale*, *Montrose*, *Walpole* and *Malcolm* and the trawlers *Arab*. *Duncton*, *Hugh Walpole*, *King Sol* and *Paynter*. At the Iceland meeting point, which was reached on 7 September, the Western Approaches ships were relieved by the Close Escort consisting of the AA ships *Alynbank* and *Ulster Queen*, the destroyers *Achates* and *Malcolm*, the corvettes *Bergamot*, *Bluebell*, *Bryony* and *Camellia*, the minesweepers *Harrier*, *Gleaner* and *Sharpshooter*, the submarines *P614* and *P615* and the trawlers *Cape Argona*, *Cape Mariato*, *Daneman* and *St Kenan*.

Even more comforting to the merchantmen was the sight of the light cruiser HMS *Scylla* (Capt I. A. P. Macintyre RN) and the sixteen destroyers (*Ashanti*, *Eskimo*, *Faulknor*, *Fury*, *Impulsive*, *Intrepid*, *Marne*, *Martin*, *Meteor*, *Milne*, *Offa*, *Onslaught*, *Onslow*, *Opportune*, *Somali* and *Tartar*) of the Fighting Destroyer Escort which joined two days later. Almost immediately the destroyers began proceeding in groups to Löwe Sound in Spitzbergen to fuel, and all ships were complete with fuel by the 13th.

The increased number of escorts meant that refuelling arrangements had to be revised. The oilers *Atheltemplar*, *Grey Ranger* and *Black Ranger* accompanied the convoy, while *Oligarch* and *Blue Ranger* remained at Löwe Sound.

As well to the destroyers, the attention of the crews of the merchant ships would have been drawn to the squat shape of the escort carrier HMS *Avenger* (Cdr A. P. Colthurst RN) ploughing through the water. *Avenger* carried twelve Sea Hurricane fighters and three Swordfish aircraft for anti-submarine and reconnaissance duties. She was escorted by two destroyers, *Wheatland* and *Wilton*, who were to remain with her—rather than augment the escort—to provide enhanced AA defence and anti-submarine screening and also to carry out rescue duties during flying operations. The fact that PQ.18 possessed its own organic air group was largely the result of successive and increasing pressure from flag officers charged with escorting convoys to the Soviet Union, culminating in Hamilton's report on PQ.17. Hamilton stressed the importance of shooting down shadowing aircraft and breaking up attacking formations before they got near the convoy to do serious damage. The provision of one Hurricane on a CAM ship was not sufficient for this purpose (even though a CAM ship, *Empire Morn*, did indeed sail with PQ.18). Privately Hamilton was incensed at the inadequacy of the naval air arm and the Government's concentration on bombing German cities. In a letter to Tovey dated 10 September he lamented the decision to 'concentrate on killing women and children in Germany as a quick road to victory',[6] and in a letter to Admiral Sir James Somerville dated 30 September 1942 he wrote:

> We all know that the RAF have behaved like shits as far as naval air is concerned: the old school tie means nothing to them. The First Lord and Winston hate the sight of Tovey and are trying their best to lever him out of his job and get a 'yes-man' in as CinC who will sit down calmly under this unsound Bombing Policy and allow the Navy to go on fighting with last war's weapons.[7]

Unfortunately Hamilton was not flying his flag at sea to see the results of his lobbying: after PQ.17 he went into hospital for minor surgery. However, his replacement was the perfect man for the job. Rear-Admiral Robert Burnett, known affectionately to his friends as 'Uncle Bob', was a destroyer officer who had also specialized in the unlikely field of sports and physical training. He was a powerful personality and, although not one of the Navy's intellectual admirals, was possessed of immense integrity, sound tactical judgement and a consummate desire to be at the enemy—qualities which were to be greatly tested through the eighteen months Burnett spent in the Arctic.

On 8 September PQ.18 was located north of Iceland and between the 10th and the 11th three U-boats were deployed along longtitude 3°W between 76°30′N and 74°30′N. Four more boats were ordered to concentrate between Bear Island and Spitzbergen and another five were instructed to close the area. At the same time, in a repeat of Operation '*Rösselsprung*', a surface task group consisting of *Scheer*, *Hipper*, *Köln* and several destroyers left Narvik and proceeded to Altenfjord in anticipation of the executive order to operate against the convoy from the *Führer*'s *Hauptquartier*. At 1037 the German ships were sighted by *Tribune* (Lt-Cdr N. J. Coe DFC RNR) but the range, ten miles, was too great for her to do anything other than report. At 1340 *Tigris* (Lt-Cdr G. R. Colvin RN) sighted the distinctive foretop of a heavy German warship at a range of about nine miles. The weather could not have been worse for an attack: visibility was clear, with a low swell accompanying a glassy calm. Colvin's difficulties were increased by the attentions of an He 115 seaplane which was wave-hopping ahead of the formation and caused him to be extremely cautious in the use of his periscope.

In spite of these difficulties, Colvin brought *Tigris* into an almost perfect firing position—1,500yds from *Köln* and 4,000yds from *Scheer* (which he erroneously identified as *Tirpitz*):

> At 1404, with still a few degrees to go to my firing course, there were still two screening destroyers yet to pass me. The nearest was close, but although they were weaving constantly, I thought I was just inside the screen. The submarine had just steadied on her firing course when the asdic operator reported very loud hydrophone effects on the starboard quarter. This was the first of the two destroyers about five cables distant and swinging towards me. I kept her under observation using an inch or two of the periscope at a time . . . When the destroyer had cleared my bow, I found that I had missed my Director Angle by between five and ten degrees.[8]

Attempts were made to 'chase' the DA and at 1414 a salvo of five individually aimed torpedoes was fired. All the torpedoes missed astern and exploded at the end of their runs, leading the Germans to believe that they were being bombed by high-flying aircraft. It was not until the *B-Dienst* teams in *Scheer* intercepted *Tigris*'s sighting report that they realized that a submarine was responsible. *Unshaken* and *Uredd* also sighted the German ships but were unable to attack. This was the last occasion during the Second World War when Allied submarines would encounter German warships at sea.

The surface threat remained latent. Hitler's obsession with the prospect of an invasion of Norway and the consequent need to preserve the Fleet proved more important than the necessity of destroying supplies bound for the Soviet Union. PQ.18 was to be left to the *Luftwaffe* and the U-boats.

The U-boats had already been making their presence felt in the shape of dubious asdic contacts or by being forced to dive while some distance from the convoy after being sighted by *Avenger*'s aircraft. At midday on the 10th *Harrier* and *Sharpshooter* depth-charged a contact astern of the convoy, and in the evening of the 12th *Malcolm* and *Impulsive* attacked a contact reported by aircraft. Both attacks were inconclusive, but a more substantial attack was carried out by *Faulknor* ahead of the convoy which resulted in *U88* (*Kapitänleutnant* Heino Bohmann) being sunk. But the U-boats were persistent, and from aircraft sightings and HF/DF bearings it was estimated that eight of them were in contact with the convoy. *Avenger*'s aircraft were proving their worth by making a thorough nuisance of themselves as far as the U-boats were concerned: although none of the latter was sunk by aircraft during this phase, the role of the aircraft in putting them down at a safe distance from the convoy and harassing them while they were trying to recharge their batteries was crucial.

The weather, which was foggy with frequent snow and rain squalls, aided the U-boats, and in the morning of 13 September they scored their first success. At 0855 two ships in the starboard column, the *Stalingrad* and the *Oliver Ellsworth*, were torpedoed. *U405* (*Korvettenkapitän* Rolf-Heinrich Hopmann), *U589* (*Kapitänleutnant* Hans Joachim Horrer) and *U408* (*Kapitänleutnant* Reinhard von Hymmen) were all in contact with the convoy at the time, and the three boats fired at roughly the same time. Both ships were probably hit by the same boat, though there is no way of determining which of three was successful. *U589* reported one 7,000-ton ship sunk and two explosions 3 minutes 35 seconds following the firing of two torpedoes against *Avenger*. *U408* observed one hit on a merchant ship after a running time of 5 minutes 27 seconds and a hit on a another ship beyond.

The *Luftwaffe* regained contact on the 12th and again on the 13th, and thereafter the convoy was continually shadowed by aircraft. The shadowers were the ubiquitous BV 138 or long-range Ju 88 and proved very difficult to deal with. They often worked in groups—nine were in contact on the 14th—and their heavy defensive armament made them a tough proposition for the lightly armed Sea Hurricanes (equipped with four .303 machine guns) to deal with. They extended their activities to protecting U-boats on the surface from attack by *Avenger*'s Swordfish.

The first air attack came at 1500 on the 13th as the screen was re-forming after the return of *Scylla* and the five destroyers which had fuelled at Spitzbergen. A force of Ju 88 bombers from *KG 30* made an unsuccessful high-altitude attack, and, directly after this, the main force of the *Luftwaffe*—forty He 111 and Ju 88 torpedo bombers—was detected coming in on the starboard bow. The Commodore. Rear-Admiral E. K. Boddam-Whetham, ordered a 45-degree turn to starboard towards the enemy but the starboard columns failed to comply. The aircraft approached in line abreast, 100 to 150yds apart and maintaining their positions in the face of the intense barrage put up by the escorts, and dropped their torpedoes within 2,000yds. Surgeon Lt-Cdr J. L. S. Coulter RN, HMS *Scylla*'s medical officer, watched the attack from the back of the ship's bridge:

They approached the convoy in line ahead from the starboard horizon. When level with the convoy they all turned towards it and attacked in line abreast. Each aircraft flew low over the water, and as the torpedoes were launched, each flew down the whole length of the convoy, firing its armament. There is no doubt that the attack was carried out with magnificent courage and precision, and in the face of tremendous gunfire from the whole convoy and its escort. The tanker in the next line abreast of us was hit early on by a torpedo which finished its run-in just above the tanker's funnel. At that second the whole tanker and aircraft were enveloped in a crimson wall of flame which seemed to roll over and over up into the sky until it dissolved into a vast cloud of black smoke. When I looked down at the sea again, apart from a small occasional flicker of flame on the water, there was no sign of either the tanker or the aircraft and I realised that they had both blown up.[9]

The attack had been extremely successful and had decimated the starboard side of convoy, sinking six of the seven remaining ships and two from the middle of the convoy—*Empire Beaumont, John Penn, Empire Stevenson, Wacosta, Africander, Oregonian, Macbeth* and *Sukhona*. There were two more attacks on the 13th, the first by a group of He 115s at 1615 and the second by some He 111s at 2035. Both were unsuccessful and were driven off by the escort.

The Germans had lost eight aircraft—one per ship—which had all been shot down by the AA fire of the escort. What of the *Avenger* and her air group? The carrier had deployed her Hurricanes against the shadowers and the Ju 88s involved in the first bombing attack, so that when the torpedo bombers arrived there were no British aircraft available. *Avenger*'s Commanding Officer, Cdr A. P. Colthurst, realized that a change in his operating method was required:

. . . with the small number of obsolete fighters at our disposal and with their slow operation in an auxiliary carrier, we must use them only to break up large attacking formations rather than destroy individuals.[10]

Colthurst also emphasized the need for *Avenger*'s radar operators to be able to differentiate between a reconnaissance in force and an attack in order that the small number of fighters available be properly deployed.

Before this change could be effected, the U-boats struck again. *U457* (*Korvetten-kapitän* Karl Brandenburg) torpedoed the oiler *Atheltemplar* at 0330. It was an extremely lucky shot, for, while it was manoeuvring, the U-boat was detected by HMS *Impulsive* passing up the port side of the convoy. Brandenburg was guilty of the sin of exaggeration, for in his patrol report he also claimed to have hit another merchant ship and to have scored two hits on a 'J' class destroyer. However, the hit on *Atheltemplar* was bad enough, for although the tanker was still afloat, there was no question of her proceeding to the Kola Inlet. Since there were still at least five U-boats in contact, there could be no possibility of detaching escorts to tow her to Spitzbergen, and the decision was taken to sink her.

Revenge came seven hours later with the sighting of a U-boat by one of *Avenger*'s Swordfish. The Swordfish was driven off by a BV 138, but Burnett dispatched HMS *Onslow* to the area. The U-boat, now known to be *U589* (*Kapitänleutnant* Hans-Joachim Horrer), was sighted on the surface at 1020 and *Onslow* went into the attack with depth charges. The destroyer continued her efforts for the next three hours, after which a quantity of oil fuel together with green vegetables and pieces of the U-boat's casing came to the surface.

The air attacks began at 1235 when twenty or more torpedo bombers came in low on the starboard bow—so low that they evaded radar detection. They divided into two groups. One, the larger, went after the *Avenger*, while the remainder concentrated on the other escorts. Evidently the barrage put up the previous day by the escorts had caused the *Luftwaffe* to revise its tactics. However, the new measures implemented by Cdr Colthurst also proved effective. *Avenger* left her station at the rear of the convoy and, with her two attendant destroyers, *Wheatland* and *Wilton*, pressed ahead of the convoy to find room to manoeuvre while flying off six fighters:

It was a fine sight to see *Avenger* peeling off Hurricanes, whilst streaking across the front of the convoy from starboard to port inside the screen with her destroyer escort blazing away with any gun that would bear and then being chased by torpedo bombers as she steamed down on the opposite course to the convoy to take cover.[11]

The AA ship *Ulster Queen* (Capt C. K. Adam RN) also left her position in the centre of the convoy to manoeuvre freely and use her six 4in HA guns to 'put up some shit'[12] and break up the attacking formation. The tactics worked: *Avenger*'s fighters drove off the attackers at long range while the gunfire forced others to drop their torpedoes early. Eleven aircraft were shot down with no loss to the convoy—'Altogether a most gratifying action,' wrote Burnett.

Shortly after this, about twelve Ju 88s made a high-level bombing attack without success, although *Avenger* and some of the escorts suffered near-misses. One aircraft was lost to AA fire. The torpedo bombers returned shortly afterwards and attacked from ahead; their target was *Avenger*, now on the convoy's starboard quarter. The carrier had ten of her Hurricanes airborne, and they accounted for eight of the 25 attackers, a ninth falling victim to the gunfire of MMS (Motor Minesweeper) *No 212*. However, one of the attackers managed to torpedo the freighter *Mary Luckenbach* on the starboard wing column. The freighter was carrying ammunition and she disintegrated an in awesome explosion, captured on film by the official Admiralty photographer accompanying the convoy on board *Avenger*. The last attack of the day came at 1430 and was made by a force of twenty Ju 88s which bombed from high level although a few made shallow bombing runs. This attack was also unsuccessful, and one of the attackers was shot down.

September 14 had seen an all-out effort by the *Luftwaffe* to inflict maximum damage on the convoy. Four attacks had been launched by *I/KG 26* and *III/KG 26*, involving about seventy aircraft. The attacks had cost the *Luftwaffe* dear: *I/KG 26* lost twelve aircraft and seven crews while *III/KG 26* lost eight aircraft and seven crews, in return for the loss of the Mary Luckenbach and three Hurricanes—all of which last had been victims of the intense AA barrage put up by escorts and merchant ships. It was hardly a successful performance by the Germans, and the loss of fourteen highly trained crews was particularly significant. The tactics adopted by *Avenger* and the AA ships, combined with the intense AA fire, were successful: the attacking formations were being broken up before they could come within launching range.

The next day the bombers returned, a force of about fifty attacking the convoy in twos and threes between 1235 and 1535. They met a vigorous response. When the aircraft came below the cloud they were met by a heavy AA barrage, while above the cloud they were harassed by *Avenger's* fighters, which made 21 sorties during the attack. Three of the German aircraft were shot down, all by AA fire. Towards the end of the attack the Germans seemed content to remain above the cloud, waiting for the ships to pass from under it before bombing. Burnett was considering ordering the convoy to remain within cloud when the 'Headache' team embarked in *Scylla* reported that the aircraft were being ordered to jettison their remaining bombs and return to base. (The 'Headache' team was a small group of German-speaking officers and ratings embarked in HMS *Scylla* for the purpose of intercepting the enemy's tactical communications, some of which would be *en clair*—as in the chatter between aircraft—and some in code. The work of these 'Headache' teams was invaluable in providing Burnett with real-time intelligence about the enemy's immediate intentions.)

Although the convoy's defences had been successful against the *Luftwaffe*, the strain of these attacks on the officers and men of the warships and merchant ships was intense. Surgeon Lt-Cdr Coulter in *Scylla* wrote in his journal for 15 September:

Afraid that I could not possibly set down the detailed events of today with any accuracy, as the noise and activity have been so extreme most of the time, that it has been rather a 'blur'. There were certainly some heavy air attacks but I am not sure whether some of them did not take place yesterday instead of today.

. . . the general noise and confusion were unbelievable. At the height of the attack, the ship was near missed, and at the same time the safety valve lifted on one of the smoke stacks and for about five mintes there was also the noise of steam escaping under pressure, which was itself deafening.[13]

Coulter's normally extensive duties as medical officer of a cruiser at war were complicated by the presence on board of nearly 400 survivors from sunken ships, mostly those lost on 12 September: 'They are all over the place asleep, and it is hard to avoid tripping over them.'[14] One of the survivors had a lucky escape:

Something hit him in the chest, with such force that he was knocked over, and received multiple contusions. He is badly bruised all over the front of his chest . . . In a pocket of his jumper, he was carrying a gunmetal cigarette case full of cigarettes, which had worked itself into a position immediately in front of his cardiac area. There were several perforations in his clothing and in the front of the cigarette case. The back of the cigarette case was intact. On opening the case, I found a number of bomb splinters inside it and the cigarettes all fragmented. There is no doubt that the cigarette case may well have saved his life.[15]

The large number of survivors present was a result of a deliberate policy decision to concentrate them on *Scylla*, which had better facilities for their care and which would be returning direct to Britain so that they would not become a charge on the Royal Navy's slim resources at Murmansk.

The air attack on the 15th was the last that PQ.18 faced while *Avenger* and the Fighting Destroyer Escort were in company. Submarines, however, were still a menace. As many as twelve were in the area, and three were in contact, although resolute and aggressive measures by the escort prevented them from breaking through. At 1340 on the 15th smoke was sighted some ten miles from the convoy. The destroyer *Opportune* was sent out to investigate and, to Burnett's relief (for he was continually aware of the surface threat), the smoke turned out to be the diesel exhaust from two U-boats condensing in the cold air.

At 0300 on the 16th *Korvettenkapitän* Karl Brandenburg judged the moment right to take *U457*, currently on the convoy's port bow, through the screen and dived. As he did so he was spotted by HMS *Impulsive*. The destroyer immmediately obtained asdic contact and held it down to 50yds before dropping a pattern of depth charges set to 50ft and a calcium flare to mark the spot. When *Impulsive* returned to the spot she found oil and wreckage, including a black leather glove, some wooden debris and pieces of paper. Before rejoining the convoy she dropped a further depth charge set to 500ft (the depth of water being 120 fathoms) over the point from where the oil was coming, and that was the end of *U457*.

During the afternoon of the 16th Burnett parted company with PQ.18 to join the homeward-bound QP.14. Besides *Scylla* and the destroyers, he took *Avenger*, the two submarines and the oilers *Grey Ranger* and *Blue Ranger*, the ships departing in three groups to confuse the constant shadowers. Their place was taken on the 17th by the Soviet destroyers *Gremyashchi, Sokrushitelny, Uritskiy* and *Kubyshev*. The first two ships each possessed a good AA armament of four 5in guns and were excellently handled. Also augmenting the escort from this date were Catalina aircraft of No 210 Squadron RAF based in northern Russia. Their arrival was timely, for, as the convoy rounded Cape Kanin on 18 September, twelve He 111s attacked from the starboard quarter. Fortunately, they were detected on *Ulster Queen*'s radar, so the escorts were ready for them. The aircraft attacked from astern and dropped their torpedoes at a distance of 3–4,000yds. The ships manoeuvred vigorously, but the *Kentucky*, the second ship in the port wing column, was hit. An hour later the aircraft were back, this time attacking from both sides of the convoy. On this occasion the bombers managed to synchronize their attacks with the torpedo carriers, and as the first wave of torpedo bombers began their run-in, the bombers began bombing through the cloud at a height of 2,500ft. Four of the aircraft were shot down, three by AA fire and one by the *Empire Morn*'s Hurricane fighter,[16] though not before one of the bombers had succeeded in finishing off the *Kentucky*, which had to be beached. Though the ship was beyond repair, the Russians managed to salvage some of her cargo. Once again the *Ulster Queen* was particularly effective in dealing with the attackers, her gunfire accounting for two of the aircraft shot down.

The convoy reached the Dvina Bar at the entrance to the White Sea in the evening of 19 September. Even so, the *Luftwaffe* maintained the pressure, for a dozen Ju 88s attacked the following afternoon as the ships were struggling to find shelter from a gale during which three merchant ships went aground. They remained, guarded by the *Ulster Queen*, and were attacked again on the 22nd, by which time the rest of the convoy had reached Archangel.

While PQ.18 had been making its way to Archangel, Burnett and the ships under his command had been heading to join convoy QP.14, which had sailed from that port on 13 September and consisted of fifteen merchant ships, including the survivors of PQ.17, under Commodore Dowding in *Ocean Voice*. The Eastern Local Escort consisted of HMS *Britomart*, *Halcyon*, *Hazard* and *Salamander*. The Ocean Escort comprised the destroyers *Blankney* and *Middleton*, the minesweepers *Bramble*, *Seagull* and *Leda*, the AA ships *Alynbank*, *Pozarica* and *Palomares*, the corvettes *Dianella*, *Lotus*, *Poppy* and *La Malouine* and the trawlers *Lord Austin*, *Lord Middleton*, *Ayrshire* and *Northern Gem*. The composition of the Fighting Destroyer Escort, cruiser covering force and battle fleet were identical to the forces allocated for the protection of PQ.18.

Burnett's forces joined QP.14 in the morning of the 17th, and for the next three days the convoy enjoyed an uneventful passage. The weather, cold with frequent snow squalls and patches of thick fog, gave some protection from the *Luftwaffe*. *Avenger* managed to keep anti-submarine patrols by her Swordfish in the air despite severe icing conditions on her flight deck and had the help of a Catalina operating from the Kola Inlet. A shadowing BV 138 appeared during the morning of the 18th but lost touch in the bad weather. Later the same day the Catalina sighted two U-boats north-east of the convoy while a Swordfish attacked another about twenty miles astern of the convoy. That evening two destroyers were detached to Spitzbergen to bring out the oiler *Oligarch* since both *Grey Ranger* and *Black Ranger* had exhausted their stocks, having supplied over 5,600 tons of fuel to the escorts since the operation began. They rejoined the following evening.

In the morning of the 19th the convoy rounded the South Cape of Spitzbergen and headed north-west along the coast. In order to deceive any shadowing U-boats about the change of route, Admiral Burnett ordered special air searches and disposed escorts astern of the convoy and on either quarter an hour before he altered course. The destroyers had orders to continue on the old course for six miles after the convoy had turned and then rejoin the main body at high speed. The Swordfish patrol was busy putting down three U-boats, but apart from a shadowing aircraft which appeared at 0820, QP.14 was unmolested that day. There was moment of excitement during the morning when an unidentified ship came into view, causing Burnett to turn his thoughts to 'the anchorage in Altenfjord', but the strange vessel turned out to be a straggler. It seemed that, after the intense pressure to which PQ.18 had been subjected, QP.14 was being ignored.

This supposition was to be rudely shattered when *U435* (*Kapitänleutnant* Siegfried Strelow) penetrated the screen and sank the minesweeper HMS *Leda* (Cdr A. H. Wynne-Edwards RN) at 0530 in the morning of the 20th. In the next forty-eight hours U-boats would sink another of the escorts, three merchant ships and a fleet oiler. Throughout the morning of the 20th, the escorts were fully occupied dealing with the U-boats, at least five of which were following the convoy. One of the two British submarine escorts, *P614*, which was returning to Blyth having been detached from the convoy with *P613* to patrol independently, unsuccessfully attacked *U408* (*Kapitänleutnant* Reinhard von Hymmen).

At 1720 that evening *U255* (*Kapitänleutnant* Reinhard Reche) torpedoed *Silver Sword*, a survivor from PQ.17, at the stern of the convoy, and the ship had to be sunk by the escorts. With the air threat receding and with evidence of a number of U-boats in company, Burnett decided that *Scylla* and *Avenger* were being unduly risked by remaining with the convoy. Moreover, Cdr Colthurst reported that his air crews had reached the limits of exhaustion and that their efficiency was decreasing daily. Accordingly, he transferred his flag to HMS *Milne* and sent both ships to Scapa Flow escorted by *Fury*, *Wheatland* and *Wilton*.

Burnett's decision to send Scylla and *Avenger* on ahead was vindicated when *U703* (*Kapitänleutnant* Heinz Bielefeld) torpedoed HMS *Somali* (Lt-Cdr C. D. Maud RN) stationed abreast the convoy as the port wing ship on the screen. She was taken in tow by *Ashanti* (Cdr R. G. Onslow RN), which provided electric power for her steering motors and submersible pump and was screened by *Eskimo*, *Opportune*, *Intrepid* and the trawler *Lord Middleton*. The Spitzbergen refuelling force consisting of the tanker *Blue Ranger* and her escorting destroyers fortuitously appeared on 22 September, which allowed *Ashanti* to fuel by the astern method from the oiler while towing *Somali*—an unusual sight under any circumstances. *Ashanti* towed *Somali* for 420 miles, and, had the weather held, *Somali* might have been saved, but during the night of 23/24 September the wind rose and rapidly turned into a full gale. Early in the morning of the 24th *Somali* broke in two and sank.

QP.14's ordeal was not over. Burnett requested air cover from Coastal Command and a Catalina did arrive on the morning of the 21st, but the aircraft was shot down by a U-boat shadowing the convoy. The air assets available to QP.14 were minimal since the slow Atlantic convoy, SC.100, was also in urgent need of air cover. Burnett parted company with the convoy on the 22nd, leaving the ships in the hands of Capt A. K. Scott-Moncrieff of HMS *Faulknor*. At 0640, an hour after Burnett's departure, the U-boats struck again. *U435* (*Kapitänleutnant* Siegfried Strelow) penetrated the screen and sank the olier *Grey Ranger*, the Commodore's ship *Ocean Voice* and the *Bellingham*, the last a survivor from PQ.17. It was a brilliant piece of work on Strelow's part, but he was undoubtedly aided by exhaustion among the crews of the escorts, who had been in almost continuous action for nearly eighteen days in conditions of extreme cold.

This was the last attack which QP.14 had to face. Regular Catalina patrols over the convoy began from the 23rd. The destroyers parted company from the convoy on

26 September while off Cape Wrath to head for Scapa Flow and the merchant ships arrived at Loch Ewe the same day.

'I do not know,' wrote Burnett after the operation, 'how far this operation may be considered to have been a success or failure.'[17] Burnett's opinion was that he had been lucky. Had the weather been worse, thereby preventing his ships from oiling, or had one of the oilers been torpedoed, had the ammunition stocks run out, or had the Germans made a co-ordinated air and surface attack, then the story might have been very different.

PQ.18 had lost thirteen ships out of forty, ten of them to aircraft and three to the U-boats; QP.14 had lost three out of fifteen together with *Somali*, *Leda* and *Grey Ranger*—all sunk by U-boats. The *Luftwaffe* was disappointed with these results and cited the presence of *Avenger* and her air group as the prime factor. Efforts to sink the escort carrier were frustrated

> . . . on account of the fighters—but . . . the wide screen of warships made the launching of torpedoes against the inner merchant vessels an extremely hazardous undertaking.[18]

Never again would the *Luftwaffe*, which lost 41 aircraft (33 torpedo bombers, six dive-bombers and two VLR[19] reconnaissance aircraft) in attacks against PQ.18, launch such massed attacks on a convoy. When the next convoy to Russia sailed, the *Luftwaffe* in Norway would be reduced to a few long-range reconnaissance planes and He 115 torpedo bombers, the majority of its strength having been withdrawn to North Africa following the Allied landings in November.

The voyage of PQ.18/QP.14 represented an important milestone in the story of the Arctic convoys. The enemy had done his best to prevent the passage of the ships and had inflicted serious losses. Yet the operation had shown that, provided a convoy had its own organic air cover and provided the escorts were furnished with suitable quantities of ammunition, massed air attacks could be driven off. The U-boats, too, could be contained, and here *Avenger*'s aircraft played a very important role. Only at the end of QP.14's journey, when the screen was weak and the officers and men of the escorts exhausted, did the U-boats make a significant impact. The threat from the *Kriegsmarine*'s surface ships did not materialize and therefore can only be considered in the abstract. However, taking into account the resources available to the convoy and the ineptitude which characterized the handling of the *Kriegsmarine*'s surface units when directed against Arctic convoys, then it is not beyond the bounds of possibility that the escort could have either driven off the attackers or held them off until superior forces arrived. Most significantly of all—and especially after the tragedy of PQ.17—the story of PQ.18/QP.14 represented a tremendous psychological victory for the Royal and Merchant Navies.

NOTES TO CHAPTER 7

1. Prime Minister's Personal Minute, M.294/2, 'Secret', 'Action This Day', 15 July 1942, Churchill Papers 20/67.

2. PRO PREM.3/463, Stalin to Churchill, 23 July 1942.

3. PRO PREM.3/76A/12, ff.81–90, Minutes of a meeting held in the Kremlin, Moscow, on 13 August 1942 at 11.15 p.m.

4. PRO WO.193/645A, Clark-Kerr to London, 29 March 1942.

5. After the passage of PQ.18/QP.14 the Hampdens were presented to the Soviets and their crews were brought back to Britain by the cruiser HMS *Argonaut* and the destroyers HMS *Intrepid* and *Obdurate*.

6. Hamilton to Tovey, 10 September 1942. Hamilton Papers, National Maritime Museum.

7. Hamilton to Somerville, 30 September 1942. Pencil draft in Hamilton Papers, National Maritime Museum.

8. Admiralty, Naval Staff History of the Second World War, 'Submarines, Vol 1: Operations in Home, Northern and Atlantic Waters', 1953, p.158. The Director Angle (DA) was the amount of 'aim-off' applied during an attack to allow for a target's speed.

9. Coulter, Surgeon-Captain J. L. S., *The Royal Naval Medical Service. Vol 2: Operations*, HMSO, London, 1956, pp.45–6.

10. PRO ADM.234/369, 'Battle Summary No 22: Arctic Convoys 1941–45', 1954, p.78.

11. *ibid.*, p.79.

12. See Chapter 3, p.48, note 11.

13. Coulter, *op. cit.*, p.48.

14. *ibid.*

15. *ibid.*, p.49.

16. The pilot managed to land at a Soviet airfield after exhausting his ammunition, thereby saving himself a swim. He had four gallons of fuel left in his tank on landing.

17. PRO ADM.234/369, *op. cit.*, p.85.

18. Air Ministry Pamphlet No 248: 'The Rise and Fall of the German Air Force'.

19. VLR = Very Long Range.

11-19-07 home

Chapter 8

New Year Triumph

They had only one idea, to give what protection they could to the convoy, and this they continued to do up to the moment of sinking.—Admiral Sir John Tovey, describing the part played by HMS *Achates* in the Battle of the Barents Sea

For the three months following PQ.18/QP.14 no convoys went to the Soviet Union as, once again, the Home Fleet headed south to the Mediterranean, this time to support the Anglo-American landings in North Africa. With such a commitment in hand, there was no question of any further convoys to Russia until the end of the year. Moreover, supplies which were earmarked for the Soviet Union, namely 154 aircraft already crated and loaded awaiting the sailing of PQ.19, were now unloaded and reallocated for the North African landings. Stalin was not impressed—and rightly so, for this was the Soviet Union's time of crisis. In October the German offensive at Stalingrad entered its final phase as both armies battled among the ruins. The Red Army was desperately mobilizing reserves of men and equipment to launch a counter-offensive on both flanks of the German Sixth Army and this was no time for the supply of Anglo-American aid to dry up.

Churchill, however, was sensitive to the tremendous struggle being waged by the Red Army and as a sop to Stalin proposed the sailing of single ships between Iceland and the Soviet Union, taking advantage of the long hours of darkness and foul weather. The scheme was not as hare-brained as it sounded. Thirteen ships sailed to the Soviet Union: five arrived, three turned back, four were sunk and one was wrecked. Twenty-three ships sailed from the Soviet Union to Iceland and only one was sunk. The trawlers *Cape Palliser, Northern Pride, Northern Spray* and *St Elstan* were disposed along the route from Iceland to act as rescue ships, while *Cape Argona, Cape Mariato* and *St Kenan* covered the eastern end of the route for the same purpose The route was also extensively patrolled by Catalinas, and it was this aspect of the operation, coupled with *Northern Spray*'s attack on a U-boat, which alerted the enemy. *Empire Gilbert* was sunk by *U586* (*Kapitänleutnant* Dietrich von der Esch) on 2 November, *Dekabrist* was sunk by aircraft on 4 November, the same day as *William Clark* was sunk by *U354* (*Kapitänleutnant* Karl-Heinz Herbschleb), and *Empire Sky* was sunk on 6 November by *U625* (*Kapitänleutnant* Hans Benker). *Chulmleigh* was beached on Spitzbergen after being bombed by a Ju 88 of *II/KG 30*. She was then sighted and torpedoed by *U625* (*Kapitänleutnant* Hans Benker) on 16 November before being bombed for a second time by another Ju 88 of *II/KG 30*. The sole westbound ship to be sunk was the Soviet tanker *Donbass* (another of PQ.17's survivors), by the German destroyer Z27 on 7 November.

At the same time it was decided to clear the mass of shipping from PQ.16, 17 and 18 which was still in Soviet ports. QP.15, consisting of 31 merchant ships, left

Archangel on 17 November. Soon after sailing, the *Ironclad* and the *Meanticut* grounded, and although they were refloated they had to return to Archangel.

The Eastern Local Escort until 20 November consisted of the destroyers *Baku* and *Sokrushitelny* and the minesweepers *Britomart, Halcyon, Hazard* and *Sharpshooter*. The Ocean Escort, which stayed with the convoy from sailing until its arrival at Loch Ewe on 30 November, consisted of the corvettes *Camellia, Bergamot, Bluebell* and *Bryony* and the minesweeper *Salamander*. The destroyers *Faulknor, Intrepid, Icarus* and *Impulsive* were with the convoy from 20 to 26 November, *Echo* from 20 to 22 November and *Musketeer* and *Orwell* from 23 to 30 November. The destroyers *Ledbury* and *Middleton* joined on 22 November and *Oakley* on 23 November, all three remaining with the convoy until 30 November. The convoy also had the protection of the AA ship *Ulster Queen* until 24 November, when the ship had to leave in order to fuel. West of Bear Island was the cruiser screen consisting of *London* and *Suffolk* accompanied by *Forester, Onslaught* and *Obdurate*, while the submarines *P312, P216, Uredd* (Norwegian) and *Junon* (Free French) patrolled the entrances to Altenfjord in the event of the ships there stirring.

The convoy encountered bad weather throughout the whole of its passage, which, when coupled with the almost complete lack of daylight, caused the ships to become very scattered. Neither of the two destroyer forces managed to make contact with the main body, and by the time the convoy had reached Bear Island it had disintegrated into a number of small groups of merchant ships and warships all heading in roughly the same direction. Fortunately the bad weather prevented air activity by the *Luftwaffe*, and although the convoy was sighted in the White Sea on 18 November, no air reconnaissance was possible and the Germans could gain no firm idea of the situation. The same could not be said for U-boat operations: on 23 November *U625* (*Kapitänleutnant* Hans Benker) torpedoed the *Goolistan* and *U601* (*Oberleutnant zur See* Peter Grau) sank the *Kuznetz Lesov*.

The only other casualty of QP.15 was the Soviet destroyer *Sokrushitelny*, which foundered as a result of the bad weather. On 20 November the two Soviet destroyers had turned back, having reached the limit of their radius of action. *Baku* was able to turn despite the heavy seas running, but *Sokrushitelny* was unable to do so and ran on for a little while, her Commanding Officer hoping that the weather would abate. It did not, and when *Sokrushitelny* did turn, she was pooped. Her machinery spaces were flooded and she lost all engine and electrical power. *Baku* had lost touch with her companion on leaving the convoy but received her distress signal at 1100 on 20 November and at once turned back to search. However, after searching in bad weather for over 25 hours, *Baku*'s Commanding Officer had to head for the Kola Inlet since his own fuel situation was critical—indeed, when *Baku* arrived in the Kola Inlet, her tanks were to all intents and purposes empty. Admiral Golovko ordered a maximum effort to save the destroyer, but by 1 December all attempts had failed and *Sokrushitelny* was drifting somewhere in the Barents Sea with no power, no wireless and a skeleton crew of fifteen officers and men on board. She eventually sank, but the exact date of her sinking is unknown.

The surviving ships of QP.15 all arrived at Loch Ewe on 30 November, whereupon the series of PQ/QP convoys came to an end. For security reasons, the

Russian convoys were now given the code letters 'JW' for the outward-bound sailings and 'RA' for the homeward-bound.

By the time the convoys re-started in December 1942 the outlook was very different from that which had obtained three months earlier. In terms of operations in the Arctic theatre, the long hours of winter darkness had arrived, giving protection against the shadowers and air attacks which had so characterized the summer convoys. Internationally, the situation was also much more favourable to the Allies. In the Western Desert, the *Afrika Korps* had been defeated at El Alamein and driven over 1,000 miles from the Egyptian frontier, while in Tunisia the Anglo-American forces under General Eisenhower were pressing toward Tunis, the sole remaining Axis stronghold in North Africa. In the Soviet Union the Red Army's winter offensive had surrounded the German Sixth Army at Stalingrad and the first stage of the long road to Berlin was under way. In the Pacific the Guadalcanal campaign had come to a successful conclusion and the Americans were poised for the next series of amphibious operations. In the Atlantic the U-boats were exacting a fearful toll of merchant shipping, but in 1943 the peak would be reached and shipping losses would decline—matched by a rise in the number of U-boats sunk.

This, then, was the position when the next series of convoys to the Soviet Union began in the winter of 1942. Although the overall situation appeared to have improved for the Allies, concern was still expressed over the number of U-boats in northern waters, and about the surface battle group, which now consisted of *Tirpitz*, *Lützow*, *Hipper*, *Köln* and *Nürnberg*, *Scheer* having returned to Germany for refit and her place having been taken by *Lützow*. The fuel shortage dominated the *Kriegsmarine*'s operational planning. Fuel oil for steam-driven ships was in very short supply—hence the decision not to send the cruiser *Prinz Eugen* to Norway but the diesel-powered *Lützow* instead (since diesel was still in plentiful supply). *Tirpitz*, however, was *hors de combat*, in need of a refit to cope with the many defects arising from her seven months in the Arctic. Hitler forbade her return to a German dockyard for fear that the British would invade Norway at any moment. Instead, she proceeded to Trondheim on 23 October and workmen were sent up from Germany to make the best job they could using such local facilities as were available.

The Admiralty proposed a convoy of 30 vessels. However, Admiral Tovey considered that such a large number of ships would be difficult to control in the poor winter weather and, as in the case of QP.15, they might become scattered into small groups which would be easy prey for U-boats or surface ships, or both. Tovey argued that two small convoys offered greater protection from both submarine and surface attack, and his views were accepted by Pound, who also insisted that the cruiser cover should go well into the Barents Sea instead of turning back on reaching 25°E as had been the practice hitherto.

Little need be said regarding the passage of JW.51A, consisting of fifteen merchant ships which sailed from Loch Ewe on 15 December and arrived at the Kola Inlet on Christmas Day having enjoyed good weather throughout the passage and having been unmolested by the enemy. The cruiser force, known as Force 'R', commanded by Rear-Admiral Robert Burnett and comprising *Sheffield* and *Jamaica*, went all the way to the Kola Inlet, where it arrived on 24 December. While at Kola,

Sheffield was visited by a concert party from the Soviet Northern Fleet on Christmas Day, the members of which ate and drank everything in sight. One singer had to be dissauded from brandishing a loaded revolver. On Boxing Day Burnett had to entertain Golovko and his staff. The traditional dinner of turkey with all the usual trimmings was provided, and the Soviet officers managed to consume everything which the concert party had left untouched. British flag officers received an allowance of table money for entertaining, and Burnett must have used up a year's worth in one lunch for the command and staff of the Soviet Northern Fleet.

The fourteen ships of convoy JW.51B sailed from Loch Ewe on 22 December. The Western Escort from 22 to 25 December consisted of the destroyers *Blankney*, *Chiddingfold* and *Ledbury*. The Ocean Escort joined on 22 December and consisted of the corvettes *Hyderabad* and *Rhododendron*, the minesweeper *Bramble* and the trawlers *Vizalma* and *Northern Gem*. On Christmas Day the destroyers *Achates*, *Obedient*, *Obdurate*, *Onslow* (Capt R. St V. Sherbrooke RN, Senior Officer), *Oribi* and *Orwell* joined. HMS *Bulldog* was also present for a twenty-four hour period on 22–23 December. The ship's companies of the destroyers had had their preparations for spending Christmas in harbour rudely interrupted. John Nicholson was a member of the crew of *Obdurate*:

> As the clouds rolled in over the mountains and darkness set in we heard the familiar voice on the loudspeaker—"Captain speaking". Everyone held his breath. When the old man spoke he had something important to communicate. This is what he said—"We have the honour, once more, to be entrusted to escort a convoy to North Russia and we shall proceed at midnight." An atmosphere of gloom settled over the ship.[1]

Cruiser cover consisted of *Sheffield* and *Jamaica* as described, with distant cover being provided by the battleship *Anson*, the cruiser *Cumberland* and the destroyers *Blankney*, *Chiddingfold*, *Icarus*, *Forester* and *Impulsive*.

The convoy was reported by a German aircraft during the morning of 24 December. During the night of 28/29 December the destroyer *Oribi*, the trawler *Vizalma* and five merchant ships lost touch with the main body during a gale. The next day the minesweeper HMS *Bramble* was sent to look for the stragglers, three of which rejoined independently on the 30th; the fourth, the *Chester Valley*, together with the *Vizalma*, joined on 1 January, while HMS *Oribi* and the fifth straggler proceeded to the Kola Inlet independently.

Admiral Burnett's cruisers had sailed from Kola on 27 December to support the convoy. He proceeded as far west as 11°E before he turned back on to an easterly course, and when he reached the meridian of Kola on the 30th he turned north-west to cross the convoy's track early the next day. Burnett intended to cover the convoy from a position 40–50 miles astern of it and a few miles north of its track. It was from this direction that the German ships would come, if they sailed. Burnett's rationale in staying north of the convoy was to gain the advantage of such light as existed while at the same time staying out of sight of any German aircraft which might be braving the weather.

However, his dispositions were ruined by the fact that the convoy was further to the south and west than he had anticipated. This was because its position as reported to him by the Commander-in-Chief at 1600 on 29 December was considerably in error. Thus, instead of crossing behind the convoy and assuming a position astern, he in fact crossed ahead of it and positioned his ships 30 miles due north of it as of 0830 on 31 December. Up to that point the Germans had shown little interest in JW.51B. There had been the aircraft sighting on the 24th, followed by the interception of a U-boat homing transmission, but that was all. In fact, the convoy had been reported by *U354* (*Kapitänleutnant* Karl-Heinz Herbschleb) south of Bear Island at noon on 30 December. The submarine managed to get off a sighting report—which described the convoy as being 'weakly protected'—before being put down by HMS *Obdurate* (Lt-Cdr C. E. L. Sclater DSC RN).

In Altenfjord the reports of JW.51B's progress were being analyzed and the moment appeared right for the implementation of Operation 'Regenbogen' (Rainbow), the *Kriegsmarine*'s latest plan for the destruction of a convoy bound for the Soviet Union. 'Regenbogen' was a complex plan involving *Lützow*, *Hipper* and six destroyers, *Friedrich Eckoldt*, *Richard Beitzen*, *Theodore Riedel*, *Z29*, *Z30* and *Z31*. *Hipper* and three of the destroyers were to circle round to the north of the convoy, engage the escort and force the merchantmen to turn south to where *Lützow* and the other three destroyers would be waiting. The plan was very optimistic, requiring much in the way of tactical skill on the part of the commanders and needing the co-ordination of the two 'arms' of the task force, neither of which qualities had been exhibited so far to any great extent by the *Kriegsmarine* during the war. A further complication was that, on the completion of the destruction of the convoy, *Lützow* would proceed independently into the Atlantic for commerce-raiding. Thus the operation encompassed two separate and unrelated aims, and the second of these almost certainly accounted for the cautious way in which *Lützow* was handled during the operation.

Needless to say, the Fleet Commander, Vice-Admiral Oscar Kummetz, was under the usual crippling restrictions in that he was prohibited from risking his ships in an engagement with superior British forces; nor was he allowed to risk his forces in a night action in which British destroyers might use their torpedoes. This gave Kummetz only two and a half hours of feeble light—which was all that was available at that time of year in those high latitudes—in which to destroy the convoy.

Kummetz was unaware of the presence of Burnett's cruisers, and this was probably the deciding factor in approval being given for the operation. The command structure under which Kummetz was forced to operate was cumbersome in the extreme. At the very top was Hitler, the overall Commander-in-Chief, who communicated his orders to Grand Admiral Erich Raeder, the Commander-in-Chief of the Navy at SKL (*Seekriegsleitung*) in Berlin. Below Raeder was Admiral Rolf Carls, Commander-in-Chief of *Gruppe Nord* with his headquarters at Kiel. Next in the chain was Flag Officer Northern Waters, Admiral Otto Klüber at Narvik, who issued the operational orders to Kummetz.

Once approval for the operation had been received from Hitler, Kummetz brought the forces under his command to a state of readiness and proceeded from Altenfjord at 1800 on 30 December. At the last minute Raeder felt it necessary to remind Kummetz of the need for caution and issued an order accordingly through Carls and Klüber which was eventually transmitted to Kummetz. As the official British historian has dryly noted,

> The German Naval Staff, though no doubt pressed in that direction by Hitler, seems to have shown a remarkable aptitude for depriving its sea-going commanders of all initiative.[2]

Yet, despite the problems of divided aims, a top heavy command structure and crippling operational restrictions, Kummetz succeeded in doing exactly what his plan required. The convoy was indeed sandwiched between *Hipper* to the north and *Lützow* to the south. Only the aggressive defence conducted by the escort against superior odds and Burnett's intervention at the critical moment, coupled with the timidity of *Kapitän zur See* Stange of *Lützow*, saved the convoy. The Battle of the Barents Sea, as the action has become known, was an epic engagement in the history of the war at sea and had consequences out of all proportion to the forces involved or to the actual results.

The situation at 0830 on 31 December was that the German battle group had left Altenfjord and was steering towards the expected track of the convoy, *Hipper* to the north and *Lützow* to the south with the six destroyers disposed between them. The convoy and associated forces were disposed into four groups, none of which was aware of the whereabouts of the others. The main convoy, now reduced to twelve merchant ships and eight escorts, was steering east. Forty-five miles to the north of the convoy were the trawler *Vizalma* and the *Chester Valley*, while the minesweeper *Bramble* (Cdr H. T. Rust DSO RN) was about fifteen miles north-east of the convoy. Finally, Burnett's cruisers were fifteen miles south-east of *Vizalma* and thirty miles north of the convoy. *Hipper* and her three destroyers had just crossed the convoy's wake, while the *Lützow* group was fifty miles away and closing from the south. The weather was clear, though visibility varied between seven and ten miles on account of frequent snow squalls. However, the temperature was below freezing and the spray which came over the destroyers' bows when they steamed at speeds in excess of 20kts froze on the upper deck, making conditions on their bridges and forward gun mountings uncomfortable in the extreme.

Capt Sherbrooke had seriously considered the possibility of an attack by German warships and at the pre-sailing conference had briefed the Commanding Officers of the escorts and the Masters of the merchant ships fully on his intentions. In such a situation the fleet destroyers would concentrate on his ship and dispose themselves between the convoy and the threat while the convoy turned away under cover of smoke. The remaining escorts were to form a close screen around the convoy while continuing to lay smoke. In the event, Sherbrooke's instructions were followed virtually to the letter and show the wisdom of a commander's taking his subordinates into his confidence.

At about 0820 the corvette HMS *Hyderabad* (Lt S. C. B. Hickman RNR) sighted two strange ships astern. She did not report them, believing that they were Soviet destroyers sent out from Kola. Ten minutes later HMS *Obdurate* reported the same ships crossing the stern of the convoy and was ordered to investigate. Sherbrooke must have had a premonition of action for, in time-honoured naval tradition, the ship's company of HMS *Onslow* was sent to breakfast and to change into clean underwear.

Obdurate was closing the unidentified ships. These were, in fact, the three destroyers of the *Hipper* group, but the British vessel was having difficulty identifying them against the dark sky, a problem which was solved at 0930 when the strangers opened fire. Sclater at once fell back on the convoy, although the Germans made no attempt to follow him. Sherbrooke had seen the gun flashes and began to implement his plan for such a contigency: *Orwell* (Lt-Cdr N. H. G. Austen DSO), *Obedient* (Lt-Cdr D. C. Kinloch[3]) and *Obdurate* were signalled to join him. At 0941 Sherbrooke made the first definite enemy report, which was received in *Sheffield* five minutes later, giving Burnett the news that the convoy was under attack and indicating the location of the escorts.

Meanwhile the convoy, escorted by *Achates* (Lt-Cdr A. H. T. Johns RN), *Northern Gem* (Lt H. C. Aisthorpe RNR), *Hyderabad* and *Rhododendron* (Lt-Cdr L. A. Sayers RNR), had begun to lay a smokescreen between the convoy and the threat. At 0939 *Hipper* appeared and opened heavy fire on *Achates*. Sherbrooke, who only had *Orwell* in company since *Obedient* had to come from the far side of the convoy, followed round, and for half an hour the two sides engaged each other in and out of the smokescreen, Sherbrooke taking every opportunity to drive off the intruders with torpedo attacks. At the same time he detached *Obedient* and *Obdurate* to join the convoy lest the German destroyers take advantage of his being engaged with *Hipper*. Shortly after 1000 a signal was received from Burnett that his ships were coming to Sherbrooke's support.

Indeed they were. However, before Burnett could intervene he was delayed by the need to investigate a radar contact detected while his ships were steaming north-west (this turned out to be the *Vizalma* and the *Chester Valley*). At 0932 gunfire was heard over the southern horizon, which must have been the German ships firing at *Obdurate*, but it soon died down and Burnett considered that it might have been AA fire. It seemed likely that the convoy might be ahead of the *Vizalma*, and accordingly he continued to steer east and north-east. Then heavy gunfire was observed to the south, and shortly afterwards Sherbrooke's sighting report was received. Though Burnett suspected that JW.51B was further south than he expected, he did not alter course until 0955 and then 'steamed to the sound of the guns'.

As the cruisers ran south they worked up to a speed of 31kts. Lt-Cdr Hubert Tresseder, on board HMS *Sheffield*, remembered:

We felt the ship heeling over as she started making a big turn to head for the sound of the guns. The decks began to quiver and the whole ship throbbed as the engines worked up to full power. By then our battle ensigns were flying at the yardarms. To those of us stationed on the upper deck, the whip and crackle of those huge flags, as *Sheffield* drove at full speed toward the enemy, were sounds none of us will ever forget.[4]

The cruisers could see *Hipper* being fought off by the destroyers but were unable to distinguish friend from foe in the poor light—nor did two radar contacts at long range help Burnett's understanding of what was going on. Burnett felt that these contacts had to be investigated, and at 1032 he turned to an easterly course, taking him away from the action. Almost immediately firing was observed on *Sheffield*'s starboard bow (which was, in fact, *Hipper* sinking HMS *Bramble*). An enemy vessel was sighted at 1045 and Burnett followed this ship round to the south. At the same time Cdr Kinloch (who had taken over command of the escort—see below) reported his position, and it was clear that both Burnett and Kinloch had not known where the other was. But now that Burnett had been informed of the convoy's position, he turned his ships south in support at 1112.

Burnett's handling of his cruisers during this stage of the battle poses some questions for the historian since it is clear that he could have intervened much earlier had he headed straight for the firing and heeded the old maxim about 'the unfailing support given in battle by one British unit to another'. However, his cautious behaviour illustrates the perpetual dilemma facing British commanders in the Arctic. Unlike their German counterparts, who could safely assume that any ship sighted was hostile and act accordingly, Burnett and his fellow commanding officers had to assess each contact individually, bearing in mind that it might be a straggler or an escort sailing independently or that it might be an enemy ship or submarine. Thus contacts could not be ignored: they had to investigated and classified—hence the Admiral's desire to establish the identity of *Vizalma* and her consort and his holding on to the east until 0955. This was the caution of a wise commander who continually bore in mind that his object was, in the traditional phrase, 'the safe and timely arrival' of the convoy, rather than rushing headlong into a confused tactical situation. His subsequent conduct in the battle showed that Burnett lacked neither drive nor tactical skill.

But to return to the convoy, which was still being unsuccessfully engaged by *Hipper*. Her attack had been rather half-hearted and her gunnery rather aimless, although the weather would have made target indentification for her relatively inexperienced fire-control teams very difficult. Whenever the range between *Hipper* and the destroyers fell to less than 11,000yds, the cruiser always turned away, probably in the hope of luring the destroyers after her but also because Kummetz could form no clear picture of what was happening.

The convoy had in the meantime turned from east to south-east at 0945, was being ably screened by *Achates* and her three dimnuitive consorts and was heading off at 9kts. However, at about 1020 *Hipper* suddenly unleashed a series of devastatingly accurate salvos on HMS *Onslow* which wrecked 'A' and 'B' guns, caused severe damage in the engine room and to the superstructure and destroyed all the radar aerials. Watching from *Obdurate* was Lt David Owen, the First Lieutenant:

Onslow, leading the chase, was firing back, but the range seemed excessive for her . . .
The unequal duel went on for some time; then the flash of bursting shells was seen on
Onslow. She seemed to be hit by three and fires sprang up. It was horrible to watch
because it was so unreal. At that distance, in that unreal light, she looked like a model,

the fires like tiny torches. In that little model, in those puny fires, our friends were dying.[5]

Sherbrooke himself was severely wounded in the face, his left eye hanging grostesquely down on his cheek so that he was temporarily blinded. Nevertheless, he refused to go below until he was sure that Cdr Kinloch, the next senior officer, was aware that he was now in command. The phrase 'in the finest traditions of the Service' comes to mind very easily when describing such an occasion, but Sherbrooke's conduct on the wrecked bridge of his ship on that day in the Barents Sea is indeed one of the finest episodes in the history of the Royal Navy.

After damaging *Onslow*, *Hipper* disengaged, presumably so that Kummetz could gain a clearer understanding of what was happening. Kinloch took his three destroyers after the convoy, which was still heading south-east. The damaged *Onslow* was in no condition to continue in the engagement, so she was stationed ahead of the merchant ships. However, the convoy was not yet out of danger, for at 1045 *Rhododendron* sighted ships to the southward. These were *Lützow* and her three destroyers. Kummetz's plan had worked and *Lützow* was perfectly in position to cause havoc among the merchant ships. Nevertheless, for some reason *Kapitän* Stange refrained from engaging because he was unsure of the position and, in the event, the only contribution made by his force was a few desultory salvos fired at the convoy by *Z31*.

Meanwhile *Hipper* was steering ENE at high speed to close the pincers of what Kummetz hoped would be a trap for JW.51B, and it was at this moment that the cruiser came upon the unfortunate minesweeper HMS *Bramble* and badly damaged her. *Bramble*'s report that she was under attack was received by *Hyderabad*, which for some unknown reason failed to pass the information on.

By 1100 Kinloch's destroyers had rejoined JW.51B—just in time, for the weather cleared and *Lützow* and her consorts were sighted. Instantly Cdr Kinloch led his destroyers round to place themselves between *Lützow* and the convoy, making smoke all the while. At 1106 *Hipper* reappeared on roughly the same course as *Lützow*. The former was firing to the east at what the Germans later claimed were British destroyers, but, since no British destroyers were in this region, her target must have been the unfortunate *Bramble*, which was eventually sunk by *Friedrich Eckoldt* (*Kapitän zur See* Hans Schemmel). At 1115 *Hipper* shifted her fire to *Achates*, which was easily visible at the stern of the convoy. The German gunnery was very accurate and *Achates* was hit hard. Lt-Cdr Johns was killed, together with 40 others of his crew. Command devolved on Lt Peyton-Jones, the First Lieutenant, who found that damage to *Achates'* machinery prevented her from conforming to Kinloch's order to station herself at the head of the convoy to screen the damaged *Onslow*. Unable to communicate his position to Kinloch, he disregarded his orders and remained at the stern of the convoy, continuing to make the smokescreen that was shielding the merchant ships. Admiral Tovey totally endorsed Peyton-Jones's conduct:

> I consider the action of Lt-Cdr A. H. T. Johns RN and subsequently Lt L. E. Peyton-Jones RN to have been gallant in the extreme. They had only one idea, to give

what protection they could to the convoy, and this they continued to do up to the moment of sinking. The behaviour of all officers and ratings was magnificent.[6]

After disposing of *Achates*, *Hipper* shifted her fire to *Obedient*, which had altered course to the north again to keep between the convoy and this new threat. *Hipper* inflicted some damage on *Obedient* before opening the range at 1130 because of a supposed torpedo attack. At the same time Kinloch and his ships fell back on the convoy. *Obedient* had lost her W/T in this engagement, and Kinloch ordered Lt-Cdr Sclater in *Obdurate* to take over while *Obedient* took station astern of *Orwell*. The British destroyers must have felt that their position was hard-pressed, but deliverance was at hand. At the very moment when *Hipper* disengaged, she suddenly came under heavy fire from the north: Force 'R' had arrived.

Burnett's cruisers had been pounding south at their best speed. *Sheffield's* log recorded that 32kts was attained and that the whole ship shook with the vibration of the engines. At about 1130 a contact was made at right angles to *Sheffield's* line of advance and moving from port to starboard. Burnett led round to a roughly parallel course and opened fire at 1130, *Jamaica* doing likewise shortly afterwards.

Hipper was taken completely by surprise and the two cruisers caused her substantial damage, including a hit in No 3 boiler room, which began to flood, and a fire in the hangar. Kummetz found himself in the unenviable position of being caught between the unknown assailant from the north and the dogged destroyers of the escort to the south, and he ordered a general withdrawal to the west. The 'Headache' teams in *Sheffield* were able to listen, with some amusement, to the outbreak of chatter on the short-wave radio between the German ships as a frantic Admiral Kummetz demanded of his escorting destroyers *Friedrich Eckoldt* and *Richard Beitzen* the identity of his assailant.

As *Hipper* turned away, so Burnett followed in order to keep up the pressure. At this crucial stage a snow squall gave *Hipper* some cover. At 1143 two German destroyers appeared in a position which was ideal for a torpedo attack. *Jamaica* fired at the distant destroyer, *Richard Beitzen*, while *Sheffield* turned toward the nearer ship, *Friedrich Eckoldt*.

At thirty-one knots [wrote Capt Clarke] the range closed with remarkable rapidity. In one minute we felt fairly certain that the ship was no friend of ours. With the director gunner's finger on the trigger, we made the battle challenge. The reply, a triangle of white lights, was unrecogizable, and a salvo of six 6in shells was sent on its way at a range of 4,000 yards. The shells, at an almost horizontal trajectory, roared towards the point-blank target.

It seemed that certainly half the salvo hit. I could see sparks of penetration, followed by the flame and smoke of detonation. Each successive salvo equally found its mark. On opening fire I had agreed with the Admiral that in the last resort I should try and ram the enemy, but it became clear in a matter of two minutes that such an extreme step would become unnecessary. As we swept down on the target she was disintegrating under our eye, and with a coup de grâce from our close range weapons as we passed her at a few hundred yards, followed for good measure by a few salvoes from our after turrets, *Friedrich Eckoldt* was left, a horrible and smoking ruin, to sink astern.[7]

Marine 'Doddie' Thorndyke was the gunlayer of *Sheffield*'s 'S2' 4in mounting (i.e. the second 4in mounting on the starboard side) and recorded the hail of fire that the ship was able to pour into the stricken destroyer:

> I was ordered to slip my guns into local [control] and managed to get off eighteen rounds at point-blank range. I could see boats being lowered, and also men manning the torpedoes, but our pom-poms took care of those. The shells were certainly passing right through these men. I could also see men jumping off the stern, and the skipper was silhouetted against the flames around his bridge. She drifted astern like a grand fireworks display.[8]

Friedrich Eckoldt had made the mistake of thinking that *Sheffield* was *Hipper*, and she had paid accordingly.

Meanwhile *Lützow* had made another attempt on the convoy. After disengaging from *Hipper*, Lt-Cdr Sclater had led the destroyers back to close the convoy. At 1138 they observed an engagement to the east which was probably *Bramble* being finished off by *Eckoldt*. Some three minutes later the convoy came under heavy fire from the north-east. This was *Lützow*, which, having failed to attack the convoy from the east, had altered course at 1126 to the north-west in order to maintain contact with *Hipper*. The smokescreen was not fully effective, and one ship, *Calobre*, was struck by a shell and damaged. The convoy made an emergency turn to the south-west to 225° while the destroyers hauled round to the east to cover the convoy while making smoke. After about five minutes the smokescreen was effective and *Lützow* ceased fire. Immediately afterwards *Hipper* was seen steering south-west with her two destroyers, so the British destroyers turned together, with *Obdurate* at the head of the line, and steered towards the new threat. Fearing a torpedo attack, *Hipper* turned away, but *Obdurate* came under fire from *Lützow*, which was streak- ing across at 24kts to rejoin *Hipper*. Although *Obdurate* was damaged by a near- miss, at 1202 the destroyers turned back to cover the convoy since it was now evident that the German ships were not going to press home their attack. This was the last the destroyers saw of the enemy, and at 1240 they steered south to overtake the convoy.

Throughout these dramatic events the damaged *Achates* had continued to shield the convoy with her smokescreen. However, by 1300 it was clear that she could not survive much longer. Her list had increased to 60 degrees and a quarter of an hour later she lost all power. Throughout the action Peyton-Jones had refrained from signalling for help since he knew that his fellow escorts were hard-pressed, but once his ship lost power then he felt that he had no choice but to ask for assistance. The *Northern Gem* came alongside just as *Achates* capsized at 1330. Eighty-one of her crew were picked up by the trawler and Skipper Lt Aisthorpe RNR was commended for the 'courageous and seamanlike handling of the *Northern Gem*'.[9]

After disposing of *Eckoldt*, Force 'R' had altered course to the west when at 1215 *Hipper* was sighted to the west on *Sheffield*'s port bow along with the destroyers, which were in a perfect position for a torpedo attack. Burnett considered the destroyers to be the more serious threat and ordered them to be engaged. After fire had been opened, those on *Sheffield*'s bridge were concerned to see that the shells

123

were passing way over the destroyers to land some distance beyond them. The crew of *Sheffield*'s director, being higher than the bridge, could see that beyond the destroyers lay *Lützow*—a far more significant target. *Lützow* replied with some rather ineffective salvos but *Hipper* joined the action with some very well-aimed fire which forced Burnett to swing round to the north to avoid being engaged on both sides at once and to lessen the risk of torpedo attack by the destroyers which were not engaged. By 1236 the battle was over as the German ships fled to the west. Burnett followed, tracking them by radar until contact was lost at 1400. Burnett did not want to distance himself too far from the convoy, so he retired and swept to the south, fearing that *Nürnberg*, which was known to have been based at Altenfjord with the other ships, might also be at sea and in the vicinity.

JW.51B enjoyed a peaceful passage for the rest of the trip, reaching the Kola Inlet on 3 January having been met by the minesweepers *Harrier* and *Seagull*. The ships in the convoy destined for Archangel arrived on 6 January. Burnett's cruisers remained at sea, patrolling to the west of JW.51B until early on 1 January 1943, when he turned to cover the homeward-bound RA.51. On 4 January he arrived at Seidisfjord and their place was taken by *Kent* and *Berwick*. On receipt of the action reports of the Barents Sea battle, Tovey took the Home Fleet, consisting of *King George V, Howe* and *Bermuda* with the destroyers *Raider, Queenborough, Musketeer, Piorun, Montrose* and *Worcester*, to sea to provide additional cover. It was an unnecessary precaution. Kummetz was heading for Altenfjord and *Lützow*'s commerce-raiding deployment to the Atlantic was abandoned. *Hipper* was sighted by the British submarine HMS *Graph*, which unsuccessfully attacked two German destroyers, one in the tow of the other, some three hours later. That was the last seen of the enemy. The German ships returned to Altenfjord on New Year's Day 1943.

The fourteen merchant ships of RA.51 had left Murmansk on 30 December escorted by six destroyers, *Faulknor* (Senior Officer), *Fury, Echo, Eclipse, Inglefield* and *Beagle*, the minesweeper HMS *Gleaner* and four trawlers, *Cape Argona, St Kenan, Daneman* and *Cape Mariato*. On the day of the battle the convoy was 150 miles to the south-east of JW.51B and so was well out of danger. Apart from having to avoid three U-boats on 1 January, of which warning had been received before sailing, RA.51's passage home had been as uneventful as JW.51A's outward journey and all the ships reached Loch Ewe on 11 January 1943.

Both sides recognized that the Barents Sea battle had been decisive. The Royal Navy had won a notable victory from a situation in which the Germans held the initiative, by boldly going on to the offensive to defend the convoy. Admiral Tovey's oft-quoted words about the battle still ring true:

> . . . that an enemy force of at least one pocket battleship, one heavy cruiser and six destroyers, with all the advantage of surprise and concentration, should be held off for four hours by five destroyers and driven from the area by two 6-inch cruisers without any loss to the convoy, is most creditable and satisfactory.[10]

Sherbrooke's tactics were governed by a clear appreciation of the objective—the defence of the convoy—and this was never forgotten, despite the difficulties and distractions of the engagements. Thus whenever the Germans broke off the action, the destroyers at once retired on the convoy. Moreover, Sherbrooke had made these aims crystal clear to his fellow commanding officers, so that, when he was wounded, Cdr Kinloch knew exactly what was expected of him, as did, in turn, did Lt-Cdr Sclater. Sherbrooke's own role in the battle was recognized with the award of the Victoria Cross.

In contrast, the Germans were hamstrung by their lack of sea experience and by poor visibility on the day. However, more important considerations are the crippling operational restraints and the divided nature of the operation. The behaviour of the six destroyers is particularly perplexing. Apart from the few shells fired by *Z31* and *Eckoldt*'s sinking of *Bramble*, they simply followed in the wake of their respective cruisers and played no further part in the action. Kummetz attempted to explain their inactivity by saying that he could not detach them for independent operations for fear of confusing them with the British destroyers. At the same time he advanced the argument that he had to keep the destroyers with him to prevent *Hipper* and *Lützow* being left without a screen. Nevertheless, it has to be said that the German destroyers of the *Lützow* group lost an important opportunity at 1045 just after they had passed ahead of the convoy.

However, the consequences of the battle as they affected the Arctic convoys were as nothing compared to the seismic events about to take place at Hitler's headquarters at Rastenburg in East Prussia. The atmosphere there was one of prevailing gloom because of the grim situation at Stalingrad. Hitler had been anticipating good news from the Arctic. At 1145 on 31 December a message had been received from Herbschleb's *U354*, saying, 'Observation of scene suggests battle has reached climax. I see only red.'[11] This could mean anything, but in Berlin and Rastenburg it was interpreted as meaning that Kummetz was annihilating the convoy. A signal from Kummetz received shortly afterwards to the effect that he was breaking off contact was likewise read as meaning that he had successfully accomplished his mission. Thereafter there was no communication from Kummetz since his ships maintained W/T silence while en route for Altenfjord and, after their arrival, the teleprinter link to Berlin broke down.

Throughout the afternoon and evening of 31 December and the morning of New Year's Day, Hitler continually pestered Vice-Admiral Theodore Krancke, SKL's representative at the *Führer*'s *Hauptquartier*, for information, and the latter's inability to provide any, coupled with the silence from Berlin and Altenfjord, drove Hitler into a frenzy of agitation. His mood turned to fury later on 1 January when he was shown the text of a BBC bulletin in which the Admiralty had announced that a strong German force attacking a Russian convoy had been driven off by the escorts without loss to the convoy (although the the loss of HMS *Achates* was admitted).

When by 1700 that afternoon Hitler still had not heard from SKL, he turned on the unfortunate Krancke and declared:

> I have made the following decision, and order you forthwith to inform the Admiralty that it is my unalterable resolve. The heavy ships are a needless drain on men and materials. They will accordingly be paid off and reduced to scrap.[12]

Krancke attempted to reason with Hitler, but to no avail. Grand-Admiral Raeder was required to report to Hitler in person on what had happened. Raeder wisely pleaded illness and waited until 6 January before appearing at Rastenburg. He found that the passage of time had not lessened Hitler's rage, and he had to listen to a 90-minute monologue which catalogued the manifold failings of the German Navy throughout its history. Raeder's response was to resign and recommend that either Admiral Carls or Admiral Dönitz replace him. Hitler, mindful of the fact that the U-boats had been the only arm of the *Kriegsmarine* to show any promise, chose the latter. It was, as Admiral Tovey said, 'a most creditable and satisfactory' conclusion.

NOTES TO CHAPTER 8

1. Morrison, John and Annie, *Lewis and Harris Seamen 1939–45*, Stornaway Gazette Publications, 1993, p.78.
2. Roskill, Capt S. W., *The War at Sea 1939–45. Vol 2: The Period of Balance*, HMSO, London, 1956, p.292.
3. Lt-Cdr Kinloch was promoted to Commander on the day of the battle as part of the usual half-yearly promotions and in this book will be referred to henceforth in his new rank.
4. Bassett, Roland, *HMS Sheffield: The Life and Times of 'Old Shiny'*, Arms & Armour Press, London, 1988, p.147.
5. Connell, G. G., *Arctic Destroyers: The 17th Flotilla*, William Kimber, 1982, p.122.
6. PRO ADM.234/369, 'Battle Summary No 22: Arctic Convoys 1941–45', 1954, p.101.
7. Bassett, *op. cit.*, p.151.
8. *ibid.*
9. PRO ADM.234/369, *op. cit.*, p.101, note 1.
10. *ibid.*, p.103.
11. Bekker, Cajus, *Hitler's Naval War*, London, 1974, p.290.
12. *ibid*, p.292.

Chapter 9

The Arctic Life

The ice came so fast upon us that it made our haires staire upright
upon our heades, it was so fearful to behold.—Gerrit de Veer, on the voyage
of William Barents to the Arctic regions in 1594

At this stage it is worth taking a break from the operational narrative to examine conditions on board the ships engaged in Arctic convoy operations and the medical provision for casualties and survivors afloat and at the Soviet ports of Murmansk and Archangel.

The cruel climate was the factor which dominated operations above all else. The area through which the convoys sailed was notorious for blizzards, fogs and gales of great intensity. Weather damage during these gales was often severe. In the merchant ships, deck cargo, tanks, wagons and locomotives would sometimes shift and necessitate turning back to port. On the return trip the ships were usually empty since there was not much cargo to bring back from Russia. In these cases the merchantmen would have their bows ballasted up so that their propellers would be submerged, and in this condition the ships would be unmanageable in a bow or beam wind. The escorts suffered too, losing boats, davits and other upper deck equipment and sometimes men. Destroyers and smaller escorts had the worst of it. In a bad gale it was often impossible for a man to go from one end of the ship to the other along the upper deck without being washed overboard. Eventually destroyers would leave their boats ashore, and later in the war some had flying bridges built to allow fore and aft communication.

But the overwhelming memories of those who served in the Arctic are of the tremendous cold and of ice. In HMS *Eclipse* in the spring of 1942, two of the 4in gun mountings were frozen solid by ice, spray froze on the backs of men working on the upper deck and the leather sea boots of one officer were frozen to his feet. During one of the many air attacks in PQ.18's voyage to Russia, a gunner was observed to break down and cry because his hands were too cold and clumsy to work his gun.

Ice in any shape or form was a menace to merchant ships and warships alike. Capt M. M. Denny RN, Commanding Officer of the cruiser HMS *Kenya*, said that 'after experience with PQ.12, I would never take a convoy near the ice, accepting almost any other risk in preference.'[1] The nearness of the ice-pack was always indicated by ice-blink[2] and a rapid fall in temperature. The temptation to give a hunting U-boat the slip by entering an ice-lead had to be resisted since this would usually end in a blind alley and was apt to close up behind the ship, leaving her stranded. Considerable damage could be done to bows, propellers and rudders in extricating a ship from such a position. Experienced officers preferred to keep at least 40 miles from the edge of pack ice and would even turn a convoy off the ice edge using light signals in darkness when U-boats were known to be about rather than risk a collision with the ice.

Heavy snow and ice would accumulate on the upper deck and, once formed, increase in bulk very rapidly. Such growth increased top-hamper and was highly dangerous. The whaler *Shera* capsized in a heavy swell and pack ice on 9 March 1942 during the passage of PQ.12 as a result of ice building up on her superstructure. Whenever possible all hands had to set to work with picks and shovels. Later, steam hoses were employed to clear away snow and ice. The working parts of weapons were kept ice-free by special grease, electric/steam heating and jacketing. These measures were effective but involved a considerable amount of extra maintenance.

In the beginning there was little that could be done to ameliorate the effects of operating in northern latitudes. The fitting of extra armament and equipment (especially radar) and the embarkation of men to operate them made considerable inroads in the space allocated to mess decks which were already overcrowded. Initially, conditions became worse rather than better. However, from the Admiralty's point of view, it had always to be borne in mind that the whole essence of the versatility of a warship lay in its suitability for active service in any part of the world and in any extreme of climate at short notice. In other words, a ship could never be completely prepared for service in the Arctic: if she were, and had then to be rushed to a theatre of operations such as the Mediterranean, she would be ill-suited for work in the hotter climate.

The PMO of the light cruiser HMS *Scylla*, Surgeon Lt-Cdr J. L. S. Coulter RNVR, described his experiences of Arctic warfare in 1942 and 1943 thus:

As far as my own ship was concerned, apart from switching off the overhead fans and, so to speak, keeping the doors and windows shut, there was no difference in the ship itself between operating inside the Arctic Circle and operating on the Equator. Such measures that were taken were aimed not at habitability but at preventing the freezing up of gun mechanisms, technical machinery and the navigation instruments on which the ship's life depended. On one occasion we went from Algiers to Murmansk in three weeks in the middle of January, which meant being transferred from a mean temperature of 70°F to one varying between 18° and minus 30°F.

There was usually a film of ice on the insides of the bulkheads of living spaces. You could get used to this, but one of the curses of the Arctic is the rapid variation in temperature due mainly to wind. There can be a rise and fall of 20° in as many minutes, particularly if the ship alters course or speed. This means that the film of ice may thaw, in which case you and your surroundings get saturated with water, after which everything freezes again. The same state of affairs prevailed even in the engine and boiler rooms, which presented a most attractive appearance with enormous icicles hanging down from the air supply trunks.

So much for between decks. But these ships weren't just travelling quietly to Russia. In the bad convoys they were fighting their way there almost mile by mile. This meant a large number of the crew being at action stations, out in the open, for days on end. We soon found that the watchkeeping system had to be drastically modified and that a four-hour watch on deck had to be reduced to a half-hour watch, which was as much as most men could endure.[3]

A BLOODY BUSINESS

Above: The AA ship *Pozarica*, which, together with her sister-ship *Palomares*, headed for Archangel, taking most of the escorts with her. Could these ships have done more to protect the merchant ships?

Below: One ship which did continue to protect her charges was the trawler *Ayrshire*, which took the freighters *Ironclad*, *Troubadour* and *Silver Sword* under her protection. (IWM FL.1284)

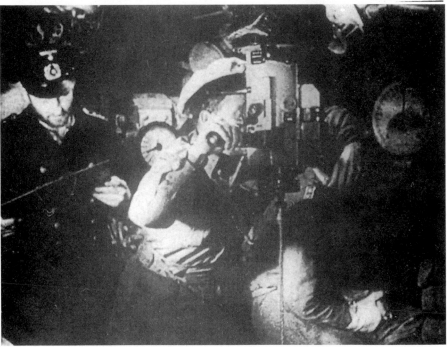

Left: A member of the crew of the *Troubadour* painting the ship's funnel white as a primitive form of camouflage. The kingposts have already been painted. (USN)

Below left: A U-boat commander at the periscope. U-boats accounted for sixteen of the 36 merchant ships that made up PQ.17. (IWM FLM.1460)

Right: The CAM ship *Empire Tide*, one of the merchant ships which did survive the attacks on PQ.17. Twenty-one of PQ.17's merchant ships were sunk after the order to scatter had been given. (USN)

Below: HMS *Dianella* was the first escort vessel to reach Archangel on 17 July and break the news of the disaster which had befallen the convoy. (IWM A.12313)

Left: Commodore Jack
Dowding, PQ.17's commodore,
who, although his own ship had
been sunk under him, rallied the
escorts which had reached
Archangel to go back and bring
in the surviving merchant ships.

FIGHTING BACK

Below left: Hampden AT109 of
No 455 Squadron RAAF, which
crashed at Vardø in northern
Norway en route to the USSR.
Luftwaffe investigators found
much valuable intelligence in
the wreck.

Right: The escort carrier HMS
Avenger. Her six Sea Hurricane
fighters are ranged on the flight
deck. (IWM FL.59)

Below: The anti-aircraft cruiser
HMS *Scylla*, Burnett's flagship
for the operation. (IWM
FL.2933)

Left, top: HMS *Ashanti* enters Löwe Sound. Spitzbergen, to fuel from the oiler *Oligarch* on 11 September 1942.

Left, centre: The classic photograph which epitomizes the Arctic convoys: PQ.18 under air attack. (IWM A.12022)

Left, bottom: A photograph taken from HMS *Avenger* on 14

September showing the destruction of the merchant ship *Mary Luckenbach*. (IWM A.12275)

Above: Survivors from sunken merchant ships are transferred from the minesweeper *Harrier* to the cruiser *Scylla*.

Below: HMS *Somali*, torpedoed on 20 September 1942 by *U703*.

The photograph shows the ship listing heavily to starboard.

Bottom: The scene on 22 September 1942 showing *Blue Ranger* (left) fuelling *Ashanti* (centre) by the astern method. *Somali*, which was being towed by *Ashanti* at the time, foundered two days later.

NEW YEAR TRIUMPH

Above: HMS *Onslow* under the command of Capt R. St V. Sherbrooke RN. This destroyer led the determined defence of JW.51B.

Left: Capt R. St V. Sherbrooke RN. His planning and foresight had much to do with the succesful defence of JW.51B and, though terribly wounded, he refused to leave the bridge of his ship until he was assured that command of the escort had been satisfactorily transferred.

Above left: The shattered funnel of HMS *Onslow* after the ship had been shelled by *Hipper*.

Above right: HMS *Onslow*'s damaged 'B' mounting. Only one member of the gun's crew remained alive after the battle.

Right: Rear-Admiral Robert Burnett, who brought the cruisers *Sheffield* and *Jamaica* into action at the critical moment. (IWM A.21758)

Left, top: Burnett's flagship, the cruiser HMS *Sheffield*.

Left, centre: The destroyer HMS *Achates*, which remained at the rear of the convoy, laying a smoke- screen, and eventually capsized after being damaged by *Hipper*.

Left, bottom: Survivors from

HMS *Achates* in defiant mood after being rescued by the trawler *Northern Gem*.

THE ARCTIC LIFE

Above: A convoy—probably one of the early series—in the half-light of a winter day. (IWM A.6888)

Below: A seaman on board HMS *Kent* proudly shows HM King George VI his 'Blue Nose' certificate, awarded to those who served north of the Arctic Circle. Such certificates may have provided the opportunity for some humour, but the reality of service in the Arctic was a decidedly different matter.

Top: A merchant ship labouring in heavy weather in early 1945. The region was, and is, notorious for gales and storms of great intensity.

Above: HMS *Lotus* at sea during the passage of JW.53. Note the ice on her forecastle, which, if allowed to accumulate,

could have the most serious effects on her stability. (IWM A.15418)

Below: Tankers of RA.53 steaming through Arctic fog, a phenomenon caused by the mixing of the warm waters of the Gulf Stream with the cold waters of the Arctic. (IWM

A.15356)

Right, top: An iced-up signal projector on board HMS *Sheffield* in the winter of 1941–42.

Right: Clearing ice from the forecastle of the cruiser HMS *Scylla* in February 1943.

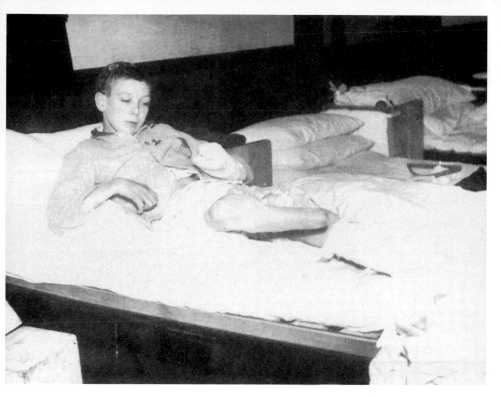

Above left: Ice and snow on the flight deck of the escort carrier HMS *Fencer* during RA.59's voyage. (IWM A.23575)

Left: Royal Marines 'closed up' at their action stations in 'X' turret on board HMS *Sheffield* in early 1942. (IWM A.6879)

Above: James Campbell, a cabin boy aged sixteen and a survivor from one of the ships in PQ.17, in hospital on his return to Britain. The boy lost one leg below the knee, half his left foot and four fingers of his left hand as a result of his immersion in icy water.

Below: The Soviet base at Polyarnoe, home for the officers and men of the Royal Navy Mission in the Arctic. (IWM A.20473)

DIFFICULT DECISIONS

Above: HMS *Belfast* off Iceland before the sailing of JW.53 on 15 February 1943.

Below: HMS *Sheffield* heads into heavy seas off Iceland. During the night of 19 February 1943 a wave tore away one-third of the armoured roof of 'A' turret.

A. J. Clarke, an Able Seaman in the minesweeper HMS *Jason*, noted similar conditions during JW.53's passage to Russia in February 1943:

> Mess decks flooded, clothing, crockery, vegetables all floating about. Can't sleep even if you want to—merely hang on and hope for the best.[4]

Clarke also noted the great variations in temperature. On 20 February 1943 the temperature was −10° but twenty-four hours later it had risen to 49°.[5] Engine Room Artificer R. J. Wood in HMS *London* noted the disruption of normal naval routine caused by Arctic operations:

> Normal routine like cleaning ship was a non-event: as the days passed so the ship became more and more untidy, spilt food on the mess decks remained there, cocoa and sugar were all over the decks. I can hear the sound of granulated sugar crunching under my feet to this day. The seamen's heads or toilets were in the forecastle and I remember seeing a line of white porcelain lavatory pans disgorging their contents in fountains every time the great ship put her bows down into the deep Arctic troughs. Handrails on the vertical ladders throughout the ship were rusty; even the main throttle valves in the Engine Room had not escaped the cold, moisture laden air. Seasickness was not uncommon, and on one occasion I saw the ship's cat being sick in a fire bucket. The cat was more considerate than some members of the ship's company.[6]

The principal measure taken to improve habitability was known as 'arcticizing', which meant diverting the ship's steam supply throughout the living and working spaces between decks and in appropriate areas on the upper deck by means of a vast array of pipes, thus providing additional heating at minimum cost and disruption to the operational readiness of the ship. 'Arcticizing' could be carried out quite quickly by any shipyard, but its effects were not always what the designers intended. Mess decks became almost sub-tropical, filled with steam, water and ice-slush. A man coming off watch had to strip off his clothes, otherwise he would be quickly bathed in his own sweat and would freeze when he went outside again. Pipes were often awkwardly situated, and the unwary would burn themselves on a hot pipe which they failed to notice or recognize.[7]

In comparison with their counterparts in the *Kriegsmarine*, Royal Navy personnel were provided with little in the way of extra clothing for service in the Arctic. Much depended on the individual's resourcefulness and the charity of family, friends and organizations ashore. Long, thick underwear and sea boots were provided from the ship's store, together with a limited number of thick duffle coats for personnel working on the upper deck. The last, however, were in short supply, so watchkeepers coming on duty had to take the coats of those coming off duty.

Those with private means could afford to purchase specially designed clothing suitable for the Arctic from well-known London stores. One-piece kapok quilted suits were popular items although not universally available. Generosity forthcoming from family and friends or stimulated by appeals in the press were left to bridge the gap caused by official disinterest. Parcels of clothing were sent to the Fleet by individuals or were sponsored by newspapers. Touching little notes were often to be found inside the clothes, for example, 'Knitted by a grateful reader of the *Daily Sketch*'. In some cases, however, the patriotism and enthusiasm of the 'knitter' exceeded her skill with the needles. One medical officer remembered receiving a balaclava helmet which had a large triangular aperture for the wearer's face. When worn, the apex of this aperture was the point of the wearer's chin while the base extended half way down his chest![8]

Air crews were especially vulnerable with regard to the lack of suitable clothing. The ordinary flying suit was clearly inadequate for conditions in the Arctic, particularly for the Swordfish crews who flew in open cockpits. Chemical heating pads were provided: when soaked in water and inserted into pockets in the flying suit, these were supposed to give off heat, but they could not be relied upon to give a constant level of warmth—the wearer was either soaked or scalded—and proved far more effective when used as rat poison. It was not until the winter of 1944 that immersion suits, together with small dinghies, were provided for air crews.

Experience was the main teacher in helping personnel to acclimatize themselves to Arctic conditions. Men soon learned, often through painful experience, not to touch metal with their bare hands lest they 'freeze' to the object concerned. Drinking with bare lips from a thin cup was another problem. Men quickly acquired the habit of remaining constipated (on account of the diet) for days on end and got used to making faces at each other as a means of checking whether or not their cheeks were frost-bitten.

Personnel received large quantities of fatty pork and butter in the rations issued to ships operating in the Arctic, but feeding a ship's company with the ship closed up at Action Stations and with the galley fires extinguished as a safety measure was a perennial problem. Often the best that could be done was to provide hot drinks using the ship's steam to heat the water. Otherwise, there was an endless diet of corned beef sandwiches.

In terms of medical ailments, apart from frostbite there was little that could be specifically attributed to the climate. The numerous minor illnesses caused by too many men living closely together were aggravated by the cold conditions. Pediculosis[9] was common in many ships and was undoubtedly made worse because men wore the same clothes for long periods. A condition known as 'Arctic Eye', whereby the eyes would become very infected and stream with pus (which would freeze in the open air), thus causing a nasty and resistant impetigo, was very common among look-outs and others required to use instruments with rubber eyepieces. The cold and the unhealthy nature of conditions on board HM ships undoubtedly contributed to a lowering of resistance to any kind of infection.

The climate also made dealing with casualties more difficult, and many of the accepted practices had to be revised. In particular, the giving of morphine to survivors had to be abandoned. One ship's doctor reported that, in the Arctic, survivors tended to give up and die more quickly than in other theatres and in this respect morphine reduced a man's will to live.

The practice of surgery on wounded men was considerably complicated by the climate. One surgeon pointed out that his fingers were so cold that they would not work properly, that sterilization and asepsis were unreliable, that the lights kept on failing and that he and his assistant were thrown about so much by the manoeuvring of the ship at high speed that they tended to do most of their work kneeling down with the patient strapped in a lower bunk. A further distracting factor was that the cold would make the glass bottles containing plasma solution—vital in the resuscitation of the wounded—very brittle. The concussion from the firing of the ship's armament and the explosion of depth charges, together with near-misses from bombs, would often cause the bottles to shatter, which was 'frightening to the patient and exasperating to the doctor'.[10] Another medical officer recorded:

> After one experience of applying a tourniquet with numbed fingers on a heaving deck covered with ice, I took pains to train my first aid parties in tourniquet drill in the open and with bare hands, just in case. It takes some doing even if you can get at the limb inside the layers of clothing that cover it.[11]

Generally speaking, casualties were few on Arctic convoy operations. A survey of the losses has produced four main reasons for this. First, a large number of deaths occurred instantaneously when ammunition ships exploded, leaving few, if any, survivors. Second, many ships sank very quickly, so that they were abandoned rapidly, and there seems no doubt that in some cases wounded men were left on board. Third, any wounded man who did get away from a sinking ship might not survive the low temperature of the water. A number of ships reported bodies, obviously badly injured, floating about near where a ship had sunk or was sinking. Finally, the nature of the weapons employed by the enemy, with U-boat and torpedo-bomber attacks predominating, meant that casualty rates were fairly low: losses from high-level bombing or dive-bombing, where there would be a greater incidence of injuries from splinters and blast, were fairly light.

Nevertheless, exposure posed a formidable problem. The Official History states that 30 per cent of all casualties needed treatment for this reason. It was found that three degrees of exposure were met with: (a) cold but dry; (b) wet, slightly shocked, but conscious; and (c) grossly shocked, with pupils widely dilated and limbs rigid, unconscious, and with stomach and lungs clogged with fuel oil. Those in the first category had usually been lucky enough to get into a lifeboat and responded quickly to warmth and hot drinks. Those in the second had usually been in the sea for about twenty minutes. Treatment consisted of removing wet clothes and wrapping the survivor in warm blankets. When his shivering had stopped, he was usually fit to be clothed. A stiff 'tot' of unadulterated Navy rum was of great value in treating men in these first two categories.

The third degree presented a more difficult problem. These men had usually been in the sea for more than half an hour and were often indifferently clothed. On being brought aboard they were stripped and wrapped in warm blankets. Artificial respiration was started immediately and intramuscular injections of camphor in oil were given. The mouth, nostrils and eyes would be gently cleansed of oil fuel. As soon as breathing became more regular, the patient was not interfered with until a pulse could be felt and the pupils began to contract. A prolonged bout of shivering would follow, after which consciousness would return. The patient would then be moved to a warm bunk and sleep would be induced, by morphine if necessary. It was found that, for these men, the giving of hot drinks was of no value as this invariably resulted in the vomiting of blood-stained froth mixed with fuel oil. These men usually took up to 48 hours to recover, provided that there were no complications.

From 1942 onwards convoys were accompanied by one or more rescue ships which had accommodation for up to 150 survivors together with appropriate medical facilities. At the end of the convoy's journey, survivors were either discharged to hospitals in the Soviet Union or returned to Britain.

One other aspect of the care for wounded and survivors in the Arctic was the maintenance of casualties ashore in north Russia while they were awaiting repatriation. This subject has been covered exhaustively in literature on the Arctic convoys, usually to the detriment of the Soviet authorities. One medical officer's impressions of the hospital at Murmansk were that

> Conditions were appalling . . . and British naval patients were taken completely out of the control of their own medical officer. The food consisted entirely of black bread, which caused patients to develop a chronic diarrhoea.[12]

It later transpired that the officer in question had never visited the hospital and had relied on others for his information. A study of the official Admiralty records, in particular the history of the Royal Naval Medical Service, shows that the picture was by no means as bleak as it has been painted.

The medical facilities in northern Russia were split between the Murmansk/Polyarnoe complex and Archangel. At Polyarnoe British patients were admitted to the hospital serving the Soviet Northern Fleet. Though regarded by the Soviets as a general hospital, it was really little more than a casualty clearing station. It was not a partcularly cheerful place, and the lack of facilities, coupled with overcrowding and an absence of sanitation, created a generally unfavourable impression.

However, reports from British medical officers do record details which were a credit to the Soviet medical authorities. Mention is often made of how British casualties were given priority, even at times when the hospital was busy dealing with large numbers of Red Army casualties from the Murman front. Russian doctors were helpful and competent, although it was considered that their training was not as thorough as British practice would have demanded. Russian nurses, though often badly trained and lacking in experience, were willing to learn and were sympathetic towards British patients, many of whom were understandably anxious at being stranded in such an alien environment.

At Vaenga and Grayaznaya, local hospital facilites consisted of the lower floor of a barrack room at the former and a converted school at the latter. At Murmansk the hospital was a one-time school in which the Soviets had placed 400 beds. The hospital was short of drugs and equipment and suffered the usual disadvantages consequent on being situated in a building designed for another purpose. Nevertheless, many of the disadvantages were overcome by international goodwill. Royal Navy medical officers were allowed to attend cases with their Soviet colleagues and were allowed to use medical supplies brought ashore from their ships.

The Medical Officer of HMS *Forester*, Surgeon Lt J. W. J. Knowles RNVR, had considerable experience of working with the hospital authorities at Murmansk, particularly after his ship landed a large number of casualties in May 1942 following the loss of *Edinburgh*. His remarks about the competence or otherwise of the Soviet medical services therefore carry more weight and authority than those by other observers whose contact was briefer. Knowles wrote of the hospital in Murmansk that

... on admission every patient was put through a regular routine. The wounded were collected in a casualty room on the ground floor, where their names and numbers were taken. Every patient, no matter from what he was suffering, was then stripped in preparation for a shower bath which was given with the greatest energy and diligence by a nurse. The patients were then seen by two admitting medical officers, one of whom was a woman whose duty was to make a rapid preliminary examination and diagnosis and to divide the patients into their various types and distribute them to the various departments of the hospital. All cases of splinter wounds, fractures or suspected fractures had x-rays taken at once before being sent off to the operating theatres or fracture wards. The whole system seemed to work very smoothly and a large number of patients was got through in quite a short time.[13]

Another, more humorous account of being admitted to a Soviet hospital, in this case the one at Archangel, comes from Third Officer Henry Phillips of RFA *Aldersdale*, a survivor from the PQ.17 convoy:

... we were ushered about six at a time into a reception room. Ranged across one end of the room was a row of trestle tables and seated behind these, like wizened oranges, were half a dozen elderly Russian matrons, who obviously spoke no English. Through sign language we understood that we were to strip to an undefined limit. In front of each woman was a notebook, and as we removed each garment, giving the name in English, it was written down phonetically in Russian. Eventually we arrived at underpants and vests, short, tall, paunchy, thin, faced by six near hysterically hilarious nurses and the dilemma of how far to go. After much discussion we reduced to the buff and made our way through an adjoining door to an enormous shower room. The showers were set high up and were controlled by a small boy. After setting the temperature some muscular nurses came in and proceeded to scrub us with ersatz loofahs on the end of a short stick, the more masculine-looking of us being singled out for some special female comments. From here we were issued with white pyjamas which were our uniform for a long time.

The hospital was fairly comfortable and the food plain and monotonous. Porridge formed the staple vegetable; we even had it with meat and gravy. The staff, being female, were hotly pursued by the more virile survivors, with varying degrees of success. Little English was spoken, though the resident medical officer was a handsome woman who spoke English with a Home Counties accent. She was a tower of strength to us.[14]

In similar circumstances, the Medical Officer of HMS *Niger* wrote:

I found the staffs of the hospitals at Polyarnoe and Murmansk most anxious to help and ready to go to extreme lengths to carry out any of my suggestions with regard to the treatment of British patients.[15]

Surgeon Lt R. Lawrie RNVR of HMS *Eclipse* echoed the praise of the Soviet authorities at Murmansk after his own ship had landed a large number of survivors in March 1942:

The arrangements for the transport of my patients to hospital were excellent. Three ambulances arrived within ten minutes, and I was pleased to notice that there were two medical officers with them. I went to the hospital with my casualties, and during the short time at my disposal I found that the arrangements, *in all respects* [author's italics], appeared very satisfactory indeed. There were numerous surgeons in attendance. I noticed that nobody was allowed inside a ward unless wearing a clean white gown.

Unfortunately owing to the movements of my ship, I was unable to stay and watch the surgeons operate on my cases. However, the naval base officer was in attendance.

But I had one other opportunity to visit the hospital, and I found that the treatment given seemed good and that my patients were quite satisfied. My own SBA[16] was a patient and, that day, had complained of a sore throat. Immediately the Russian throat specialist for the Northern Fleet had been sent for in consultation.

My only complaints were that the beds seemed rather close together and the food was far below our standard. But I talked to some 60 survivors from British merchant ships who said that they were all well looked after and were pleased with the attention which they had received. Their chief difficulty was lack of interpreters.[17]

These remarks are all the more relevant in that they were made at a time when Murmansk was experiencing very heavy air attacks which caused considerable disruption to local services.

In general, battle casualties in the Arctic were no different from those in any other theatre. However, there is evidence to show that the incidence of mental stress was higher in officers and men serving in the Arctic than elsewhere. *Scylla*'s Medical Officer wrote:

In my opinion the greatest danger in time of war afloat is the mental effect of the climate. I have no doubt at all that fear against an Arctic background is a far more difficult thing to control than fear in other theatres of war . . . behind it all was the awe-inspiring beauty of the Arctic with its cruel cold, its dreadful loneliness and what seemed to be the utter hopelessness of survival if the worst should happen.[18]

There was much discussion in the Navy at the time about the relative hardships endured by those engaged in Malta convoy operations and those in the Arctic. Both had to pass through waters near enemy air and surface-ship bases and suffered attacks accordingly. However, Malta convoys were generally faster and took less time to reach their destination: the 'Pedestal' convoy of August 1942, for example, took five days to travel from Gibraltar to Malta whereas the equivalent Arctic convoy, PQ.18 out and QP.14 back, entailed a three-week round trip for the escorts. It was this continual strain which was the main factor in the incidence of stress among officers and ratings.

One sign of the extended strain under which men were operating came in the shape of an increasing sick-list. Surgeon Lt R. Lawrie RNVR, the Medical Officer of the destroyer HMS *Eclipse*, noted in March 1942, after his ship had been heavily engaged in some of the early PQ convoys, that

Since our visit to North Russia, with its action with enemy surface craft and the unrest of daily bombing attacks, there has been a marked increase in the sick parade. On one day recently I have had to send twelve men for medical and surgical consultations. Of these twelve, eight have already been discharged to hospital and four are awaiting relief. The important thing is that these men had been suffering from their complaints for months and in some cases for years without reporting sick . . . The extreme cold off North Russia, combined with prolonged action conditions, had a most marked effect on our crew . . . These conditions greatly affected the nerves of the crew, with the consequent results that complaints which they previously hid have become aggravated, and are now disclosed.

These twelve men were good, conscientious workers who had been in the Navy since before the outbreak of war. It is only now that they feel the strain on their nervous systems to such an extent that they must report sick with a long standing physical disability.[19]

Scylla's surgeon commented:

Our men seemed to get hyper-emotional and disorientated on this convoy [PQ.18/QP.14] and I must admit that a lot of it is a mental blur to me. But one thing I do remember is that in the Arctic men seemed to be less philosophical than in warmer climates.

As the days passed and we became so weary, my office became a sort of focal point for visitors whenever there was a lull in the action, and here I used to dispense teaspoonfuls of whiskey in hot tea to my combatant colleagues. I found it common enough for a responsible officer or rating to sit alone with me and weep a little, and dry his eyes, and go back to his job.[20]

The strain of continual operations could be made worse by the presence on board a warship of a large number of survivors, all of whom were in some state of shock having endured the sinking of their own ship. During an air attack on QP.14 (one of many the convoy endured), Fred Herman, a survivor on board *Scylla* from one of PQ.18's American ships, wrote:

The infernal cacophony of exploding bombs went on, with the massive thunder of the ship's own guns beating through the other waves of sound again and again.

One man began to pound on a table with his fist. A coloured man sat up cross-legged, swaying to and fro, holding his ears and rolling his eyes at the deck above. Under the impact of sound alone men seemed to go to pieces. Some tried to talk but could only stammer. One crawled under a table and curled up there. Even among the quieter, self-controlled men you could watch the tension increasing like a coiled spring. It showed in the nervous way they drew back their lips. It came into their eyes and into their drained white faces.[21]

During this attack, one of *Scylla*'s ship's company, a seaman sent aboard from HMS *Standard*,[22] felt that he simply could not cope with the strain, abandoned his post and hid himself deep inside the ship.

Air crews faced particular problems in dealing with stress. They spent long hours in their cockpits or in ready rooms waiting for the order to take off. These periods of inactivity were then followed by brief periods of intense action and concentration as they flew off on patrol or in search of a U-boat contact. They often had to fly in atrocious conditions, and at the back of their minds was the dreadful thought that if they got lost or if their radio or radar ceased to work, then there was the grim prospect of ditching in the ocean with little likelihood of survival. After one four-hour flight from HMS *Nairana* (Capt V. N. Surtees DSO RN), the pilot and observer of a Swordfish of 811 Squadron were frozen solid and had to be physically lifted from their cockpit and carried below.

Rough weather and the constant need to be at a state of readiness made air crews constantly tired. On 27 October 1944, seven days after sailing with JW.61, Lt-Cdr E. R. Barringer, a pilot with 835 Squadron in HMS *Nairana*, noted that

. . . the ships were now rolling more than 40° from side to side. Living conditions on board the ships were chaotic and everyone had to work, eat and sleep in a world which rolled inexorably through 80° or more. The air crews who were spending most their time in flying gear in the Ready Room were already beginning to feel tired and short of sleep.[23]

The growing fatigue and tiredness among aircraft crews manifested itself in a growing accident rate. During the return trip of RA.61, 811 Squadron in HMS *Vindex* (Capt H. P. T. Baylis RN) wrote off 75 per cent of their aircraft (eight out of twelve Swordfish and three out of four Wildcats) in accidents. 853 Squadron flying Avengers from HMS *Tracker* experienced similar problems. The Squadron needed resting as air crews and flight deck crews had lost confidence in themselves. *Vindex* did not sail with JW.62. In the words of one of 835 Squadron's pilots in HMS *Nairana*, 'they [811 Squadron] had reached or exceeded the physical limits of their endurance'.[24] In the same way, 825 Squadron had to be withdrawn from front-line service after the JW.59/RA.59 convoys in the summer of 1944.

Things were not made any easier for the air crews by the unhelpful attitude to their problems shown by some of the ships' officers. One of the main complaints by air crews was that they never managed to get a decent hot meal since their flying operations did not fit in with the wardroom mealtimes or the ship's cooks' routine. As a result, they lived on hastily prepared corned beef sandwiches and tea. One New Zealand pilot in *Nairana* expressed himself in typically forthright fashion:

Al Burgham, who was one of the mildest of men, really got steamed up on one occasion and pointed out with typical Kiwi bluntness that the new commander should bear in mind that the ship was there for the pilots to fly off and not for him to exercise his Dartmouth rules and regulations.[25]

Nairana seems to be have been a particularly unhappy ship for the air crews since her Commanding Officer, though possessed of a laudable desire always to be engaged with the enemy, simply refused to consider the strain under which his air crews were operating. He continually wanted the aircraft airborne, regardless of the weather or advice offered to him by his Air Staff. Relations between Capt Surtees and Cdr Val Jones RN, the Commander (Flying), deteriorated sharply as Jones attempted to protect his men from 'the Captain's seemingly insatiable and unreasonable demands'.[26]

Matters came to a head during the return journey of RA.62 in November 1944. The air crews of 835 Squadron were out flying in all weathers, and morale fell particularly when they knew that the Swordfish squadron in the other escort carrier with the convoy, HMS *Campania*, was stood down because of the bad weather:

> Swordfish aircrew of 835 began to feel 'put upon' and being asked to do not only more than their fair share of flying but to take off in conditions which were almost impossible and in which the chances of achieving any success were minimal. The aircrews began actively to dislike and even fear Captain Surtees and his insatiable demands for aircraft to be flown off.[27]

Nairana's PMO, Surgeon Lt-Cdr Waterman RN, became so concerned about the state of health of the flyers that he asked Surtees if they could be stood down from operations. Surtees refused, but Waterman was not to be bested. Bypassing Surtees, he fell back on an Admiralty Fleet Order which allowed him to declare air crews unfit for flying. Surtees was furious, but there was little that he could do—indeed, Waterman's action had been given the Admiralty's approval.

When *Nairana* returned home, Jones succeeded in having the Central Air Medical Board from the Fleet Air Arm's headquarters at Lee-on-Solent visit the Squadron. The CAMB found that 50 per cent of the air crews should be relieved from operational flying immediately and another 25 per cent should be relieved within a month. This was a vindication of Cdr Jones's action, but his victory was to be short-lived. Capt Surtees had complained to the Admiralty about him, and Jones was offered the appointment of Commanding Officer of 737 Squadron, an observer training unit. Barringer's portrait of the state of 835 Squadron in *Nairana* may be extreme but it exemplifies the strain under which air crews operated in the Arctic. Lt-Cdr John Godley RNVR, who assumed command of 835 Squadron, is more favourable in his treatment of Surtees but acknowledges the fact that the air crews were desperately tired and overworked.[28]

Although the survivors and wounded were temporary 'residents' in north Russia, for a small group of officers and men, together with a number of minesweepers, the ports of Murmansk and Polyarnoe were 'home'. Throughout the war a Royal Navy Liaison Mission was present in the region throughout the war, while a small number of minesweepers were based at Murmansk for local escort and sweeping duties.

A British Naval Liaison Mission had left for the USSR as early as 25 June 1941. Rear-Admiral G. J. A. Miles was given a staff of six, including the Naval Attaché at Moscow and charged with ensuring

> ... the prolongation of Russian resistance as this is obviously of very great importance to British interests ... obtaining some co-ordination of Russian strategy with our own and concert measures and action so that the Germans are denied material and economic advantages of any victory they may achieve.[29]

In contrast to Churchill's ebullient tone, the Admiralty took a more pessimistic view and Admiral Miles' orders were written in such a way as to leave no doubt that the Admiralty expected Soviet resistance to collapse fairly quickly. Consequently a large element in his instructions was given over to plans for the destruction of port facilities in north Russia in the event of a Soviet capitulation or an armistice. It was not until 1943 that all references to defeat were removed from the orders.

Miles became Senior British Naval Officer North Russia and was based at Murmansk with the staff of the C-in-C Northern Fleet. Another SBNO was appointed to Archangel, and when SBNONR moved to Polyarnoe another officer was appointed to Murmansk to handle matters there.

In the spring of 1943 there were 202 officers and men distributed among Archangel, Murmansk, Polyarnoe and Vaenga for operational duties in support of convoys and their escorts. Additionally there were eight members of the Military Mission and the crews of two minesweepers and a trawler based at Polyarnoe. Since there were only six shipping control officers of the Red Navy in Britain and Iceland, with thirteen others in the Soviet Military Mission in London, the Soviet Government used this disparity in numbers as a pretext for harassing the British contingent in northern Russia following the decision to suspend the convoys in the spring of 1943. The harassment took the form of the searching of personal belongings by Soviet customs officials, restrictions on the movements of British warships in the Kola Inlet and the closure of a jammer used against German U-boat homing beacons in Norway. The closure of British-operated wireless stations at Polyarnoe and Archangel was also demanded and complied with.

For the officers and men actually in north Russia it became impossible to move from base to base in the Murmansk area without having first acquired a multitude of passes from various Soviet bodies (including the dreaded NKVD). The rules for obtaining such passes were complex and seemed to change with the circumstances of each applicant. But by far the most resented aspect of Soviet intransigence was their withholding of mail. In June 1943 the Soviets seized what was only the second delivery of private mail for RN personnel in the Murmansk area that year and carted it off to Moscow on the grounds that some of the bags had been tampered with. The British officers and men could not even hope for reliefs since the Soviet Embassy in London would not grant visas to replacement personnel: by September 1943, 153 of the 198 men serving there were due for relief but could see no imminent end to their sojourn in northern waters.

Representations to the Soviet Ambassador in London and by the British Ambassador in Moscow resulted in no modification of the Soviet attitude. There is no doubt that the decision to suspend the convoys for the summer of 1943 played a large part in determining Soviet policy, as did the seeming inability of the Anglo-Americans to launch the oft-promised 'Second Front'. A more subtle reason is that, with tide of the war running in their favour, the Soviets resented the presence of a large British contingent on their soil, many of whose number had entered the USSR without visas and without clearing the usual customs and immigration formalities. It can be argued that the large British presence did little other than provoke Soviet xenophobia, and it is interesting to note that there was no equivalent official US Navy representation and that Americans were not harassed to the same degree as their British allies—a distinction which was not lost on the Royal Navy.[30]

In July 1943 the Soviet authorities jailed two British seamen for two and five years respectively for assaulting a Communist official.[31] The matter was taken up at the highest level, Churchill suggesting that ostentatious preparations be made for withdrawing the British presence:

> This of course would mean that no more convoys would come by the Arctic route. We would be sorry for this as it is the best route and if the aforesaid operation succeeds it may become much easier.[32]

Wiser counsels, however, prevailed, the Foreign Office arguing that such a course would lead to a diplomatic defeat while the Admiralty, mindful of a forthcoming operation against *Tirpitz* code-named 'Source', did not want the Soviet facilities abandoned in case they were needed. Moreover, there were three warships and 24 merchant ships in the Kola Inlet, and it was unimaginable that they should be left there without shore support, both material and moral.

The matter was eventually settled in October 1943 by direct consultation during the tripartite Teheran Conference between the British Foreign Secretary, Anthony Eden and his Soviet counterpart, V. I. Molotov. The Soviets agreed that they would not press for parity of numbers in the missions in Britain and the Soviet Union but they did complain about the arrogance and insensitivity displayed by British officers and ratings in north Russia. The sessions of the main conference, which was the first meeting of the 'Big Three', provided much more balm for the troubled waters. For the first time the Soviets were given detailed explanations of Anglo-American aims and felt that they were, at last, being treated as equal partners in the alliance. The effects of the *rapprochement* were immediate and visible. Visas were granted for replacement personnel, some of the more irritating restrictions were lifted and an additional naval hospital was permitted at Archangel. The Naval Mission left the USSR with the ships of the last convoy, and relations during the last months of their stay had been better—though never cordial.

As well as the Naval Mission, British minesweepers of the 1st and 6th Minesweeper Flotillas were stationed in north Russia (although this may seem curious in view of the Russians' historic interest in this method of warfare). British minesweepers of the *Halcyon* class would sail out with an outward-bound convoy and then remain in north Russian waters throughout the next winter, returning to Britain in the spring when they were relieved. While in Soviet waters their duties consisted mainly of sweeping ahead of the homeward-bound convoys and then meeting the inward convoys, usually 48 hours away from Murmansk. However, many other duties fell their way, and the ships became general 'maids of all work', acting as dispatch vessels, local convoy escorts, AA guardships, communications links and training ships.

The minesweepers were small, and they were utterly unsuited to Arctic conditions. Recreational facilities ashore were very rudimentary and consisted of football in summer and skiing in winter. Larger ships of the Fleet which called at north Russian ports between convoys could provide stores and also a change of scene for the minesweeper crews, but on the whole their lot of the latter was a dull and cheerless one. The diary of Able Seaman J. Clarke, who served in HMS *Jason* throughout her north Russian sojourn in 1943, reflects the sheer boredom of the existence, with nothing but mail and the eventual prospect of relief to look forward to:

> *27 Feb:* People seem very friendly and everyone in some kind of uniform. You can get anything here for a packet of cigs or bar of nutty.
> *1 March:* I think the main worry is going to be boredom as the Russians don't seem to be very sociable.
> *6 October:* Eight months in this joint is enough to drive anyone screwy.[33]

The majority of the British naval staff left north Russia with RA.67, although some remained until September 1945. The last of the minesweepers returned with RA.57. Theirs had been a dull and monotonous war in which the climate and the intractability of their Soviet hosts were as much a menace as the enemy.

NOTES TO CHAPTER 9

1. PRO ADM.234/369, 'Battle Summary No 22: Arctic Convoys 1941–45', 1954, p.8.
2. Bright sunlight which reflected off the ice and made the look-outs' task very difficult, not to mention uncomfortable.
3. Coulter, Surgeon Capt J. L. S., *The Royal Naval Medical Service. Vol 2: Operations*, HMSO, London, 1956, p.420.
4. Diary of Able Seaman A. J. Clarke, Department of Documents, Imperial War Museum, 87/15/1.
5. *ibid.*
6. TS account by ERA R. J. Wood, Department of Documents, Imperial War Museum, 89/3/1.
7. In one cruiser the pipes ran behind the officers' heads, with the result that the 'sitter' always ran the risk of burning himself on the intimate portion of his anatomy, particularly if the ship were rolling.
8. Coulter, op. cit., p.421.
9 Louse infestation.
10 Coulter, *op. cit.*, p.423.
11. *ibid.*, pp.423–4.
12. *ibid.*, p.433
13. *ibid.*
14. Ludlam, Harry, and Lund, Paul, *PQ.17 Convoy to Hell: The Survivors' Story*, W. Foulsham & Co, London, 1968, p.142.
15. Coulter, *op. cit.*, p.434.
16. Sick Berth Attendant—a medically trained naval rating.
17. Coulter, *op. cit.*, p.434.
18. *ibid.*, p.424.
19. Report of Surgeon Lt R. Lawrie RNVR, quoted in Coulter, *op. cit.*, pp.466–7.
20. *ibid.*, pp.424–5.

21. Herman, Fred, *Dynamite Cargo—Convoy to Russia*, Cassell & Co., London, 1943.
22. HMS *Standard* was the Royal Navy's establishment for men suffering from exhaustion or battle fatigue. It operated on a policy of restoring a man's self-respect by a mixture of discipline, compassion and healthy exercise in a stimulating environment.
23. TS memoirs of Lt-Cdr E. R. Barringer RNVR, Department of Documents, Imperial War Museum, 91/17/1, p.209.
24. *ibid.*, p.227.
25. *ibid.*
26. *ibid.*
27. *ibid.*, p.233.
28. Kilbracken, Lord, *Bring Back My Stringbag*, Peter Davis, London, 1979.
29. PRO ADM.199/604 (M.06888/43).
30. PRO ADM.199/604.
31. PRO ADM.199/604, Monthly Report of Proceedings of the Senior British Naval Officer North Russia, 1–31 July 1943.
32. PRO ADM.199/606.
33. Diary of Able Seaman A. J. Clarke, *op. cit.*

Chapter 10

Difficult Decisions

A very impressive sight this, to see these big merchantmen battering
their way through the gale—only wish I felt well enough to enjoy it.—Able
Seaman A. J. Clarke aboard HMS *Jason* describing JW.53

After the great events of December 1942, the first convoys of 1943 enjoyed comparatively uneventful passages. Of immediate concern was the return to the United Kingdom of the officers and men wounded in the Barents Sea action, including Captain Sherbrooke. Accordingly, *Obdurate* and *Obedient* left the Kola Inlet on 11 January and made a fast passage to Scapa Flow, where they arrived without incident on 15 January.

JW.52, comprising fifteen ships, sailed from Loch Ewe on 17 January and arrived in the Kola Inlet on 27 January without loss. The escort arrangements consisted of the destroyers *Blankney*, *Ledbury* and *Middleton* from 17 to 21 January, when the Ocean Escort—the corvettes *Lotus* and *Starwort*, the minesweeper *Britomart* and the trawlers *Northern Pride* and *St Elstan*—took over. The destroyer escort consisted of *Onslaught* (Cdr W. H. Selby RN, Senior Officer), *Beagle*, *Bulldog*, *Matchless*, *Musketeer*, *Offa* and the Polish *Piorun* (whose crew must have been as puzzled by their role in this operation as were *Garland*'s for PQ.16). Cruiser cover was provided by *Kent* (Flag, Rear-Admiral L. H. K. Hamilton), *Bermuda* and *Glasgow* from 21 January. The cruisers covered the convoy from 10°E until the Kola Inlet was reached. Distant cover was provided by the battleship *Anson* (Flag, Vice-Admiral Sir Bruce Fraser) and the cruiser *Sheffield* screened by *Echo*, *Eclipse*, *Faulknor*, *Inglefield*, *Montrose*, *Queenborough*, *Raider* and the Polish *Orkan*. JW.52 was located on 23 January, but those U-boats which made contact were driven off by the escort while Cdr Selby ordered several evasive alterations of course. Four Ju 88s put in a half-hearted appearance on 24 January and lost two of their number without result. Clearly, things had changed for the *Luftwaffe* in the Arctic since the heady days of the summer of 1942.

However, one unforeseen disadvantage of Cdr Selby's evasive manoeuvring was that for the majority of the trip Rear-Admiral Hamilton had no idea where the convoy was. At one stage Hamilton thought that his cruisers were forty miles off the convoy's port bow when in fact his ships were twenty miles astern in an area which he described as 'the hornet's nest which swarms astern of any shadowed convoy and which is the obvious place to avoid'.[1] While Hamilton gave every credit to Selby for his diversionary tactics, he correctly pointed out that, should an attack by surface forces materialize, his cruisers would not be a position to intervene effectively.

The homeward-bound RA.52, of ten ships, left Kola on 29 January. The Ocean Escort consisted of the destroyers *Beagle*, *Bulldog*, *Forester* (to 4 February), *Icarus*,

Matchless, Musketeer, Offa, Onslaught and *Piorun*, the corvettes *Honeysuckle, Hyderabad, Rhododendron* and *Oxlip*, the minesweepers *Harrier* and *Seagull* and the trawlers *Lady Madeleine, Northern Gem, Northern Wave* and *Vizalma*. The destroyers remained with the convoy until 5 February, whereupon *Harrier* took over as Senior Officer and the escort was augmented by the destroyers *Blankney, Middleton* and *Vivacious* for the last stage of the journey to Loch Ewe. The covering forces were identical to those provided for JW.52. Also with the escort was the destroyer *Onslow*, which was returning to Britain for repairs following the Barents Sea action (though she was nominally part of the escort, her fighting capability was very limited and she left the convoy on 2 February to proceed to Scapa).

There was only one incident of note. On 3 February *U255* (*Kapitänleutnant* Reinhard Reche) sank *Greylock*, though fortunately all her crew were taken off by *Harrier, Oxlip* and the three trawlers. The success of the attack was probably due to the men of the escorts being exhausted with the inevitable decline in efficiency. Many of the ships, particularly those who had come out with JW.51B, had been in the Arctic for over a month. As Tovey rightly concluded in his report,

This occurred on what was the nineteenth consecutive day in these wintry northern waters for the majority of the escort, and it is not to be expected that the personnel and *matériel* were then at their best.[2]

However, the loss of *Greylock* was the only success for the enemy, and the convoy arrived at Loch Ewe between 8/9 February.

The next convoy, JW.53, assembled in Loch Ewe throughout early February 1943 under the command of the Commodore, Rear-Admiral E. W. Leir DSO.[3] Difficulties in loading cargo meant that the sailing date had to be put back to 15 February, and, even so, only 25 of the 30 ships were ready to sail. The escort arrangements for JW.53 differed from those of its predecessors because by the middle of February there would be nearly seven hours of daylight, which would give plenty of opportunity for the *Luftwaffe*. It was decided that the convoy should be accompanied by a strong escort whose composition reflected the multitude of threats to which the merchant ships would be exposed. The Close Escort, which would go all the way to Murmansk, was under the command of Cdr H. G. A. Lewis RN in the minesweeper HMS *Jason* and consisted of three 'Hunt' class destroyers, three corvettes, one minesweeper and two trawlers. Off Iceland the convoy would be joined by the Ocean Escort, which was under the command of Capt I. M. R. Campbell in HMS *Milne* and consisted of the cruiser HMS *Scylla* (the veteran of PQ.18/QP.14 and recently returned to the Arctic after participating in the 'Torch' landings in North Africa), the escort carrier HMS *Dasher* (with two 'Hunt' class destroyers for rescue purposes) and the destroyers *Boadicea, Faulknor, Inglefield, Milne, Obdurate, Obedient, Opportune, Orwell, Eclipse, Fury, Impulsive, Intrepid* and *Orkan*. To provide immediate cover against an attack by German warships was Rear-Admiral Burnett's 10th Cruiser Squadron, consisting of *Belfast* (Flag), *Sheffield* and *Cumberland*, known collectively as Force 'R'. *Belfast* had recently completed a two-year refit following extensive mine damage sustained in December 1939, and this would be her first operation with a new ship's company, many of whom had never been to sea before. Burnett's ships would screen the convoy from 5°E to 35°E and then head directly for the Kola Inlet. Providing distant cover were the battleships HMS *King George V* and *Howe*, together with the cruiser HMS *Norfolk*, under the command of Admiral Sir John Tovey, Commander-in-Chief Home Fleet. Tovey's ships would cruise as far as 32°E to cover the convoy, always mindful of the fuel state of his escorting destroyers and the need to avoid being detected by German air reconnaissance. Finally, though not strictly part of the escort, the submarines *Truculent*, *Sportsman*, *Simoom* and *Sea Nymph* were ordered to patrol off the Norwegian coast to warn of any move by *Tirpitz* or her consorts.

The pre-sailing conference for the Masters of the merchant ships and the Commanding Officers of the warships in the Close Escort was held at Loch Ewe on 14 February and was attended by Rear-Admiral Burnett. Burnett had intended to sail for Seidisfjord on the east coast of Iceland immediately afterwards with the other two cruisers in his squadron and the destroyers of the Ocean Escort which were sailing from Scapa. At Seidisfjord the warships would top up with fuel before joining the convoy. However, problems with a recalcitrant capstan engine delayed *Belfast*'s departure until 16 February.

The convoy had sailed a day early, on 15 February, and as the heavily loaded merchant ships rounded the Butt of Lewis and lost the shelter of the Hebrides they met the full force of an Atlantic gale. A. J. Clarke, in HMS *Jason*, remembered seeing the convoy heading into the open sea:

A very impressive sight this, to see these big merchantmen battering their way through the gale—only wish I felt well enough to enjoy it.[4]

Many of the ships carried tanks or heavy locomotives as deck cargo, and five vessels, *Empire Baffin*, *Explorer*, *James Bowie*, *John Lawrence* and *Joseph E. Johnstone*, had to return with weather damage or to secure cargo which had come adrift. On 17 February the Soviet merchantship *Komiles* reported that the lashings securing her deck cargo had broken and that she was proceeding to the Faeroe Islands to make good the damage. However, on the 19th her Master reported that she was beginning to break up in the heavy seas: a search was organized but nothing was found and Cdr Lewis feared the worst for her. However, *Komiles* had not sunk . . .[5]

Under the buffeting of the gale, the ships in the convoy rapidly became scattered. Cdr Lewis reported

Heavy seas and swell from NW . . . visual communication with escorts difficult due to low visibility and height of waves. Convoy somewhat scattered and escorts out of position.[6]

The Ocean Escort faired no better at the hands of the gale as the ships made their way to join the convoy. The escort carrier HMS *Dasher* was forced to return with storm damage, and a subsequent inspection of the American-built vessel revealed that

. . . no attempt had been made to fit [the] ship for Arctic service. Few if any of the exposed essential hydraulic fittings required for the operation of aircraft are fitted with heating . . . consider her operational value has been prejudiced by these omissions.[7]

The bad weather severely disrupted the arrangements for the Ocean Escort to join the convoy. Admiral Burnett, having finally got away from Loch Ewe on 16 February, described the weather conditions encountered during the voyage to Iceland:

> All the time the wind and sea were increasing . . . the wind was force 9, the sea state 7 and *Belfast* was rolling heavily. The average height of the waves was 40ft and distance between the crests was 500ft to 600ft.[8]

Belfast arrived off Seidisfjord in the afternoon of 18 February, but the weather was so bad that she could not enter the fjord to fuel. The cruisers *Scylla* and *Cumberland* together with the destroyers *Intrepid*, *Fury*, *Eclipse*, *Impulsive* and *Orkan* were in the same predicament, so Burnett took all the ships under his command and led them round to Akureyi on Iceland's north coast, where they arrived on the 20th. The remaining destroyers of the Ocean Escort, *Milne*, *Faulknor*, *Boadicea*, *Obedient*, *Opportune*, *Orwell*, *Obdurate* and *Inglefield*, had sailed from Scapa on 14 February and had arrived at Seidisfjord on the 15th, but the appalling weather prevented them from fuelling until the 19th. Even so, fuelling was no easy task, as *Milne*'s experiences show:

> Gusts of gale force came leaping at her from every direction, sometimes whistling down the length of the fjord, at others rebounding from the sheer cliffs that flanked it, driving her bodily sideways as she made her way anxiously up to the oiler moored in the middle. Twice Campbell got *Milne* alongside only to have all berthing wires snap like string before she could be hove in snugly to the tanker's side.[9]

Only seamanship of the highest order succeeded in getting the destroyers alongside the oiler and fuelled.

The cruiser HMS *Sheffield*, proceeding to Iceland from Scapa, was another casualty of the storm. Seen from the bridge, the waves seemed to be coming at the ship from above eye level. During 19 February the ship appeared to miss her step and plunge her bows deep into an enormous swell. The forecastle disappeared under a green sea and *Sheffield* shuddered as if struck by a massive fist. As her bows laboriously came up and free, hundreds of tons of water piled aft and against the side of 'A' turret, forcing it inward. As a result, the roof of the turret, made of 1¾in armoured steel, simply popped off and was peeled back for a third of its area.[10] The experience must have been an unusual one for the 27 men of the turret's crew, but fortunately only three men were hurt, one suffering a broken jaw. At noon the Meteorological Officer reported that the wind had gone off the Beaufort Scale and that the anemometer on the foremast had been blown away.

On arrival at Iceland, it was decided to replace *Sheffield* with her sister ship HMS *Glasgow*. However, *Glasgow* was another storm victim, having dragged her anchors

146

and gone aground, so HMS *Norfolk* was detached from the Home Fleet, her place being taken by HMS *Berwick*.

By 20 February fuelling was complete. *Milne* and her seven destroyers had sailed from Seidisfjord on 20 February and joined JW.53 the next day, while *Scylla* and her destroyers sailed from Akureyi in the evening of the 20th and joined the convoy on 22 February. Finally, Burnett's cruisers got under way on 21 February, although in doing so *Belfast* nearly suffered the same fate as the luckless *Glasgow*:

> It was a day of ill-omen for *Belfast* . . . the capstan engine had failed to respond for treatment, the cable of the port anchor took a complete turn around the fluke of the starboard anchor, thus providing an interesting seamanship problem. A strong squall arose just as the cable had been cleared and the ship was anchored with two shackles in 24 fathoms and the engine room reported no steam on the main engines due to water in the fuel oil.[11]

Fortunately these problems were all overcome, and by 23 February Burnett's cruisers were steaming in position eight miles ahead of the convoy. After nearly four days the gale blew itself out and the escorts began the task of shepherding the scattered merchant ships back into some kind of formation. In the course of the night of 19/20 February the battle fleet came within radar range of the convoy, enabling *King George V* to plot the positions of the merchant ships on her radar and pass the information to the escorts.

One advantage of the appalling weather was that the convoy was hidden from the prying eyes of the *Luftwaffe*. But, as the skies began to clear from 22 February, this state of affairs could not continue. It would only be a matter of time before German aircraft found JW.53: the ice-edge extended unusually far south, forcing the convoy to adopt a course which would take it within 250 miles of the enemy's anchorage at Altenfjord and the air base at Banak.

The familiar sight of two BV 138 reconnaissance aircraft appeared over the convoy on 23 February, and the next day shadowing aircraft were sighted at 1135 and 1315, both of which were heard to transmit homing signals, presumably for the benefit of U-boats lying in wait for the convoy. Between 1800 and 2130 the convoy was repeatedly harassed by two or three U-boats, but each contact was rigorously prosecuted by the escorts—with apparent success, for no attack developed. Reche's *U255* attacked two destroyers but missed.

The major alarm of the day came at 1730 when HMS *Obedient* obtained a radar contact which she classified as a large surface ship. The destroyer immediately broadcast the code-word 'Strike', indicating that an attack by German surface ships was imminent. Burnett clearly relished the prospect of administering another drubbing to the *Kriegsmarine* so soon after the Battle of the Barents Sea, and he immediately swung *Belfast*, with *Cumberland* and *Norfolk* following, round to the south-west in order to meet the threat. Burnett obviously had no fears about taking on the Germans in the dark, but, as he later wrote,

> I had the greatest doubts as to the truth that enemy surface forces were in contact with the convoy. The Germans must have been well aware of the composition of the escort

147

and I could not believe that even Admiral Dönitz could throw heavy ships in the dark on such a force. Neither was I prepared to plunge with Force R into a mêlée of our own fighting destroyers. My intention was to steam southwards towards the Norwegian coast and get between any enemy who might have been foolish enough to take such a great risk and his home port, getting in touch with Captain (D) 3 by signal so that he could track the retiring enemy for my benefit and then get out of the way before I went in to destroy him.[12]

Nothing epitomizes Burnett's fighting spirit more than the text of this report: there is no talk of 'engaging' the enemy or of 'sinking' him, only of *destroying* him. It was the uncomplicated nature of his fighting philosophy that made Burnett one of the Royal Navy's finest tactical commanders of the Second World War. However, his hopes were to be frustrated, for at 1745 *Obedient* signalled that the 'Strike' call had been a false alarm. The contact had probably been a U-boat shadowing the convoy and caught beam-on by the destroyer's radar. At daybreak on 25 February the BV 138 returned, and at 1115 a signal was received from SBNO North Russia that a force of Ju 88 and Me 109 aircraft had been seen crossing the coast. Fifteen minutes later fourteen Ju 88s, which came from *I/KG 30*, were detected astern of the convoy at a height of 13,000ft. The aircraft made a shallow glide attack which

> . . . was not well pressed home and few aircraft rendered a clean dive. It was an inspiring sight to see *Scylla* steering across the convoy, listing heavily under wheel and helm, with every gun spitting skywards.[13]

A few bombs fell near the tanker *British Governor*, but no ships were damaged and the convoy ploughed on. Subsequently two of the Ju 88s returned for a high-altitude bombing attack, but to no effect. The shadowers, however, stayed in contact until nightfall, evidently broadcasting homing signals for U-boats. During the night there was considerable U-boat activity, in which the value of HF/DF apparatus was amply demonstrated. Time after time a U-boat which was unwise enough to give her position away by transmitting a homing signal would find herself illuminated by starshell and attacked by the escorts. Several alterations of course had to be made during the night because of U-boat alarms, but the aggressive tactics of the escorts paid off, denying the U-boats any success.

On 26 February a shadowing aircraft was back in company and circled the convoy at a range of 20–30 miles, transmitting homing signals all the while. At 1225, without warning, German aircraft approached the convoy from all points, a tactic possibly designed to confuse and divide the anti-aircraft defences. If so, it did not work, for a heavy and varied blind barrage was put up—with some success, since intercepted German R/T was heard ordering the pilots to fly higher, drop their bombs and return to Petsamo as quickly as possible. The aircraft flew above the cloud base so were not observed at any time, but it was thought that twelve Ju 88s were involved. Like the first attack, it was unsuccessful. Reche's *U255* was still stub- bornly in contact, but no opportunity for an attack presented itself.

Early in the morning of 26 February the convoy divided. Seven merchant ships, escorted by *Inglefield*, *Intrepid*, *Fury* and *Bluebell*, went to Archangel, where they arrived on the 29th. The remainder went to Murmansk, reached on 27 February. JW.53 had arrived without loss, but sadly the freighter *Ocean Freedom* was sunk and the *Doverhill*, *British Governor* and *Ocean Kinsman* were damaged in bombing raids by Ju 87 aircraft while they lay at anchor.

The homeward-bound convoy, RA.53, enjoyed a much tougher passage. The 30 ships of the convoy left the Kola Inlet on 1 March escorted by *Scylla*, the destroyers *Intrepid*, *Obedient*, *Obdurate*, *Boadicea*, *Eclipse*, *Faulknor*, *Impulsive*, *Fury*, *Opportune*, *Milne*, *Orwell*, *Orkan* and *Inglefield*, the corvettes *Bergamot*, *Poppy*, *Lotus* and *Starwort* and the trawlers *Northern Pride* and *St Elstan*. The destroyers departed in groups between 7 and 11 March and were replaced by *Ledbury*, *Pytchley*, *Meynell* and *Vivacious* for the last stage of the journey to Loch Ewe. Cruiser cover was provided by *Belfast*, *Cumberland* and *Norfolk*, while the battleships *King George V* and *Howe*, screened by *Glasgow*, *Forester*, *Icarus*, *Musketeer*, *Offa*, *Onslaught* and *Piorun*, were the distant cover.

RA.53 ran into very heavy weather, causing the ships to become scattered. This state of affairs was exploited by the U-boats: they were able to penetrate the screen, which was far more widely dispersed than usual. Reche's *U255* torpedoed the *Richard Bland* and the *Executive* on 5 March; the latter went down immediately, but the *Richard Bland* had to be finished off by the same submarine five days later. On 9 March *U586* (*Kapitänleutnant* Dietrich von der Esch) sank the *Puerto Rican*. A fourth ship, *J. L. M. Curry*, foundered on 7 March as a result of the weather, but *Opportune* prevented a fifth loss by towing the broken-down *John H. B. Latrobe* to Seidisfjord.

While the convoy was on passage, news was received that *Scharnhorst* had left Gdynia, where she had been under repair following the 'Channel Dash', and was heading towards Norway. In the event that the move might presage a direct attack on RA.53, the disposition of the ships of the Home Fleet was altered to meet the threat. The battleship *Anson* proceeded immediately to Seidisfjord and the carriers *Furious* and *Indomitable* stood by on the Clyde. In case *Scharnhorst* were heading for the Atlantic, the anti-breakout patrols in the Denmark Strait and the Faeroes–Iceland passage were stepped up, while additional cruisers sailed from Iceland to cover RA.53, which latter arrived at Loch Ewe on 14 March.

Scharnhorst's move to Norway was the first manifestation of Dönitz's assumption of command of the *Kriegsmarine*. Under the cover of heavy weather, *Scharnhorst* (*Kapitän zur See* Julius Hinze) had left Gotenhafen and then proceeded to Trondheim via Bergen under heavy escort and with massive air cover, the operation being known as '*Zauberflotte*'. From Trondheim she proceeded, with *Tirpitz*, to join *Lützow* in Bogen Bay near Narvik, where she arrived on 12 March. Ten days later all three ships moved to Altenfjord, where they arrived on 24 March.

Dönitz had won a considerable personal victory in securing Hitler's approval for the transfer, and it was a measure of how he was able to use the successes won by his U-boats in the Atlantic to strengthen his position in the hierarchy. At first Dönitz seemed to agree with Hitler about the disposal of the remnants of Germany's surface fleet: already officers and men were being drafted away from the surface ships to the ever-expanding U-boat arm. Eventually, though, the classic arguments about the merits of a 'fleet in being' convinced him that, whatever the short-term gains, Hitler's order was counter-productive.

On 9 February 1943 he secured Hitler's agreement that the capital ships be ordered out when the next favourable opportunity occurred. More importantly, he secured his approval of the force commander's being allowed act on his own initiative without being hamstrung by restrictive instructions from Hitler himself or from SKL. However, on 26 February, when Dönitz proposed moving *Scharnhorst* to Norway, he encountered considerable opposition. The *Führer*'s view was that, since *Graf Spee*'s performance at the River Plate, the capital ships had led to one loss after another, with incaculable damage to German morale and prestige:

> The time for great ships is over. I would rather have the steel and nickel from these ships than send them into battle again.[14]

Hitler correctly pointed out that, in the Pacific, the value of capital ships had been lessened by carrier-borne aircraft and that the *Kriegsmarine* and the *Luftwaffe* had not developed satisfactory co-operating procedures. Dönitz disputed this and craftily suggested that the only reason for the lack of success was the restrictive operating instructions given to the force commander, implying that if the commander had a free hand, success was guaranteed. Thus it was in the nature of a bet between the two men that Hitler agreed to *Scharnhorst*'s going to Norway: Dönitz had challenged Hitler's wisdom on the subject, and now he was being given the chance to prove himself correct. Interestingly enough, British Intelligence, in its summary on Dönitz's personality and likely intentions when he took over as Commander-in-Chief, predicted that he would adopt a more aggressive stance in the Arctic and that he would seek to exploit the surface units available to him.[15]

The reinforcement of the German squadron in Norway took the shine off what had been a very satisfactory series of convoys in the winter of 1942–43. From the four outward- and three homeward-bound convoys, a total of three ships had been sunk by enemy action and a fourth had foundered in bad weather. Additionally, the Soviet ships *Bureya* and *Leonid Krasin* had made successful independent passages to Iceland, although the *Uffa* and the *Krazny Partizan*, also making independent passages to Iceland in January 1943, were both sunk by *U255* (Reche) on 26 January. The result of all this endeavour was that a huge quantity of supplies was delivered to the USSR.

However, the arrival of *Scharnhorst* in northern waters and the concentration of the three capital ships in Altenfjord with a supporting destroyer flotilla caused Tovey to view the sailing of convoys to the USSR throughout the summer of 1943 with grave anxiety. To counter an attack by such a strong task force, he would have to take his fleet all the way into the Barents Sea—a risk which he felt was not worth the object. Consequently, he recommended that the convoys be suspended throughout the summer of 1943.

In the event, Tovey never had to argue his case with the Admiralty, for events in the Atlantic intervened. The struggle there was reaching a climax, and since the Atlantic and the Arctic could not be covered simultaneously, the decision was taken to transfer every available escort, other than those required for screening the battle fleet, to Western Approaches Command. This decision automatically entailed the cancellation of JW/RA.54. However, it would fall to the politicians to convey this disagreeable decision to the Soviets.

Churchill told Roosevelt first in a telegram sent on 18 March. He cited the pressure the Navy was under in the Atlantic, where the U-boats were on the offensive. In particular, he told Roosevelt of the disaster which had befallen convoys HX.229 and SC.122, which had lost 21 ships. Churchill noted that the cancellation of JW/RA.53 would be a 'heavy blow to Stalin and his Government', that the decision would certainly arouse their 'grievous resentment' and that, therefore, Stalin had to be informed of the world-wide position the Royal Navy was facing, particularly in the Atlantic:

> I feel that it will be right and wise to place the picture before him as a whole, dark though it be.[16]

Roosevelt agreed, and on 30 March the news was delivered to Stalin. Churchill told the latter of the delicate balance of events in the Atlantic and added that the loss of one or more capital ships while *Tirpitz* remained in northern waters would alter the balance of power irreversibly:

> We are doing our utmost to increase the flow of supplies by the southern route. If this is achieved the monthly delivery will have been increased eightfold in twelve months and would in some way offset both your disappointment and ours at the interruption of the northern convoys.[17]

Stalin's reaction was curiously muted:

> I understand this unexpected action as a catastrophic diminuition of supplies of arms and raw materials to the USSR on behalf of Britain and the United States of America . . . this cannot fail to affect the position of the Soviet troops.[18]

Stalin was not particularly interested in the southern route via the Persian Gulf, since the supplies required a lengthy voyage to their destination followed by a long journey overland by rail to the front. Although this route was comparatively safe, its capacity was limited to what the rail link between Persia and the USSR could handle. A secondary consideration of importance to the Soviet Union was that Stalin did not want the British establishing a foothold in Persia. However, Churchill thought he had got off lightly: 'My own feeling,' wrote Churchill to the British Ambassador in Moscow, 'is that they took it like men.'[19]

In any case, the strategic situation was not as desperate as it had been twelve months earlier. The danger of a Soviet collapse had vanished with the surrender of the German Sixth Army at Stalingrad on 2 February 1943 and with the sweeping Soviet advances in the Ukraine and the Caucasus which had followed. Soviet industry, having recovered from the gigantic relocation to sites east of the Urals, was beginning to turn out massive quantities of equipment for the Red Army—crude but effective equipment like the T-34 tank and the *Katyushka* rocket, small arms which would turn the Soviet infantryman into a walking arsenal, the *Stormovik* 'flying tank' ground-attack aircraft—which would give Soviet generals the wherewithal to take on the Germans, who had hitherto held the qualitative and quantitative edge. The Red Army was now on an inexorable march westwards which would end in the ruins of Berlin.

Furthermore, the Anglo-American campaign in the Mediterranean was taking some of the pressure off the Eastern Front. The Germans would surrender in North Africa in May 1943, and plans for the invasion of Sicily in July were well advanced. There was no longer the overriding political requirement for convoys to the Soviet Union which had governed their sailing in 1942. Nevertheless, the decision to suspend sailings throughout the summer meant that the Red Army would have to endure the bloody tank battles of Kursk without the benefit of Anglo-American aid.

On 8 May 1943 Admiral Sir John Tovey struck his flag as Commander-in-Chief of the Home Fleet and was replaced by Admiral Sir Bruce Fraser. Fraser was as different a personality from Tovey as chalk from cheese. He was urbane, cultivated and enjoyed good living. However, beneath the exterior was a highly disciplined mind: Fraser was an outstanding gunnery officer who had played a leading role in the development of the 14in gun which provided the main armament of newest battleships, the *King George V* class. He had also served as Tovey's deputy for some time, so he needed little time to get to grips with is command. One of his first tasks was to review the possibility of sending a summer convoy to the Soviet Union. In a letter to Pound dated 30 June 1943, Fraser dismissed the idea unless the German surface threat could be reduced.

The suspension of convoys to the Soviet Union for the summer meant that many of the ships of the Home Fleet were deployed to the Mediterranean for Operation 'Husky', the invasion of Sicily. *Tirpitz* remained a potent threat, however, so to guard against her breaking out into the Atlantic the Home Fleet received reinforcements from the United States Navy. The battleships *South Dakota* and *Alabama* with the five destroyers of DESRON 8 under the command of Rear-Admiral O. M. Husvedt USN were transferred from Argentia, Newfoundland, to Fraser's command. Fraser now had two 'KGVs' with their combined main armament broadside of twenty 14in guns, backed up by the two *South Dakota*s with eighteen 16in between them, to deal with such an eventuality.

The transfer of this US Navy force in many ways marked the end of an era. It was the last time when it would be appropriate for US naval forces to come under British command and to conform with British signalling and tactical practice. When the time came for the the Royal Navy to join the US Navy in the Pacific, the boot would be on the other foot.

The Americans brought a breath of fresh air to the anchorage at Scapa Flow. They were extremely enthusiastic, but inexperienced in the methods of the Royal Navy when operating in potential hostile seas:

When the Americans came over to join us they seemed to have no experience of submarines at all. They really didn't take many anti-submarine precautions—we had

152

great difficulty making them take proper precautions. I took them up with me to Iceland, which was where we'd be restarting the convoys from. We went out for a range-finding exercise as well and I sent the Americans up north of me, and they disappeared over the horizon. I asked them afterwards why they'd disappeared. and they said. 'Actually we only wanted to make sure we'd cross the Arctic Circle.' Then the fog came down, we'd come in two detachments, and all of a sudden we heard depth charges going off left and right. Of course, we knew it had to be porpoises, or basking sharks, or something.[20]

On the social side, the fact that the American ships were 'dry' led to an epidemic of visits to their British counterparts every evening.

Though no convoys ran throughout the summer, the problem posed by *Tirpitz* was right at the top of Fraser's agenda. While she remained in Norway she completely tied down the Home Fleet and her likely movements had to be considered before any operation was planned. Since the battleship would not venture forth, she had to be destroyed at her anchorage at Kaafjord—a branch of Altenfjord—and herein lay the problem. Kaafjord was over 1,000 miles from the nearest British bases, and the necessary long-range aircraft were not available to bomb her. Carrier-borne aircraft were not an alternative as they lacked the capability of carrying a bomb sufficiently large enough to damage the ship. The idea was often expressed of using a submarine to penetrate the anchorage in the same way that British submarines had penetrated the Sea of Marmara in the First World War. However, the formidable net and defences of the various German anchorages in Norway ruled this option out altogether.

In the summer of 1943 a solution to the problem came to hand—the 'X-craft' midget submarine. At the end of 1941 Churchill had ordered the Royal Navy to investigate the development of 'human torpedoes' and midget submarines. His interest in these weapons came about as a result of the exploits of the Italian Navy's *Decima MAS* (10th Light Flotilla) in the Mediterranean and in particular their crippling of the battleships *Queen Elizabeth* and *Valiant* in December 1941 at Alexandria.

The first attempt to use a 'chariot' against *Tirpitz* ended in failure when it broke free from its parent craft. However, in the X-craft the Royal Navy had a much more potent weapon. Each was 51ft long, of 30 tons, with a beam of 5ft 9in and a depth from casing to keel of 5ft 9in. A 42bhp diesel engine—the same as that used in a London bus—gave a speed of 6.5kts on the surface while a 25hp electric motor gave a top submerged speed of 5kts. Each craft had a range of 1,500 miles at 4kts. The crew consisted of three officers and an engine room artificer—all volunteers—who would be expected to endure life in the tiny malodorous interior for up to a fortnight if required. The X-craft's armament consisted of two 1-ton explosive charges of Amatol carried on either side which would be dropped on the sea bed beneath the target or fixed to the hull of the target ship, using magnetic clamps, by a diver. who was able to leave the craft by means of a 'wet and dry' chamber.

To maximize their endurance, X-craft would be towed to the operational area by other submarines specially fitted for the purpose, and in order to ensure that the crew would be as rested as possible each vessel would be manned by a 'passage crew' during the outward journey who would change with the operational crew just before the tow was abandoned. The crew would then have the task of navigating their way to the target while avoiding net defences and minefields, place their charges and then make their escape before the charges were blown by time fuzes.

Prototypes of the X-craft had been successfully tested in 'attacks' on ships of the Home Fleet, and, thanks to air reconnaissance and 'Ultra' intelligence, by September 1943 the Admiralty had a clear picture of the whereabouts of the German task group in northern Norway and in particular knew that all three big ships, *Tirpitz*, *Scharnhorst* and *Lützow*, were in inlets off Altenfjord. Operation 'Source' was given the go-ahead.

Six X-craft were allocated for the operation: *X5* (Lt H. Henty-Creer RNVR), *X6* (Lt D. Cameron RNR) and *X7* (Lt B. G. Place DSC RN) were assigned to *Tirpitz*, *X9* (Lt T L Martin RN) and *X10* (Lt K. R. Hudspeth RANVR) to *Scharnhorst* and *X8* (Lt B. M. McFarlane RAN) to *Lützow*. The towing submarines *Thrasher* (*X5*), *Truculent* (*X6*), *Stubborn* (*X7*), *Syrtis* (*X9*), *Sceptre* (*X10*) and *Sea Nymph* (*X8*) left Loch Cairnbawn on the north-west coast of Scotland during the night of 11/12 September and by 20 September were in position for the exchange between the passage and operational crews. Tragically *X9* broke her tow and foundered in unknown circumstances and *X8* encountered difficulties after her charges flooded and had to be released, their subsequent explosion (despite the 'safe' fuze setting) damaging the craft beyond repair and dictating that she be scuttled.

X10 encountered a multiplicity of mechanical problems which left her without compass or periscope, and Hudspeth took the correct but disappointing decision to abandon the operation and headed back out to sea, where, after five miserable and uncomfortable days, he made contact with HMS *Stubborn*. On 3 October the craft had to be abandoned in worsening weather only 400 miles from the Shetlands. As it happened, *Scharnhorst* was at sea on gunnery exercises that day. Her absence had been noted, but it had proved impossible to notify the submarines.

X5 simply disappeared, her exact fate unknown, but the remaining pair, *X6* and *X7*, carried out their assignment perfectly. Both craft passed through the anti-submarine boom in Kaafjord in the morning of 22 September. Place's *X7* became entangled in some nets when forced to dive by a German patrol craft, and it took two hours to extricate her. *X6* crept through the defences, with Cameron having to raise and lower the periscope by hand since the motor had burned out. Despite these problems, and after being spotted by the battleship's gunners and becoming the target for a barrage of small-arms fire, Cameron brought *X6* virtually alongside *Tirpitz*, where he released his charges on the port side abreast 'B' turret. He and his crew abandoned the sinking submarine and were picked up to be taken on board the German vessel.

Meanwhile Place had also encountered navigational problems after his compass failed. After struggling through a series of almost impenetrable nets, *X7* literally bumped into *Tirpitz* before dropping beneath her, where Place released his charges, one under 'B' turret and the other under 'C' turret. Place then tried to make his escape but became entangled in another net. When all four charges exploded, *X7* was badly shaken and became impossible to control, porpoising up and down so much that the submarine actually went over the top of one net, Place being able to notice that, alas, *Tirpitz* was still afloat. Place eventually went alongside a German practice target to let his crew escape, abandoned the submarine and simply waited to be picked up. However, as he left *X7* she sank beneath him and only one other member of the crew, Sub-Lt R. Aitken RNVR, survived to be taken prisoner.

They were taken on board the battleship to join Cameron and his crew, who were being almost fêted by the ship's officers on the bridge and being given hot drinks and schnapps. The Germans expressed open admiration for their valour, although at the time of the explosions *Kapitän* Hans Meyer had lost his temper completely and ordered that Cameron's crew be shot at once! Cameron and Place, together with their crews, eventually went to a prisoner-of-war camp. The two commanders were awarded the Victoria Cross, but they were lucky to survive to receive it, for, had Hitler's orders regarding the treatment of saboteurs and special forces parties—the notorious 'Commando Order'—been implemented, they would both have been executed.

The sighting of the X-craft in a supposedly secure anchorage had caused a fit of collective panic on board the battleship. Almost immediately after *X6* had been sighted, the order to close all watertight doors was given. The bottom was dragged from bow to stern in case charges were attached to the hull, and it was suggested that the ship leave her berth. However, *Kapitän* Meyer felt that more of the submarines might be waiting outside the net enclosure, so he decided to remain inside the nets, despite not knowing what was lying beneath his ship. He did order the ship to be winched to starboard, away from where the charges had been dropped, using the anchor cables. All the while the ship's armament was manned, and although the main and secondary guns could not depress to fire at *X6*, the close-range weapons let loose a barrage of fire while enterprising members of the ship's company threw grenades into the water.

At 0812 the charges went off with a spectacular explosion. It is not clear how many of the four actually detonated, but a post-war examination of the fjord failed to discover any of the charges remaining. Topp's decision to swing the bows of his ship bodily to starboard using the cable undoubtedly saved her from worse damage or complete destruction. As it was, the effect of the explosion was terrific. The whole ship whipped viciously, all electric lights were extinguished, any items of equipment not secured fell about and glass from broken scuttles and mirrors cascaded everywhere. Anyone standing up was thrown off his feet. The ship's log recorded that

> . . . at 0812, two heavy consecutive detonations to port at 1/10 second intervals. Ship vibrates strongly in vertical direction and sways slightly between her anchors.[21]

A seamen who subsequently served on board *Scharnhorst* and who survived the sinking of his ship in December 1943 confessed to his interrogators that

> We've had torpedo hits, we've had bomb hits. We've hit two mines in the Channel, but there's never been an explosion like that![22]

It was not until *Tirpitz* could be fully surveyed that the extent of her injuries could be established. The damage was extensive. Although her hull remained intact, there was considerable shock damage in the machinery spaces. All turbine feet, propeller-shaft plummers and thrust blocks and auxiliary machinery bearers were cracked and distorted. The port turbine casing and condenser casing were fractured. The propellers could not be turned and the port rudder was inoperable owing to the steering compartment having flooded through a stern gland. The four 38cm (15in) turrets had jumped off their roller paths, although 'B' and 'D' turrets were quickly repaired. The optical rangefinders, except those in 'B' turret and the foretop, had been rendered useless. Three of the four flak directors were out of action and the aircraft catapult was unserviceable. One seaman had been killed and 40 more injured.

It was clear that *Tirpitz* needed the services of a major shipyard, but her return to Germany was out of the question in the face of determined Allied air, surface and submarine attack. The *Luftwaffe* could not provide the massive air umbrella with which it had protected *Scharnhorst* and *Gneisenau* during the 'Channel Dash' and there were insufficient naval forces to protect *Tirpitz* against the Home Fleet. Hitler agreed that the ship should be repaired *in situ*, with workers and materials being sent up from Germany. Docking was out of the question, since the *Kriegsmarine* possessed only one floating dock large enough to take her, and it was inconceivable that this could be transferred to Norway. Divers repaired the cracks in the battleship's hull using underwater cement, while a coffer dam had to be constructed around the port rudder to allow the gland to be repacked.

Through 'Ultra' decrypts the Admiralty learned that the ship would not be fit for service until March 1944 at the earliest. On 15 March *Tirpitz* carried out harbour trials of her machinery and armament in Altenfjord before going to sea for full power trials and degaussing calibration. Her restoration in such a short time represented a considerable achievement for her ship's company and the repair workers.

Operation 'Source' had transformed the strategic situation in the Arctic at a stroke. Fraser could now contemplate the resumption of convoy sailings during the winter of 1943–44. Another bonus came with the return to Germany of *Lützow* in the last week of September. Although the opportunity to sink her on the journey was lost, she was at least out of the picture as far as Arctic operations were concerned. Scharnhorst was now the Kriegsmarine's only heavy unit in northern waters.

The year 1943 had seen many changes in the high commands of both sides. The last occurred on 21 October when Admiral of the Fleet Sir Dudley Pound died after suffering a stroke during the Quebec Conference. Pound was not one of the Royal Navy's greatest First Sea Lords but he was by no means one of the worst. He had had to deal with conflicting priorities with meagre resources while at the same time restraining Churchill's wilder schemes. His successor was Admiral Sir Andrew Cunningham, fresh from his triumphs in the Mediterranean. Within three months of his appointment the Royal Navy would win a smashing victory in the Arctic.

NOTES TO CHAPTER 10

1. PRO ADM.234/369, 'Battle Summary No 22: Arctic Convoys 1941–45', 1954, p.105.
2. PRO ADM.199/73, Commander-in-Chief Home Fleet's remarks on the passage of RA.52.

3. A First World War submariner, Leir was known as the 'Arch Thief' after his practice of relieving His Majesty's Government of anything that was portable. It is said that only his DSO was earned honestly!

4. Diary of Able Seaman A. J. Clarke, Department of Documents, Imperial War Museum, 87/15/1.

5. The official record for JW.53 in PRO ADM.199/73 indicates that *Komiles* foundered in the gale, a conclusion also noted in Able Seaman Clarke's diary. The author is grateful to Arnold Hague of the World Ship Society for providing the information that the vessel, in fact, survived the gale.

6. PRO ADM.199/73, Report of Proceedings of the Commanding Officer of HMS *Jason*.

7. PRO ADM. 199/73, CinC Home Fleet to Admiralty, 15 February 1943.

8. PRO ADM.199/73, Report of Proceedings of the Rear-Admiral Commanding 10th Cruiser Squadron, 17 February 1943.

9. Campbell, Vice-Admiral Sir Ian, and MacIntyre, Capt Donald, *The Kola Run: A Record of the Arctic Convoys 1941–45*, Frederick Muller, 1958, p.166.

10. PRO ADM. 53/118525. Deck Log of HMS *Sheffield*, 19 February 1943.

11. PRO ADM.199/73: Report of Proceedings of the Rear-Admiral Commanding 10th Cruiser Squadron, 17 February 1943.

12. *ibid.*

13. PRO ADM.199/73, Report of Proceedings of Capt I. M. R. Campbell RN of HMS *Milne*, 25 February 1943.

14. Padfield, Peter, *Dönitz: The Last Führer*, Gollancz, London, 1984, p.273, note 10.

15. Hinsley, F., *British Intelligence in the Second World War*, HMSO, London, 1981. p.531.

16. Prime Minister's Personal Telegram T.325/3 No 1783 to Washington for Eden and Halifax to send on to Roosevelt, 18 March 1943, Churchill Papers 20/108.

17. Prime Minister's Personal Telegram T.404/3, 'Personal and Most Secret', 30 March 1943, Churchill Papers 20/109.

18. Stalin to Churchill, 2 April 1943, Churchill Papers 20/109.

19. Prime Minister's Personal Telegram T.454/3 to Moscow, 'Personal and Most Secret', 4 April 1945, Churchill Papers 20/109.

20. Humble, Richard, *Fraser of North Cape: The Life of Admiral of the Fleet Lord Fraser (1888–1981)*, Routledge & Kegan Paul, 1983, pp.167–8.

21. Admiralty: 'Battle Summary No 29: The Attack on the *Tirpitz* by Midget Submarines (Operation Source), 22 September 1943', 1948, p. 17.

22. *ibid.*

11-23-07

Chapter 11

'Admiralty Appreciates *Scharnhorst* is at Sea'

Situation today. Enemy will probably attack us today with U-boat and
possibly surface craft. Four more Home Fleet destroyers should join us p.m.
today. Duke of York *is astern, coming up at 19 knots or more. Three heavy cruisers*
somewhere ahead. Happy Christmas.—Capt J. 'Bes' McCoy to Commodore
of Convoy JW.55B 25 December 1943

By September 1943 it was clear that the tide of war was running against the German
Army on the Eastern Front. The surrender of Field Marshal von Paulus's Sixth Army
at Stalingrad in February had been followed by the smashing of the German
offensive in the Kursk Salient in July. By September the *Wehrmacht* was in
headlong retreat all along the southern sector of the front, from Moscow down to
Baku. Smolensk was retaken on 25 September, and by early October the Red Army
was across the Dneiper river and sweeping north around the Ukrainian capital Kiev.

It was at this juncture that on 21 September Molotov requested that the convoy
sailings be resumed. The diplomatic exchange which followed was one of the most
acrimonious of the war. The Defence Committee (Operations) met on 28 September
in London with Admiral Fraser in attendance. The circumstances for resuming
convoy sailings were favourable. The long winter nights were approaching, and,
with *Tirpitz* out of action following Operation 'Source' and *Lützow*'s return to
Germany, only *Scharnhorst* was left in Norway to menace the convoys. Churchill
proposed the sailing of four convoys between November and February, each of 35
ships. In his telegram to Stalin he stressed that the commitment was a 'declaration of
our solemn and earnest resolve'.[1] Stalin's reply was couched in such offensive terms
that Churchill refused to receive it and returned it to the Soviet Ambassador.

Nevertheless, the convoys were to sail again. The first priority was to organize
the return to Britain of the merchant ships which had been at Kola since the last
outward-bound convoy in March. Capt Ian Campbell in the destroyer HMS *Milne*
with the destroyers *Musketeer, Mahratta, Matchless, Savage, Scorpion, Scourge,*
Saumarez and *Westcott*, the minesweepers *Harriet* and *Seagull* and the corvette
Eglantine sailed from Seidisfjord on 23 October, taking with him five minesweepers
and six submarine-chasers supplied to the Soviet Union under Lend-Lease.

Campbell arrived at Polyarnoe and at once noticed a more friendly attitude among
his Russian hosts. To begin with, his ships were allowed to berth alongside the jetty
at Polyarnoe rather than anchor in Vaenga Bay where the holding ground was very
poor. Visits were exchanged and calls were paid on senior Russian naval officers.
including the C-in-C Northern Fleet, Admiral Arsenii Golovko. But, as Campbell
later wrote,

It was uphill work. The language difficulty could have been overcome with goodwill, but all gaiety and light-hearted talk was smothered by the dour, unsmiling political commissars who attended every occasion, their mean suspicious eyes flickering like [those of] cornered animals.[2]

The return convoy, RA.54, consisting of thirteen merchant ships, left Kola on 1 November and arrived without incident at Loch Ewe on the 14th. It was delayed by thick fog and bad weather which, though uncomfortable and miserable for the merchant ships and their escorts, shielded them from the prying eyes of the *Luftwaffe*.

The first outward-bound convoy of the winter cycle, JW.54A, left Loch Ewe on 15 November escorted by the destroyers *Onslow* (Capt J. A. McCoy, Senior Officer), *Onslaught*, *Orwell*, *Impulsive*, *Iroquois*, *Haida*, *Huron*, *Inconstant* and *Whitehall* with the minesweepers *Heather* and *Hussar*. The cruiser covering force, which shielded JW.54A all the way to the Kola Inlet, consisted of *Kent* (Rear-Admiral A. F. E. Palliser, Flag), *Jamaica* and *Bermuda*. Distant cover was provided by Vice-Admiral Sir Henry Moore in HMS *Anson* with the American cruiser *Tuscaloosa*.

Although the Admiralty had promised to send the Russians forty ships a month, Fraser, like Tovey before him, considered that this was too large a number for a single convoy, especially during the winter when bad weather would scatter the merchantmen as had happened to JW.53 earlier in the year. Accordingly, JW.54A consisted of eighteen merchant ships which left Loch Ewe on 15 November, arriving at Kola on the 24th, from where some of the ships proceeded under Soviet escort to Archangel. On 22 November the fourteen ships of JW.54B sailed from Loch Ewe escorted by the destroyers *Saumarez*, *Savage*, *Scorpion*, *Stord* (Royal Norwegian Navy), *Scourge*, *Venus*, *Vigilant*, *Hardy* and *Beagle*, the corvettes *Rhododendron* and *Poppy* and the minesweeper *Halcyon*. The cruiser force of *Kent*, *Jamaica* and *Bermuda* covered the convoy during its passage through the danger area south of Bear Island. Vice-Admiral Sir Henry Moore's battleship force was also at sea, but, after the sailing of JW.54A, USS *Tuscaloosa* was replaced by HMS *Belfast*.

Because of delays in unloading the merchant ships at Kola, just one homeward-bound convoy, RA.54B, left Archangel on 26 November. Only eight ships were in the convoy, which reached Loch Ewe on 19 December without loss, although *U307* of the 'Eisenbart' group had attempted to attack on 28 November but had been put down by the escort.

Thus the 1943–44 winter cycle of convoys had got off to a good start. Thirty-two loaded ships had reached Russia and 21 had returned to the United Kingdom, all unscathed. Although the German Navy's *B-Dienst* monitoring service had detected the passage of JW.54A, no attempt had been made to oppose it. The German Naval Staff began a belated review of the situation.

The year 1943 had been a very quiet one for the officers and men of the *Kriegsmarine*'s Northern Battle Group. Admiral Dönitz may have succeeded in saving the ships from the breaker's yard, but he had in truth achieved no more than his predecessor, Raeder. By October 1943 the Northern Battle Group consisted of *Scharnhorst* (*Kapitän zur See* Julius Hintze) and the 4th and 6th Destroyer Flotillas. However, on 17 November the 6th Destroyer Flotilla was ordered back to the Baltic,

Top: JW.53 ploughing through light pack-ice.

Above: The Kola Inlet at sunset showing, in the centre, the disguised RFA oiler *Oligarch*. Her funnel has been cut down and fitted with a spark arrester and a dummy fuunnel had been erected amidships. (IWM A.15421)

Right: Vice-Admiral Sir Bruce Fraser, who took over command of the Home Fleet on 8 May 1943 from Admiral Sir John Tovey. (IWM A.15345)

Above: The German
battlecruiser *Scharnhorst*. Her
appearance in northern waters in
early 1943 caused the
suspension of the convoys to the
USSR.

Left: Rear-Admiral Erich Bey,
Commander of the German task
force.

Above right: The cruiser HMS
Norfolk, which succeeded in
hitting *Scharnhorst* three times
and destroying her radar
equipment. (IWM FL.1861)

Right: The gash in *Norfolk*'s
deck made by an 11in shell from
Scharnhorst.

'TO THE LAST SHELL'

Above: HMS *Duke of York*, flagship of Admiral Sir Bruce Fraser at the Battle of the North Cape.

Below: The shattered Director Control Tower of HMS *Saumarez*, hit by an 11in shell which killed all but one of the crew.

Right, top: Damage to *Duke of York*'s tripod foremast caused by an 11in shell which passed through one of legs without exploding. The flagship suffered more damage from the blast of her own guns.

Right, bottom: Guns' crews of HMS *Duke of York* don their anti-flash hoods and gloves and pose proudly for the official photographer after the battle.

Above: Some of *Scharnhorst*'s 36 survivors leave the drifter *St Ninian* at Scapa Flow on their way to a prisoner-of-war camp.

Below: Admiral Fraser with the Commanding Officers of some of the ships which participated in the Battle of the North Cape. From the left are Capt The Hon Guy Russell RN (*Duke of York*), Cdr La Barber DSO RN (*Opportune*), Cdr R. L. Fisher DSO (*Musketeer*), Cdr G. Meyrick RN (*Savage*), Fraser, Capt J. Hughes-Hallett DSO RN (*Jamaica*) and four other destroyer officers.

DIFFICULT DECISIONS

Right, top: The escort carrier HMS *Chaser*, which was detached from Western Approaches Command to join the escort for JW/RA.57.

Right, bottom: The crew of Swordfish 'B' of 816 Squadron after their sinking of *U472* on 4 March 1944. From left to right are Sub-Lt W. P. Laing, Sub-Lt P. T. Beresford and LA J. Beech.

Above: *U288* under attack by aircraft from HMS *Tracker* and *Activity* on 3 April 1944. The heavy losses inflicted on the Germans in the first convoys of 1944 showed that the tide was now definitely running in the Allies' favour.

Below: Soviet officers embarked in HMS *Fencer* and taking a keen interest in flying operations.

Above: The battleship *Royal
Sovereign* with two of the eight
destroyers and four submarines
transferred to the USSR in the
summer of 1944.

Below: The mixed Soviet and
British crews of the submarine
V1 (ex HMS *Sunfish*). The
smiles are contrived: the British
ratings did not like the life in the

Red Navy and only three
actually sailed with the
submarine.

Above: A photograph taken from the escort carrier *Emperor* showing the strike force for Operation 'Tungsten'. Astern are *Furious*, *Pursuer* and *Searcher*.

Below: Barracuda crews on board HMS *Furious* attend a final briefing before the attack on 3 April 1944.

Right, top: Smoke rises from *Tirpitz*, indicating a hit. The damage caused during the 'Tungsten' operation was largely superficial and the Home Fleet kept up the pressure with strikes throughout the summer of 1944.

Right, centre: A Barracuda lands on HMS *Furious* after the 'Tungsten' attack.

Right, bottom: Sub-Lt E. D. Knight RNVR gives personnel on *Furious*'s exposed bridge a description of the attack.

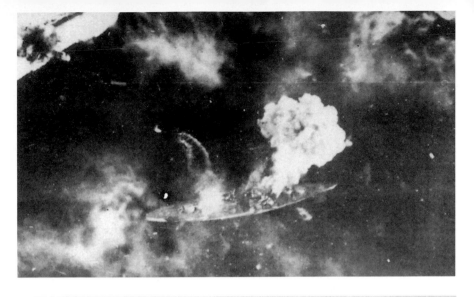

Left: Vice-Admiral Sir Henry Moore, who took over command of the Home Fleet from Admiral Fraser.

Right: Wg Cdr J. B. Tait DSO DFC RAF, Officer Commanding No 617 Squadron, who led the final bomber attacks on *Tirpitz*.

Below: An aerial reconniasance photograph showing the capsized battleship. Salvage craft are alongside attempting to reach those trapped in the hull.

Bottom: *Tirpitz* post-war. The *Kriegsmarine* removed her propellers and much of the armour belt on the starboard side, but it was the Norwegians who benefited most from the wreck.

VICTORY

Left, top: Some of the 11,000 Russians captured in Norway and sent back to the USSR in JW.61A.

Left, centre: The *Empress of Australia* entering the Kola Inlet on 6 November 1944.

Left, bottom: The escort carrier *Nairana* seen from HMS *Campania* in rough weather during the JW/RA.64 convoys. That any flying at all was possible in these conditons was due to consummate skills of the pilots and flight-deck crews.

Right, top: Rear-Admiral Rhoderick McGrigor on the bridge of HMS *Campania* during the passage of JW.64. The carriers were used as flagships because of their superior facilities, but, even so, the bridge here looks remarkably cramped.

Right, centre: Operation 'Open Door': Norwegians from Sorøy after their evacuation from the island in February 1945. (IWM A.27543)

Below: A merchant ship in the storm which repeatedly battered the homeward-bound RA.64.

Left: Heavy seas seen from the bridge of HMS *Bellona*.

Below: The corvette HMS *Bluebell* was torpedoed by *U711* on 16 February 1945 and was one of the last British warships to be sunk while escorting an Arctic convoy.

leaving *Kapitän zur See* Hans Johannesson's five destroyers of the 4th Flotilla to keep *Scharnhorst* company. These latter vessels were large new destroyers of the 'Z' class. Each was over 400ft long and armed with five 15cm guns and eight torpedo tubes. They were bigger, faster and more powerfully armed than, though not as seaworthy as, their British counterparts.

On 8 November Vice-Admiral Oscar Kummetz went on extended leave for medical treatment in Germany. He had not been a particularly successful commander—his ineptness had been largely responsible for the Barents Sea débâcle in January. His replacement was Rear-Admiral Erich 'Achmed' Bey, whose previous appointment had been Flag Officer (Destroyers). Bey was 'a man of massive build, an excellent seaman and a born destroyer captain. A soft heart beat beneath a rather forbidding exterior.'[3] He had seen considerable action during the war, including minelaying operations off the British coast in 1940 and the fiasco at Narvik, where his force had been wiped out, and he had commanded the destroyer forces during the famous 'Channel Dash'.

He took up his appointment under difficult circumstances. To begin with, he had no proper staff. Many of Kummetz's people had gone back to Germany with him, while Bey's staff had yet to be appointed or to join. He was also given very little in the way of guidance from OKM as to what he was supposed to achieve and how he was to do it. A planning document issued on 20 November 1943 indicated that *Scharnhorst* was to be used against convoy traffic, but this was so hedged with restrictions and caveats that it was unworkable. The chief restrictions were that, before any operation could proceed, there had to be accurate knowledge from reconnaissance, U-boats or other intelligence of the convoy's whereabouts and the composition of the escort, together with the requisite meteorological information. The only advice which he received from Kummetz was to wait until repairs to *Tirpitz* had been completed.

On 22 November Bey produced his own assessment of the situation, and this echoed the pessimism at OKM. He had discussed the relative roles of *Scharnhorst* and the five destroyers of Johannesson's 4th Flotilla. Bey considered that in winter *Scharnhorst* was acutely vulnerable to torpedo attacks by the very heavy destroyer escort now accompanying the convoys. He therefore considered that it would be better for the destroyers to attack the convoy while *Scharnhorst* distracted the cruiser escort. However, five destroyers were not nearly enough to attack a heavily defended convoy, and, since *Scharnhorst* herself would need some sort of screen, Bey arrived at the surprising conclusion that three destroyers should deal with the convoy while the other two ships screened the battlecruiser. It seemed as if Bey could not make up his mind whether the destroyers should support *Scharnhorst* or *vice versa*. Bey's pessimism was echoed by Admiral Schniewind at Kiel. In a document issued on 5 December, the latter reinforced the requirement for accurate knowledge of the convoy's position but considered that in the middle of the Arctic winter the chance of finding a convoy was not very good.

Amid the prevailing gloom in the German Naval High Command, only Admiral Dönitz seemed to have any optimism about using *Scharnhorst* against the convoys. Dönitz, of course, had pledged to Hitler that the big ships still had a viable role, so to a certain extent his professional reputation and standing in the *Führer*'s 'court circle' depended on his being able to turn his pledge into reality. On 19 December Dönitz assured Hitler that *Scharnhorst* would attack the next convoy. He told him that a convoy

> . . . carrying war material for Russia and protected by a cruiser escort which was no match for our battleship was sailing through an area within easy reach of our battle group. Its position, course and speed were known.[4] Because of ice in the vicinity of Bear Island, which prevented evasive action, and the superior speed of the German ships, it could not hope to avoid our attack.
>
> Our reconnaissance had not discovered the presence of any heavy enemy formation, though that, of course, did not mean that no such formation was at sea. But if it were, it must have been a long way from the convoy and the *Scharnhorst* seemed to have every chance of delivering a rapid and successful attack.[5]

By December the convoy cycle had settled down and so both eastbound and westbound convoys (JW/RA.55) were divided into two parts, the whole cycle occupying 27 days (from 12 December 1943 to 8 January 1944). Cruiser cover was provided by the 10th Cruiser Squadron consisting of *Belfast* (Vice-Admiral Robert Burnett, Capt F. R. Parham RN; Flag), *Sheffield* (Capt C. T. Addis RN) and *Norfolk* (Capt D. K. Bain RN), while Admiral Fraser in HMS *Duke of York* (Capt G. H. Russell RN) provided heavy cover with HMS *Jamaica* (Capt J. Hughes-Hallett RN).

Convoy JW.55A, consisting of nineteen merchant ships, left Loch Ewe on 12 December. The minesweepers *Harrier* and *Cockatrice* formed the Local Escort until 15 December, when they were joined by the destroyer HMS *Westcott*, the minesweeper HMS *Speedwell* and the Norwegian corvette *Acanthus*. On 15 December the destroyer screen consisting of *Milne* (Capt I. Campbell RN, Senior Officer), *Musketeer*, *Meteor*, *Matchless*, *Opportune*, *Ashanti*, *Virago* and the Canadian *Athabaskan*, joined until 21 December, when they departed to pick up the westbound RA.55A. The Eastern Local Escort, consisting of HMS *Hussar* and three Soviet destroyers, joined on 20 December and saw the convoy through to Kola, where twelve ships arrived on 21 December, the remainder going on to Archangel, where they arrived on 22 December.

Though unmolested by the Germans, the convoy had been sighted by *U386* (*Oberleutnant* Fritz Albrecht) one of four U-boats on patrol east of Bear Island. There was a resulting flurry of German radio activity which suggested that, given the reduced risk of air attack in the winter darkness, a sortie by *Scharnhorst* might be imminent. Accordingly, Fraser took the unprecedented step of sailing *Duke of York*, *Jamaica* and the four escorting destroyers all the way through to the Kola Inlet, ostensibly to pay a good-will call on Admiral Golovko. At Kola there was the usual exchange of visits and entertainments, but the Russians remained extremely suspicious: 'I still do not grasp for what reason the C-in-C of the British Home Fleet has decided to pay us a visit at the height of the Polar night season,' confided Golovko to his diary.[6]

Fraser left Kola on 18 December to return to Akureyi in Iceland to fuel. Meanwhile the second eastbound convoy, JW.55B, consisting of nineteen ships, had sailed from Loch Ewe on 20 December. The Western Local Escort, which stayed with the convoy until 22 December, consisted of the corvettes *Borage* and *Wallflower* with the minesweepers *Hound* and *Hydra*. On 22 December the Ocean Escort joined, consisting of the destroyers *Whitehall* and *Wrestler*, the minesweeper *Gleaner* and the corvettes *Honeysuckle* and *Oxlip*. The Fighting Destroyer Escort consisting of *Onslow* (Capt J. A. 'Bes' McCoy DSO RN, Senior Officer), *Impulsive*, *Onslaught*, *Orwell*, *Scourge*, *Haida*, *Huron* and *Iroquois*, joined the same day and remained with the convoy until 29 December.

JW.55B was expected to pass Bear Island on Christmas Day, roughly the same time as the homeward-bound RA.55A, which had left Kola on 22 December. It was escorted by the destroyers *Westcott* and *Beagle*, the corvettes *Acanthus*, *Dianella* and *Poppy* and the minesweeper *Speedwell* and had been met by Capt Campbell's eight destroyers which had covered JW.55A. Cruiser cover east of Bear Island was provided by *Belfast*, *Sheffield* and *Norfolk*, which sailed from Kola on 22 December, while the same evening Fraser took *Duke of York* and *Jamaica* to sea for the usual heavy-ship covering position.

At 1059 on 22 December JW.55B was detected by a Dornier Do 217 bomber on a routine meteorological flight. The convoy was reported as a troop convoy, which was immediately interpreted as an invasion force bound for Norway—a favourite obsession of Hitler's which spread down into the ranks of the *Kriegsmarine*. Admiral Schniewind ordered a series of preparatory measures, which included increasing the number of air patrols by the *Luftwaffe*, redeploying the U-boats of the '*Eisenbart*' group to new positions off Vestfjord and ordering *Scharnhorst* and her destroyers to three hours' notice for sea. But at 1430 that afternoon the sighting was re-evaluated as a convoy. Aircraft succeeded in maintaining contact throughout 23 and 24 December. At 1220 on the 24th the *Luftwaffe* reported the convoy as steering a course of 050° at a speed of 8kts in position 70°27′N 03°35′E. The oft-derided air reconnaissance skills of the *Luftwaffe* now provided the Germans with the course, composition and speed of the convoy.

Fraser decided that JW.55B was dangerously exposed: although the Germans had never made a sortie to the westward before, the convoy was unsupported. Accordingly, he broke radio silence twice to amend the disposition of the British forces at sea. At 1201 he asked that, 'if the situation develops',[7] the westbound convoy RA.55A be diverted to the north after passing Bear Island, thus clearing the area. At the same time he ordered four destroyers to leave the escort of RA.55A and join that of JW.55B, since it was apparent that the homeward-bound convoy had escaped detection.

At 1325 he broke radio silence for the second time to order JW.55B to reverse its course for three hours; at the same time he ordered *Duke of York* and *Jamaica* to increase speed to 19kts. Although the increase in speed would not have brought the convoy any closer to Fraser, ordering JW.55B to reverse course would mean that if *Scharnhorst* did come out, then she would not find the convoy until after nightfall. In the event, it proved nearly impossible to get JW.55B to go back. Station-keeping and signalling among the merchant ships appear to have been far less satisfactory than usual, and McCoy felt that it would be virtually impossible to turn the convoy through 360 degrees in the dark and rough weather while at the same time keeping it together. All he could manage was to obey the spirit of Fraser's orders and reduce speed to 8kts.

By the evening of 24 December Fraser was able to review the situation. The two convoys were now approaching each other on opposite courses and *Scharnhorst* could still launch an attack. However, there was no word that she had quit her moorings in Altenfjord. JW.55B had definitely been sighted, but RA.54A had so far escaped detection.

On the morning of Christmas Day Capt McCoy signalled across to the convoy commodore, Rear-Admiral M. W. S. Boucher DSO, in *Fort Kullyspell*:

> Situation today. Enemy will probably attack us today with U-boat and possibly surface craft. Four more Home Fleet destroyers should join us p.m. today. *Duke of York* is astern, coming up at 19 knots or more. Three heavy cruisers somewhere ahead. Happy Christmas.[8]

The four Home Fleet destroyers, *Musketeer*, *Opportune*, *Virago* and *Matchless*, joined the convoy at 1250. With their arrival Fraser felt that the escort was strong enough either to drive *Scharnhorst* off with a massed torpedo attack or to inflict such damage as would slow the battlecruiser down until *Duke of York* could catch up and finish her off.

The wind was now Force 8 from the SSW and U-boat homing transmissions were detected on more than one bearing. The seven '*Eisenbart*' U-boats which had been redeployed off Vestfjord in case of an invasion of Norway had been sent back to their patrol line off Bear Island when JW.55B was identified as a convoy. At 1800 on 24 December they had been ordered to take up specific attacking positions. At 0900 on the 25th *U601* (*Kapitänleutnant* Hansen) reported the convoy on a course of 060° in position 72°25′N 12°30′E and at 1045 the remainder of the boats in this group were ordered to operate on the basis of Hansen's transmissions. *U716* (*Oberleutnant* Hans Dunkelberg) closed the convoy that evening and fired a T5 acoustic 'Gnat' torpedo at a destroyer but missed. *U701* was put down by a depth-charge counter-attack. Subsequently the '*Eisenbart*' boats were ordered to take up new positions to the east.

So far there was no news of *Scharnhorst*. Fraser, however, had one other asset at his disposal—one which gave him unparalleled access to the German's radio traffic. For some time the British had been breaking the German naval ciphers and making operational use of the resulting intelligence. Such material was assigned the code-word 'Ultra', treated with the utmost secrecy and passed on to only a few senior officers, for such intelligence was almost a dubious asset: the Admiralty always had to guard against the risk of compromising the source of their information, and against losing such a priceless asset by letting the enemy suspect that his traffic was being read.

It was through 'Ultra' that Fraser had learned of the German air and submarine contacts with JW.55B and through the absence of any signal traffic that he was able to assume that RA.55A had escaped detection. Now, at 0216 in the morning of 26

December, an 'emergency' 'Ultra' message arrived, stating baldly that '*Scharnhorst* probably sailed 6 p.m., 25 December'.[9] Both Fraser and Burnett were on the select list of commanders who received 'Ultra' decrypts at sea. However, Capt McCoy of JW.55B was not. He, too, needed to be told that *Scharnhorst* was at sea and after the merchantmen in his care, yet the source of the information could not be risked. It was better for the Admiralty to tell McCoy rather than let Fraser or Burnett break radio silence. Accordingly, at 0319 on 26 December the Admiralty told McCoy that 'Admiralty appreciates *Scharnhorst* is at sea'.

The news was greeted in the British ships with surprise underpinned by sublime confidence that they would sink her. That, after all, was what their crews had trained to do. Marine Ernie Heather, at his action station in HMS *Duke of York*'s Transmitting Station,[10] deep in the bowels of the ship, wrote:

> We had confidence in the ship we were sailing in, our confidence in our officers, and—though nobody would ever speak about it—our confidence in each other. So that, should we come into contact with the enemy, then we were going to do our utmost and our level best to annihilate it.[11]

The beast was out. Dönitz, having reviewed all the available intelligence and having concluded that JW.55B was not supported by a battleship (despite some evidence from DF to the contrary), ordered the battle group to sea at 1415 on Christmas Day. At 1527 Admiral Northern Waters at Narvik issued the executive order '*Ostwind*' and confirmed that *Scharnhorst* and the ships of the 4th Destroyer Flotilla were to sail at 1700.

Christmas Day had already been spoiled for the crew of the *Scharnhorst* by an order from Bey to be at one hour's notice for sea from 1300 that afternoon. At 1630 *Scharnhorst* and the destroyers reported that they were ready for sea. But she did not sail at 1700: Admiral Bey and his skeleton staff were still on board *Tirpitz*, and it was not until 1955 that she passed through the net barrier of Lange Fjord into Altenfjord and headed up the long length of Stjernsund at 17kts.

Scharnhorst had hardly left her berth when doubts as to her mission began to assail the German commanders afloat and ashore. Both Bey and Schniewind were concerned about the weather. South-westerly gales of between Force 6 to 9 were expected, and concern was expressed about the ability of Johannesson's destroyers to operate in such seas. When the *Luftwaffe* reported that, because of bad weather, there would be no reconnaissance flights on 26 December, Schniewind realized that two of the vital elements would be missing—no reconnaissance, and no destroyer screen for the battlecruiser.

Dönitz was having none of this faint-heartedness. In signal which was received in *Scharnhorst* just before midnight, Bey was left in no doubt as to what was required of him and the officers and men under his command:

> 1. Enemy attempting to aggravate the difficulties of our eastern land forces in their heroic struggle by sending an important convoy of provisions and arms for Russians. We must help.
> 2. Convoy to be attacked by *Scharnhorst* and destroyers.

3. Tactical situation to be exploited skilfully and boldly. Engagement not to be broken off until full success achieved. Every advantage to be pressed. *Scharnhorst's* superior fire power crucial. Her deployment therefore urgent. Destroyers to engage as suitable.
4. Disengagement at own discretion and automatically if heavy forces encountered.
5. Crews to be briefed accordingly. I am confident of your offensive spirit. *Heil und Sieg.* Dönitz. Grand Admiral.[12]

Scharnhorst headed north into worsening weather at 25kts. She was overtaking a quartering sea, but every now and then she would seem to slip uneasily into the side of a large wave before staggering up and out again. It was a most unpleasant motion and there were many in her company who were chronically affected by seasickness. If conditions in the *Scharnhorst* were bad, then they must have been unbearable in the destroyers, which were continually being washed down over the complete length of their upper decks by huge waves.

At about 0300 *Scharnhorst* received a message from Schniewind confirming that '*Ostwind*' was to proceed, with *Scharnhorst* acting alone if the destroyers were unable to keep up. Bey asked Johannesson for his opinion and the latter, ever an optimist, indicated that his ships could still proceed. Bey's plan was for *Scharnhorst* to go north to a position ahead of the convoy and then turn towards it and, using the destroyers as a screen, search for the convoy. At 1238 and 1251 he received *Luftwaffe* sighting reports, but these were over twelve hours old by the time they were received in *Scharnhorst*. JW.55B was still being tracked by U-boats. *U716* (Dunkelberg) reported the convoy at 0328 and gave a position using the *Kriegsmarine's* grid reference chart which tallied with where *Korvettenkäpitan* Lanz, *Scharnhorst's* Navigating Officer, thought the convoy would be. By 0700 Lanz calculated that his ship was within 30 miles of the convoy and was ahead of it. Bey now ordered *Scharnhorst* and the destroyers to steer 250° and start reconnaissance. The five destroyers accordingly turned into the wind and weather and spread out in line abreast with *Scharnhorst* ten miles astern of them. At 0755 Bey ordered another alteration to the south-west to 230°.

Although he was unaware of it, Bey had nearly succeeded in bringing about the perfect interception. Not since Operation '*Berlin*'[13] in 1941 had the Germans come so close to a convoy with such chances of success. Another forty minutes, and the convoy would be in view . . .

At 0820, for some unexplained reason, Bey altered course to the north. It may have been a fleeting radar contact, but this is unlikely given that the *Kriegsmarine's* standing orders forbade the indiscriminate use of either the *Seetakt* or the *Hohentwiel* set with which *Scharnhorst* was equipped. Whatever the reason for the alteration of course, Bey neglected to inform Johannesson, so that the destroyers continue to plough away to the south-west. Soon *Scharnhorst* was steaming at 90 degrees to the destroyers. She lost touch with them and never regained it.

In the latitude of 73°N, nautical twilight, which is when the sun is 12 degrees below the horizon or higher, begins at 0839. At 0900, in the bleak lightening of the darkness, Johannesson saw the shape of a destroyer to the northward. He thought it was one of the convoy's escorts and signalled the sighting report to *Scharnhorst*. The ship was in fact *Z38*, out of position. Beyond her, away to the north-east, Johannesson saw a pale pink glow on the horizon like starshell. He was puzzled, for German starshell gave a bright white light. Time had run out for Admiral Bey. Whether he received Johannesson's signal or not was immaterial. At 0926, without any warning from radar or lookouts, starshell exploded overhead, bathing *Scharnhorst* in its cold, terrifying and totally unexpected light.

Scharnhorst might have been surprised, but no one else was. After receiving the 'Ultra' decrypt informing him that the German battlecruiser was at sea, Fraser began to pull the threads of his command together. At 0344 Force 2 was ordered to raise steam for full speed. At 0401 he ordered McCoy to turn JW.55B to a northerly course out of *Scharnhorst*'s way, and at the same time he signalled his own position to Burnett in *Belfast*. Once again he had balanced the risks and decided that it was worth breaking radio silence in order to keep the widespread forces under his command in touch with each other. There was to be none of the chaos which had characterized Tovey's attempts to catch *Tirpitz* in March 1942.

At 0628 he ordered JW.55B to resume an easterly course of 045 and told Burnett to close the convoy for mutual support. By 0712 Burnett reckoned that he had gone far enough south so he turned to the west. There was a south-westerly gale blowing and he wanted to approach the convoy from well to the southward so that in the event of action he would not be steaming directly into the wind and seas. He held this course for an hour, and after receiving the position, course and speed of the convoy, altered course to 300° at 0815, at the same time increasing speed to 24kts.

By now all the British forces were aware of each other's locations. As a final precaution, Capt McCoy disposed the destroyers *Musketeer, Matchless, Opportune* and *Virago* on a line of bearing of 165° from the centre of the convoy on the starboard and threatened side. At 0925, almost along that line, McCoy could see the intermittent glow of starshell. The first stage of the battle had begun.

At 0840 *Belfast* got a contact on her Type 273 search radar at a range of 35,000yds and bearing 295°. At that time the cruiser was steering 325° and Burnett estimated that the convoy bore 287° from *Belfast*, range 48 miles. *Scharnhorst*, if that is what the contact was, was directly between Force 1 and the convoy, and if Bey had any determination he could go on to win the *Kriegsmarine*'s greatest victory of the war.

At 0901 Burnett formed his cruisers on a line of bearing of 180° in the order *Belfast, Sheffield* and *Norfolk, Belfast* being the northern ship, roughly at right angles to the bearing of the enemy contact. At 0906 *Norfolk* was in radar contact, bearing 261°, range 12 miles, followed at 0907 by *Sheffield*, bearing 258°, range 10 miles. The bearing was moving left and south. At some time Bey must have decided that he had gone far enough to the north and swung round to search to the south. At 0915 the main echo bore 250°, range 13,000yds. Burnett ordered the cruisers to form a line of bearing of 160° from him, but as the bearing of the contact continued to draw left and aft there was the danger that one of the cruisers might foul the range of any cruiser on the starboard or disengaged side of her.

At 0921 it was *Sheffield* which sighted the *Scharnhorst* first and made the thrilling signal 'Enemy in sight, bearing 222 degrees, range 13,000 yards'. Three minutes later *Belfast*'s 4in guns opened fire with starshell but failed to spot the enemy. At 0929 Burnett ordered his ships to engage with their main armament and the course was altered to 265° to close the enemy. *Norfolk* then opened fire with her 8in guns at a range of 9,800yds but had to drop back to clear *Belfast*'s range.

Norfolk continued firing until 0940 and obtained two hits with her second or third salvo. She was the only ship of the three not to have flashless cordite, and the flash of her eight 8in guns going off blinded everybody above decks. *Norfolk*'s fire was fast and accurate: she loosed off six eight-gun broadsides in two minutes, a testimony to the high standard of training of her gun crews, who had to perform what was the largely manual operation of loading the guns as the ship ploughed through the heavy seas.

Scharnhorst was taken completely by surprise. *Oberbootsmannsmaat* Wilhelm Godde, on the port forward searchlight control platform, suddenly saw huge nine-foot columns of water rising up out of the darkness. 'Caesar' turret[14] trained round and opened fire. *Steurmannsgefreiter* Wilhelm Kruse, on the Admiral's bridge, said that the three cruisers were visible, together with the flashes of *Norfolk*'s gunfire.

The first of *Norfolk*'s hits landed between No 3 15cm mounting on the port side and the port-side torpedo tubes, penetrated the upper deck and ended up in the Technical Petty Officers' Mess without exploding. The second hit was crucial. The 240lb projectile smashed into the *Seetakt* radar on the foremast, destroying the mattress aerial. It also destroyed the port HA director and wounded four of *Scharnhorst*'s crew.

At 0938 Burnett brought Force 1 round to port to a course of 105°: he had now steamed around the enemy and was between him and the convoy. *Scharnhorst* had altered course to port to 150° at 0927 and increased speed to disengage. By 0946 she was doing nearly 30kts and the range had opened to 24,000yds.

At this stage in the action Burnett decided to break contact with *Scharnhorst* and return to a course of 305° to close the convoy, and at 1020 contact was lost. In the prevailing weather conditions he knew that *Scharnhorst* had a speed advantage over him of 3–4kts. Now *Scharnhorst* bore 078° at a range of 36,000yds and was steering north-east at about 28kts. It was apparent that Bey was trying to avoid damage and work his way round to the north to have another attempt at finding the convoy. Perhaps a more imaginative commander might have deduced the convoy's whereabouts by studying the behaviour of the cruisers: Burnett's ships had, after all, steamed right past *Scharnhorst* and only opened fire when they were between her and the convoy.

Bey now appears to have made a last attempt to locate his destroyers, in order either to enable them rejoin him or to launch a concerted attack with them, the destroyers from the south and *Scharnhorst* from the north. At 1135 he signalled his position to Johannesson, who had stolidly been steering his westerly course, having received no orders to the contrary despite seeing the starshell, and ordered him to steer 030°. At the same time he received a sighting report from *U277* (Lübsen) indicating that the convoy was in square AB6365 on the German Navy's grid chart. At 1158 he ordered Johannesson's ships to steer for this location. Bey was trying to tie his threads together and was doing his best with his improvised staff and with units which had not worked up in each other's company. In Dönitz's post-war memoirs, Bey is severely censured. Dönitz considered that 'tactical co-ordination' between *Scharnhorst* and D4 was non-existent and that the action with the cruisers 'should have been fought out to its conclusion', whereupon the convoy would have fallen into *Scharnhorst*'s hands like 'ripe fruit'.[15] Bey may not have been the perfect commander, but such simplistic criticism is hardly justified. Bey had nearly brought off the perfect interception, he had avoided becoming entangled with the cruisers (although a more determined commander but have tried to brush them aside) and he was still trying to locate the convoy.

Ironically, Burnett's decision to break off the action and rejoin the convoy became the object of criticism by the tactical experts at the Admiralty. The point of their criticism was that *Scharnhorst* had turned south-east at 0927, three minutes after *Belfast* fired starshell, but it was not until 0938 that Burnett had came round to port to 105°, which was eleven minutes after *Scharnhorst* had turned and eighteen minutes after *Sheffield* had reported the enemy as being in sight:

> I did not immediately alter course to port as I wished to place Force 1 between the enemy and the convoy should he break away to the west and north further to gain what advantage there was in the light.[16]

The critics argued that *Scharnhorst*'s alteration of course had already accomplished this by 0930 and Burnett could have altered to port immediately. At 1020, when contact was lost, *Belfast* was eighteen miles nearer the convoy and it was physically impossible for *Scharnhorst* to have reached the convoy before Burnett. If *Belfast* had steered north at 17kts she could have remained in radar contact while still keeping between the *Scharnhorst* and the convoy.

At 1035 Burnett signalled to Fraser, 'Have lost touch with the enemy who was steering north. Am closing convoy.' Fraser may have approved Burnett's decision, but it was the start of a very worrying period for him in which he had doubts about the outcome of the day. His uncertainty prompted Fraser to signal Burnett at 1058, 'Unless touch can be regained by some unit, there is no chance of my finding enemy.' This signal precipitated Burnett into a a crisis of confidence. His Flag Captain, Capt Frederick Parham, recalled that

> When he'd taken the decision to stay with the convoy he called me down to the chart house, one deck below the bridge. He cleared the chart house of everybody else and said to me, 'Freddie have I done the right thing?' I said to him, 'I'm absolutely certain you have.' Shortly after that we received a signal from the C-in-C [at 1058] which, roughly speaking, said, 'Unless somebody keeps their eye on the *Scharnhorst*, how d'you think I'm going to bring her to action?'
>
> Poor old Bob—he was a terribly emotional chap and was very nearly in tears about it. I was able to reassure him. And afterwards his judgement was proved absolutely spot-on because *Scharnhorst* turned up for another attack on the convoy and ran straight into us. There is no question in my mind that Bob was right—absolutely right.[17]

Burnett considered that the protection of the convoy was his first priority, even though that meant ignoring the Fighting Instructions which held that 'very good reasons must exist before touch with the enemy is relinquished'. In his dispatch to Fraser he defended his decision thus:

I received your signal 261058 at 1104. Considering my chief object to be the safe and timely arrival of the convoy and being convinced that I should shortly make contact again, it would not have been correct tactics to have left the merchant ships in daylight to search for the enemy, nor to have split my force by detaching one or more ships to search, in view of the enemy's high speed and the weather conditions which limited a cruiser's speed to 24 knots. Feeling confident that the enemy would return to the attack from the north or north-east and keeping in mind the object of the operation, I decided to carry out a broad zig-zag ahead of the convoy.[18]

Burnett's actions were given the final imprimatur by Capt Stephen Roskill, the official historian, who, after an exhaustive study of the track charts, considered that under the conditions prevailing it would have been impossible for the three cruisers to have remained in radar contact. 'Criticism of Admiral Burnett's actions can therefore hardly be sustained,'[19] he concluded.

Meanwhile Burnett had been joined by the four destroyers of the 36th Division (*Matchless*, *Musketeer*, *Virago* and *Opportune*), which had originally been detached from RA.55A for JW.55B and were now being sent on to join Force 1. At 1050 Force 1 took station ahead of the convoy with the four destroyers about a mile ahead. Expectations were high that *Scharnhorst* would reappear at any moment. Taking advantage of the lull in the action, the ships' companies were fed at their action stations. On *Belfast* the 'action messing' was hot soup, a meat pie and a jam tart for each man.

Admiral Fraser on board *Duke of York* was having a worrying and frustrating forenoon. After contact with *Scharnhorst* was broken he began to consider his options. She could be intending to mount another attack on the convoy or she might have given up and gone home. Alternatively, a far worse scenario was that she had given Force 1 the slip and was heading into the Atlantic. He also had to consider the fuel state of his destroyers—he either had to go back to Iceland or go on towards the Kola Inlet. At 1203 he ordered Force 2 back on to a course of 260°. If *Scharnhorst* were headed into the Atlantic, then at least Force 2 was on a roughly parallel course, ahead of the German and to the south; if she were after the convoy, then Force 1 would have to take care of her.

For *Duke of York*, *Jamaica* and the four destroyers to turn in the heavy seas then running required seamanship of a high order. But the turn had hardly been completed when a signal came through from *Belfast* at 1205: 'Unknown radar contact, bearing 075 degrees, range 13 miles.' Force 1 was back in contact. 'Turn 'em round again,' ordered Fraser.

Sheffield acquired the contact at 1211 and *Norfolk* was in contact at 1214. The quarry was closing rapidly and moving right. Burnett had been correct. Bey had wasted three hours in looking for the convoy but he was back. Force 1 altered course to starboard at 1216 to head *Scharnhorst* off and made a further alteration to starboard at 1219. By this time the two forces were approaching each other at a combined speed of nearly 40kts. At 1220 Burnett ordered his ships to open fire, and at 1221 it was *Sheffield* which made the signal 'Enemy in sight' for the second time that day.

NOTES TO CHAPTER 11

1. Winton, J., *The Death of the Scharnhorst*, Anthony Bird Publications, 1983, p.46.
2. Campbell, Vice-Admiral Sir Ian, and MacIntyre, Capt Donald, *The Kola Run: A Record of the Arctic Convoys 1941–45*, Frederick Muller, 1958.
3. Busch, Franz-Otto, *The Drama of the Scharnhorst*, Robert Hale, London, 1956, pp.49–50.
4. The convoy referred to here was JW.55B.
5. Winton, *op. cit.*, p.72.
6. Golovko, Admiral Arsenii, *With the Red Fleet*, Putnam & Co, 1965, pp.180–1.
7. Winton, *op. cit.*, p.67.
8. *ibid*, p.68.
9. PRO ADM.223/36: 'Signals connected with the sinking of the *Scharnhorst*'.
10. The Transmitting Station was the ship's fire control centre, where data concerning the target's range, course and speed, together with other required information, was converted into the required elevation and azimuth for the guns.
11. Winton, *op. cit.*, p.70.
12. Bekker, Cajus, *Hitler's Naval War*, Macdonald & Janes, 1974, p.352.
13. Operation '*Berlin*' was a combined commerce-raiding operation in the Atlantic by *Scharnhorst* and *Gneisenau*.
14. In German naval parlance the turrets were identified as 'Anton', 'Bruno', 'Caesar' and (in four-turret ships) 'Dora'. 'Caesar' was therefore the after 11in turret.
15. Dönitz, Karl, *Ten Years and Twenty Days*, Greenhill Books, London, 1990, p.380.
16. PRO ADM.199/913: 'Report of Proceedings of the Flag Officer Commanding the 10th Cruiser Squadron (CS10)'.
17. Admiral Sir Frederick Parham to author, 7 September 1985.
18. PRO ADM.199/913, *op. cit.*
19. Roskill, Capt S. W., *The War at Sea*, Vol III, Pt 1, HMSO, London, 1960, p.84.

11 -24-07

Chapter 12

'To the Last Shell'

The cruisers handed Scharnhorst *to* Duke of York *on a plate*—Rear-Admiral Robert Burnett to the ship's company of HMS *Sheffield* after the Battle of the North Cape

For the second time that day *Scharnhorst* was taken by surprise. She made an alteration of course to the west and then, at 1225, when the range had come down to 4,100yds, she swung round to port to steer south on a course of 135°. As she turned, she opened fire with all three 11in turrets and her shooting was unpleasantly accurate. One early salvo pitched in between *Norfolk* and *Sheffield*, close to the latter's starboard side and sweeping her upper deck with a hail of splinters 'up to football size'.[1]

It was *Norfolk* which bore the brunt of *Scharnhorst*'s fire: it will be recalled that she had no flashless cordite for her 8in guns, and as a result she gave *Scharnhorst*'s fire control team the perfect aiming point. At about 1223 the German battlecruiser scored hits on the British warship. One 11in shell struck the barbette of 'X' turret, rendering the latter inoperable and requiring the magazine to be flooded as a precaution. The second shell hit *Norfolk* amidships on the starboard side, penetrating to the main deck and exploding near the ship's secondary damage control headquarters, killing six men and wounding another two so seriously that they later died of their injuries. Fumes and smoke from the explosion poured down into the machinery spaces, but the engine room personnel displayed a phenomenal amount of *sang froid*. Chief Engine Room Artificer (CERA) Cardey was on duty in the forward engine room when *Norfolk* was hit:

I was standing in the middle of the compartment by the dials when there was a vivid flash and bits of metal rained down. One hit an engine room rating, who was just beside me, in the leg. Another piece of metal tore off the tops of two fingers of a man who had his hand on a lever. He did not know it had happened until a quarter of an hour later. Water began to pour down through the engine room hatches. Some fuel oil came with it, and I saw one fellow looking like a polished ebony statue because he had been covered from head to foot with the black oil. He was carrying on as if nothing had happened. I went across to the dials and found that the pressure was not affected. Some of the lights had gone out and there was a good deal of smoke, and we knew by the smell that the fire was raging somewhere. They were too busy to come and tell us what happened. Every man in the engine room had his work to do so we just carried on and only heard odd bits of information when they brought the sandwiches down and so on. We kept the engines going at full speed for six hours after the ship was hit. There was about three feet of water swishing about in the bilges below the engine room and the lower plates were covered.[2]

173

Many of *Norfolk*'s engine room ratings were 'HO' (Hostilities Only) men who had joined the Navy for the duration of the war. For many it was their first taste of action. CERA Davies wrote:

As an old RN man I can tell you they were something to be proud of. Not one faltered, and I suppose we all were, at the back of our minds, expecting something to happen at any minute.[3]

Capt D. K. 'Batchy' Bain wrote in his report of proceedings that

The men in the engine room continued to give *Norfolk* more knots than she ever had before and, instead of dropping back, we were there in the final phase of the action.[4]

Meanwhile the four destroyers of the 36th Division under the command of Cdr Ralph Fisher in HMS *Musketeer* had sighted *Scharnhorst* steaming straight towards them at 1216. Fisher had anticipated being given the order to split his force into two sub-divisions and launch a torpedo attack from either bow. Such an order was given by Burnett at 1222 but, for one reason or another, was not passed to the bridge after being received in *Musketeer*'s Signal Office. Despite later criticism by the Admiralty, who considered that a torpedo attack could have been made at 1225, Fisher did not consider such an attack to be a viable option at this time. *Scharnhorst* was approaching head on, and Fisher had no way of knowing which way she might turn in order to avoid an attack. Nevertheless, *Musketeer* fired some 52 rounds of 4.7in and got close enough to *Scharnhorst* to observe shells hitting her.

By 1231 *Scharnhorst* was steering a course of 110° and had increased speed to 28kts. At that speed she slowly began to draw away from Force 1. Fisher's destroyers increased speed to 26kts and came round to 135°. At 1241 the range had opened considerably, to 13,000yds. Burnett's ships ceased fire, and he resolved to shadow *Scharnhorst* until Force 2 was in a position to intercept her. As he later wrote to Fraser,

Realising that he [the enemy] had been, up to date, most obliging and that if he continued to act as he was doing he would walk into you, I decided to withhold fire until you had engaged in order to avoid scaring him into drastic alterations of course and not to disturb you by various echoes.[5]

The whole engagement had lasted twenty minutes. The British ships had all used radar in one way or another to direct their gunnery. *Sheffield*'s Type 284 fire control set was unserviceable so the target was held using the ship's Type 273 warning set (which was also able to give some indication of fall of shot) while using her Type 285 secondary armament fire control set for all-round warning. *Norfolk*'s Type 273 was put out of action by *Scharnhorst*'s fire, as was her Type 284 main armament fire control set. However the latter was swiftly repaired so that *Norfolk* was able to fire 31 radar-directed broadsides during the course of the day. *Belfast*'s radar outfit of Types 273, 284 and 285 worked perfectly throughout the day and the ship fired 38 broadsides, fourteen of them visually directed.

Shortly after *Scharnhorst* broke away, JW.55B narrowly escaped interception by Johannesson's destroyers. These ships had been sweeping to the south-west until 1030, when Bey had ordered them to alter course to 070° and increase speed to 25kts. They were then, of course, widely separated from *Scharnhorst*, which was racing north after her first engagement with Burnett's cruisers. An hour later Bey ordered a further alteration to 030 and at 1218, as a result of a U-boat report, he ordered them to operate in an area considerably to the west of their position.

In order to reach the new area, Johannesson steered 280°, a course on which he passed about eight miles to the southward of the convoy, coming down on its south-easterly track just after 1300. Had Bey delayed his orders by a little as fifteen minutes, then contact between the destroyers and the convoy could hardly have been avoided. As it was, Johannesson held on to the westward until 1418, when Bey ordered the destroyers to return to harbour. The German destroyers took no further part in proceedings.

Force 1 had taken up station on *Scharnhorst*'s port quarter at about 7½ miles—just out of visibility. Fisher's destroyers were disposed to the west. Burnett ordered his ships to form on a line of bearing of 220°, roughly at right angles to *Scharnhorst*'s course, and at 1256 sent out the first of many sighting reports to Fraser which were to be of such importance in the eventual destruction of the German battlecruiser.

At 1300 *Scharnhorst* swung round to 155°, a course which would take her back to base. Bey was following his orders, which allowed him to break off the operation if challenged by superior forces. He had made two good attempts to attack the convoy, and each time he had been thwarted by the cruisers. Accordingly, he headed for home and at 1525 signalled his ETA at Altenfjord as being just after midnight.

Dönitz was very critical of Bey's decision to break off the action:

> ... at this time the *Scharnhorst* was in a much better tactical position and it was the enemy who were silhouetted against the brighter south-western horizon while *Scharnhorst* had the dark northern sector behind her. The correct thing to have done now would have been to continue the fight and finish off the weaker British forces, particularly as it was plain that they had already been hit hard. Had this been done, an excellent opportunity would, of course, have been created for a successful attack on the convoy.[6]

The truth of the matter was that Bey and his staff were probably very weary. They had all been up since the previous night and, after two engagements with the very determined ships of Force 1, their nerves were probably rather frayed. The prospect of a quick dash back to Altenfjord and the safety of the boom defences must have been very appealing.

Unknown to Bey, the net began to close around him as the afternoon wore on. One of the great mysteries of the battle is why the Germans did so little to warn Bey of the disaster which was threatening him. It was not for want of intelligence. The *Luftwaffe* were in contact with Force 2 up to 1300 and probably after that as well. Bey received a sighting report at 1530. Moreover, the code-breakers in the *B-Dienst* service, in the Naval Staffs at Kiel and Narvik and in Berlin all had a mass of sigint[7] which showed that *Scharnhorst* was being threatened from the south-west. As one historian of the battle has succinctly remarked,

The Germans could hear 'DGO' [call-sign of Force 2] chatting to 'JLP' [call-sign of Force 1], clearly exchanging operational information. After a short while they could even read what had been said. 'DGO' went on hobbing and nobbing with 'JLP', like a conspirator talking to his mate, nodding now and again to 'Scapa' and to 'IJV' [call -sign of McCoy in the convoy]. As the bearings slowly drew together, their import became unmistakable. The Germans knew that all this signal traffic vitally concerned the lives of men in their own service. They knew that they were overhearing two parties planning to kill their fellow countrymen. One wonders why nobody in Germany or Norway had the nerve or the authority to send out one top-priority 'flash emergency signal, in plain language if need be, at that last desperate moment, to warn *Scharnhorst* of what was coming. But the Germans did nothing: they were like school children standing aghast on the river bank, hands in their mouths, helplessly watching their father's model yacht sail downstream and over the weir.[8]

Throughout the afternoon Burnett's ships hung on to *Scharnhorst*. Bey's choice of a south-easterly course unconsciously aided the British ships, for it placed the wind and sea on their beam. Had Bey steered more to the east, into the wind and sea, and maintained a speed of 28kts, he would have slipped away into the night, for in those conditions none of the British ships could have kept up with her.

Every twenty minutes or so Burnett would report the position, course and speed of his quarry. It was a superb piece of shadowing, described by Fraser as 'exemplary'. Admiral Sir John Tovey, a former Commander-in-Chief Home Fleet, later wrote to Capt Frederick Parham of HMS *Belfast*:

I was following your intercepts on the chart, and I know that you and your fine ship would never let go of the brute unless the weather made it absolutely impossible for you to keep up. The combination of the gallant attack you and other cruisers made on the *Scharnhorst*, coupled with your magnificent shadowing, is as fine an example of cruiser work as has ever been seen.[9]

Fraser was still concerned that *Scharnhorst* might have her destroyers with her—a scenario which would complicate his plans enormously. Accordingly, at 1318 he signalled Burnett for details of the make-up of the German force. Burnett's signal that he was in contact with 'one heavy ship' removed the last doubts. Fraser now believed that, unless something very unusual happened, action with *Scharnhorst* would be joined at around 1630.

At about 1600 Burnett's by now routine shadowing report contained the ominous postscript 'by myself'. This was not quite fair on *Musketeer* and the three other destroyers, which were flogging along at 30kts into a head sea, regardless of any damage they might do their hulls, but he told Fraser that both *Sheffield* and *Norfolk* had had to drop back and that *Belfast* was on her own. At 1545 Capt Bain in *Norfolk* had signalled that he would have to reduce speed in order to fight a fire in a wing compartment; he would also have to alter to a steadier course, which meant that he would lose bearing. However, *Norfolk*'s damage control parties fought the fire and she rejoined Burnett at 1700. No sooner had Burnett taken this in than *Sheffield* began to fall back. Her port inner set of main gearing had failed, the shaft had to be locked and her speed was only 8kts. Repairs were made, but *Sheffield* remained ten miles behind Burnett's force for the rest of the engagement.

That left *Belfast* on her own, chasing *Scharnhorst*. *Belfast*'s engineering department were getting speeds of 28, 29 and 30kts out of the ship, despite her having been fourteen months out of dock, but she was very vulnerable and exposed. *Scharnhorst*'s after radar set was still working, and she must have had some indication that she was being followed. Capt Parham could not understand why *Scharnhorst* did not swing round and dispose of her solitary shadower:

> The *Norfolk* was damaged and *Sheffield* had dropped behind with engine trouble. We were alone, shadowing that huge ship. She was a much bigger ship than us and she only had to turn around for ten minutes to have finished us off completely.[10]

At 1617 *Scharnhorst* was picked up on *Duke of York*'s Type 273 radar bearing 20° at a range of 45,000yds. The bearing of the target remained steady, and Fraser withheld from opening fire until the range had come down to 6½ miles. At 1632 *Scharnhorst* appeared on *Duke of York*'s Type 284 main fire control radar, and shortly after that *Belfast*'s Type 273 picked up *Duke of York* bearing 176°, range 40,000yds. The plots in both ships could now be married together. At 1637 Fraser ordered his destroyers to take up positions in two sub-divisions on either side of *Duke of York*'s bow, *Savage* and *Saumarez* to port and *Stord* and *Scorpion* to starboard. At 1642 Force 2 altered course to 080° in order to clear 'A' arcs. At 1645 Fraser judged that the range was close enough to begin the action and ordered *Belfast* to illuminate the target with starshell.

Belfast opened fire at 1647 but her shells failed to illuminate the target sufficiently for *Duke of York*. Consequently, at 1647 the battleship fired four 5.25in starshell from 'P1' and 'P2' mountings. The shells burst perfectly behind the target, lighting her up as clearly as daylight. 'At first impression *Scharnhorst* appeared of enormous length and grey in colour,' wrote *Duke of York*'s Gunnery Officer, Lt-Cdr Richard Crawford RN. She was indeed a magnificent sight, with her long, raked bow powering through the tremendous seas. But the critical gaze of the watchers in *Duke of York*, *Jamaica*, *Belfast* and the other ships was concentrated on the fact that *Scharnhorst*'s three 11in turrets were trained fore and aft. For the third time that day she had been caught by surprise.

For the guns' crews on the various British ships, the waiting was over. Admiral Sir Henry Leach was, at that time, the Turret Officer in *Duke of York*'s 'A' turret:

> Then came the long-awaited order 'All positions stand to!' In an instant, tiredness, cold and seasickness were shed and all hands became poised for their individual tasks. 'Follow Director', and the huge turret swung round in line with the Director Control Tower. 'All guns load with armour-piercing and full-charge—load, load, *load*!'; the clatter of hoists as they brought up the shells and cordite charges from the magazines, the rattle of the rammers as they drove them into the chambers of the guns and the slam of the breeches as they closed were music to all. Then a great stillness for

seemingly endless minutes, disturbed only by the squelch of hydraulics as layers and trainers followed the pointers in their receivers from the Director. 'Broadsides!', and the interceptors, connecting the firing circuits right up to the Director Layer's trigger, were closed; a glance at the range receiver, whose counters were steadily, inexorably ticking down until . . . 12,000 yards . . . the fire gong rang and *crash*—all guns fired and the Battle of the North Cape had started.[11]

Duke of York's ten-gun broadside boomed out at 1651. Simultaneously two huge Battle Ensigns, the biggest White Ensigns the Signal Boatswain could find, were broken out at each masthead. In the Arctic twilight they served little to aid recognition as was their traditional purpose, but they were nevertheless an inspiring sight when illuminated by the flash of *Duke of York*'s guns.

The British battleship's first salvo straddled *Scharnhorst*, striking her low down on her hull and forward, the latter hit rendering 'A' turret inoperable. *Jamaica* joined the battle shortly after *Duke of York*, as did *Belfast* from the northward. *Norfolk*, racing to catch up after dealing with the fire, announced her arrival with a full eight-gun broadside at 1700. The vivid flash from her eight 8in guns going off together took everyone on *Belfast*'s bridge by surprise.

Despite her apparent unpreparedness, *Scharnhorst* reacted very quickly. Her first return salvo was fired at 1656—only five minutes after *Duke of York* had opened fire. She began with 5.9in starshell and followed this with a six-gun 11in broadside from 'B' and 'C' turrets. *Scharnhorst*'s shells initially fell some 2,500yds short, but she soon picked up the range and began to straddle *Duke of York* quite accurately.

The German battlecruiser had recovered well from her surprise and was proving to be a very able opponent. She steered east and kept up a constant and accurate fire with the three guns of 'Caesar' turret. However, every so often she would swing to the south the clear the arcs of 'Bruno' turret, which would loose off a few salvos before she headed east again. It was a very effective tactic and one which placed a great strain on the men in *Duke of York* and *Jamaica*. As *Duke of York*'s gunnery narrative later noted, this was the

. . . most testing time of all, for no visible effects of our own fire but large orange enemy flashes on the horizon which appeared extremely menacing. He could hit at any time.[12]

Leading Seaman Bob Thomas was 'Rate Officer' in the port forward 5.25in director. He wrote:

When the action began, the darkness soon filled with indescribable noise, the stench of cordite and flash. But more than anything else it was the approach of the red and yellow tracer that made me so very frightened. Fear was mounting [so much] that if I could have escaped from the scene I would have bolted like a rabbit.[13]

At 1713 Fraser ordered his four destroyers to attack with torpedoes. However, a great opportunity for torpedo attack had been missed. Earlier in the afternoon (at 1637) Fraser had ordered the four destroyers to be prepared to launch torpedo attacks but not to do so without a direct order from him. Fraser justified this decision on the grounds that he was best placed to judge when the destroyers could most usefully be employed. However, when at 1650 Cdr Michael Meyrick in HMS *Savage* had sighted *Scharnhorst*, he was in the ideal position—so close to *Scharnhorst* that *Duke of York*'s starshell illuminated his ship as clearly as the target. In fact, the distance between *Scharnhorst* and *Savage* became so close that the latter was obliged to retire to the south in order to open the range.

It was inevitable that, sooner or later, *Duke of York* would be hit. As the afternoon wore on, *Scharnhorst*'s gunnery got better and better. Admiral Fraser later gave three reasons for this discomforting turn of events: first, *Scharnhorst*'s gunners were settling down after being taken by surprise; second, flashless cordite was not being used by *Duke of York*'s 5.25in guns, making them a good aiming point; and last, *Duke of York*'s radar-jamming ceased when her foremast was hit and the jamming set consequently put out of action.

An 11in shell from *Scharnhorst* passed through one of the legs of *Duke of York*'s tripod foremast, travelling only feet beneath the Type 273 radar office and its three occupants, who were considerably shaken up by the experience though unharmed. However, the Type 273 warning set for which they were responsible ceased working, even though all appeared to be in order. After picking himself up, Lt H. R. K. Bates RNVR, the Radar Officer, knew that the set had to be mended:

> I switched off the 'office' lights and climbed up into the aerial compartment. By feeling about, and aided by letting a pocket torch peep between my fingers, I found the aerials pointing to the sky. I got the aerials horizontal and stabilised again by their gyroscope and the sea echoes and the echo of *Scharnhorst* were restored. So it was the terrific shock of the German eleven-inch shell passing through the mast which had made the aerials topple over.[14]

Nevertheless, the legend grew in *Duke of York*, and eventually throughout the Fleet, that the miraculous repair of the radar was due to Bates' having climbed the mast and held the wires together single-handedly. He received the nickname 'Barehand Bates', and no claims to the contrary on his part could dispel the legend, which was given official encouragement throughout Britain.

In another straddle, the mainmast was hit, causing the loss of the after receiver for the Type 281 air warning set, while one of *Scharnhorst*'s 5.9in shells wrecked Fraser's barge. However, this was the least of the Admiral's worries, for by 1708 it looked as if *Scharnhorst* was going to get away. *Scharnhorst* was far faster than *Duke of York*, and she slowly began to open the range. By 1717 she was out of sight from *Duke of York*, which had to fire her main armament by radar. By 1800 the range had opened to 18,000yds and Fraser was asking Meyrick's destroyers to spot his ship's fall of shot. Finally, at 1824 *Duke of York* checked fire, *Jamaica* having already done so at 1742. The atmosphere on the battleship's bridge was grim to say the least. Fraser signalled to Burnett and the Admiralty that he was going to cover the convoy since he felt that there was no hope of catching *Scharnhorst*. Sub-Lt Henry Leach in *Duke of York*'s 'A' turret wrote:

... steadily, gallingly, the range counters clicked up as the enemy drew away. I cannot adequately describe the frustration of those few who were in a position to realise what was happening: to have achieved surprise, got so close, and apparently done so well, and all for nothing as the enemy outpaced us into the night.[15]

But suddenly the range counters steadied and then started to close: *Scharnhorst* was slowing down, and her pursuers were gaining on her.

There is every indication from the survivors that *Scharnhorst* was again taken by surprise. However, it will never be fully known how aware Bey and Hintze were of the tactical position around them. At 1617 Bey signalled *Gruppe Nord* that he was being followed by a large ship, but he did nothing to engage the shadower or shake her off. It is also doubtful whether *Scharnhorst* was using her radar as both Bey and Hintze were afraid that the transmissions could be picked up by the British. However, many of the survivors remember announcements being made warning of radar contacts to starboard, which could only be the *Duke of York*. Why, then, was the main armament not trained on the appropriate bearing? We shall never know.

Most of *Scharnhorst*'s ship's company were stood down when the alarm went at 1600. It came as an unpleasant surprise to most of them to learn that, instead of heading for home, they were to be engaged by a capital ship.

Duke of York's first salvo scored one hit in Section XIII, about two or three feet above the waterline. The hole was swiftly patched. A second 14in shell wrecked 'A' turret. The flash ignited charges in 'A' magazine and the fire spread to 'B' magazine with potentially catastrophic consequences. Both magazines were partially flooded. However, because of the need to keep 'B' turret in action, the magazine crew were left floundering about up to their waists in icy water, trying to salvage usable ammunition to pass to the guns.

Although *Scharnhorst*'s 11in armament was well fought, her close-range weapons were poorly handled. At the beginning of the action the crews for the open 105mm mountings had to take cover. While this was an eminently practical step in view of the fact that *Scharnhorst*'s upper deck was being swept with 14in shell splinters, the order was not countermanded later, with serious consequences for the ship. *Kapitänleutnant* Wieting, the Second Gunnery Officer, ordered the 105mm guns loaded with starshell, but this order was almost immediately countermanded by *Korvettenkapitän* Walther Bredenbreuker, the Gunnery Officer, who ordered the guns loaded with armour-piercing shell. Evidently there was not much unity of purpose in *Scharnhorst*'s gunnery team.

Bey continued to inform Norway of his position, at 1656, 1732 and 1819. The last signal read: 'Opponent is firing by radar location at more than 18,000 yards. My position AC4965 [79°09´N 28°30´E]. Course 110 degrees, speed 26 knots.' At around 1820 *Scharnhorst*'s speed fell off after a 14in shell hit the starboard side and placed the starboard boiler room out of action. *Matrosenobergefreiter* Hubert Witte, a messenger on the Admiral's bridge, recalled seeing the speed recorder on the bulkhead in front of him drop rapidly from 29 to 22kts. *Korvettenkapitän (Ing)* König, *Scharnhorst*'s Engineer Officer, told Hintze that the ship could only do 8kts. However, herculean labours by his damage control parties in effecting repairs and cross-connecting other machinery got the ship going again, and she began to work up to 22kts.

At 1830 'shadows' were reported coming up on either beam. When told, Bredenbreuker snapped that he needed targets not shadows. Hubert Witte commented bitterly that those '"shadows" were tangible enough to pump us full of to pedoes'.[16]

By 1840 Cdr Meyrick's four destroyers were rapidly gaining on the enemy. The first sub-division (*Savage* and *Saumarez*) were 10,000yds off *Scharnhorst*'s stern while *Stord* and *Scorpion* were off her starboard beam. *Scharnhorst* opened fire when the destroyers had closed to below 8,000yds, but because her 105mm guns' crews were still below decks, she lacked proper anti-destroyer fire at this critical moment. She used her 20mm and 37mm weapons to fire tracer to illuminate the destroyers for her 5.9in armament, and even some 11in rounds were lobbed in the direction of the destroyers.

Savage and *Saumarez* approached from the north-west and drew most of *Scharnhorst*'s fire while *Stord* and *Scorpion* came up, apparently unseen, from the south-east. At 1849 *Scharnhorst* was illuminated by starshell fired by *Savage* and she was seen to be turning to the south. *Scorpion* and *Stord* immediately swung to starboard, each firing eight torpedoes, at a range of 21,000 and 18,000yds respectively.

For the Norwegians in *Stord* there was a sense of grim satisfaction in being able to strike back against those who had occupied their country, forced them into exile and in many cases tortured them or their families. Lt-Cdr S. Storeheill RNorN was determined that his torpedoes should not miss and pressed home his attack to the limit. *Scorpion*'s Commanding Officer thought that Storeheill was going to ram *Scharnhorst*, while Leading Telegraphist Catlow, attached to *Stord* for communications liaison duties, wrote:

> As we followed *Scorpion* into the torpedo attack, I for one did not expect to come out of it . . . We were bracing ourselves for the turn as we fired our torpedoes and the expected sound of tearing metal as *Scharnhorst* opened fire on us, but neither came. I shouted up the voicepipe to the Leading Signalman to find out what was happening. His comforting answer was 'The Captain thinks she's a U-boat. He's going in to ram. At the moment I'm trying to squeeze myself into this voicepipe and pull my tin hat over my shoulders.'[17]

Scorpion and *Stord* got one hit between them—it is practically impossible to ascribe the hit to one particular destroyer—probably because *Scharnhorst* combed the tracks. However, in manoeuvring to avoid the attack from *Scorpion* and *Stord*, *Scharnhorst* now placed herself in a perfect position for *Savage* and *Saumarez* to launch their attack. At 1853 *Savage* fired eight torpedoes and scored at least three hits on *Scharnhorst*'s port side. *Saumarez* had to endure heavy fire from the German ship during her approach and was badly damaged. An 11in shell passed through her Director Control Tower, killing eleven officers and men and wounding another eleven. A second 11in shell exploded alongside the starboard side of the ship and peppered the side and upper deck with splinters. The forced lubrication system for the starboard engine was damaged and the shaft had to be stopped. As a result,

Saumarez could only proceed at 8kts, but she nevertheless managed to fire four torpedoes at a range of 1,800yds. Admiral Fraser later wrote:

This gallant attack was practically unsupported and [was] carried out, particularly in the case of the first sub-division, in the face of heavy fire from the enemy.[18]

One torpedo struck *Scharnhorst* in a boiler room, a second hit aft and the third struck forward. However, it is impossible to be sure of the number and location of hits, on account of the many inconsistencies in the survivors' statements.

To those watching from *Duke of York*, *Jamaica*, *Belfast* and the other cruisers, the destroyer engagement was an awesome display of tracer and gun flashes. *Duke of York*'s Type 284 radar was repaired and started to track *Scharnhorst* at a range of 22,000yds at 1842. From then on, the battleship's fire control team were able to switch effortlessly from blind to visual control as *Scharnhorst*, illuminated by her gunfire, provided a point of aim.

For a time *Scharnhorst* was steering south-west, almost directly towards *Duke of York*, and the range came down rapidly. At 1901, after turning 90 degrees to starboard to open 'A' arcs, *Duke of York* and *Jamaica* opened fire at a range of 10,400yds. It seems that *Scharnhorst* was yet again taken completely by surprise, and *Duke of York*'s salvo hit aft, causing immense damage. *Duke of York* now began to fire rapid 14in salvos at the German and scored many hits which literally tore the ship apart.

It was now clear to Bey and Hintze that there was no escape, and their signals to *Gruppe Nord* took on a desperate yet defiant tone. At 1732 Bey signalled that he was 'surrounded by heavy units'. At 1825 he signalled: 'To the *Führer*. We shall fight to the last shell.' At 1902 he signalled to Dönitz: 'Most immediate. *Scharnhorst* will ever reign supreme.' Just as this last signal was being sent, its recipient was probably having the most difficult interview of his career as he informed Hitler of *Scharnhorst*'s predicament. The *Führer* took the news well, doubtless comforted by Dönitz's hopes that *Scharnhorst* would be able to fight her way out of trouble.[19]

While *Duke of York* and *Jamaica* contined to fire at *Scharnhorst* from the west, *Norfolk* opened fire from the northward but checked after only a couple of salvos as she had trouble in picking out the right target. *Belfast*, too, opened fire and scored a number of hits.

The battle was now approaching its end. Between 1901 and 1928 *Scharnhorst*'s speed fell to 5kts and she steadied on to a northerly course. Lt Vernon Merry RNVR, Fraser's Flag Lieutenant, watched as *Duke of York*'s gunfire slammed into the German ship:

Every time we hit her, it was just like stoking up a huge fire, with flames and sparks flying up the chimney. Every time a salvo landed, there was this great gust of flame roaring up into the air, just as though we were prodding a huge fire with a poker.[20]

The range was now so low that *Duke of York* was firing on a virtually flat trajectory, and it was possible for those on board the battleship to watch the tracer bands on the shells glowing as they sped toward the target now less than three miles away.

At 1919 Fraser ordered *Belfast* and *Jamaica* to close *Scharnhorst* and finish her off with torpedoes. *Duke of York* continued firing, loosing off over 28 broadsides in all and getting 21 straddles. At 1928 she checked fire to allow *Belfast* and *Jamaica* to launch their torpedoes.

By this time *Scharnhorst* was barely moving, with unco-ordinated fire coming from her secondary armament. *Jamaica* fired three torpedoes to port at 1925, one of which misfired, but claimed no hits. Two minutes later *Belfast* fired three torpedoes, one of which may have hit (this is considered unlikely, although Burnett would claim to his dying day that it was his flagship which had administered the *coup de grâce*). Both cruisers then hauled round to fire their remaining torpedoes. At 1937 *Jamaica* fired three to starboard at *Scharnhorst*, which was lying dead in the water and beam-on to her attacker. No hits were observed as the battlecruiser was now almost completely obscured by smoke, but underwater explosions were heard after the correct running interval and it was assumed that two torpedoes had gone home. Two minutes earlier, at 1935, *Belfast* had turned to fire her port tubes, but by this time *Musketeer* and the three destroyers of the 36th Division had joined the mêlée, and there were so many ships in the area that the cruiser broke away to the southward to clear the area and await a more favourable opportunity.

The four destroyers of the 36th Division (*Musketeer*, *Matchless*, *Virago* and *Opportune*) had had a long haul from the west to catch up with the *Scharnhorst*:

After the *Duke of York* got into action, I streaked at 32–33 knots to the east, keeping outside *Scharnhorst*'s radar range to the north of her, trying to gain bearing for a torpedo attack should she attempt to break away to the north-east.[21]

Fisher had tried to contact Meyrick in *Savage* to launch a co-ordinated attack but had been unable to do so. However, after such a long chase through the rough seas, Fisher was not to be baulked of his prey at the last moment and his four destroyers raced into the attack. As they closed they could see *Scharnhorst* under attack:

At the end we were coming up fast astern of *Scharnhorst* and as starshell cast an orange glow over the scene we could smell the fires raging in her as she was pounded by *Duke of York*'s guns. It was sight never to be forgotten as these salvos of shells, showing red tracer lights in their bases, curved through a graceful arc in the night sky, some of them to produce a great, slowly rising, red glow in the target.[22]

The four destroyers closed *Scharnhorst* by sub-divisions from the north and astern. The battlecruiser was by then steering an erratic course from north-east to south-west, but by the time they fired she was lying stopped on a south-westerly heading. At 1930 *Musketeer* and *Matchless* attacked from the port side, followed by *Opportune* and *Virago* from starboard. *Opportune* fired two salvos at 1931 and 1933 at ranges of 2,100 and 2,800yds respectively and claimed two hits. *Virago*, a ship less than two months out of the builders and with 70 per cent of her company having never been to sea before, followed her in and fired seven torpedoes at 1934 at a range of 2,800yds and observed two hits.

Matchless went in as close as 1,000yds and fired four torpedoes at 1933 and observed two, possibly three, hits between the funnel and the base of the mainmast and then withdrew to the west. She was unable to fire because the training gear of her torpedo tubes had been strained by a heavy sea. As the attack developed, her tubes had to be trained round by hand from port to starboard. As this was being done, waves broke over the bridge and severed all communication between the command and the torpedo men, with the result that the tubes were not turned in time. She came round without firing but ran in for another attack, but by that time *Scharnhorst* had sunk.

The torpedoes of the 26th Division administered the *coup de grâce*. *Duke of York* steered north to clear the area since three cruisers and eight destroyers were milling around the stricken battlecruiser. All that was visible of *Scharnhorst* was a dull glow through the smoke. No ship saw her sink, but it seems fairly certain that she went down after a heavy explosion which was heard and felt in several ships at about 1945. She was last seen by *Jamaica*, *Matchless* and *Virago* at about 1938. Ten minutes later, when *Belfast* came round to deliver her second torpedo attack, it was clear from the amount of wreckage in the water that the ship had gone. The position was marked as approximately 72°16′N 28°41′E.

In *Duke of York*, *Scharnhorst* suddenly disappeared off the PPI[23] and there was a sharp exchange between the officers on the bridge, who, disbelieving of radar's properties, felt that the target had got away and wanted her found again—and quickly. In fact, the radar was so accurate that those watching the screen could see the 'blip' that had once been the pride of the *Kriegsmarine* became smaller and smaller and eventually fade away. At 1948 *Belfast* fired starshell to illuminate the area. Capt Parham remembered that he saw 'a raft packed with shouting or screaming oil-covered German sailors. It was a dreadful sight.'[24]

The lack of hard information about whether or not *Scharnhorst* had sunk was alarming to Fraser. Having worn a mask of apparent indifference all day, he now began sending signals asking Burnett if *Scharnhorst* had in fact gone down. At 1951 he ordered the area to be cleared except for ships with torpedoes and one destroyer with a searchlight. One of these vessels was *Matchless*, which had been unable to attack earlier. However as her ship's company were preparing for action, at 2000 they were ordered to 'Rescue Stations' instead. A large scrambling net was hung over the side and sailors stood ready with lines, lifejackets and boat hooks. Those on deck could see a good deal of wreckage and red lights from lifejackets winking in the darkness. In the heavy sea running, rescue was going was going to be a difficult business. Six ratings were picked up from a liferaft. They were cold, wet through and covered in oil fuel. In the same fashion as other survivors, they were stripped, washed, given dry clothing and rum to fetch up any oil they had swallowed and put to sleep in hammocks in the forward mess deck.

HMS *Scorpion* was also in the area, sweeping the water with her searchlight. Like those on board *Matchless*, her ship's company could see the wreckage and fuel oil in the water and hear the cries of men swimming in the icy sea. Lt-Cdr W. S. Clouston RN, *Scorpion*'s Commanding Officer, stopped up-wind from a large group of men in the water, leaving them in his ship's lee, and drifted gently down on them. His seamanship won the admiration of those whom he rescued. *Scorpion* picked up thirty of the many men swimming around her; Clouston estimated the number to be as many as one hundred, although he believed that a lot of these were dead. Several drifted away or were too cold to grasp the heaving lines thrown to them. The heavy seas hampered the rescue, as did the large amount of wooden wreckage in the water through which the frozen men had to be pulled.

Fraser now had the evidence that *Scharnhorst* had sunk. At 2004 *Scorpion* signalled that she was picking up *Scharnhorst*'s survivors. At 2018 Fraser asked if *Scharnhorst* had sunk and received confirmation from Clouston at 2030. At 2035 *Duke of York* broadcast at full power to Scapa W/T, and to anyone else who was listening,[25] '*Scharnhorst* sunk', to which he received the reply at 2136, 'Your 26/2035. Grand. Well done.'

Fraser ordered the search for survivors to be ended at 2040. 'Ultra' reports indicated that U-boats of the '*Eisenbart*' group had been sent to the area to search for survivors and had been released from the restriction on attacking warships. After a brief, and insecure, exchange of signals with Burnett over the TBS (Talk Between Ships) R/T, Fraser headed for the Kola Inlet, followed by Burnett's cruisers and the destroyers, the ships arriving there at various times on the 27th. *Saumarez*, which had been badly damaged by *Scharnhorst*'s fire, was lagging behind, doing 8kts on her port engine. Just after 2000 her Commanding Officer, Lt-Cdr E. W. Walmsley DSC RN, made a very optimistic efficiency signal stating that two of his four 4.7in guns were in action together with three torpedoes. She was later joned by *Savage* and *Scorpion* as escorts, and Walmsley gradually raised speed until *Saumarez* was making 15kts. At noon on 27 December she stopped and half-masted colours to bury her dead, and that evening she secured alongside the Vaenga Pier in the Kola Inlet.

The German survivors were able to provide some details of the end of *Scharnhorst*. From when *Duke of York* had opened fire at 1901, *Scharnhorst* had been pounded to pieces. 'C' turret had continued to fire until the end, using local control, until all ammuntion had been exhausted. The order had then been given to pass ammunition aft from 'A' turret. None of *Duke of York*'s shells had penetrated the armoured deck, although they did terrible execution above it, leaving mangled wreckage through which the aid parties had struggled to remove an increasing number of casualties. Since none of *Scharnhorst*'s medical staff survived, it is presumed that they, like their colleagues on *Bismarck* two and half years earlier, had stayed with their patients until the end.

Above the armoured deck, the 'P1' 15cm mounting had been hit and wrecked, the hangar had been hit and the aircraft destroyed, causing a large fire, the starboard forward 105mm mounting had been hit, a shell had landed on the starboard side near the funnel and another had landed on the 'tween deck on the port side. Others had hit in Section X, on the Battery Deck, on the starboard after single 15cm mounting and on a quadruple 20mm mounting on the starboard side which was seen to fly through the air. The starboard anchor had been carried away while another hit had broken the cable, which had begun to run out. *Scharnhorst*'s boatswain had gone out on to the forecastle to check on the damage but he had been washed overboard. 'B' turret had been hit and the ventilation system put out of action. Conditions in the turret had become unbearable: every time the breeches were opened thick black smoke had poured out, which had made it impossible to see a thing despite the bright lamps. The upper deck was littered with the bodies of the dead, slowly being washed overboard as the ship heeled.

Despite this pounding, *Scharnhorst* had been in no imminent danger of sinking. As her survivors cockily claimed, gunfire alone would never have sunk her. When *Duke of York* had checked fire at 1928, *Scharnhorst* had suffered hits by fourteen 14in shells. She had also been hit by about a dozen 8in and 6in shells from *Norfolk*, *Jamaica*, *Belfast* and *Sheffield* and 5.25in shells from *Duke of York*'s secondary armament together with uncounted projectiles from *Savage*'s 4.5in and the other destroyers' 4.7in guns. Excluding 155 rounds of starshell fired by *Duke of York* and the innumerable rounds from the destroyers, Forces 1 and 2 had fired a total of 2,195 shells of various calibres that day.

It was the torpedoes that had done the damage. After the torpedo hit in No 1 boiler room on the starboard side, the water had risen above the plates and the crew had been ordered to leave after drawing the fires. Despite König's efforts, speed could not be restored. The torpedo hits had had the effect of preventing the damage control teams from dealing with the problems caused by the previous hit, thus dissipating their efforts and ensuring that very little could be achieved. After a torpedo had struck Section III on the starboard side, the damage control party sent to deal with it had found that flooding could only be controlled by sealing off the whole section, trapping the 25 men of the after damage control team who were already there. A torpedo had finally put 'B' turret out of action, jamming the training and elevating mechanism. The handling room crews had climbed up to the turret to escape but had found the doors jammed. Minutes of frantic wrestling had finally got one door open just as the ship was sinking, but only *Matrosegefreiter* Rudi Birke survived.

At about 1930 Hintze had ordered that 'Manoeuvre V' be carried out. This involved the destruction of codes and other secret equipment but also the shutting of watertight doors to ensure that the ship would stay afloat longer and that more men would have the chance to escape. Another torpedo hit had been noted on the starboard side at this time—the eighth on that side of the ship. By 1940 the list to starboard had become extreme, and some time between 1940 and 1945 Hintze had given the order to abandon ship.

In the confusion of *Scharnhorst*'s last moments, it had been each man for himself. *Matrosengefreiter* Helmut Boekhoff, a loader on a starboard twin 37mm mounting, remembered that the ship had been on fire from stem to stern; he had climbed, with others, to the top of the bridge superstructure and had been slung into the water as the ship capsized. Rudi Birke had been washed into the sea as he climbed out of the turret. The Executive Officer, *Fregattenkapitän* Dominick, had stood on the upper deck, behaving as if the whole affair were nothing more than an excercise in Kiel Bay, helping seamen who had clambered up from below to put on their lifejackets.

Oberbootmansmaat Wilhelm Godde, on the Admiral's bridge, had waited until the sea was washing over the bridge wing before leaving. He, like every other man on the bridge, had shaken hands with *Kapitän zur See* Hintze and *Konteradmiral*

Bey. Hintze had given his lifejacket to a junior seaman who had mislaid his own. Godde made a point of mentioning later, as did many other survivors, that there had been no breakdown of discipline and no panic: *Scharnhorst*'s ship's company had conducted themselves splendidly in this, their most terrible hour. Both Bey and Hintze survived the ship and were seen swimming in the water (thus disposing of the rumours that they had killed themselves on the bridge). Both men subsequently drowned, but at one stage Hintze was very near to be being picked up by HMS *Scorpion*.

The men in the water had either used their lifejackets for support or had clung to rafts and other wreckage. The sea had been rough, but fuel oil from the ship had had the effect of calming the waves. Wilhelm Goode had found a raft but it had been overloaded: instead, he had clung to a baulk of timber used by the damage control parties. While clinging to this log, he had seen *Mechanikergefreiter* Johann Merkle, a Quarters Armourer from 'C' turret, walking along the upturned hull of the doomed ship, before he swam off on a raft. The survivors had cheered or sung while in the water; the British had interpreted this noise as screaming, but the men were probably doing something to stay warm. Helmut Boekhoff remembered:

> I saw all the blokes screaming and shouting '*Scharnhorst*—hip, hip, hooray, hip, hip, hooray!' and then I was certain that the song was coming up, 'On the Seaman's Grave No Roses Grow'. By that time I looked round and saw the ship turn right round and I saw the propeller still turning because . . . the English had shot a starshot across us. Then all of a sudden I saw her going down, come back up again, then all of a sudden finally she went down. And as she went down I heard this tremendous trummel in my stomach and my legs, you know. There was a big explosion below. And by that time all I thought about was to get away . . . you know, get saved. . . When I looked round I see these blokes, they're swimming between all these bits and still shouting 'Heil, our *Führer*', and, you know, '*Scharnhorst*—hip, hip, hooray' again and again, and I thought '*Pscht*, what a waste.'[26]

Thirty-six men were picked up out of *Scharnhorst*'s ship's company of over 1,900. No officers were rescued, the senior survivor being *Oberbootmansmaat* Wilhelm Godde. The survivors were taken to Kola, where they were transferred to *Duke of York* for the journey to Britain. There was a brief moment of panic when they saw that the vessel transferring them to *Duke of York* was a Soviet tug and they feared that they were destined for Siberia. But their worries were groundless, and they soon found themslves being well looked after on board the British battleship.

Duke of York arrived back at Scapa Flow on New Year's Day 1944. She appeared out of the mist to greet the war correspondents who had not been allowed to sail and who were bobbing about in a fleet of drifters waiting for her. Flying her Battle Ensign, and followed by *Jamaica* and seven destroyers, she proceeded to her moorings, receiving the cheers of every ship's company of the vessels in the Flow. It was an emotional homecoming. Just as soon as the battleship was secured and the prisoners were disembarked, Fraser declared the day to be Christmas Day for everyone who had taken part in the action, the sailors having spent the real Christmas Day at sea and closed up at their action stations.

Now that the battle was over, there was time for celebration. Messages of congratulation poured in to HMS *Duke of York* from the War Cabinet, from the First Lord of the Admiralty, from President Roosevelt and even from Marshal Stalin. But there was also time for reflection. The gaiety was tinged by the thought that nearly 2,000 German sailors had gone to their deaths in the icy waters of the Arctic. Lt Stanley Walker RN, in HMS *Sheffield*, wrote:

All that was left of a 26,000-ton ship was some 36 survivors and a few pieces of shrapnel. One couldn't help feeling a little sorry for those who had perished. It was a cold, dark night, with little chance of survival in those icy waters. However, it might just as easily have been one, or indeed all, of us.[27]

Sub-Lt Henry Leach, in *Duke of York*, expressed very similar sentiments:

Almost a blankness or shock at what had been done. Some relief that it had gone the way it had. Little exultation—the closing scenes were too grim for that and the remoteness of actions at sea precludes hate between sailors. Pride in achievement. And a great weariness.[28]

Capt Frederick Parham of HMS *Belfast* echoed the feeling of weariness:

The best way of remembering that day would be to read the dispatches while being rocked about in a refrigerator lit by a single candle with someone banging on the outside with a large hammer.[29]

Although the British ships had all escaped serious damage from *Scharnhorst*, they had all suffered from the blast effects of their own gunfire. In *Duke of York* every mushroom-head ventilator on the forecastle had been torn off and water had flooded down on to the mess decks, which had to be pumped out by the 14in turrets' crews working in two watches. Every ship had sustained similar damage to a greater or lesser degree.

Fraser was now free to write his Report of Proceedings to the Admiralty, containing a full account of the battle. He gave his flagship full credit for her role:

Duke of York fought hard and well, having drawn, for over an hour and a half, the whole of the enemy's fire. She was frequently straddled ahead, astern and on the beam. That she was not hit was probably due to masterly handling aided by accurate advice from the plot. There is no doubt that *Duke of York* was the principle factor in the battle. She fought the *Scharnhorst* at night and she won. This in no way detracts from the achievements of the 'S' class destroyers, who with very great gallantry and dash pressed in unsupported, to the closest ranges, to deliver their attacks, being subjected the while to the whole firepower of the enemy.[30]

Fraser's praise of his flagship was not universally shared. Surgeon Lt J. C. H. Dunlop RN, the junior Medical Officer in HMS *Sheffield*, wrote:

They fought each other for about three hours—and fought extremely well—and as a matter of fact at the end of that time old *Duke of York* hadn't achieved a great deal (in spite of all the blah in the papers). The critical blow was delivered in the form of a very courageous attack by a Norwegian destroyer which (under 'cover' of darkness made into daylight by starshells etc) closed to within 400 yards of the big ship's guns (one shell from which could have sunk her) and delivered a torpedo attack which completely changed the whole picture.[31]

Fraser's dispatch also included the traditional recommendations for gallantry awards. The suggestions were acted upon with considerable speed by the Admiralty and the first list was published on 4 January, three days after *Duke of York* had secured at Scapa. There was a GCB for Fraser (who would later collect the Order of Suvorov from the USSR), a KBE for Burnett, DSOs for Addis (*Sheffield*), Bain (*Norfolk*), Parham (*Belfast*) and Russell (*Duke of York*), a Bar to his DSC for Walmsley (*Saumarez*) and DSCs for Fisher (*Musketeer*) and Clouston (*Scorpion*). There was also a DSC for 'Barehand' Bates and a DSM each for the two seamen who had been in the radar office with him when *Scharnhorst*'s shell roared beneath them. The award of a DSC to Bates and the DSM to his two ratings, Able Seamen Badkin and Whitton, reflected the role which radar had played in the battle. Radar enabled *Duke of York* to 'find, fix and fight the *Scharnhorst*'.[32] Without it the German ship would have simply slipped away into the night. Fraser could not mention, however, that other asset which had proved instrumental in providing him with information about German intentions: 'Ultra''s role in the battle would remain secret for another twenty-odd years.

Writing on 2 January 1944, the Defence Correspondent of *The Sunday Times*, Capt Russell Grenfell, remarked that the sinking of *Scharnhorst* was

. . . a model operation of its kind, in which all concerned on our side seem to have played their parts with almost text-book correctitude. By comparison with this masterly British performance, the *Scharnhorst*'s conduct seems extraordinarily vacillating and irresolute. She should have been quite strong enough to break through the British cruiser screen and play havoc with the convoy. Yet she waited about three vital hours between two half-hearted and ineffectual advances, and finally went down with great loss of life without achieving anything at all.[33]

What of the two convoys whose presence had been the cause of the action? RA.55A went through unscathed to the United Kingdom with only one *Luftwaffe* sighting report on 27 December to indicate that the Germans had ever been aware of her presence. The outward-bound convoy, JW.55B, still had several U-boats in contact on the 26th, but by the next day there was only one left on the convoy's starboard quarter—the remainder had departed to search the area where *Scharnhorst* had sunk for survivors.

On 29 December JW.55B entered the Kola Inlet at 1030 intact, although one ship, *Ocean Gypsy*, which had straggled from the convoy, came in alone some hours later. The sailing of the eight ships of RA.55B on New Year's Eve completed the picture for 1943: all eight arrived at Loch Ewe on 8 January 1944 without loss.

The sinking of *Scharnhorst* eliminated the immediate surface threat to the convoys since *Tirpitz* was still under repair following the damage inflicted during

Operation 'Source'. However, throughout the summer of 1944 the presence of 'The Lone Queen of the North' in her Arctic lair would exert a considerable influence on convoy operations.

NOTES TO CHAPTER 12

1. PRO ADM.199/913, 'Report of Proceedings of the Flag Officer Commanding the 10th Cruiser Squadron (CS10)'.
2. Holman, Gordon, *The King's Cruisers*, Hodder & Stoughton, London, 1947, p.162.
3. *ibid.*
4. PRO ADM/199/913, 'Report of Proceedings of the Commanding Officer of HMS *Norfolk*'.
5. PRO ADM.199/913, 'Report of Proceedings of the Flag Officer Commanding the 10th Cruiser Squadron (CS10)'.
6. Dönitz, Karl, *Ten Years and Twenty Days*, Greenhill Books, 1990., p.217
7. Signals intelligence.
8. Winton, John, *Death of the Scharnhorst*, Antony Bird Publications, 1983, p.166.
9. Admiral Sir Frederick Parham to author, 7 September 1985.
10. *ibid.*
11. Admiral Sir Henry Leach, quoted in Winton, *op. cit.*, p.183.
12. PRO ADM.199/913.
13. Thomas, R. O. L., *HMS Duke of York 1941–45*, unpublished TS account.
14. H. R. Bates to John Winton, 25 February 1982, quoted in Winton, *op. cit.*.
15. Leach, *ibid.*
16. PRO ADM1/16833, 'Interrogation of *Scharnhorst* survivors: Interrogation of *Marineobergefreiter* Hubert Witte'.
17. Winton, *op. cit.*, p.126.
18. PRO ADM.199/913, 'Commander in Chief's Despatch'.
19. *Führer*'s Conferences on Naval Affairs.
20. Merry, quoted in Winton, *op. cit.*, p.134.
21. PRO ADM.199/913, Commander Fisher's despatch, para. 76.
22. *ibid.*
23. Plan Position Indicator, an early form of radar screen.
24. Admiral Sir Frederick Parham to author, 7 September 1985.
25. Because of problems encountered in contacting Scapa W/T early in the battle, Cdr Peter Dawnay, the Fleet Wireless Officer, ordered all signals to be transmitted direct to the Admiralty by ship/shore frequency. These signals were re-broadcast by the Admiralty so that staff officers all over the world were able to follow the course of the battle.
26. BBC documentary, 'The Life and Death of the *Scharnhorst*', 26 December 1971.
27. TS account by Cdr Stanley Walker RN, included in the papers of Surgeon Lt J. C. H. Dunlop RNVR, Department of Documents, Imperial War Museum 82/13/1.
28. Leach, quoted in Winton, *op. cit.*
29. Admiral Sir Frederick Parham to author, 7 September 1985.
30. PRO ADM.199/913, Commander-in-Chief's Despatch.
31. Papers of Surgeon Lt J. C. H. Dunlop RNVR, *op. cit.*
32. PRO ADM.199/913, HMS *Duke of York*, gunnery narrative.
33. *The Sunday Times*, 2 January 1944.

Chapter 13

'The Lone Queen of the North'

It is a great relief to us to have this brute where we have long wanted her.—Winston Churchill, on the sinking of *Tirpitz*

The sinking of *Scharnhorst* left the *Kriegsmarine* with no sea-going capital ships in northern waters. *Tirpitz* was still under repair, so there was no longer any need for the Admiralty to give each convoy battleship cover, and all efforts were directed against the two dozen U-boats based in Norway which now constituted the main threat—enhanced with the recent introduction by the Germans of the new T5 acoustic torpedo, which homed in on the noise generated by the target's propellers.

Between January and April 1944 four eastbound and four westbound convoys were run, with the loss of only five merchant ships and two escorts, all torpedoed by U-boats. In the summer of 1944 the convoys were suspended because, in addition to the long hours of daylight in northern latitudes (which favoured the Germans), all shipping was required for Operation 'Overlord', the invasion of Normandy (and the long-promised 'Second Front'). These convoys were all heavily escorted, and they threw a great strain on the ships and men of the fleet required to escort them. The inhospitable climate was also a constant factor. Yet the convoys run in the first part of 1944 went virtually unmolested compared to the ordeal suffered by those of 1942. Lastly, the year saw the end of the big bogeyman of the convoys, the German battleship *Tirpitz*, which, having survived a multiplicity of attacks by submarines and various land- and carrier-based aircraft, was finally dispatched on 12 November 1944.

The first convoy of 1944, JW.56A, consisted of twenty ships and left Loch Ewe on 12 January. Local Escort was provided by the minesweepers *Orestes* and *Ready* (to 22 January), the corvettes *Borage* and *Wallflower* (to 18 January) and *Poppy* and *Dianella* and the destroyer *Inconstant* (all three to 27 January). The convoy was also covered by the sloop *Cygnet* from 12 to 15 January and the destroyers *Savage* and *Stord* (RNorN) from 16 to 27 January.

Three days after sailing, the convoy ran into heavy weather and was compelled to seek shelter in Akureyi, where it arrived on 18 January. The bad weather forced the ships to remain there until 21 January, but five of them, *Charles Bullfinch*, *Jefferson Davis*, *John A. Quitman*, *Joseph N. Nicollet* and *Nathaniel Alexander*, did not proceed owing to storm damage. From Akureyi to the Kola Inlet the escort was provided by *Hardy* (Senior Officer), *Inconstant*, *Obdurate*, *Offa*, *Savage*, *Venus*, *Vigilant*, *Virago* and *Stord*. Although there was no battleship cover, the cruisers *Kent* (Flag-Rear Admiral A. F. E. Palliser), *Berwick* and *Bermuda* were present. The Soviet destroyers *Gremyashchi*, *Grozny* and *Razumny* provided the Eastern Local Escort from 27 January.

The *Luftwaffe* failed to find JW.56A, but the Germans had been forewarned of the convoy's sailing by agents in Iceland.[1] As a result of these reports, ten U-boats were formed into the *'Isegrim'* group and ordered to form a patrol line between Bear Island and the North Cape. From midday on 25 January contact was made by *U739*, the most northerly boat, and the convoy was attacked in the dark during the afternoon of 25 and night of 25/26 January. This was the first concentrated attack on an Arctic convoy by a U-boat pack. *U965* (*Kapitänleutnant* Klaus Ohling), *U601* (*Kapitänleutnant* Otto Hansen) and *U360* (*Kapitänleutnant* Klaus Becker) each went in four times and *U425* (*Kapitänleutnant* Heinz Bentzien) twice, while *U737* (*Kapitänleutnant* Paul Brasack), *U278* (*Kapitänleutnant* Joachim Franze) and *U314* (*Kapitänleutnant* Georg-Wilhelm Basse) all engaged the escorts with T5 acoustic torpedoes.

The results of this concerted effort were quite meagre. At 1833 on 25 January Becker in *U360* fired a T5 at HMS *Obdurate* which wrecked the starboard propeller and badly buckled the destroyer's stern. For over four hours the ship was virtually helpless until very efficient damage control had shored up the stern and restored power steering. *Obdurate* parted company and returned to the Kola Inlet independently. At 2012 on 25 January *U278* (*Kapitänleutnant* Joachim Franze) sank the Commodore's ship, *Penelope Barker*. The Commodore, Capt I. W. Whitehorn RN, transferred to *Fort Bellingham*, which was in turn torpedoed by *U360* at 0015 on the 26th. Five minutes later *U716* (*Oberleutant zur See* Hans Dunkelberg) sank the *Andrew G. Curtin*. *Fort Bellingham* stubbornly refused to sink, and *Obdurate* went alongside to transfer her Medical Officer, Surgeon Lt M. Hood RNVR. Five hours later *Fort Bellingham* was finally dispatched by *U957* (*Oberleutant zur See* Gerd Schaar). Schaar surfaced to rescue survivors, but Hood had refused to leave a patient on board the sinking merchant ship and was drowned. These were the only attacks on the convoy, which arrived in the Kola Inlet on 28 January. Nevertheless, the increased scale of the U-boat attacks on JW.56A caused Admiral Fraser to modify the arrangements that had been made for other convoys: the sailing of the homeward-bound RA.56A was postponed, and JW.56A's escorts were ordered to meet the following JW.56B and reinforce it in the danger area.

The seventeen ships of JW.56B had left Loch Ewe on 22 January. The Local Escort consisted of the destroyers *Wrestler*, *Whitehall* and *Westcott*, the corvettes *Rhododendron* and *Honeysuckle* and the minesweepers *Onyx* and *Hydra*. On 26 January the destroyer escort joined, consisting of *Milne* (Senior Officer), *Mahratta*, *Musketeer*, *Opportune*, *Scourge* and *Huron* (RCN). *Meteor* arrived on 28 January. On 29 January the destroyers from JW.56A, less *Obdurate*, joined. Cruiser cover was provided by *Kent* (Flag), *Berwick* and *Bermuda*.

The convoy was sighted at midday on 29 January by *U956* (*Kapitänleutnant* Hans-Dieter Mohs) and reported. However, Mohs had a hard time defending himself from the escorts, who must have picked up his sighting report and run down the bearing. He fired three T5 torpedoes at escorts but without success. Nevertheless, his report had got through, for *Kapitän zur See* Peters, the U-boat commander in Norway, formed the *'Werewolf'* group, made up of the *'Isegrim'* boats reinforced by *U956*, *U472*, *U313*, *U973* and *U990*.

By the morning of 30 January *U957* had attacked four times and *U737, U601, U278* and *U472* twice, while *U313* (Schweiger) had fired T5s at the escorts. The sole result of all this this endeavour was the torpedoing of HMS *Hardy* (Capt W. G. A. Robson RN) by U278. The destroyer's wreck later had to be finished off by HMS *Venus*. The U-boats did not escape unscathed: on 30 January *U314* was sunk by *Whitehall* and *Westcott*. As with JW.56A, the U-boats confined their efforts to one night's work, and the convoy entered the Kola Inlet without loss on 1 February, the ships destined for Archangel arriving a day later.

The Germans made much of their operations against the two convoys, claiming to have sunk seven destroyers and four merchant ships and to have damaged another four destroyers and six merchant ships. The basis of such optimistic reports was undoubtedly the extensive use of the T5 acoustic torpedo, which had a tendency to explode in the target ship's wake if it missed astern. Such explosions were often interpreted as hits, and the shore staff were frequently not over-insistent on corroborative evidence in support of a claim. However, a further reason for the German claims must have been Dönitz's desire to recover some prestige following the loss of *Scharnhorst*.

The experience of JW.56B convinced Fraser that a single large convoy would allow him to use his forces more effectively, and so the 39 ships in north Russia were returned to the United Kingdom in one sailing, RA.56, which had an escort which never fell below 26 vessels, including the cruiser cover. The Eastern Local Escort was provided by the minesweepers *Gleaner* and *Seagull*. The Close Escort consisted of *Westcott* and *Whitehall, Cygnet, Dianella, Oxlip, Poppy, Rhododendron, Halcyon, Hussar* and *Speedwell*. The Destroyer Escort was immense and consisted of *Offa, Opportune, Savage, Venus, Vigilant, Inconstant, Mahratta, Meteor, Milne, Musketeer, Scourge, Huron* and *Stord*; three extra destroyers, *Swift, Verulam* and *Obedient*, were specially sailed from Scapa Flow to augment these ships. The Western Local Escort consisted of *Wrestler, Borage, Honeysuckle, Wallflower, Cockatrice, Loyalty, Rattlesnake* and *Ready*, while cruiser cover was provided by *Kent, Berwick* and *Bermuda*. RA.56 neatly avoided the boats of the 'Werewolf' group which were deployed across its path. A *Luftwaffe* sighting report on 6 February obligingly indicated that the convoy was sailing on a reciprocal course, so the U-boats searched in the wrong direction. RA.56 arrived in Loch Ewe without loss on 11 February.

The idea of a single large convoy continued with the next outward-bound sailing, JW.57, which comprised 43 ships. In view of the increasing tempo of U-boat attacks on convoys to the Soviet Union, it was decided to augment the escort with a light cruiser configured as a flagship to control aircraft operations. The improved situation in the Atlantic meant that it was also possible to release, from Western Approaches Command, an escort carrier with dedicated anti-submarine aircraft embarked. For JW.57 the cruiser HMS *Black Prince* and the escort carrier HMS *Chaser* were allocated.

The convoy sailed on 20 February. The Local Escort, which was present until 22 February, consisted of *Hydra, Loyalty, Orestes, Rattlesnake, Burdock* and *Dianella*. The Close Escort from 20 to 28 February consisted of *Beagle, Boadicea, Keppel,*

Walker, Bluebell, Camellia, Lotus and *Rhododendron.* On 22 February HMS *Black Prince,* wearing the flag of Vice-Admiral I. G. Glennie, joined with the destroyers *Mahratta, Matchless, Meteor, Milne, Obedient, Offa, Onslaught, Oribi, Savage, Serapis, Swift, Verulam* and *Vigilant.* *Chaser* also arrived on 22 February with a Western Approaches Support Group, B1, consisting of *Wanderer, Watchman, Byron* and *Strule.* *Chaser* and the B1 ships would remain with the convoy until it had cleared the Bear Island danger area.

A Ju 88 picked up the convoy on 23 February, followed by an FW 200. On receipt of their signals, the *'Werewolf'* group (*U956, U674, U425, U601, U362, U739, U713, U313, U312* and *U990*) deployed across its path together with the *'Hartmut'* group consisting of *U472, U315, U673* and *U366.* On 24 February an FW 200 maintained contact with the convoy, despite being attacked by Martlet fighters from HMS *Chaser,* and homed *U425, U601, U739* and *U713* on to the convoy. However, *U713* was sunk by HMS *Keppel.* The Swordfish aircraft from HMS *Chaser* played a considerable role in driving the U-boats off with frequent depth-charge and rocket-projectile attacks. On 25 February Catalina 'M' of No 201 Squadron, operating at maximum range from Sullom Voe in the Shetlands, found and attacked *U601* (*Kapitänleutnant* Otto Hansen). The aircraft dropped both its depth charges and the U-boat was seen to sink. A small group of eight or ten survivors was spotted struggling in the water but were later lost to sight in a snowstorm. In the face of such a determined defence, the U-boat attack was frustrated, and on 28 February the convoy entered the Kola Inlet without loss to any of the merchant ships.

However, on 25 February *U990* (*Kapitänleutnant* Hubert Nordheimer) had torpedoed the destroyer HMS *Mahratta* (Lt-Cdr E. A. F. Drought RN), which had been stationed at the stern of the convoy. The loss of *Mahratta* might not have occurred had the Home Fleet's destroyers been as well honed in anti-submarine warfare as their colleagues in Western Approaches Command: the latter specialized in U-boat hunting and were wise to the *modus operandi* of, and the latest weapons used by, the U-boats.[2] Lt-Cdr Reginald Whinney was in command of HMS *Wanderer,* one of the ships of the B1 group, and wrote of his concern that only two destroyers were covering the stern of the convoy when it had been promulgated that U-boats were making successful attacks undetected down-wind and down-sea. However, he did not signal his concern to Glennie because 'I've already had one flea in the ear today and the air is already humming with signals'.[3] Whinney then recalled that

Later it happened. The destroyer *Mahratta,* one of the two ships astern of the convoy, called up the Admiral on R/T. Up on the bridge I heard the educated and entirely calm voice—it could have been [of] Drought, the Commanding Officer who had been at prep school and again at Dartmouth with me: 'Have been hit by a torpedo aft and am stopped.' This was obviously a Gnat which had homed on the destroyer's propeller noises. This report was followed by a pause before the next: 'Have been struck by a second torpedo.'

Then there was another pause; probably Drought was trying to get all watertight doors shut and summing up the desperate situation. 'Life-saving equipment is being cleared away.' Still the same calm, unemotional tones. Then, probably due to a fault in the R/T set, an unhappy warble developed in the voice: 'We are abandoning ship. We are sinking. We cannot last much longer.'

And that was it. It appeared that the Admiral set two destroyers to rescue survivors. There were very few rescued. I believe at least some of the life-saving gear was frozen up. So far as we in *Wanderer* could make out, no ship was sent out after the U-boat. Personally, from sheer incompetence and rasping anguish, the *Mahratta* incident compared with . . . the staggering horror of the sinking of the mighty *Hood*.[4]

The destroyer *Impulsive* was sent back and picked up seventeen survivors from *Mahratta*.

The next homeward-bound convoy, RA.57, left the Kola Inlet on 2 March and consisted of 33 ships. The Close Escort consisted of the destroyers *Beagle, Boadicea, Keppel* and *Walker*, the corvettes *Bluebell, Camellia, Lotus* and *Rhododendron* and the minesweepers *Gleaner* and *Seagull*. *Gleaner* and *Seagull* were the last of the British minesweepers to be stationed in north Russia. Since 1941 such vessels had provided Local Eastern Escorts for the convoys and also assisted the Soviet authorities in running the feeder convoys to and from Murmansk, Archangel and other ports in the area, but, with the expansion of the Soviet Navy, it had been adjudged that their services were no longer necessary. Their departure coincided with an attempt by the Soviet naval authorities to exclude SBNO and his staff from the planning conferences for the local convoys, presumably on the grounds that, since the Soviets were wholly responsible for the convoys, they no longer needed British advice. However, a vigorous protest from Rear-Admiral Archer ensured that the British would continue to be involved. The work of the minesweepers had been a lonely and thankless task spent in a desolate theatre with an ally who seemed to place little value on their presence. Yet the work of the minesweepers, which went largely unnoticed compared to the greater events out at sea, was extremely important to the smooth running of the convoy cycle.

The Close Escort stayed with the convoy until 10 March, except for *Beagle* and *Seagull*, which departed on 9 March. The Destroyer Escort consisted of *Black Prince, Chaser, Impulsive, Matchless, Meteor, Milne, Obedient, Offa, Onslaught, Oribi, Savage, Serapis, Swift, Verulam* and *Vigilant* and sailed with the convoy on 2 March, remaining until 8 March although some individual ships departed on the 7th. The Local Escort at the western end consisted of the minesweepers *Hydra, Loyalty, Onyx, Orestes* and *Ready*.

Admiral Fraser anticipated that the U-boats would wait for the convoy in the approaches to the Kola Inlet. He therefore arranged a series of patrols by Soviet aircraft to cover the area to seaward and to keep the U-boats down while the convoy made a wide diversion to the east on leaving the Inlet. The ruse was successful, for it was not until 4 March that air reconnaissance located the convoy. The aircraft sent out homing signals and during the night of 4 March *U739* (*Oberleutant zur See* Mangold) just missed the destroyer *Swift*. *U472* (*Korvettenkapitän* Siegfried Freiherr von Forstner) was less fortunate. She was badly damaged by Swordfish 'B' of 816 Squadron embarked in HMS *Chaser* and was unable to dive. Von Forstner later had to scuttle the submarine under gunfire from HMS *Onslaught*. The next day *U703*

(*Oberleutant zur See* Joachim Brunner) sank the freighter *Empire Tourist* with an FAT torpedo[5] and just missed the destroyer *Milne* with a T5.

The *Luftwaffe* maintained contact throughout 5, 6 and 7 March but only *U278* (*Kapitänleutnant* Joachim Franze), *U288* (Meyer), *U959* (*Oberleutant zur See* Friedrich Weitz) and *U673* (Sauer) were able to make attacks—unsuccessfully—on the escorts using the T.5 torpedo. The bad weather made the operation of the U-boats' anti-aircraft guns very difficult because of icing. This greatly aided *Chaser*'s aircraft, for Swordfish 'F' sank *U366* (*Oberleutant zur See der Reserve* Bruno Langenburg) on 5 March and Swordfish 'X' sank *U973* on the 6th, despite bad weather which made the launching and recovery of aircraft extremely hazardous. *Chaser* kept her Swordfish flying anti-submarine patrols until 7 March, but there were no more sightings and the convoy arrived in Loch Ewe on 10 March, less the crane ship *Empire Bard*, which had straggled on the first night and turned up at Iokanka.

Empire Bard was one of two crane ships sent to north Russia with PQ.15 to augment the primitive cargo handling facilities there. However, no sooner had she arrived than the Ministry of War Transport demanded her return. Eventually the Soviet authorities agreed that she could leave with RA.57, and the speed of the convoy was specially reduced to 8½kts on her account. SBNO's report continues:

A general sigh of relief went up as she cleared the harbour. That was 2 March. Forty-eight hours later, to our horror, a signal was received from VA(D) that the *Empire Bard* was missing after the first night, having straggled. Sure enough, the following day, 5 March, the lost sheep turned up at Iokanka and was on our hands again. Steering trouble was alleged, but lack of speed was probably the main cause as she only averaged six knots on passage back to Kola Inlet, with a burst up to eight knots when one of the escorts in desperation 'sighted' a submarine.[6]

The next pair of convoys, JW/RA.58, were modelled on the same pattern except for the inclusion of two escort carriers, *Activity* and *Tracker*, and the Second Escort Group, under the command of the redoubtable Capt F. J. Walker. The assignment of two escort carriers was a major step forward since the convoy now possessed sufficient air assets to deal with both the U-boat threat and the persistent *Luftwaffe* shadowers. *Activity* embarked three Swordfish and seven Wildcat fighters while *Tracker* had twelve Avengers and seven Wildcats. The intention was that the Wildcats should suppress the U-boats' AA fire while the Swordfish and Avengers dropped depth charges to finish a victim off.

JW.58, of 50 ships, left Loch Ewe on 27 March. Also included in the convoy was the old American cruiser *Milwaukee*, which was being handed over to the Soviets in lieu of their portion of the surrendered Italian Fleet. The Local Escort from 27 to 29 March consisted of *Rattlesnake, Onyx, Orestes, Rhododendron* and *Starwort*. The Close Escort consisted of the destroyers *Westcott* (Senior Officer), *Whitehall* and *Wrestler* with the corvettes *Bluebell, Honeysuckle* and *Lotus*, which were present from 27 March to 4 April. On 27 March the main body of the escort joined, consisting of *Diadem* (Rear-Admiral F. Dalrymple-Hamilton, Flag), *Activity*, *Tracker, Impulsive, Inconstant, Obedient, Offa, Onslow, Opportune, Oribi, Orwell*,

Saumarez, Serapis, Scorpion, Stord and *Venus*. The Second Escort Group also joined on 29 March, consisting of *Starling* (Senior Officer), *Magpie, Wild Goose, Whimbrel* and *Wren* plus *Beagle, Boadicea, Keppel* and *Walker*. On 3 April the Soviet destroyers *Gremyashchi, Kuibyshev, Razumny* and *Razyarenny* joined.

Three days after the convoy had set sail the *Luftwaffe* made contact. However, the days when a shadower could circle the convoy unmolested while broadcasting its course and position to the world were long past. The air activity was intense and the fighters shot down no fewer than fiveof the shadowers, a Ju 88 on 30 March, two FW 200s on 31 March, one BV 138 on 1 April and a Ju 88 on 2 April. A further success came on 29 March when *U961*, outward-bound to the Atlantic, was sunk by Capt Walker's *Starling*.

The U-boat opposition to the convoy was intense. Three packs were disposed across its route, *'Thor'* (*U278, U312, U313* and *U674*), *'Blitz'* (*U277, U355, U711* and *U956*) and *'Hammer'* (*U288, U315, U354* and *U968*). In addition to the three packs, the U-boat Command had directed *U716, U739, U360, U361* and *U990*, which were heading for the Atlantic, on to the convoy. Contact was made shortly after midnight on 1 April, and most boats made at least one attack.

All this effort was to no avail, for the escorts succeeded in keeping the submarines at bay and, indeed, sank three of their number. *U355* (*Kapitänleutnant* Günther la Baume) was damaged by an Avenger of 846 Squadron from HMS *Tracker* and finished off by HMS *Beagle* on 1 April. On 2 April *U360* (*Kapitänleutnant* Klaus Becker) was sunk by HMS *Keppel* using her 'Hedgehog' ahead-throwing weapon and on 3 April Swordfish 'C' of 819 Squadron from HMS *Activity* sighted *U288* on the surface. She summoned up an Avenger and a Wildcat from *Tracker*'s 846 Squadron and sank the submarine in a combined effort.

The convoy arrived in the Kola Inlet on 4 April without loss. Sub-Lt David Chance RNVR was a member of SBNO's staff and had sailed with the Soviet minesweeper *MS.119* to meet the incoming convoy:

> We went to the north to meet the inbound convoy and saw nothing but one lone merchant ship escorted by a corvette and a destroyer—the Russian captain laughingly asked me if that was all he had to expect. Half an hour later the horizon dead ahead of us was a solid line of ships.[7]

The passage of JW.58 represented a substantial achievement: four U-boats had been sunk and five shadowers had been shot down at no cost. The German Command was disturbed by this turn of events and in particular by the efficiency of the convoy's air cover. Yet appeals from the *Kriegsmarine* to the *Luftwaffe* went unheeded. There is no doubt that, had the *Luftwaffe* possessed the same strength in Norway as it had in September 1942, then JW.58 would have had a much harder passage. Once again, the total lack of co-operation between the *Kriegsmarine* and the *Luftwaffe* favoured the Allied cause.

It is, therefore, hardly surprising that the homeward-bound convoy RA.58, of 38 ships and with the same escort as JW.58, enjoyed a trouble-free passage. After the heavy losses of reconnaissance aircraft against JW.58, the *Luftwaffe* refused to fly daylight missions and confined its activities to night-time radar searches. After sailing on 7 April the convoy was detected on the 9th, but the lack of hard intelligence as to its whereabouts meant that the ten U-boats formed into the 'Donner' and 'Keil' groups made only desultory attacks and the convoy arrived in Loch Ewe on 14 April.

JW/RA.58 marked the last pair of convoys for the first half of 1944. There were, however, 44 ships lying empty in Soviet ports, and since there was not going to be another JW convoy given the Royal Navy's concentration on the planning for 'Overlord', it was decided to bring these vessels home as quickly as possible; at the same time they could carry the 1,336 officers and men of Milwaukee, who were returning to the USA having handed over their ship, and 1,430 Red Navy officers and men required to man ex-Royal Navy ships and submarines being transferred to the Soviet Union. Accordingly the cruiser Diadem, the escort carriers Activity and Fencer, the destroyers Beagle, Boadicea, Inconstant, Keppel, Marne, Matchless, Meteor, Milne, Musketeer, Ulysses, Verulam, Virago, Walker, Westcott, Whitehall and Wrestler and the RCN frigates Cape Breton, Grou, Outremont and Wakesieu were ordered to proceed to Kola as quickly as possible. Also included was the personnel ship Nea Hellas, which unfortunately was obliged to return with defects, leaving the force without a vessel large enough to take all the American and Soviet passengers in one lift. Swift reorganization was required by the British Naval Staff in northern Russia to redistribute the 'passengers' among the merchant ships and warships. Generally speaking, the Soviet personnel were accommodated in the merchant ships while the American officers and men travelled with the escorts. The exception was Rear-Admiral V. I. Levchenko, who travelled in Fencer, where he and his staff observed the operations of the carrier with much interest.

The convoy sailed on 28 April and was detected by the Luftwaffe towards midnight on the 28th/29th. Four U-boats of the 'Donner' group and seven of the 'Keil' group were disposed across its path. U387 (Korvettenkapitän Rudolf Buchler) and U711 (Kapitänleutnant Hans-Günther Lange) made repated attacks on the convoy towards midnight on 30 April and Lange succeeded in sinking the William S. Thayer; 43 of this ship's crew and passengers were lost, but 192 were rescued by HMS Whitehall.

The atrocious weather made flying operations very difficult. At one stage over six inches of snow was recorded on flight decks. The deck crews worked doggedly to overcome the conditions and keep the aircraft flying, and their efforts were rewarded, for over the next two days Fencer's aircraft sank three U-boats. Swordfish 'C' of 842 Squadron sank U277 (Kapitänleutnant Robert Lubsen) on 1 May, while Swordfish 'B' of the same unit accounted for U959 (Oberleutant zur See Friedrich Weitz) and U674 (Oberleutnant zur See Harald Muhs) on 2 May. Alas, early on 3 May one of Fencer's Martlets was shot down by U278 (Kapitänleutnant Joachim Franze), which boat also escaped the attentions of two attacking Swordfish. Nevertheless, the aircraft prevented any further attacks on the convoy, and the latter arrived at Loch Ewe and the Clyde on 6 and 7 May.

This was another extremely satisfactory result—three U-boats sunk for the loss of one merchant ship. Admiral Fraser noted that

With the return of RA.59 the convoy season may be said to have come to a close. . . Taken as a whole the campaign can be claimed as a success. A large volume of valuable supplies has reached Russia almost intact and the enemy has sustained far greater losses in attempting to hinder them than he has inflicted on our forces.[8]

Well might Fraser be pleased. From the eight convoys running to and from the USSR, four merchant ships and two warships had been sunk in return for the loss of at least five valuable long-range reconnaissance aircraft and thirteen U-boats ranged against the enemy. The Germans could not view these events with anything but the deepest despondency. Since no increase in air power was forthcoming from the *Luftwaffe*, the U-boats were forced to abandon their attacks by day and revert to striking by night, endeavouring to get clear of the convoy before dawn. The coming of the long period of summer daylight (30 April–12 August) would mean that U-boat operations would become less effective, particularly in the face of such efficient air cover as was now being given to the convoys.

No convoy would run to the Soviet Union until August, but the Arctic was far from quiet. In particular, the problem of *Tirpitz* dominated Home Fleet operations until she was finally sunk in November. That this ship exercised such an influence without straying beyond her defended anchorage is proof of the validity of the 'fleet in being' concept.

A close watch had been maintained on the progress of repairs following the X-craft attack, using photographic intelligence, radio intercepts and reports from the Norwegian Resistance. The Admiralty were unaware that SKL was unsure how to employ the great ship once her repairs were complete so decided that, once repaired, she should be sunk or sufficiently damaged as to be unfit for service. Planning for a carrier-borne air strike code-named 'Tungsten' began at the end of 1943 under the direction of the Deputy C-in-C Home Fleet, Vice-Admiral Sir Henry Moore.

By the beginning of 1944 the Royal Navy possessed sufficient resources to employ two fast fleet carriers (*Victorious* and *Furious*) for the bombers, three escort carriers (*Emperor, Pursuer* and *Searcher*) carrying fighters and a single escort carrier (*Fencer*) to provide the carrier group with anti-submarine and fighter defence. Between them the ships carried 42 Barracuda dive-bombers; 28 F4U-1B Corsairs, 20 Grumman F6F-3 Hellcats and 40 Grumman FM-1 Wildcats, all to be used as escort fighters; fourteen Supermarine Seafires and eight Grumman F4F-4B Wildcats for fighter defence; and six Swordfish for anti-submarine work.

Training began in earnest in early 1944 using a full-scale mock up of *Tirpitz* complete with dummy AA batteries and smoke generators at Loch Eriboll. However, delays were encountered because *Victorious* was under refit and her air group was dispersed and not fully worked up. As a result, the attack, which had been scheduled for between 7 and 16 March, was postponed by a fortnight. In the event, the delay proved beneficial, for the aircraft were permitted extra training, including a 'full-dress' rehearsal on the Loch Eriboll range on 28 March. The delay also enabled more of the Barracudas to be strengthened to carry the 1,600lb armour-piercing bomb which had only recently been cleared for use with the aircraft. It was hoped that this bomb, just arrived from the USA, would inflict serious damage on the ship.

The strike plan was for *Victorious* to fly off two groups of Barracudas from 827 and 829 Squadrons and *Furious* to fly off the nine Barracudas of 831 Squadron. The fighter escort for each wave was to consist of twelve Corsairs as protection against air interception, ten Hellcats to strafe the land-based AA batteries and 20 Wildcats to suppress *Tirpitz*'s considerable close-range AA armament.

The forces for 'Tungsten' sailed in two parts. Force 1 left Scapa Flow on 30 March and consisted of *Victorious, Duke of York, Anson*, a light cruiser and five destroyers. Until 1 April this force was to provide heavy cover for JW.58. Force 2, consisting of *Furious, Pursuer, Searcher, Emperor, Fencer*, three cruisers, two oilers and ten destroyers, left Scapa later on 30 March under the command of Rear-Admiral A. W. La Touche Bissett. The plan called for the two groups to rendezvous on 3 April for a strike early on the 4th. However, the reports that JW.58's escort was more than capable of looking after the convoy enabled Fraser to bring the operation forward twenty-four hours.

Forces 1 and 2 joined during the afternoon of 2 April. Fraser, in *Duke of York*, moved with two destroyers to a position north-west of Bear Island while the oilers, with two destroyers for cover, proceeded to a point 300 miles north-west of the North Cape. Meanwhile Vice-Admiral Moore in *Anson* took the remaining ships to the flying-off position, 120 miles north of Kaafjord, where the force arrived at 0415 on 3 April. Throughout the night there was considerable activity on board the carriers as aircraft on deck had their engines warmed up and were then exchanged for aircraft which had been in the hangars beneath the flight decks. The whole operation was carried out in darkness, and when the aircraft of the first strike started their engines at 0405 there was not one failure and all 61 planes took off safely.

The first strike consisted of 21 Barracudas led by Lt-Cdr R. Baker-Faulkner RN and carried seven 1,600lb armour-piercing bombs, twenty-four 500lb semi-armour-piercing bombs and twelve 500lb and four 600lb bombs for surface or underwater blast effect. The strike aircraft formed up at low level and took their departure at 0437, flying low to minimize the possibility of detection. When the aircraft were twenty-five miles from the coast they climbed to 10,000ft, and they made landfall at 0508.

German radar detected the incoming aircraft at 0505 but the warning did not reach *Tirpitz* until 0524, four minutes before the attack commenced. At the time she was getting ready to proceed to sea for trials: the port anchor had been raised and the cable for the starboard anchor was 'up and down'. Though the close-range armament was fully manned, the ship was not at a state of readiness and many of the watertight doors were open.

The aircraft attacked from as many directions as possible, in order to divide the anti-aircraft fire. The Hellcats of 800 Squadron vigorously strafed the ground-based AA batteries while the Wildcats of 881 and 882 Squadrons put the battleship's flak directors out of action and caused severe casualties among the AA guns' crews in their exposed positions. The Barracudas experienced intense AA fire as they began their dive, but the flak had been much reduced by the fighters. Three of the 1,600lb bombs hit. The first reached the armoured deck above the port engine room, where it exploded but failed to penetrate the armour. Nevertheless, it caused serious damage, starting a fire that was fed by petrol escaping from the ruptured aircraft refuelling pipes. The second 1,600lb bomb passed through the roof of 'S1' 150mm turret, was deflected on penetrating the upper deck and exploded at the base of the funnel, causing another large fire. The third 1,600lb bomb hit under water, below the lower belt, and exploded outside the protected bulkhead, which was dished inwards over a length of 15ft, causing the wing compartments to flood and making a hole three feet wide and eighteen inches deep in the outer plating.

Of the five 500lb bombs which struck, one penetrated the quarterdeck abreast 'D' turret, where it caused a serious fire in a mess deck, and a second passed through a boat at the foot of the mainmast and exploded in the wardroom, causing another large fire. The other three exploded on hitting the 2in armour. One 600lb bomb had burst in the air on hitting the funnel, crushing the port side of the funnel and blowing in the roof of the port hangar, which had already been damaged, causing a fire. The second 600lb bomb caused more problems than any of the 1,600lb bombs. It exploded about 10ft away from the starboard side and 30ft below the belt armour. Extensive damage was done to the frames and the starboard bilge keel, and the hull was split, along a welding line, for a length of 50ft. The shock of the explosion travelled up a sea-water inlet pipe and did more damage to the boiler room at the inboard end. Only one Barracuda was lost during the attack, 'M' of 830 Squadron, which was last seen flying up Kaafjord in a controlled glide. Nothing more was heard of this aircraft.

The attack had lasted exactly one minute. *Tirpitz* was left lying across the fjord, and, although her main engines were working, the helm indicator and engine room telegraphs were inoperable. It had been decided to abandon the trials and return inside the nets when, at 0636, the second wave arrived. The second strike had taken off just as the first wave were attacking and the aircraft followed the same procedures except that the target area was now clearly visible, thanks to the brown pall of *Tirpitz*'s smokescreen and the smoke from her many fires.

The smokescreen had barely begun to take effect when the first wave had attacked, but by the time the second wave came in it had spread considerably. However, it proved more of a handicap to *Tirpitz*'s gunners than it did to the aircraft, since it obscured the former's view of the attacking aircraft while failing to mask the outline of the ship. Because their directors were out of action, the gunners were forced to fire blind—a mode for which the weapons were neither intended nor equipped. Sound-detection was also useless, for the steam siren had jammed in the open position with a deafening noise. The flak-suppression Hellcats and Wildcats were extremely effective, and, again, only one of the Barracudas was lost.

Nothing was seen from *Tirpitz* of the Barracudas' attack on account of the smokescreen, but a further five hits were scored. One 1,600lb bomb penetrated the forecastle but then failed to explode. Two 500lb bombs exploded on the upper deck, causing considerable splinter damage, but one 500lb SAP bomb went through the roof of the starboard hangar and exploded near 'S1' 150mm turret, compounding the damage done in that area by the 1,600lb bomb from the first wave. The fifth hit from the second wave was a 500lb SAP bomb which exploded as it was passing through the upper deck and started a large fire below 'P1' 150mm turret, which was also damaged. A near-miss abreast the starboard propeller bracket caused minor splits in the hull together with dishing around the bracket and some flooding.

The second strike was delivered equally swiftly and the aircraft returned to the carriers, where one 800 Squadron Hellcat had to ditch alongside after the aircraft's arrester hook had failed to lower. Thirty-seven aircraft had dropped 92 bombs with a gross weight of 25 tons. The fighters had not concentrated on *Tirpitz*. As the first wave withdrew, they attacked enemy craft in the area and sank the patrol boat *Vp6103* and strafed a netlayer, a cargo steamer and a heavy repair ship, the *C. A. Larsen*. The fighters of the second wave damaged two anti-submarine craft, *UJ1212* and *UJ1218* and wounded several of their crewmen.

As soon as the results of the attack were known, Admiral Moore wished to launch another strike the next morning, but he changed his mind on the grounds that the air crews were fatigued after the nervous strain of the lead-up to and execution of 'Tungsten'. In any case, during the night of 3/4 April the weather broke, so the force returned to a rousing welcome at Scapa Flow on 6 April.

The damage to *Tirpitz* was severe but superficial. The ship could still steam, and her main armament was still in order. Repairs to her hull took a month to complete, with divers working in freezing water. The internal damage took longer to repair since large quantities of telephone and electric cable needed to be replaced after the fires. What was significant was the extent of the casualties: 120 officers and men were killed, together with two civilian workmen, and another 316 were wounded, including the Commanding Officer—in total, some 15 per cent of the ship's company. Considering that no bomb penetrated the main belt and that only five bombs got through the upper deck, it is surprising that casualties should have been so high, although the majority of these were among the flak crews in their exposed positions.

The repair work proceeded unhindered, despite the efforts of the Royal Navy. Admiral Cunningham had wanted Fraser to repeat the operation as quickly as possible on the grounds that an injured enemy should be continually hammered until defeated. Fraser demurred, pointing out that the increasing hours of daylight made the possibility of surprise more remote and that next time there would be no convoy at sea to divert the U-boats. There was a testy exchange of signals on the matter, but eventually Fraser did agree to repeat the operation, provided the weather was favourable and that surprise could be guaranteed. Luck was not on Fraser's side. On 24 April Operation 'Planet' was cancelled, as was Operation 'Brawn' on 15 May because of bad weather over the target area. On 28 May Operation 'Tiger Claw' was abandoned for the same reason. *Victorious* left the Home Fleet after this, and there was a seven-week delay before two more fleet carriers, *Formidable* and *Indefatigable*, were ready.

Between 17 July and 29 August 1944 the Home Fleet carried out five strikes against *Tirpitz* using *Indefatigable* and *Formidable*, sometimes reinforced by the old but still game *Furious*. For such a huge expenditure of effort, and the risk involved in taking valuable capital ships so close to an enemy-held coast, the sole results were a hit by a 500lb bomb (which struck the roof of 'B' turret, doing little other than denting the armour plate) and one by a 600lb bomb (which failed to explode and which, on examination by the Germans, was found to contain less than half of the

215lb charge) during the attack on 24 August. No more clear warning of the dangers involved in such operations came on 22 August 1944, when *U354* (*Oberleutnant zur See* Hans-Jurgen Sthamer) torpedoed the escort carrier *Nabob*, which was carrying fighter aircraft in support of the fleet carriers. Sthamer fired an FAT spread which hit the carrier aft, causing serious damage and flooding. He then tried to finish her off with a T5; this hit the frigate *Bickerton* instead, which later had to be sunk.

It became evident to Fraser that *Tirpitz* had not yet been immobilized, despite the aggregate expenditure of 52 tons of bombs in 95 bomber sorties and 73 escort and support sorties which had involved the loss of eight aircraft. But the most interesting aspect of these operations is that, during each of the carrier strikes, not a single *Luftwaffe* aircraft had appeared overhead in support—a reflection on the state of liaison between the two services. It was clear that *Tirpitz*'s good fortune could not last for ever.

Towards the end of August 1944 the Joint Planning Staff in London met to consider how *Tirpitz* could finally be eliminated. The Air Staff favoured the use of shore-based aircraft to sink the ship, provided General Eisenhower would consent to such aircraft being diverted from bombing targets in Europe and that the Soviets would consent to the use of their airfields. The Soviets agreed, and the plan was passed to Air Chief Marshal Sir Arthur Harris, C-in-C Bomber Command, to implement it. In fact, the RAF's involvement in trying to sink *Tirpitz* went back to January 1942 when Halifax bombers had ineffectually attempted to bomb the ship at Trondheim. Between January and April 1942 Bomber Command had launched four raids on the battleship, but to no effect. At one stage it was proposed to use a modified version of the 'bouncing bomb' against the ship. Code-named 'Highball', the weapon was given extensive trials, but the Norwegian fjords did not suit the low-level delivery required for this weapon so the plan was dropped. However, by 1944 the RAF possessed the 12,000lb 'Tallboy' bomb, which had great powers of penetration when dropped on concrete or other toughened surfaces. The 5,100lb torpex charge would have a cataclysmic effect if exploded inside a ship, while the mining effect from a near-miss at a depth of 50ft would be considerable.

Harris planned to send 39 Lancaster bombers armed with 12,000lb bombs from Scottish airfields in the evening of 11 September, to attack the next morning and fly on to airfields near Archangel. He had originally wanted to use the faster Mosquito aircraft, but though Eisenhower was prepared to release Lancasters, his consent being given on 2 September, he was not prepared to part with the more versatile Mosquito. The plan had to be changed when the weather deteriorated sharply during the evening of the 11th. Harris was unperturbed and ordered the aircraft, from Nos 617 and 9 Squadrons, to fly to the USSR direct, refuel, carry out the operation and return to the United Kingdom. Things worked out very differently in reality, for although the aircraft managed to land in the USSR, six were rendered useless by the shabby state of the runways. Refuelling took two days, and it was not until the 15th that Wg Cdr J. B. Tait DSO DFC of No 617 Squadron led the 27 surviving aircraft into the attack. The attack was admirably executed and one hit and two near-misses were obtained. The Lancasters returned to their temporary Soviet base before flying off to England between 16 and 21 September.

The 12,000lb bomb that hit tore a 32ft deep by 48ft long hole in the starboard bow and the ship's structure below the armoured deck was wrecked for a distance of 118ft back from the stem. Flooding was complete in the damaged area, causing 1,500 tons of water to come aboard. The shock from the explosion and two near-misses damaged the main machinery, which remained unserviceable for eight days.

At a conference in Germany on 23 September it was decided that *Tirpitz* would not be repaired for sea-going service but would instead be patched up to a sufficient standard for her to move to a berth off Haakøy Island near Tromsø to act as a floating battery in a series of defensive works being prepared in the Lygenfjord area. German surveyors estimated that there would be only four feet of water under her keel in her new berth, and the bottom consisted of three feet of sand on top of rock—in other words, the ship would be unsinkable. She made the move on 15 October under her own power and arrived at her new berth the next day. It was her last journey.

She was discovered by a Firefly from HMS *Implacable*, which had been alerted when *Tirpitz*'s absence from Kaafjord was noticed by a Mosquito from No 540 Squadron in an eleven-hour round trip from Britain. The Mosquito mission demonstrated one disadvantage of the Tromsø berth—it was within flying distance of the British Isles. A second disadvantage was that the minimum depth under her keel was 20ft rather than 4ft and that the bottom was sand on top of mud! To overcome this problem, it was proposed that one million cubic feet of rubble be dumped around the ship, filling in the sea bed and reducing the depth of water. However, before this work could commence, the Royal Air Force returned.

Bomber Command had wished to repeat the attack as soon as possible, but it was not until late October that the operation could be mounted. As *Tirpitz*'s new berth was 200 miles nearer the RAF's bases, there was no need for Soviet facilities—the Lancasters could make the trip in one journey, albeit that they had to be modified. The mid upper turret was removed, and fuel tanks containing 300 Imperial gallons were installed in the fuselage. The 1,460hp Rolls-Royce Merlin 22 engines were replaced with 1,620hp Merlin 24s to enable to overloaded aircraft to take off.

Thirty-two Lancasters took off on 29 October, although low cloud over the target prevented accurate aiming. All the aircraft dropped their bombs, but the only injuries inflicted were from a near-miss which caused some flooding and some shaft damage right aft. Repairs could only be effected in a dockyard, however, and, when considered with the damage to her bow already inflicted, this attack ended *Tirpitz*'s career as a warship. Henceforth she was referred to as '*Die Schwimmende Batterie*', and her ship's company was reduced, particularly the engine room department, to little more than a care and maintenance party to keep domestic services running. It was a far cry from the proud ship which had been commissioned in December 1940 with such high hopes for success.

On 12 November another force of twenty-nine Lancasters from Nos 9 and 617 Squadrons, again led by Wg Cdr Tait, went back to repeat the operation. This time the conditions were perfect: the weather was clear and the smokescreen caused little interference. Furthermore, the fighter cover from Bardufoss which had been promised by the *Luftwaffe* never materialized, owing to what Admiral Ciliax, the Naval C-in-C Norway, described as 'a whole series of unhappy coincidences and failures'.[9] The Lancasters enjoyed a trouble-free operation, unmolested by fighters and unimpeded by smoke.

It was this attack which finally ended the chequered career of 'The Lone Queen of the North'. The first group of Lancasters scored two hits just after 0941, one to port of 'B' turret and the other on the port side amidships which opened the battleship's side from bilge keel to upper deck. The port No 1 boiler room, centre boiler room and port engine room flooded immediately, causing a list of between 15 and 20 degrees. A third 12,000lb bomb struck on the port side abreast 'P3' 150mm turret, causing massive flooding in its magazine and shell room, a gyro compartment and a fan room. Another near-missed alongside 'P2', opening the port No 2 boiler room and 'P2' magazine and shell room to the sea. The list increased to 40 degrees and *Kapitän zur See* Wolf Junge ordered the lower decks to be evacuated. By 0950 the list was 70 degrees and a fire which had started near 'P3' turret spread to 'C' magazine, which exploded. Two minutes later the ship capsized. The mass of smoke created by the first hits obscured the target for the remaining Lancasters, but more than half the bombs fell within 250yds of the ship. One bomb exploded on Haakøy Island, where the crater much impressed the locals and the German occupiers.

Casualties were heavy, and over 1,000 officers and men were trapped in the upturned hull despite Junge's order to clear lower decks. Eighty-five officers and men made a remarkable journey up through the ship to the double bottom, from where they were released by teams of rescue workers cutting through the shell plating of the outer bottom on the starboard side. As they worked, the rescuers could hear those trapped deep inside the ship singing '*Deutschland über Alles*' before the rising water silenced them for ever.

The news of *Tirpitz*'s destruction was received with grim pleasure in Britain. Churchill summed up the national mood accurately when he told Roosevelt, 'It is a great relief to us to have this brute where we have long wanted her.'[10] The Germans carried out many investigations, but the damage was done. The selection of the berth was an error, but a more glaring failure was the lack of fighter cover. Nearly 600 British aircraft had attacked *Tirpitz* in her brief life, yet the only air defence provided had been that when the ship's own Ar 196 attacked an Albacore back in March 1942.

Thus ended the career of *Tirpitz*. Expectations of her potential grossly exceeded her achievements, yet she had forced the Royal Navy to maintain an overwhelming presence in home waters merely by lurking in the various fjords in which she made her home. By tying up substantial British and American forces, she had more than justified her existence. Her greatest triumph, the destruction of PQ.17, had been achieved simply by her moving from one defended anchorage to another.

It was the good citizens of Tromsø who gained most from her loss. During the inter-war years the German people had sacrificed consumer goods in favour of arms production—the famous 'Guns Before Butter' campaign. After the war the wreck of *Tirpitz* was broken up *in situ* and the proceeds from the sale of this scrap did much for the local economy. It was one form of reparation for the Nazi occupation not specified in any peace treaty.

NOTES TO CHAPTER 13

1. Rohwer, J., and Hummelchen, G., *Chronology of the War at Sea 1939–1945*, Greenhill Books, p.256. Neither the source of the information nor the nature of the 'agents' is given.

2. However, in fairness, in the Atlantic the surface threat was non-existent and the air threat negligible, so that the Western Approaches forces could concentrate on U-boat hunting. They also had the benefit of an operational research division ashore in Liverpool where U-boat and escort tactics could be analyzed, but this information was not generally available.

3. Whinney, Capt R., *The U-boat Peril: An Anti-Submarine Commander's War*, Blandford Press, 1985, p.119.

4. *ibid.*

5. *Federapparat*, a torpedo which ran in a zigzag course on being fired and was suitable for long-distance attacks against shipping formations. Hits were often achieved more by luck than judgement.

6. PRO ADM.199/1104, 30th Monthly Report of the SBNO North Russia, 1–31 March 1944.

7. David Chance to author, 3 July 1993.

8. PRO ADM.234/369, 'Battle Summary No 22: Arctic Convoys 1941–45', 1954, p.117.

9. Roskill, Capt S. W., *The War at Sea 1939–1945*, Vol III, Pt II, HMSO, 1961, p.168.

10. Prime Minister's Personal Telegram T.2122/4 No 822 from Prime Minister to President, 15 November 1944, Churchill Papers 20/175.

Chapter 14

Victory

There must be the beginning of any great matter, but the
continuing unto the end until it be thoroughly finished yields
the true glory.—Sir Francis Drake

By August 1944 the invasion of Europe was sufficiently well advanced to allow the Home Fleet forces to be released for a resumption of convoys to the Soviet Union. Admiral Sir Henry Moore had succeeded Fraser in June 1944 as Commander-in-Chief Home Fleet on the latter's departure for the Far East. He found the situation much as it had been in the spring. *Tirpitz* and her five destroyer escorts were still at Altenfjord and were receiving regular visits from the Fleet Air Arm as described in the previous chapter. The *Luftwaffe's* strength in the Arctic was still marginal on account of its other commitments. However, the number of U-boats in the theatre was increasing, partly as a result of their growing inability to operate in the Atlantic in the face of very tough anti-submarine measures but mainly because the American drive through Brittany and south-west France had robbed them of their bases on the Atlantic coast. The 11th and 13th U-boat Flotillas were already based in Norway, but, with the fall of the French ports, they would be joined by the 2nd, 3rd and 7th Flotillas. Norway was now the most convenient location for their bases in terms of operations against both Atlantic convoys and those going to the USSR. As well as appearing in larger numbers, the U-boats were now being fitted with the *Schnorkel* underwater breathing tube, which allowed them to run their diesels while submerged and greatly enhanced their operational capability. This final 'season' of Arctic convoys would see those U-boats fitted with *Schnorkel* gear operating right up to the entrance of the Kola Inlet.

JW.59, the first of the new series of convoys, sailed from Loch Ewe on 15 August 1944. It consisted of 34 ships. The Close Escort from 15 to 25 August comprised the sloop *Cygnet*, the frigate *Loch Dunvegan* and the corvettes *Bluebell, Camellia, Charlock, Honeysuckle* and *Oxlip*. The sloops *Kite, Mermaid* and *Peacock* and the destroyers *Keppel* and *Whitehall* of the 22nd Escort Group from Western Approaches Command operated ahead of the convoy to put down any U-boats which might be lying in wait. On 17 August the main body of the escort joined, consisting of the cruiser *Jamaica* (Capt J. Hughes-Hallett RN), the escort carriers *Vindex* (Capt H. T. T. Bayliss RN) and *Striker* (Capt W. P. Carne RN) and the destroyers *Caprice, Marne, Meteor, Milne* and *Musketeer*. Also with the convoy was the Soviet battleship *Archangelsk* (ex HMS *Royal Sovereign*) and twelve Soviet submarine-chasers.

Royal Sovereign was part of package of British and American warships transferred to the USSR in May 1944 as compensation for that country's not

207

receiving a share of the surrendered Italian Fleet. It comprised one battleship, one cruiser (USS *Milwaukee*, which, as already described, had gone to the Soviet Union with JW.58), eight destroyers and four submarines. The transfer was very much a token gesture since the ships were of considerable vintage, having all been built at the end of the First World War and hard-driven in the Second. The submarines were relatively new, but two of them, the former HMS *Unbroken* and HMS *Sunfish*, had been damaged by enemy action and were certainly past their best.

Archangelsk and eight destroyers sailed with JW.59, but the submarines proceeded independently, small Royal Navy parties being embarked to assist the Soviet crews in operating the machinery. Theirs was not a happy experience. They found the discipline in the Soviet Fleet to be harsh and unbending and discovered that Soviet society was anything but classless as they observed the officers appropriate the main accommodation area for conversion to cabins while condemning the crew to a cheerless and cramped existence packed into the fore-ends with the reload torpedoes. The also found the influence of the Political Officers to be all-pervasive. On one occasion in *V1* (ex *Sunfish*), a British Leading Stoker and a Soviet stoker were rigging a chain purchase to lift a cylinder head in the Engine Room. The Political Officer appeared and told the pair that in a socialist society such tasks were done by hand; evidently dogma was more important than sound engineering practice. Worst of all, vodka was substituted for the beloved 'tot'. There were representations to naval authority and threats to desert and let the submarine sail without the RN personnel, but to no avail. Anglo-Soviet co-operation and good relations were at stake, so the full weight of naval discipline was applied to ensure that the ratings stayed at their posts—though only three of the party actually sailed with the submarine.[1]

Three of the submarines arrived safely, but *V1*, under the command of Capt 3rd Class Israel Fisanovich, failed to arrive at Murmansk when expected. A report was received from an RAF Liberator that it had attacked and sunk a submarine in the Norwegian Sea on 27 July 1944, and Rear-Admiral Egerton, the SBNO, considered that this submarine could have been *V1*. His initial impression was confirmed when *V2* (ex HMS *Unbroken*) arrived on 3 August. Egerton interviewed Leading Telegraphist C. A. Wilkes, a member of the British liaison party on board the submarine, who told him that the Soviet Commanding Officer had not kept to the 'safe' route allocated to him and that recognition signals were never kept on the bridge where they were immediately accessible. Egerton concluded:

> It seems more than possible, therefore, that the submarine attacked on 27 July was in fact *V1*, who was off her route and who had no recognition signals at immediate notice.[2]

Egerton was correct. *V1* had been allocated a 'safe haven' in which bombing was restricted during the submarine's passage from Lerwick to the Kola Inlet. The position of the 'haven' was adjusted each day to correspond to the submarine's track. To allow for navigational errors, a strip 20 miles either side of the 'haven' was made a total bombing restriction area by night and a submerged bombing restriction area by day. Since aircraft navigation was even more hit-and-miss, a further safety zone of 20 miles was added either side for the benefit of the aircraft. The most likely hypothesis for *VI*'s end was that she was way out of position, had no recognition signals to hand when the Liberator was sighted and so dived and was attacked. It is worth noting that the aircraft carrying out the attack was 90 miles away from the 'safe' corridor.

Vice-Admiral F. H. G. Dalrymple-Hamilton was in command of JW.59 but on this occasion chose to fly his flag in *Vindex* rather than the cruiser since the carrier possessed much better command facilities. Heavy cover was provided by the Home Fleet, which was simultaneously engaged in an attack on the *Tirpitz*, Operation 'Goodwood'.

The convoy had an uneventful passage. The continuous daylight allowed the carriers to keep their aircraft airborne throughout the twenty-four-hour period. A Ju 88 reported the convoy east of Jan Mayen Island, and early on 21 August the convoy reached the patrol line of the '*Trutz*' group (*U344, U668, U394, U363* and *U997*), which had been deployed across its path. *U344* (*Kapitänleutnant* Ulrich Pietsch), ahead of the convoy, attacked the 22nd Escort Group with a T5 salvo and then sank the sloop HMS *Kite* (Lt-Cdr W. F. R. Seagrave DSC RN) on 21 August with heavy loss of life, only nine of her crew being rescued.

Pietsch sent off a sighting report which resulted in a fresh patrol line being formed from *U703, U354, U365* and *U711*, but all these boats were successfully kept down by the air patrols from the carriers and a Catalina from the 118th Reconnaissance Regiment, Soviet Air Force. By 23 August only *U394, U711* and *U365* were in contact, the other boats have fallen behind. The U-boats kept up the pressure, *U668, U363* and *U997* all firing T5s at the escort but missing. In return, a Swordfish from *Vindex* sank *U344*, thus avenging HMS *Kite*, and on 23 August *U354* (*Kapitänleutnant* Hans-Jurgen Sthamer) was sunk by HMS *Mermaid* (Lt-Cdr J. P. Mosse RN), *Loch Dunvegan* (Cdr E. Wheeler RNR), *Keppel* (Cdr L. J. Tyson RN) and *Peacock* (Lt-Cdr R. B. Stannard VC RNR) following a hunt which had lasted twelve hours. This sinking was poetic justice, for the day before Sthamer had sunk the frigate *Bickerton* and crippled the carrier *Nabob*.

The U-boats were withdrawn on 25 August in order to regroup before the homeward-bound convoy sailed, and the convoy proceeded without further incident. Fighter cover from the Soviet Air Force appeared on 24 August and the next day the convoy entered the Kola Inlet.

The homeward-bound convoy, RA.59A, comprised nine ships and sailed on 28 August with the same escorts as JW.59. Present were the heavy lift ships *Empire Elgar* and *Empire Bard*, which had come out to northern Russia with PQ.16 and RA.57 respectively. They were fitted with large derricks and could supplement the meagre unloading facilities at either Murmansk or Archangel. The Senior British Naval Officer North Russia was glad to see them go:

I must confess to a feeling of relief that *Empire Elgar* and *Empire Bard* are returning to the United Kingdom in convoy RA.59A. The crews of these two ships have been a constant source of embarrassment to SBNO Murmansk, who has many times been involved in negotiations with the Soviet authorities over the misbehaviour of these seamen ashore. There is no doubt that their conduct has lowered British prestige in North Russia.[3]

The convoy had an uninterrupted passage, and although the boats of the '*Trutz*' group had been disposed across its likely path, neither they nor the *Luftwaffe* made contact. Nevertheless, the carriers kept up a full flying programme, which was justified on 1 September when one of the Swordfish from 825 Squadron in *Vindex* picked up a high-frequency homing signal from a U-boat, ran down the bearing and damaged *U394* (*Kapitänleutnant* Borger). In the early days of Western Approaches Command, an instructional poster drawn by the well-known Commander Jack Broome warned escort commanders, with a suitably pithy drawing, that if a U-boat sighted a convoy he would 'tell his friends'. The situation was now reversed, for the Swordfish 'told his friends' and summoned *Keppel, Loch Dunvegan, Mermaid* and *Peacock* to finish off *U394* in a massed, creeping attack which lasted six hours. The convoy arrived without loss at Loch Ewe on 5 September.

The JW/RA.59 operations had demonstrated the value of having dedicated anti-submarine support groups attached to the convoy. During the double operation, the 20th and 22nd Escort Groups had sunk two U-boats but had taken over eighteen hours of hunting to do so. Had those ships been part of the screen, they could have done no more than plaster the contact area with depth charges before returning to the convoy; now, as more escorts were available, the U-boats could be hunted to destruction while the convoy steamed by.

The next pair of convoys, JW/RA.60, enjoyed an equally quiet voyage. JW.60, of 31 ships, sailed from Loch Ewe on 15 September. The Close Escort consisted of the sloop *Cygnet*, the destroyers *Bulldog, Keppel* and *Whitehall* and the corvettes *Allington Castle* and *Bamborough Castle*. The Main Escort consisted of the cruiser *Jamaica*, the escort carriers *Campania* and *Striker* and the destroyers *Marne, Meteor, Milne, Musketeer, Saumarez, Scorpion, Venus, Verulam, Virago, Volage, Algonquin* (RCN) and *Sioux* (RCN).

Admiral Moore was concerned that *Tirpitz* might be in a sea-going condition following repairs to the damage suffered during Operation 'Tungsten', so he sailed with the convoy in the battleship HMS *Rodney*. In the event, the precaution was unnecessary, for on 15 September, the day the convoy sailed, Nos 9 and 617 Squadrons RAF launched their first attack from north Russia and seriously damaged the ship. On hearing the news of the success of the raid, Moore decided to take *Rodney* through to the Kola Inlet anyway, as it would give him an opportunity to meet with Admiral Golovko. The convoy passed unobserved by the enemy and, evading the seven boats of the '*Grimm*' group, arrived on 23 September.

The homeward-bound RA.60, of 32 ships, left Kola on 28 September with the same escorts as JW.60. The convoy avoided the '*Grimm*' group and also the twelve boats of the '*Zorn*' group which had just deployed to the area. Only *U310* (*Oberleutnant zur See* Wolfgang Ley) of the latter group made contact when she accidentally blundered into the convoy on 29 September. Ley fired two salvos of FAT pattern-running torpedoes and succeeded in sinking the *Edward H. Crockett* and the *Samsuva*. These were the only losses suffered by the convoy, which arrived in Loch Ewe on 5 October.

JW.61, composed of 30 ships, sailed five days later. With *Tirpitz* out of action and the air threat negligible, the U-boats were the main anxiety for the convoy, and so JW.61 had the strongest escort of any sailing to date. The Close Escort, provided by Western Approaches Command, consisted of the 8th Escort Group comprising the destroyer *Walker*, the sloops *Lapwing* and *Lark* and the corvettes *Camellia*, *Oxlip* and *Rhododendron*. The main body of the escort joined on 22 October and consisted of the cruiser *Dido* and the destroyers *Obedient*, *Onslow*, *Offa*, *Opportune*, *Oribi* and *Orwell*. On the same day the carriers *Vindex*, *Nairana* and *Tracker* joined, supported by two more Western Approaches Escort Groups (EG), the 21st consisting of the frigates *Conn*, *Byron*, *Fitzroy*. *Reane*, *Redmill* and *Rupert* and the 24th comprising *Louis*, *Inglis*, *Lawson*, *Loring*, *Narborough* and *Mounsey*.

Flying conditions during the passage of the convoy were atrocious. Lt-Cdr Peter Barringer, of 835 Squadron aboard *Nairana*, recalled that

> Only Swordfish were employed on the outward run, due to the appalling weather and poor light. At this time of year there was barely two hours of daylight and very minimal at that . . . ships were darkened at 1400. This meant that all flying duties had to be borne by 811 Squadron [embarked in *Vindex*] and 835 Squadron. The *Tracker*'s Avengers were for the most part passengers. particularly as they did not carry ASV equipment.[4]

The perils of flying in such conditions are well illustrated in this account of a landing on board *Nairana* by Lt John Cridland:

> I was within a few feet of touching down when the flight deck corkscrewed away from me. I had to take rapid and violent action with a frighteningly steep bank to starboard to avoid hitting the ship's bridge. No other aircraft but a Swordfish would have remained in the air . . . my wing caught the aerials between the mast above the bridge but we remained airborne and in spite of it all I was able to go round again and make a normal landing, much to the relief of my observer.[5]

Cridland was less popular with the Petty Officer Telegraphist who had to climb the mast in a howling gale to replace the aerials.

No U-boats were encountered until 26 October, when the convoy passed east of Bear Island and ran in to a very heavy concentration of submarines, nineteen in all, of the 'Panther' group. The escort groups went ahead of the convoy to keep the U-boats down, and in this they were successful, for only five of the latter managed to make contact (and were only able to launch T5s against the escorts, without result). Bad asdic conditions hampered the escorts and no U-boats were sunk, and the convoy arrived at Kola without loss on 28 October.

During the interval before the sailing of the next homeward-bound convoy there was little to do while the escorts lay at anchor at Vaenga. The wardroom bars of the carriers were particularly busy since air crewmen were not allowed to drink while at sea. The officers and men of *Nairana* established a special relationship with the crew of the Canadian destroyer *Sioux*, which would always be the last to come alongside the carrier to fuel and would then remain alongside all night while much serious 'partying' went on.

Tactics similar to those employed for JW.61 were adopted for the homeward-bound RA.61, of 33 ships: the frigates sailed early to keep the U-boats down while the convoy left the narrow waters of the Kola Inlet. The boats of the *'Panther'* group were disposed at the entrance to the Inlet, but the aggressive tactics of the escorts frustrated their attempts to attack the convoy. Their sole success was the torpedoing of the frigate *Mounsey* (Lt F. A. J. Andrew RN) by *U295* (*Kapitänleutnant* Günther Wiebolt) with a T5. *Mounsey* had to return to Kola Inlet for repair. Otherwise, the convoy enjoyed an uninterrupted passage and reached Loch Ewe on 9 November. Once again, poor asdic conditions, caused by the mixing of the warm waters of the Gulf Stream with the colder waters of the Arctic, had prevented the escorts from reaping the rewards of their labours. Too often a firm contact would disappear as the U-boat slipped beneath the thermocline into colder water. One escort commander described U-boat hunting in such conditions as 'trying to catch several irritated and offensively minded snakes with six harmless rabbits to oppose them.'[6]

While the JW/RA.61 convoys were at sea, the most unusual convoy of the series was en route for the Soviet Union—JW.61A, consisting of two large liners carrying over 11,000 Soviet nationals. These men were liberated former German prisoners of war or former soldiers of the Red Army who had been taken prisoner by the Germans and who, for one reason or another, had chosen to enter either ethnic Russian formations in the *Waffen SS* or the *Wehrmacht* or had been conscripted willy-nilly into construction battalions of the *Organisation Todt*. After the invasion of France in June 1944 they had either given themselves up or had been captured in their thousands. Theirs was an anomalous position in Britain. They were not quite prisoners of war, neither were they the soldiers of the army of an allied nation. Moreover, among the Russian soldiers were civilians who had been caught up in the war, including women and children. The civilians could not, legally, be treated in the same way as the soldiers and under British law could not be detained since they had committed no crime.

The Soviet Government wanted its nationals returned, and, since their accommodation in Britain was a charge on the War Office, it seemed best for all concerned that they be sent back to the USSR as quickly as possible, especially as it became crystal clear that many of the Russians did not actually want to return. To avoid controversy and the possible raising of the matter in Parliament, it was decided that all the Russians, regardless of their status, should go back whether or not they wanted to. This decision automatically accepted that force would have to be used if necessary.

The problem exercised Patrick Dean of the Foreign Office's Legal Department. On 15 October 1944 he wrote to the Home Office, urging that

> . . . the obvious course is to ensure that all the Russian nationals at present in the London reception centre are sent home among the first batch, since this will relieve you of the responsibility and will avoid the legal and political difficulties which are

likely to arise if these people are detained as civilians in the UK much longer. . . It is rather a nuisance that some of these Russians are women, since I understand that they require more accommodation, but fortunately their number is comparatively low, and we very much hope that it will be possible to get them home as soon as possible.[7]

On 17 October 1944, during their meeting in Moscow, Churchill told Stalin that 11,000 'ex-prisoners of war'[8] would be sent back. Stalin commented that the prisoners were Russians 'who had been made to fight for the Germans while others had done so willingly', whereupon Churchill pointed out the difficulty of differentiating between the two. At that time it did not look as though a speedy repatriation could be arranged, but with the unexpected cancellation of the assault on Rangoon, the Secretary to the Chiefs of Staff Committee notified the Foreign Office in November that

. . . the shipping situation has altered and the Chiefs of Staff have instructed me to state that shipping can be made available to lift 11,000 personnel, provided the move takes place to ensure the return of the ships by the end of November 1944.[9]

The Admiralty's insistence that the ships be back by the end of November lent weight to Eden's demand that the Russians be sent home quickly. As soon as the War Cabinet had given its consent to the repatriation, the task began of gathering the prisoners together from camps all over Yorkshire. Each man would be issued with a complete set of standard British Army clothing and equipment (less, of course, small arms). All their *Wehrmacht, Organisation Todt* or Red Army clothing would be withdrawn from them. At the same time, Maj-Gen E. C. Gepp, head of the Directorate of Prisoners of War, told Gen Vasiliev, Head of the Soviet Army Mission in London, that 10,220 Soviet nationals would go with the first party. The British were concerned about the reaction of some prisoners who had forcibly indicated that they did not wish to return to the USSR. Brig Firebrace of the PoW Directorate enquired of Vasiliev if the Soviets would be prepared to provide Red Army personnel to guard the transports. Vasiliev refused and insisted that the prisoners be guarded by British troops throughout the journey. Accordingly, Firebrace issued the following order to the commandants of the camps where the Russians were held:

. . . possibility exists that certain Russians will not want to leave England and may attempt to escape . . . provide armed guards from trains to port but guards will not repeat not use arms except in self-defence . . . retain sufficient train escorts at port until sailing of ships to prevent escapes at port. This should be done as inconspicuously as possible.[10]

The ships selected to take the prisoners back were the Canadian Pacific liner *Empress of Australia* and the Cunarder *Scythia*. The ships were allocated the convoy number JW.61A. The escort was provided by the cruiser HMS *Berwick* (Capt S. H. T. Arliss RN), the escort carrier HMS *Campania* (Capt K. A. Short RN) and the destroyers *Cambrian, Caprice, Cassandra, Saumarez, Scourge* and *Serapis*. In addition to the Soviet nationals, *Berwick* carried a contingent of Norwegian troops who were to join the Soviet forces about to enter northern Norway and ensure the sovereignty of their country.

The ships sailed from Liverpool on 31 October 1943 carrying 10,139 male prisoners, 30 women and 44 boys and, after an uninterrupted passage, arrived in the Kola Inlet on 6 November. William Birch was a seaman on board the *Empress of Australia* at the time, and he recalled that the Russians were

> . . . very docile. They knew they were going to be shot. We wouldn't believe it, we couldn't believe it. We kept saying, 'Oh no, they wouldn't do that.' But evidently they did. They knew, more than we did, what was going to happen to them.

On arrival in the Kola Inlet, the two liners were not allowed to come alongside. Instead, they had to anchor in the Inlet itself, the passengers being taken off in lighters. As soon as disembarkation was complete, the liners fuelled and left on 11 November for the Clyde, where they arrived on the 17th after a trouble-free voyage. The Soviet News Agency TASS painted a rosy picture of the arrival of the prisoners:

> They were warmly welcomed by plenipotentiary representatives of the Council of Peoples' Commissars for Matters Concerning Repatriation of Soviet Citizens from Germany and Countries Occupied by Her, as well as representatives of local State Organs and of the Soviet Public.
> It was an exciting picture when the Soviet citizens returning from Fascist captivity met the working people of Murmansk. A spontaneous meeting started. On an improvised platform Soviet citizens, who had been forcibly torn from their Motherland by the Fascist scoundrels, rose one after the other to express their deep gratitude to the Soviet Government and to Comrade Stalin for their solicitude. . . The local State Organs display great solicitude for the repatriated people. They are provided with food and lodgings. The Soviet people who have regained their Motherland show tremendous interest in the happy events of the war fronts and life in the Soviet Union. On 6 November they heard Stalin's speech. They are being sent in groups to their native places. The orphaned children are going into children's homes.[11]

However, a more accurate account of the arrival of the prisoners was provided by Maj S. J. Cregeen, a British officer on the staff of SBNO:

> On November 7th, in Murmansk, I was in a car returning from the Naval Mission Headquarters to the War Port. En route we passed by a long column of Russian repatriated nationals, who were being marched from their transport, the Sythia, under armed guard to the camp just outside the town. It appeared that they were being treated as having the status of nothing more than enemy prisoners of war. The guards were armed with rifles and were probably allotted at the rate of one per 10/15 nationals. There was no sign of a welcome reception being arranged for these repatriates, whose demeanour was added proof of their unfortunate status. They were all dressed in British battledress, carrying a small parcel of personal belongings in most cases, and at that stage they had not been provided with any Russian equipment, insignia or 'comforts'.[12]

For the 'repatriates', the camp at Murmansk would lead into the maw of the *Gulag* from which few, if any, would return. Though there would be more forced repatriation convoys, in future the Mediterranean and Black Sea routes to Odessa would be used.

The last pair of convoys of 1944, JW/RA.62, were the first to sail without the threat of intervention by *Tirpitz*. Yet this pair suffered more opposition than their predecessors, for the *Luftwaffe* had finally given in to the *Kriegsmarine*'s pleas for more aircraft in Norway and had sent two *Gruppen* containing approximately 70 Ju 88 torpedo bombers back to Norway.

Despite this reinforcement of the *Luftwaffe* in the Arctic and the concentration of seventeen U-boats in two groups, '*Stock*' and '*Grubbe*', the JW.62 convoy of 31 ships went unchallenged throughout the passage, apart from a shadower which gained contact on 27 November and was promptly shot down, and reached Kola on 7 December. The homeward-bound RA.62 had a more interesting time. The 29 ships left Kola on 10 December together with the damaged *Mounsey*, now returning to Britain for permanent repair. The escort comprised the cruiser *Bellona*, the escort carriers *Campania* and *Nairana*, the destroyers *Beagle*, *Bulldog*, *Caesar*, *Cambrian*, *Caprice*, *Cassandra*, *Keppel*, *Obedient*, *Offa*, *Onslaught*, *Onslow*, *Oribi*, *Orwell* and *Westcott*, the sloops *Cygnet*, *Lapwing* and *Lark*, the frigates *Bahamas*, *Loch Alvie*, *Somaliland*, *Tavy*, *Tortola*, *Monnow*, *Nene*, *Port Colborne*, *St John* and *Stormont* (the last five all Canadian) and the corvettes *Allington Castle*, *Bamborough Castle*, *Tunsberg Castle* (Norwegian) and *Eglantine*.

The day before the convoy sailed, the frigates and a Soviet force under the command of Rear-Admiral Fokin and composed of *Baku*, *Gremyashchi*, *Razumny*, *Derzki*, *Doblestni* and *Zhivuchi*, sailed to clear the U-boats away from the Kola Inlet. During the sweep, *U997* (*Oberleutnant* Hans Lehmann) fired a T5 salvo at *Zhivuchi* and *Razumny* but missed. *U387* was even more unfortunate for she was depth-charged by HMS *Bamborough Castle* (Lt M. S. Work DSC RNR), although Soviet sources claim that she was rammed by *Zhivuchi*. However, *U365* (*Oberleutnant* Dieter Todenhagen) was able to evade the escorts and settled down to shadow the main body of the convoy. On 10 December Todenhagen tried to torpedo the oiler *Laurelwood* but missed. He was luckier on the 11th, for he torpedoed the destroyer *Cassandra* (Lt G. C. Leslie RN) and blew her bows off, and the crippled ship had to limp back to Murmansk for repair. More misfortune came on 12 December when the Norwegian corvette *Tunsberg Castle* hit a German mine off Makkaur and sank.

The *Luftwaffe* made an appearance on 12 December when nine Ju 88s of I/KG 26 tried to attack the convoy south-west of Bear Island. The attack was unsuccessful and resulted in two of the aircraft being shot down by the fighters. Finally, on 13 December, *U365*, which had been doggedly tailing the convoy, was sunk by Swordfish 'L' and 'Q' from 813 Squadron on board *Campania*.

RA.62 was the last convoy of 1944. It had been a successful series, 159 ships having been sent to the USSR with not a single loss; of the 100 ships which had returned, only two had been lost. Six U-boats had been destroyed by the convoy's escorts and a further three by long-range patrol aircraft of RAF Coastal Command.

A huge quantity of supplies had been delivered to the USSR, where the Red Army stood poised for the final thrust to Berlin.

The start of 1945 was marked by an audacious attempt on the part of the *Kriegsmarine* to attack shipping in the Kola Inlet. Operation '*Caesar*' involved the use of *Biber* midget submarines[13] of *K-Flotilla 265* which would be carried to the target area by three specially converted Type VIIC U-boats, *U295*, *U318* and *U716*. The U-boats were to carry the *Biber*s to within 40 miles of the target area, release the deck clamps and submerge beneath them. The *Biber*s had twelve hours to penetrate the Inlet and attack on 8 January at 1500. Following the attack the craft were to lie on the shallow bottom and send acoustic signals to their parent submarines. After the pilots were picked up, the *Biber*s would be destroyed. Alternatively, the operators were given directions to make their way to a rendezvous at the Fischer Peninsula or to head for neutral Sweden. The three U-boats left Harstadt on 5 January 1945. However, the vibration from the boats' diesel engines, used when the craft were on the surface, started leaks in the *Biber*s' fuel lines and, despite efforts to repair the faults, the operation had to be abandoned.

The first pair of convoys in 1945, JW/RA.63, consisting of 38 and 31 ships respectively, went undetected by the Germans. JW.63 arrived safely on 8 January and RA.63 returned safely to the Clyde on 23 January.

The passage of the last series of convoys in 1944 had been rather uneventful compared to what had gone before. However, the JW/RA.64 pair were to endure the full Arctic repertoire of foul weather together with frequent air and submarine attack. JW.64 sailed from the Clyde (the Loch Ewe anchorage having been closed down) on 3 February 1945 with 29 merchant ships. The Close Escort consisted of the sloops *Cygnet* and *Lark*, the destroyer *Whitehall* and the corvettes *Alnwick Castle*, *Bamborough Castle*, *Bluebell* and *Rhododendron*. On 6 February the cruiser *Bellona* joined, together with the escort carriers *Campania* (flying the flag of Rear-Admiral R. M. McGrigor) and *Striker*, the sloop *Lapwing*, the corvette *Denbigh Castle*, the Norwegian trawler *Osky* and the destroyers *Onslaught*, *Onslow*, *Opportune*, *Orwell*, *Serapis*, *Zambesi*, *Zealous*, *Zest* and *Sioux*. The destroyer *Zebra* was to have joined the escort but had to return to the Faeroe Islands with defects.

Shortly after the main body of the escort joined, the convoy was sighted by a routine *Luftwaffe* meteorological flight and in the afternoon of the 6th a Ju 88 arrived to shadow the convoy. The latter was shot down by two Wildcats from *Campania*, one of which was lost with its pilot, Sub-Lt A. Smyth RNVR. From then the *Luftwaffe* were to be in continuous contact with the convoy.

Shadowers returned on the 7th, together with a number of Ju 88 torpedo bombers; one of these latter was shot down by *Denbigh Castle* (Lt-Cdr G. Butcher RNVR). McGrigor anticipated an early-morning torpedo attack so ordered the convoy to make a 90-degree alteration of course to starboard in order to to bring the enemy's most favourable attacking sector astern. The plot in *Campania* indicated that there were about a dozen aircraft operating in two groups to the north and south-west of the convoy. The aircraft were from a force of 48 Ju 88s from *KG 26*. The main body of the force failed to find the convoy and those aircraft that did were deterred from pressing home their attack by the fighters and the AA gunfire of the escort. Seven of the Ju 88s failed to return as a result of accident or through having to ditch in the sea after running out of fuel.

During the 8th and 9th the *Luftwaffe* shadowers were constantly prowling round the convoy and U-boat homing signals were intercepted. In the evening of the 8th McGrigor ordered the convoy's only night fighter, a converted Fulmar, to be flown off from *Campania* to deal with the shadower. The sortie failed owing to the darkness and poor R/T communication. The Fulmar then made a bad landing on *Campania* and was wrecked when it ran into the barrier. Thus the convoy lost its only dedicated night fighter, a crucial asset in the long hours of winter darkness. Consideration was given to using an ASV-equipped Swordfish in the role and some sorties were flown, but the experiment was not particularly successful.

Despite the interest shown by the Germans in the convoy, no attacks materialized on the 8th or 9th. McGrigor took the convoy slightly north of the usual track and in doing so he passed around the northern end of the '*Rasmus*' U-boat pack (*U286, U307, U425, U636, U711, U716, U739* and *U968*) which had deployed across his perceived track.

The *Luftwaffe* returned on 10 February when the convoy was only 250 miles from Bardufoss. The attack was launched by 32 aircraft from *II* and *III/KG 26*. There was no warning of the attack other than the appearance of a lone Ju 88 which was damaged by *Sioux* but managed to release its torpedo. At 1019 the main body of the raid was detected on radar coming in from the starboard bow. The destroyer *Whitehall* (Lt-Cdr P. J. Cowell RN) was in the most exposed position, being the right-hand ship of the extended screen ahead, but defended herself with distinction. She and *Lark* (Cdr H. Lambton RN) broke up the attacking formation of about eight aircraft, causing them to take evasive action:

> . . . she sent one away damaged, shot down the second, shared a third with the *Lark* and successfully avoided all torpedoes. Fine work by a veteran with a close-range armament of only two Oerlikons each side.[14]

Orwell, Cygnet, Sioux and *Onslow* all claimed 'probables' or to have inflicted damage, but the day really belonged to the air crews. This description of the raid is by Lt-Cdr E. E. Barringer RNVR from HMS *Nairana*:

> The convoy was being constantly shadowed and it was only a matter of time before the next air attack would be launched. John Godley and John Cridland with George Strong and Paddy Hall took off at 0815 on 10 February on a routine anti-submarine patrol. While they were airborne the long-awaited attack materialized. John Godley sighted some Ju 88s as they came in at low altitude and George Strong got away a warning message to the *Nairana*.
>
> It was now the turn of the fighter pilots, and the Wildcats rose to meet the incoming enemy aircraft. There were about thirty Ju 88s, which approached in groups of 6 or 8 aircraft each from different directions. Sammy Mears and Ron Moss went after the first wave. Sammy made a quick attack from the starboard quarter on a Ju 88 closing to close range and shooting it down—'all in one swipe, as it were'. He then made another long stern chase on a Ju 88 but broke off the pursuit when he found himself

being drawn too far from the convoy and was already out of R/T touch. Sam had to resort to his homing beacon to get back to the carrier. Meanwhile Ron Moss was making his own attack and attacked another Ju 88 which was severely damaged and presumed to have been shot down. Bill Armitage and Norman Sargent scrambled to meet another formation which scattered as they approached and fled into the cloud.

Meanwhile some low-flying Ju 88s broke through and bore down on the convoy. The warships and merchant ships threw up a terrific curtain of fire and two enemy aircaft crashed in flames amidst the convoy. This third torpedo attack was carried out with skill and determination and one German pilot flew low over the forward line of ships, taking careful aim before dropping his torpedo. He left the convoy with both engines on fire and later crashed into the sea. There was an enthusiastic audience on *Nairana*'s flight deck and a running commentary was being broadcast on the ship's tannoy system. All the ship's company cheered as each enemy crash was reported.

The two carriers were operating in their box in the centre rear of the convoy and the guns' crews joined in with enthusiasm, firing at everything and anything in sight. Unfortunately, as some of Wildcats came into land, two of *Campania*'s fighters were shot down by the convoy's own anti-aircraft gunfire. One pilot was saved.

The attacks continued and the carriers became the prime targets. Both carriers had to take instant evasive action. In one particular violent turn the *Nairana*'s rudder jammed and for a few desperate minutes she went round in circles, but her luck held and she did not collide any of the other vessels.

George Gordon and Pete Blanco were the next to scramble, but after a few minutes in the air, George, to his chagrin, had to return home with engine trouble. Despite this and also coming under fire from ships in the convoy which was fortunately inaccurate, he managed to land back on safely. The remaining Wildcats in the air were vectored on to approaching enemy formations and several attacks were broken up before they could reach the convoy.

The attacks appeared to be slackening off as the last two pilots, Al Burgham and Ken Atkinson, stood by to take-off . . . they were vectored on to a bogey approaching in cloud on the port side of the convoy. The trigger-happy gunners in the convoy below saw the enemy aircraft at the same time and gave it, and the two Wildcats, a rousing reception. As soon as the Ju 88 saw the fighters the German pilot made a very unorthodox high-level torpedo drop. Having shed his load, he sought the sanctuary of the nearest cloud as quickly as he could but Al Burgham followed him, instructing Ken to remain below the cloud in case the Ju 88 decided to dive to sea level to make his getaway. Al got in several good bursts and repeatedly hit the enemy plane, which was well ablaze as it flew into a bank of low cloud. He followed the burning aircraft into the cloud, from which he emerged just in time to see the stricken aircraft, trailing a plume of smoke, splash into the sea. It was a definite kill but there was still work to do. Al engaged another Ju 88 as it emerged from the clouds. As soon as it saw the emerging Wildcats the torpedo bomber raced back into the safety of the clouds with great urgency.

While all this was going on, the two Swordfish which had taken off at 0815 were getting anxious to land-on. They had been circling the carrier, carefully trying to avoid the AA fire, and waiting for a lull in the fighting. When this lull came the two Swordfish were called in. John Cridland was first to land but as he came in he could see another aircraft closing on him. Ken Hall calmly but depressingly advised him that it was a Ju 88. It was then a matter of time before John reached the carrier before the Ju 88 reached him. John just made it, but coming, understandably, with a little more throttle than was needed, he floated over the arrester wires and crashed into the barrier. His aircraft was swiftly disengaged from the barrier and manhandled forward while the barrier was re-erected for the next landing by John Godley. Just as he was about to touch down, all the guns opened up as two Ju 88s flashed across *Nairana*'s bows . . . but he made a safe landing.

So the enemy air attacks ended. No ships were hit and two Wildcats and one pilot [were] lost (shot down by their own AA fire) against 7 Ju 88s destroyed, four more probably shot down and eight more so seriously damaged that they were unlikely to get back safely to their Norwegian base. It was a very significant victory for the convoy, its escorts and, above all, its carrier-borne fighter aircraft.[15]

In fact, five of the Ju 88s were shot down but an unknown number were damaged. The problem of aircraft casualties caused by friendly fire was a serious one. Orders were subsequently issued that all friendly aircraft should only approach the convoy from astern and that Wildcats should do so with their undercarriage down. Additionally, air crews not required for flying duties were stationed at *Nairana*'s gun positions to assist the gunners in identification. In his report, McGrigor admitted that fire discipline was very poor among both the merchant ships and escorts:

> [They] showed a quite inexcusable lack of fire discipline, even taking into account the bad visibility, low cloud and pace of events. There is little resemblance between a Ju 88 and a Wildcat and none with a Swordfish.[16]

However, the air crews could be said to have had their revenge some days later when an armourer working on a Wildcat's .50-calibre armament in the hangar accidently touched the firing button, sending a spray of bullets through the flight deck and causing consternation in a gunners' mess nearby. Fortunately, no one was injured.

After this attack, the rest of the journey was fairly uneventful. Ice, snow showers and poor visibility hampered flying operations for both sides. However, the convoy still had to pass through a concentration of U-boats off the Kola Inlet consisting of the '*Rasmus*' group—which was hurriedly redeployed when it was realized that the convoy had skirted round it—together with *U293*, *U318*, *U992* and *U995*.

On 12 February the Soviet escort arrived and the Archangel section of the convoy departed, covered by *Lark*, *Lapwing* and *Alnwick Castle* as far as the entrance to the White Sea. On 13 February *U992* torpedoed *Denbigh Castle* right at the entrance to the Kola Inlet. HMS *Bluebell* (Lt G. H. Walker RN) took the ship in tow, but she had to be beached before reaching the anchorage and she later capsized, becoming a total loss.

The convoy entered the Kola Inlet on 15 February and two of the merchant ships, the *Fort Crivecouer* and the *Arunah S. Abell*, managed to collide at the entrance to the Inlet. Fortunately the convoy evaded the bulk of the U-boats, which went seeking targets elsewhere: on 14 February *U968* (*Oberleutnant zur See* Otto Westphalen) sank the *Horace Gray* and the tanker *Norfjell* proceeding towards Murmansk in the White Sea feeder convoy BK.3 to join RA.64.

While the escort was at Kola awaiting the homeward-bound convoy there was an interesting diversion when it was decided to rescue the inhabitants of Sorøy. In their search for slave labour, the Germans had raided the island, burned the inhabitants' dwellings and forced the people to take shelter in caves in the hills. The islanders' plight was reported to the Admiralty by the Norwegian Military Mission on the island and action was not long in coming. The Norwegian mission was told to have the inhabitants ready for evacuation, and a Catalina of the Norwegian Air Force landed off Sorøy to warn them of their impending departure. In the afternoon of 15 February Operation 'Open Door' was implemented. The destroyers *Zambesi* (Capt J. H. Allison DSO RN, Senior Officer), *Zealous*, *Zest* and *Sioux*, which had been detached from the convoy, swept up Galten Fjord with their White Ensigns proudly flying—watched impotently by German shore garrisons—and anchored off Sorøy. Five hundred and twenty men, women and children were embarked on the four ships, which returned the way they had come without opposition. The destroyers sailed to Murmansk, the children being plied with chocolate (a luxury some of them had never seen) and being outrageously spoiled during the voyage. The inhabitants were then distributed among the merchant ships sailing back to the United Kingdom with RA.64.

The escort for RA.64 was identical to that for JW.64 except that the destroyers *Cavalier*, *Myngs* and *Scorpion* reinforced it on 25 February. Admiral McGrigor was very concerned that the large number of U-boats which he had successfully evaded on the outward journey were congregating off the Kola Inlet, waiting for the homeward-bound convoy to sail:

> ... on sailing, RA.64 would have to force its way through a strong concentration of U-boats ... one U-boat was working right in the entrance, where it had torpedoed three ships in the last few days,[17] while HF/DF fixes and Russian reports showed that others were clustered along the first 40 miles of the convoy route and could not be avoided. Russian countermeasures were confined to day flying and a few small craft patrolling the entrance and were quite ineffective. There was no night flying, no hunting groups and no thought on their part of taking the offensive against the U-boats so handily placed.[18]

Accordingly, he ordered the ships of the Close Escort—*Cygnet*, *Lapwing*, *Alnwick Castle*, *Bamborough Castle*, *Rhododendron*, *Lark* and *Bluebell*—to sail on 16 February for an anti-U-boat sweep in the approaches to the Kola Inlet, assisted by Soviet aircraft. During the night *Lark* and *Alnwick Castle* sank *U425* (*Kapitänleutnant* Hans Bentzien), and this success seemed to get the operation off to a good start.

The main body of RA.64, consisting of 33 ships, sailed from the Kola Inlet on 17 February 1945:

> It was a bitterly cold morning. 40° of frost was recorded on *Nairana*'s flight deck. The sea was flat and dead calm with a metallic sheen and spirals of mist rising from the sea. This was the dreaded 'arctic' mist and created a most eerie effect.[19]

McGrigor's worst fears were about to be realized, for there was an unexpectedly stong concentration of U-boats waiting for the convoy which had not been discouraged by the pre-sailing sweep. Ten boats were stationed off the peninsula, *U286*, *U310*, *U318*, *U425*, *U636*, *U711*, *U739*, *U968*, *U992* and *U995*. The convoy was very slow in leaving the Inlet, and it was not long before the first U-boat attacks materialized. At 1024 *U968* blew the stern off HMS *Lark* and sank the freighter *Thomas Scott*. A third success for the U-boats came in the afternoon when *U711* (*Kapitänleutnant* Hans Lange) torpedoed HMS *Bluebell* (Lt H. G. Walker RN). The little corvette, a veteran of so many Arctic convoys,[20] blew up and sank with the loss of all her crew except one.

The weather deteriorated quickly. On 17 February Lts Ron Brown and Jock Beyan were taking off on anti-submarine patrol from HMS *Nairana* when their aircraft hit an Oerlikon mounting on the starboard side forward of the bridge and went over into the sea. The two air crewmen managed to get out of the aircraft and inflate their dinghy, but it was fortunate that they were wearing their immersion suits because it was 25 minutes before the destroyer HMS *Onslaught* found them, her Commanding Officer (Cdr The Hon A. Pleydell-Bouverie RN) having taken the courageous decision to use his searchlight to look for the two men in waters where U-boats were known to be present.

As the gale worsened, flying operations were suspended on 18 February. The ships began to labour in the heavy seas and great rolls of up to 45 degrees were experienced. The merchant ships, many of which were in ballast, had an especially rough time. However, in *Nairana*'s hangar an unexpected hazard arose

   . . . as aircraft, doubly and trebly lashed down, began to weaken some of the ring bolts in the deck. No sooner had this been resolved when, just after midnight on 19 February, all squadron personnel were summoned to the hangar on the tannoy broadcast. An electrically powered tractor which weighed over a ton and which was designed for moving aircraft had broken loose and was running rogue on the hangar deck.[21]

Eventually the beast was secured, but not before two Swordfish had been written off and another three badly damaged.

At the height of the gale two merchant ships were reduced to steering with block and tackle on the rudder head and twelve of the destroyers had to be docked on their return to Britain with damage to their frail hulls. The gale carried on throughout the 19th, and by the morning of the 20th the escorts had their work cut out as they sought to round up the scattered ships. This work was made all the more important as at 0420 there was the familiar sight and sound of a shadower, and it would not therefore be long before an air attack was mounted. The task of gathering in the merchant ships was not easy: HMS *Zambesi* steamed over 1,000 miles in heavy seas at high speed in order to bring in the scattered ships. The threat materialized an hour after the shadower had gained contact. A force of 25 Ju 88s attacked without success, being driven off by the fighters from *Nairana* (all of *Campania*'s fighters bar one having been damaged in the storm), the AA fire from the escorts and vigorous handling of the convoy by Admiral McGrigor.

Throughout the 21st and 22nd the convoy was shadowed by both aircraft and U-boats, but no attacks developed. However, in the evening of the 22nd the gale increased again, undoing all the hard work of the escorts, which had managed to gather 31 ships out of 33. The convoy became scattered again and, as Admiral McGrigor subsequently wrote,

These persistent gales caused much difficulty in keeping stragglers with the convoy. Engine trouble, defective steering, ice-chipped propellers, shifting cargoes and splitting decks were among the very genuine reasons for dropping astern and at times stopping.[22]

In the evening of the 22nd the gale worsened dramatically. The convoy broke up, with some ships following the Commodore on a course of 160° while others, including the flagship HMS *Campania*, which was suffering 45-degree rolls, hove-to.

The shadowers found the convoy again on the 23rd but must have sent an inaccurate position report because the force of Ju 88s flown out to attack the battered merchant ships and their exhausted crews did not arrive. The aircraft did find one straggler, the *Henry Bacon*, which was attacked and sunk by a formation of nineteen Ju 88s. The *Luftwaffe* raid commander immediately radioed his success to Bardufoss and the signal was picked up in *Campania* by direction-finding. McGrigor was therefore able to send fighters down the bearing to find the *Henry Bacon*, which was sinking 50 miles to the east of the convoy. More importantly, the destoyers *Zambesi*, *Zest* and *Opportune* were dispatched to rescue the 65 survivors, this total including some of the Norwegian refugees from Sorøy.

The gale continued to buffet the convoy for the next two days, reducing its speed to about 3½kts. By this stage nearly all the escorts were running low on fuel, and the destroyers were detached to proceed independently to the Faeroes, fuel, and then return to the convoy as speedily as possible. Fortunately, the bad weather also hampered the *Luftwaffe* and the U-boats, for no further attacks materialized by either. RA.64's sufferings were nearly at an end. On 26 February McGrigor parted company, taking the two carriers and four destroyers with him and leaving the convoy in the hands of Capt R. F. Jessel of HMS *Zealous*. The latter brought the ships down to the Clyde, where they arrived without further incident on 1 March.

TheJW/RA.64 pair were the last convoys to endure the full horrors of the Arctic. Three more pairs of convoys, JW/RA.65, 66 and 67, ran to the USSR before the cycle was suspended. JW.65 encountered no opposition throughout the majority of its passage, although on the last leg of the approach to Kola a snowstorm brought flying operations from the carriers *Campania* and *Trumpeter*, together with sorties by Soviet aircraft from bases ashore, to a halt just as the convoy was passing through a concentration of thirteen U-boats. Losses were inevitable, and *U995* (Hess) sank the steamer *Horace Bushnell* on 20 March while *U968* (Westphalen) sank the sloop *Lapwing* and the merchant ship *Thomas Donaldson*.

As with RA.64, Rear-Admiral Dalrymple-Hamilton arranged elaborate manoeuvres to disguise RA.65's departure. A new route was used while four destroyers sailed out on the old route firing flares, dropping depth charges and making all manner of commotion to draw the U-boats away from the convoy. The ruse succeeded, and the 26 ships of the convoy, undetected by U-boats or aircraft, arrived at Scapa on 1 April.

The next pair of convoys, JW/RA.66, saw even more determined measures to beat the U-boats. The 27 ships of JW.66 entered the Kola Inlet behind a screen of escorts, deploying their A/S weapons in a ferocious blind barrage to deter the enemy. Despite this assault on the U-boats, poor asdic conditions ensured that only one was damaged. Nevertheless, the convoy went through unscathed and arrived on 25 April.

To deter the U-boats from lying in wait off the Kola Inlet, and given the poor performance of asdic in this region, the British had requested permission from the Soviets to lay a minefield at such a depth that ships would pass over safely but in which any U-boats driven deep by the escort would be caught. The Soviet authorities were reluctant on the grounds that their own ships might be caught but were eventually persuaded to agree. The operation was code-named 'Trammel' and involved the use of the fast minelayer HMS *Apollo* (Capt C. Grindle RN) with the destroyers *Opportune*, *Obedient* and *Orwell*, which had been fitted with mine rails. The ships arrived in the Inlet on 21 April, and on 22 April, covered by the 19th Escort Group, they laid a field which consisted of 276 mines in six lanes moored at a depth of 60ft. Admiral Egerton, the SBNO, had already told Capt Grindle about the Soviets' concerns. The result was that Grindle

> . . . set their minds at rest simply but effectively by steaming over the minefield on the completion of the lay. I am told that the many Russian officers embarked in *Apollo* for the operation were all seen to be perspiring freely, although the day was not hot.[23]

The 26 ships of RA.63 were the first to enjoy the protection of this field and the last Arctic convoy to be molested by the enemy. The day before the convoy sailed, 29 April, the escorts conducted their usual pre-sailing sweep of the approaches to the Kola Inlet with mixed results. *U307* (Krüger) was sunk on 29 April by HMS *Loch Shin* but *U968* (Westphalen) managed to close the convoy and torpedo the frigate *Goodall* (Lt-Cdr J. V. Fulton RNVR). The corvette HMS *Honeysuckle* (Lt H. H. D. McKillican DSC RNVR) went alongside to rescue the crew but was badly damaged in the process. *Goodall* was the last Allied escort vessel to be sunk in home waters. However, her loss was avenged the next day when *Loch Shin*, *Anguilla* and *Cotton* sank *U286* (Dietrich) off the Kola Inlet in the last encounter between U-boats and escorts in home waters during the Second World War. Once clear of the concentration of U-boats off the Kola Inlet, RA.66 proceeded without further incident and arrived in the Clyde on, appropriately enough, VE-Day, 8 May 1945.

Only one more pair of convoys went to and from the Soviet Union before the cycle was discontinued. JW./RA.67 ran after the end of hostilities but were escorted in case there were any fanatical U-boat commanders unwilling to heed the surrender order. The precautions proved unnecessary, and both convoys proceeded without incident. When the 25 ships of RA.67 arrived in the Clyde on 30 May 1945, the story of the Arctic convoys ended.

Unfortunately, the end was shrouded in acrimony and bitterness. The wartime coalition comprising Britain, the United States and the USSR fell apart almost as quickly as it had come together. The cause was twofold. First, there was an unwillingness among the Western allies to supply aid to the USSR for any purpose other than Soviet participation in the war against Japan. This decision was partly the result of disenchantment with Soviet policy towards the countries of Eastern Europe, particularly Poland, which had been 'liberated' by the Red Army. However, another reason—and this is of special relevance when considering British aid—was that the requirements for reconstruction in the West were now so great that little could be spared for the USSR. The four Protocols under which Britain had supplied the Soviet Union with aid had been uniquely sacrificial on Britain's part and had sprung from the dark days of the summer of 1941 when only Britain and the Soviet Union had stood against Hitler. The end of hostilities in Europe meant that normality was bound to return.

The Soviet Government could not understand this. It felt that the Western preoccupation with civil rights in Eastern Europe ignored legitimate Soviet concerns about security; it also considered that aid for reconstruction was the Soviet Union's by right. With some justice, the Soviets believed that the Red Army had vanquished the Germans on the battlefield and had won the European war. Certainly it had destroyed the bulk of the German Army, and, more than any other country, the USSR had paid the price for the defeat of Nazism with the lives of its people and the devastation of its land.

The story of the break-up of the wartime alliance lies outside the scope of this book. Suffice it to say that within weeks of the end of the war the former allies were squaring up to each another as potential adversaries. The 'Cold War' had begun, and there would be no place for the commemoration of the Arctic convoys as examples of Allied co-operation.

NOTES TO CHAPTER 14

1. Compton-Hall, Cdr Richard, *The Underwater War*, Blandford Books, 1982, p.131.
2. PRO ADM.199/1104, Report of Proceedings No 3, June and July 1944, Senior British Naval Officer, North Russia.
3. *ibid*. The last straw was when *Empire Bard*'s Boatswain was found stealing chocolate from life rafts to sell ashore.
4. Papers of Lt-Cdr Barringer RNVR, Department of Documents, Imperial War Museum, 91/17/1, p.209. ASV is Air to Surface Vessel radar.
5. *ibid*.
6. Roskill, Capt S. W., *The War At Sea 1939–45*, Vol III Pt II, HMSO, 1961, p.167.
7. PRO WO.32/11137,65A, Dean to Home Office, 15 October 1944.
8. Gilbert, Martin, *Road to Victory—Winston Churchill 1941–45*, Heinemann, 1986, p.1024.
9. PRO PREM.3/364.
10. PRO WO.32/11141, 2A.
11. PRO FO.371/43382, 174.
12. PRO WO.32/11119, 184A–B.
13. The *Biber* was a one-man submarine which displaced 6.5 tons with its armament of two G7e 21in torpedoes. It was 29ft 6in long and 5ft 3in in the beam and had a draught of 4ft 6in.

Surface propulsion was provided by a 32hp Opel Blitz Otto petrol engine, which gave a range of 100nm at 6.5kts. A 13hp electric motor powered by three Type 13 T210 battery troughs gave a submerged range of 8½nm at 5.3kts.

14. PRO ADM.234/369, 'Battle Summary No 22: Arctic Convoys 1941–45', p.121.

15. Barringer, *op. cit.*, pp.292–6.

16. PRO ADM.234/369, *op. cit.*, p.121.

17. There were in fact two boats, *U711*, which had sunk the *Horace Grey* and the *Norfjell*, and *U286*, which had attacked another feeder convoy but without result.

18. PRO ADM.234/369, *op. cit.*, p.122.

19. Barringer, *op. cit.*, p.299.

20. *Bluebell* had covered PQ.18, QP.15, JW.53, JW.57, JW.58, JW.59, JW.64, QP.15, RA.57, RA.58, RA.59A and RA.64.

21. Barringer, *op. cit.*, p.302.

22. PRO ADM.234/369, *op. cit.*, p.124.

23. PRO ADM.199/1104, Report of Proceedings, 20 March to 31 May 1945, Senior British Naval Officer, North Russia.

El Fin

9:30 pm. 11-26-07

Quite unusual for me to read a book This quickly, < 1 month

I remember well my Senior H.S. research paper for mrs. Feight at Hemlock H.S. in The Spring of 1960- "The Battle of The Atlantic". I wish I had a copy of That paper

Chapter 15

Conclusions and Reflections

Without the great influx of American aeroplanes, American motor transport, a thousand other things we lacked, what would have been the fate of Soviet resistance?—Victor Kravchenko, Soviet official, on the value of Anglo-American aid

What can be said of the convoys which battled their way through to the Soviet Union, and was the effort and sacrifice worth it? In the overall context of Anglo-American aid to the USSR, the Arctic convoys delivered slightly under a quarter—22.5 per cent—of the total amount. The brief balance sheet for these operations shows that £428,000,000 worth of supplies, including 5,000 tanks, 7,000 aircraft and immense quantities of munitions were shipped to the Soviet Union.[1] This equipment was of immeasurable value to the Red Army, giving it the resources to stem and then hurl back the German invasion. Initially the equipment supplied to the USSR may not have been particularly suited to that country's requirements or to the rigours of the Russian winter. British tanks such as the Matilda were criticized as being too slow and underarmed for dealing with the Panzers; the Eighth Army thought much the same in the Western Desert. However, once the United States became a full belligerent instead of a benevolent neutral, the supplies came in quantity and were of considerable quality. American-built trucks were particularly praised by the Soviets. These criticisms notwithstanding, every item of Anglo-American equipment sent to the USSR gave that country time—time to relocate Soviet industry and time to start the production lines which would turn the Red Army into an awesomely equipped fighting machine.

The cost of sending this equipment to the USSR was heavy. Eighteen Allied warships[2] and 104 merchant ships were sunk, and 829 men of the Royal and Merchant Navies lost their lives. The German losses were heavier,[3] and thus the balance of success lay very much with the Allies, and with the Royal Navy, which provided most of the escorts, in particular.

Opponents and detractors of these operations argue that the convoys were unnecessary: that they constituted too great a drain on scarce resources; that the risks were not worth the gain; and that other, safer routes existed for supplying the USSR. These arguments have some merit but ignore the fact that the Arctic route was the swiftest and the most flexible way of giving help to that country. The arguments also ignore the question of honour. The conduct of nations cannot be measured like a balance sheet. In the dark days of 1941–42, the Soviet Union was Britain's only ally: the latter could hardly have stood by while the German Army won yet another victory. Moreover, unlike Britain's miserable allies of the 1940 campaign, the Russians were doggedly resisting. As Churchill said, 'These people have shown themselves worth backing.' The detractors also ignore the fact that the convoys were a visible guarantee of Anglo-American involvement in the war effort. Three trainloads of trucks coming up from the Persian Gulf was one thing, but the sight of HMS *Duke of York* lying in the Kola Inlet on 27 December 1943 with her Battle Ensigns flying and her hull and superstructure showing the scars from the Battle of the North Cape was different altogether. The convoys represented commitment: while they were running, relations with the Soviet Union were amicable; when they stopped, relations froze, for not only did the Soviets mind losing the aid, the paranoia which was inbuilt into the Soviet system feared that all sorts of capitalist tricks were afoot.

There is still in Great Britain the feeling among some historians and among those who served on the Arctic convoys that they were irrelevant and that they were organized on political rather than military grounds. This in turn leads to the theory, oft advanced, that the convoys were the bait laid out by a callous Admiralty to entice the German capital ships out into a fleet action. This argument puts the cart before the horse. The political decision had been made to send these convoys to the USSR via the Arctic and the build-up of German forces in Norway was a response to that decision. However, it must be said that none of the Home Fleet commanders who organized the convoys would have minded an engagement with *Tirpitz* or any other German capital ship, had they shown themselves, for all took steps to prepare against such an eventuality. But to say that this constitutes trailing the convoys across the North Cape like a sacrificial lamb is stretching the point. Of course, hanging over this debate lies the shadow of PQ.17, which will always be a matter of controversy for as long a historians debate the subject.

Western aid played a considerable part in the Soviet victory, particularly in the early days, but we shall never really know the extent of the Anglo-American contribution. How vital was it? Soviet historiography on the subject is tinged with paranoia and has tended to play down, or ignore, the role of Western aid in the achievement of the final victory. This example will suffice. Writing of the decision to suspend the convoys in the summer of 1942, the Soviet historians V. I. Achkasov and N. B. Pavlovich remarked that

> The British Admiralty attributed the suspensions of Allied convoy movements to the north to a number of factors, in particular the difficulty of protecting them from enemy submarines and aircraft during the period of the midnight sun, the great demand for escort ships in the Mediterranean, the destruction of convoy PQ.17, and the losses suffered by the Atlantic convoys and by convoy PQ.18. As a matter of fact this was all merely a pretext. The real reason for the suspension of northern convoy movements was the persistent attempt by the Allies to curtail delivery of necessary equipment and supplies to the USSR, and thereby hamper the operations of the Red Army, whose successes were increasing daily.[4]

This is unfair. Western historiography has rightly given the Red Army full measure for its role in the defeat of Germany, but the part played by Western aid in that victory remains undocumented. The Soviets' attitude also ignores the privations that Britain suffered on their behalf, particularly in the period of the First Protocol in

1941–42. During this time Britain sacrificed her own interests to maintain her commitments to the USSR. The British Government cast aside the reservations expressed by the Chiefs of Staff and provided more in the way of major military aid than the United States, despite the huge disparity in resources: the goodwill and the readiness to fulfil obligations which the Soviets claimed were lacking dominated its thinking. Perhaps, with the liberalization of Soviet society, historians in the former Soviet Union will no longer have to cloak their country's history in socialist rhetoric and we shall see a truer picture emerge.

However, it is possible to find glimpses of a more realistic view of events. A different perspective comes from a former Soviet engineer, Victor Kravchenko, who held high office in the Defence Procurement Section of the RFSR[5] before defecting to the United States in 1943 and was therefore in a position to know:

> Day after day, I had the direct and tragic proofs of my country's failure to prepare for this life and death crisis. I came to know more intimately than the high-ranking generals and admirals how valuable American Lend-Lease weapons, material and machinery were in achieving victory. Americans may have some doubts about this, but not the Soviet leaders. For them it is a fact. God knows we paid them back in full—in Russian lives—for Allied help, but that does not alter the fact itself. Without the great influx of American aeroplanes, American motor transport, a thousand other things we lacked, what would have been the fate of Soviet resistance?[6]

The question poses another in return: what would have been the fate of British resistance had the Soviet Union been defeated? Over two-thirds of the German Army was deployed on the Eastern Front, and had the Germans been able to concentrate all their forces in the West, then the outcome of the invasion of Europe might have been very different. The fates of Britain and the Soviet Union were totally linked together.

Kravchenko's memoirs throw an interesting sidelight on how the Soviet leadership viewed Anglo-American aid. While the USSR desperately needed the aid, that fact had to be concealed in order to preserve the illusion that Stalin's government was virtually infallible. Western aid was explained to the Party faithful as a 'contribution' towards victory, after which the socialist nations would give the rotten capitalists their just deserts.

The ingratitude of the Soviet authorities and the way in which a lot of aid—particularly food aid—went not to the deserving or needy but into the mouths and stomachs of the Communist élite, the *nomenklatura*, caused those who had to fight the convoys through, enduring the cold and awful weather, to consider whether their labours were worth it. In his last Report of Proceedings, written in March 1944 before being relieved, Rear-Admiral E. R. Archer, the Senior British Naval Officer in North Russia, considered the point:

> Escorts of JW convoys often ask if their journeys are really necessary, having the impression that the sailing of these convoys is dictated by political expediency rather than necessity. From all the information at my disposal, I feel confident that the munitions, fuel, food and transport etc . . . brought out here are all very much in demand. I have even been told on more than one occasion, by Russians who should be

able to speak with authority, that but for this source of supply it is doubtful if Leningrad would have been held. It is to be admitted, however, that the general attitude of the Russians might give the impression quoted above. They are a sensitive people, loath to admit that outside help is needed and rather grudging in expressing any appreciation when such is given.

However, anyone who attends meetings about these convoys cannot fail to be impressed by the dismay displayed if there is any question of delay or reductions in the number of ships.[7]

The paranoia and insularity of the Soviet system during the war prevented Soviet officials from expressing their gratitude or appreciation. This is surprising, for the Russians are a warm-hearted people. Time and time again in the Letters of Proceedings from the SBNO North Russia one reads of how the Political Officers prevented the development of normal professional relationships between the Royal and Soviet Navies.

The Cold War buried any chance of the Soviet authorities' giving recognition to the efforts made by the Royal Navy on their behalf. This has denied the Arctic convoys their place as an epic in the history of twentieth century naval warfare. There can be few campaigns where there has been such concentrated heroism shown in the face of such appalling conditions. One considers HMS *Eclipse* tearing after Z26 through the gale, the spray freezing round her gunners' feet; the trawler *Ayrshire* driving her three charges into the ice-pack after the scattering of PQ.17; the struggle to save *Somali*; Capt Sherbrooke on the wrecked bridge of HMS *Onslow*; the destroyer *Achates* protecting JW.51B until she sank; Lts Place and Cameron in their submarines penetrating the heart of Altenfjord; the air crews on the escort carriers in the winter of 1944–45 who kept flying despite the freezing conditions . . . these are just some of the examples.

There was heroism on the German side too: the pilots who kept on flying into ferocious barrages of AA fire knowing that their chances of survival if forced to ditch were minimal; the U-boat commanders who faced the full panoply of A/S measures deployed against them as they engaged the later convoys; and the gunners on board *Scharnhorst* who did indeed 'fight to the last shell'.

Truly the Arctic convoys deserve the description as a 'northern saga of bravery, heroism and endurance' given them by Ivan Maisky. But there is more to it than that: the running of these convoys was a matter of honour. That the aid given was often ignored or only grudgingly acknowledged does not alter the fact that British and American assistance to the USSR laid the basis for a wartime alliance which alone could defeat the menace of Nazi Germany.

NOTES TO CHAPTER 15

1. See Appendix 3 for details of Allied aid to the USSR.
2. See Appendix 1 for full details of Allied warship losses.
3. See Appendix 2 for details of Axis warship losses.

4. Achkasov, V. I., and Pavlovich, N. B., *Soviet Naval Operations in the Great Patriotic War 1941-45*, Naval Institute Press, 1981, p.310.

5. Russian Federated Soviet Republic, the largest of the constituent republics which made up the former USSR.

6. Kravchenko, Victor, *I Chose Freedom*, Robert Hale, 1958, p.193.

7. PRO ADM.199/1104, 30th Monthly Report of SBNO North Russia, 1-31 March 1944.

Appendices

APPENDIX 1: BRITISH AND ALLIED WARSHIPS SUNK DURING ARCTIC CONVOY OPERATIONS, 1941–45

Cruisers

Edinburgh Sunk 2.5.42 by *Foresight* after being torpedoed by *U456* 30/4/42.

Trinidad Damaged by own torpedo 29/3/42; bombed and sunk while returning to UK 14/5/42; eventually torpedoed by *Matchless*.

Destroyers

Achates Capsized 31/12/42 following damage sustained in Battle of Barents Sea.

Hardy Torpedoed by *U278* 30/1/44; wreck sunk by *Venus*.

Mahratta Torpedoed by *U990* 25/2/44

Matabele Torpedoed by *U454* 17/1/44.

Punjabi Rammed by *King George V* 1/5/42.

Sokrushitelny Foundered in gale 22/1142.

Somali Torpedoed by *U703* 20/9/42; sank while under tow 24/9/42.

Sloops

Kite Torpedoed by *U344* 21/8/44.

Lark Torpedoed by *U968* 17/2/45; wreck towed into Kola and abandoned.

Lapwing Torpedoed by *U968* 20/3/43.

Frigate

Goodall Torpedoed by *U968* 29/3/45.

Corvettes

Bluebell Torpedoed by *U711* 17/2/45.

Denbigh Castle Torpedoed by *U992* 13/2/45; wreck towed into Kola and abandoned.

Tunsberg Castle Mined 12/12/44.

Minesweepers

Bramble Sunk by *Admiral Hipper* and *Friedrich Eckholdt* 31/12/42.

Gossamer Bombed in Kola Inlet 24/6/42.

Leda Torpedoed by U435 20/9/42.

Niger Mined in British minefield 5/7/42.

Submarines

Jastrzab Sunk in error by *St Albans* and *Seagull* 2/5/42.

Armed Whaler

Shera Capsized by icing on upper deck 9/3/42.

233

APPENDIX 2: GERMAN WARSHIPS SUNK DURING ARCTIC CONVOY OPERATIONS, 1941–45

Battlecruiser

Scharnhorst   Sunk in action with Home
Fleet 26/12/43.

Destroyers

Friedrich   Sunk by *Sheffield* 31/12/42.
Eckholdt

Z26   Sunk in action with *Trinidad*
and *Eclipse* 29/3/42.

Auxiliary vessels

Bremse   Sunk by *Nigeria* amd *Aurora*
7/9/41.

Ulm   Sunk by *Marne, Martin* and
Onslaught 25/8/42.

Submarines

U88   Sunk by *Faulknor* and
Swordfish of 825 Sqn
(*Avenger*)14/9/42.

U286   Sunk by *Anguilla, Cotton* and
Loch Shin 29/4/45.

U277   Sunk by Swordfish from
*Fencer*1/5/44.

U288   Sunk by aircraft from *Activity*
and *Tracker* 3/4/44.

U307   Sunk by *Cygnet, Loch Shin*
and *Loch Insh* 29/4/45.

U314   Sunk by *Meteor* and
Whitehall 30/1/44.

U344   Sunk by Swordfish of 835
Sqn (*Vindex*) 22/8/44.

U347   Sunk by Catalina of 210 Sqn
RAF 17/7/44.

U354   Sunk by *Keppel, Loch Shin,*
Mermaid, Peacock and
Swordfish of 825 Sqn
(*Vindex*) 24/8/44.

U355   Sunk by *Beagle* and Avenger
from *Tracker* 1/3/44.

U360   Sunk by *Keppel* 2/4/44.

U361   Sunk by Catalina of 210 Sqn
RAF 17/7/44.

U365   Sunk by a Swordfish of 813
Sqn (*Campania*) 13/12/44.

U366   Sunk by a Swordfish of 816
Sqn (*Chaser*) 5/3/44.

U387   Sunk by *Bamborough Castle*
9/12/44.

U394   Sunk by *Keppel, Whitehall,*
Mermaid, Peacock and a
Swordfish of 825 Sqn
(*Vindex*) 2/9/44.

U425   Sunk by *Alnwick Castle* and
Lark 17/2/45.

U457   Sunk by *Impulsive* 16/9/42.

U472   Sunk by *Onslaught* and
Swordfish of 816 Sqn
(*Chaser*) 4/3/44.

U585   Mined off Murmansk 30/3/42.

U589   Sunk by *Onslow* and
Swordfish of 825 Sqn
(*Avenger*) 14/9/42.

U601   Sunk by Catalina of 210 Sqn
25/2/44.

U644   Sunk by *Tuna* 7/4/43.

U655   Sunk by *Sharpshooter*
24/3/42.

U674   Sunk by Swordfish of 842
Sqn (*Fencer*) 2/5/44.

U713   Sunk by *Keppel* 21/2/44.

U742   Sunk by Catalina of 210 Sqn
18/7/42.

U921   Sunk by Swordfish of 813
Sqn (*Campania*) 30/9/44.

U959   Sunk by Swordfish of 842
Sqn (*Fencer*) 2/5/44.

U961   Sunk by *Starling* 29/3/44.

U973   Sunk by Swordfish of 816
Sqn (*Chaser*) 6/3/44.

Tirpitz 12 Nov '44
Sunk but not due to convoy action

APPENDIX 3: AID TO THE USSR 1941–45

Cargo Shipped from the Western Hemisphere to the Soviet Union, 22 June 1941 to 20 September 1945

Route	Amount shipped (gross long tons)	Arrived (%)	Lost (%)
North Russia	3,964,000	93	7
Persian Gulf*	4,160,000	96	4
Black Sea	681,000	99	1
Far East	8,244,000	99	1
Soviet Arctic	452,000	100	0

Totals (gross long tons):		
	Amount shipped:	17,501,000
	Arrived in USSR:	16,587,000
	Lost:	488,000
	Discharged in UK:**	343,000

* Shipment to the Persian Gulf was by a variety of routes. The figures include all routes.
** The major portion of this amount was discharged in the United Kingdom but subsequently re-shipped to North Russia without loss.

Supplies Despatched to the USSR by Great Britain between 1 October 1941 and 31 March 1946

Item	Number
Admiralty Supplies	
Battleship	1
Destroyers	9
Submarines	4
Motor Minesweepers	5
Minesweeeping Trawlers	9
ASDIC	293 sets
Radar	329 sets
Submarine Batteries (complete)	41
6" guns (complete)	2
5.25" guns (complete)	56
4" guns complete with 16 spare barrels	36
12pdr guns complete with 12 spare barrels	22
20mm Oerlikons with 54 spare barrels	162
.5" Vickers machine guns with 52 spare barrels	384
.5" Browning complete with 120 spare barrels	240
.30" Martin	210
2" Rocket Projectors	36 sets
AAD Type L Projectors with ammunition	16 sets

Misc gun mountings	530
Mines (various)	3,206
Paravanes	318
Depth Charges	6,800
Hedgehog Projectiles	2,304
Torpedoes	361
Smoke generators, candles and Lachrymatory candles	5,124 sets
Grenade throwing eqpt	67 sets
Ammunition	
15"	2,000 rounds
6	2,400 rounds
4.7", 4.5", 4" & 3"	13,600 rounds
12pdr	31,000 rounds
2pdr	93,000 rounds
20mm	882,000 rounds
.5" Vickers	5,792,000 rounds
.5" Browning	1,399,000 rounds
.455" SA	26,000 rounds
.303" SA	359,000 rounds
.30" SA	889,000 rounds
2" Rockets	4,000 rounds
Flares & misc pyrotechnics	8,273

War Office Supplies
Vehicles
 Tanks (various) all
 supplied with
 ammunition 5,218
 MT vehicles 4,343
 Bren Carriers 2,550
 Motor Cycle 1,721
 AFV and MT spares 4,090 tons
Weapons
 PIAT projector 1,000
 Thompson SMG 103
 2pdr AT Rifle 636
 6pdr AT gun 96
 Boys AT Rifles 3,200
 Bren guns 2,487
 7.92mm Besa guns 581
 Smoke Generators 303,000
Ammunition
 PIAT 100,000 rounds
 2pdr AT gun 2,807,000 rounds
 .45" SMG 20,786,000 rounds
 6pdr AT 776,000 rounds
 Boys AT 1,761,000 rounds
 .303" SA 89,332,000 rounds
 7.92mm BESA 53,411,000 rounds
 2" Mortar (HE &
 Smoke) 1,163,000 rounds
 3" Mortar (HE &
 Smoke) 162,000 rounds
 Signal Cartridges 2,204,000
 Clams 159,000
Electronic Equipment
 Radar 1,474 sets
 Radio 4,338 sets

Valves 42,850
Misc Radio Test Eqpt 850 items
Charging &
 Generating Eqpt 160 sets
Telephone Equipment
 Telephone Cable 30,227 miles
 Telephones 2,000 sets
 Switchboards 40 line 60
 Switchboards 10 line 400
Miscellaneous Items
 Exploder Cable 1,070 miles
 Camouflage Netting 3,013,000 metres
 Camouflage Face
 Veils 1,199,500
 Surveying &
 Meteorological Eqpt 925 items
 Specialloid Pistons 159,000
 Tyres 72,000

Air Ministry Supplies
Aircraft (all types) 7,411
Aircraft Engines 976
MT Vehicles 724
Petrol, oil & other
 products 14,146 tons
Ammunition
 .303" 162,000,000 rounds
 .30 66,450,000 rounds
 .5" 24,000,000 rounds
 20mm 17,500,000 rounds
Aircraft Engines and
 MT Spares worth £15,981,000
Misc aircraft eqpt
 worth £1,734,000

Raw Materials, Foodstuffs, Machinery & Industrial Plant Supplied by the UK*

Raw Materials

Commodity	Quantity	Value
Aluminium	32,000 tons	£3,803,000
Copper	40,000 tons	£2,204,000
Industrial Diamonds	N/A	£1,424,000
Jute	100,435 tons	£4,975,000
Rubber	114,539 tons	£239,000
Graphite	3,300 ton	£160,000
Tin	28,050 tons	£7,774,000
Wool	29,610 tons	£5,521,000
Total Value of these and other Raw Materials:		£47,841,000

236

Foodstuffs
These included tea, cocoa beans, palm oil, palm kernels, groundnuts, coconut oil, pepper and spices.

Total Value of Foodstuffs supplied: £8,210,000

Machine Tools, Plant and Associated Eqpt.
Commodity	Value
Machine Tools	£13,081,000
Power Plant	£12,264,000
Electrical Eqpt	£9,091,000
Misc Eqpt (e.g.: communications, food processing, textile plant, port and salvage eqpt.	£4,691,000
Misc industrial plant	£5,201,000
Total Value of Machine Tools etc	£45,616,000

Medical Equipment, Comforts and Hospital Supplies
Surgical & Medical Items and Clothing**	£5,260,000
Clothing Grant by HMG	£2,500,000

*Source: Official Report presented to the House of Commons, 16 April 1946: *Parliamentary Debates*, Vol.421, cols 2516–19.
**Money exclusively raised by charitable donations.

Major Supplies from the United States to the USSR, 11 March 1941–1 October 1945

Item	Quantity/Value		
Aircraft (67% fighters, 26% bombers, 7% misc)	14,795	Explosives	345,735 tons
		Locomotives	1,981
		Rolling Stock	11,155 units
		Rails	540,000 tons
Tanks	7,537	Field Telephone Cable	1,050,000 miles
Jeeps	51,503	Food	$1,312,000,000
Motorcycles	35,170	Gasoline	2,670,000 tons
Tractors	8,701	Industrial Chemicals	842,000 tons
Trucks	375,883	Tyres	3,786,000
AA Guns	8,218	Leather	49,000 tons
Sub Machine Guns	131,633	Boots (pairs)	15,000,000

APPENDIX 4: A DESCRIPTION OF THE PORT FACILITIES IN NORTH RUSSIA BY SBNO NORTH RUSSIA AND DATED JUNE 1944

The following notes have been compiled for the information of those in Britain who have to work with us here in Murmansk, and for those who may be appointed to work out here.

The Kola Inlet

The Kola Inlet runs roughly north and south from 69.18N to the town (village) of Kola in 68.53N where the River Kola runs in, thereafter the inlet is known as the River Tuloma.

On the western shore and about five and a half miles inside the inlet lies Polyarnoe where the Commander in Chief of the Russian Northern Fleet has his adminstration and where the Senior British Naval Officer, North Russia is also placed. The latter is a Rear Admiral and administers Archangel, Murmansk, Polyarnoe and Vaenga and has the operational control of our warships and the JW and RA convoys to and from these waters. Eight miles by water and on the opposite shore lies Vaenga where we have an Auxiliary Hospital with beds for 74 patients and the necessary staff. A large Russian operational aerodrome is there and a pier at which destroyers and smaller craft can berth serves the village from the water. There is no power of any kind on this pier but water is laid on—not fit for drinking. Vaenga is the northern terminus of the railroad, a single track from Murmansk which only appears to be used for goods traffic for war stores; the road from Murmansk also stops there. Twelve miles down this road is Rosta, a naval repair yard with two dry docks, the larger capable of holding a 9,000 ton cruiser, the smaller a fleet destroyer, there are also an oil and coaling jetty. Four miles further south comes Murmansk

From the above it will be seen that our administrative centre and Murmansk are 16 miles by road plus eight miles by water apart or 21 miles by water. During many months of the year, for perhaps three days at a stretch, ice, snow and blizzards will render the road impassable, fog and gales in the Inlet will render the same disservice for boat traffic and a highly temperamental telephone is all that remains. There it is in the highest degree important that the correct address for stores and correspondence be used. SBNO North Russia is at Polyarnoe, SBNO Murmansk is in that delectable city and has to do with the merchant ships from convoys: many authorities still appear to be believe that both these post are the same.

Murmansk

Murmansk lies along the eastern shore of the inlet from 69N to 68.57N and from 33.03E to 33.05E. Further expansion to the east is problematical as the country is hilly and very rocky in that direction. Up until 1928 it was a small town of wooden buildings with some coastal traffic and fairly extensive fisheries. Then it was decided to expand it as the Soviet's ice-free Northern port and an ambitious building programme in brick and cement was embarked on, while the quays were added to and an adequate system of lines was laid to serve these quays by rail. The outbreak of war stopped this scheme and, in 1942, it was subjected to the most severe bombing attack then inflicted on any European city, Valletta perhaps excepted. The wooden construction of so many buildings and almost all of the quays rendered large areas of the town only too susceptible to incendiary attack, while the unreliability of cement under arctic conditions produced unhappy results in the larger buildings. Throughout the summer of 1942 the town continued to smoulder and by the end, almost all the Northern half of the town had gone, while a considerable part of the remainder was heavily damaged: at a rough estimate in June 1944, one third has been entirely demolished, one third is not fit for habitation and not one single building has a half of its full complement of glass. Repairs and a little new building have been started recently.

Quite recently two provision shops have blossomed out ito the most appetising windows displaying hams, sausages and fish, made of wood. They avoid the charge of acquiring one's roubles under false pretences by having nothing on sale within whatever. Later on the individual citizen may dispose of his surplus vegetables there, otherwise they are merely two of the food centres where the Comrades may draw their daily rations. Otherwise the only things to draw one's eye are crude war posters. The social life appears to be confined to clubs, in Murmansk there are four, one army, two navy and an international sailors' club. Only the latter has made the slightest attempt at extending hospitality to the British and American missions here and, during convoys, it is rather a place to be avoided. We lend films for showing there and that is the only evening amusement except that, at times, the films are followed by a dance.

Recreations are very few. In winter there is ski-ing and it is good fun from February until the middle of April but the country does not lend itself to real running, the Russians chiefly confine themselves to cross-country work and, at the beginning of April, held a northern winter sports meeting at which 5,7 and 10 kilometre races for men and women were held.

Occasional travelling concert parties of the ENSA type, and equally mediocre, visit a hall in one of the clubs and charge one an extortionate number of roubles for a very hard seat. Once the snow is off the low lying land, about the first half of June, football starts. Our own experience has been that the games are well conducted, the men are fit but not very expert, though that may only be so at the start of the season, and the crowd is friendly to British sides.

Sporadic gardening, strictly utilitarian, is also in evidence, but its outward appearance would shame any Village Allotment committee out of business in Britain. It appears that the state provides the seeds or seedlings and demands a third or less of the crop, depending on the type of seed provided, ie potatoes or seedlings – one third, but seeds – less. For the information of ships visiting here, it shoud be noted that the Russian audiences at any entertainment – football, concert or film, are very well behaved, enthusiastic and critical, though the small-boy element at football matches can be excluded from the first category.

General Conditions

From 3rd December until 19th January the sun does not rise above the horizon, so from 3 to 5 hours twilight around midday are little help to working conditions. The opposite obtains from 3rd June to 19th July and print can be read in the open at any hour of the day from the end of April until late in August.

In winter the snow and Northern Lights prevent absolute darkness except during blizzards, which have been rare in the winter of 1943/44 and snow squalls. The lowest observed day temperature was −10F, with the night temperature 15 degrees or more lower. In still weather this temperature is not really troublesome to those who are well-nourished and adequately clothed, with wind accompanying these temperatures one feels it on ears and face, though walking will keep the rest of one's body quite warm. Snow continues to fall until some time in June and will start again at the end of August or early in September. A general thaw set in about mid-April 1944, low lying snow had gone by the end of May, but patches still lie on the hills at the time of writing, the end of June. The main inlet remains ice-free though bays and spaces between the quays become frozen over, however the rise and fall of the tide and the constant movements of shipping prevent this ice becoming thick enough to be troublesome.

239

In trying to picture the working of this Port by British eyes, the above conditions must constantly be borne in mind, other factors which materially affect a true estimate are that the artificial light necessary to work cargoes for months of the year must obviously be kept at a minimum with the front a bare 30 miles away and are subject to constant interruptions for Air Alerts.

Steam machinery must be constantly watched and warmed or it will become frozen up and the same applies to all mechanical vehicles. Roads become filled with powdery snow, constantly churned up, which yet acquires sufficient solidity between the wheel tracks to suspend a vehicle from its under-carriage leaving the wheels air borne. Constant snow falls bury items of cargo feet deep on the quays and these can quite easily disappear until the thaw. Gloves can only be discarded for short spells, so that such simple operations as screwing a shackle through a cargo sling or passing a wire strop will take a vast time and will probably be inefficiently done.

Interpreters, of whom there are never enough, are girls from the Technical College in Moscow and the simplest nautical terms are a sealed book to them. Russia possesses no race of seamen. Authorities in the dock are usually drawn from civil engineers. As an example, the Chief Dock Pilot, wearing the uniform of a Lieutenant Commander of the Reserve, asked the writer whether the Duke of York, then in the Inlet, was a destroyer!

Authorities (a) Town

The military side of life in Murmansk, which means nine tenths of its existence, is administered by an Engineer Rear Admiral who is also Admiral Superintendant to the Northern Fleet based on Polyarnoe. In the last resort he can galvanise any department into activitiy though his staff is prone to 'pass the baby'.

The Diplomatic Representative is the link between the Foreign Missions and the Russian Departments and can be most helpful, or the reverse. Entry and exit visas on passports, many types of local permits and similar snags, are, or can be, dealt with by him.

The Commissar of Militzia—relative rank of Major-General—is in charge of that Force, ie: Police, this latter name having been changed owing to unhappy associations in the peoples' minds. He can be of real help in connection with obstreperous seamen ashore, driving offences and so on.

The Mayor has to do with town accommodation, though the majority now comes under one or other of the services.

Intourist-Manager. Hotel for travellers, victualling of Foreign Missions, railway tickets and seat reservations, domestic staff for the Missions and can provide an excellent meal if a dinner party becomes necessary.

(b) Port

The general work of discharging cargoes and the supply of return cargoes is under the control of the Representative of the Department of Foreign Trade. Our Shipping Officers have maintained a close liaison with this official and that is an absolute essential requirement to efficient work.

The Manager of the Port is the executive in the Port and is assisted by despatchers who berth ships and arrange rail movements and dock pilots.

Customs are much the same as in other ports though a quite amazing number of permits are needed to bring one box of bacon from a ship to the Mission or to a railway waggon for onward despatch. A close liaison and much patience with the determination not to attempt to smuggle or bounce them, have produced reasonably happy relations and satisfactory results.

'Inflot' are the Ships' Representatives and carry out all the domestic necessities for ships in foreign ports.

The Frontier Guard supply sentries on the dock gates for the control of personnel and cargo entering and leaving the port and at the ships' gangways. Either they, or the Northern Fleet or the Army, depending on the locality, also supply the guards at the road barriers which exist in considerable profusion on Murmansk's two roads, to the north and the south.

The Convoy Captain arranges ships' anchor berths in the Inlet on arrival and before sailing in convoy and provides Pilots for movements in the Inlet, this is done by officers from the Northern Fleet. Except when convoys are moving he works from Polyarnoe.

The Port of Murmansk

The port consists of a number of woden quays along most of the water frontage of the town.

Sudno Verf (Ship Wharf): This quay is situated at the southern extemity of the port area. Mainly used for repairing small naval vessels ad submarines. The quay is of wood and in a very dilapidated condition. Wooden bollards (in number 12) are used for securing vessels. The quay is served by a single track line of rails from which three loop lines run to connect up with repair shops situated close by.

No facilities for storage of cargo. No cranes on this quay. Fresh water is laid on.

Approach to the quay is bad owing to the close proximity of a Reef and great care has to be taken when berthing. There are six slips suitable for Trawlers and 'Coastal' type submarines in the area of which the Sudno Verf forms the quay wall. The area is completely fenced off and served by a single track railway line.

Used for the first time by merchant ships other than of Soviet nationality during the convoy season of 1943/44. For ballasting sand and timber supplied direct from trucks. Two merchant ships, one LIBERTY type and one EMPIRE type have been berthed at the one time at the quay, occupying the extreme southern end. The crane ships EMPIRE BARD, EMPIRE ELGAR and LAPLAND have also used this berth for discharging.

To date it has not been possible to obtain entrance to any of the repair shops in this area and repair facilities can only be guessed at, but judging from the dismantled state of submarines seen at various times along the jetty, it can be assumed that considerable facilities exist for almost all types of regular work. This area has suffered very little from bomb damage.

Fish Quay: This area is situated between the Sudno Verf and the Cabotajnee quay. Wooden construction throughout. Berths for two vessels. No bollards mooring chains and rings. Two lines of rails serve the quay. On part of the north side of the quay the flooring slopes upwards and permits cargo being easily handled into Trucks or Flat cars, which are cleared by a single track railway. One large warehouse, in a good state of repair, is situated along the shore end berth. There is a coal elevator built on to the end of this warehouse but it is in a very dilapidated condition. The elevator has been used once or twice this season for bunkering Russian trawlers. Fresh water is available from the quay. There is a coaling berth suitable for small coastal type vessels of shallow draft situated at the extreme shore end of the quay.

Cabotajnee Quay (Coasting Quay): This quay is situted between the Fish Quay and the War Port. Of wooden construction throughout with five wooden bollards, permits of one vessel of LIBERTY, OCEAN or EMPIRE type. No railway lines serve the quay, there are no cranes and no warehouses for the storage of cargo. The area surrounding the quay has been badly damaged by bombing, but is very suitable for dumping cargo. Clearance from this area can be effected in winter by use of sledges and this method was successfuly used in the 1943/44 Convoy Season. So far as is known the season just ended saw the use of this quay for the first time by British and USA merchant vessels.

Commercial Port

Railway lines serving this area:

     5 lines from the Main Port
     1 line from the Timber Quay
     1 line from the War Port Area

It should be noted that all railway lines serving the various quays in the Commercial Port area eventually merge into the five lines referred to above, and these lines then pass through a narrow bottleneck at the entrance to the port. Clearance of cargo by rail from the area is therefore easily disrupted.

War Port

Although this area is included under the heading COMMERCIAL PORT no merchant vessels are able to discharge at the quay, which can only accommodate one medium sized tug or similar craft, and various small boats used by the Russian Northern Fleet.

The Commericial Port of Murmansk has suffered heavy damage as the result of bombing, with the result that little in the way of warehouse storage now exists. There is one large shed (referred to as Shed 47) situated alongside berths 10 and 11, a small shed situated at Berth 7, and a medium sized shed situated in the angle formed by berths 3 and 4. All cargo which cannot be accommodated in the sheds mentioned above, must of necessity be dumped on the quays, and when possible covered with tarpaulins against weather.

Berths 1 & 2

Rails serving the quay 3 in number, plus 2 outer lines. This area is timbered and in good repair (result of work by the Port Authority during summer 1943). No iron bollards, vessels moor with wire strops. No cranes. Fresh water laid on. It should be noted that the area lying between berths 1,2,3,4 & 5 is the largest 'timber floored' area in the port.

Berth 3

This is only used as a 'lightening' berth. It is not served by rail; no cranes available; fresh water is laid on. This quay is in a bad state of repair.

Berths 4 & 5

Rails serving quay, 4 in number. Ring bolts for mooring, plus four wooden bollards faced with iron. Despatcher's Office opposite berth 4, and the shed (medium sized) referred to in the port notes is also adjacent. Fresh water is laid on. No cranes. Air Raid shelter opposite berth 4.

     Length of quays about 900 feet.

Berths 6 & 7

Rails serving quays, 3 in number. No bollards, 7 or 8 mooring rings. No cranes. Fresh water laid on. Shed opposite berth 7 in a fair state of repair. Large Air Raid shelter opposite berth 6. Length of quays about 900 feet.

Berth 8

This quay is very badly damaged. Chiefly used for bunkering: a conveyer is fitted for this purpose. No rails or cranes serve this berth. Fresh water is not available. There is considerable storage available for coal in the area of this quay, but in the Convoy Season it is chiefly occupied by cargo awaiting removal from the docks.

Berths 9, 10 & 11

Rails serving quays, 2 in number plus three outer lines serving berths 9 and 10. Berths 10 and 11 faced with concrete. Bollards 10 (iron), 3 (wood-iron faced). Quays are timber floored, in a fair state of repair. One electric travelling 'Luffing' crane, believed capable of lifting up to 11 tons. Fresh water is laid on. 1 large shed (concrete) No. 47 opposite berths 10 and 11. Air Raid shelter adjacent to Berth 11.

Note: Berth 9, which was previously known to be a foul berth (cement faced quay blown into the water by bombing) may now be clear. Divers have been working at this berth recently and a large block of concrete was noted being raised. This may well have caused the damage sustained by EMPIRE CELIA to her bilge keel. The entrance to these berths is bad being served by a narrow channel in which vessels find it impossible to turn round.

Timber Quay Berths 12, 13 & 14

Accommodates two merchant ships. Can also accommodate, at shore end of quays, several tugs and motor boats. Quays constructed of timber, covered in some places with sand and stone. Condition of quay 'good'. Fresh water laid on. One main railway line serves the area. No bollards, 9 mooring rings. There are six lines of rails within this area, of which three directly serve the quays. No storage sheds. Length of quays about 1,000 feet.

Cranes	Dockside	3, 3, 6 and 5 tons.
	Shoreside	2, 5 and 8 tons.

Cranes are English construction and were brought to Murmansk from Archangel in the summer of 1943 by EMPIRE BARD and EMPIRE ELGAR.

Shore end of quay dries out at low water. Reef in close proximity to berth 12.

Considerable quantities of cargo can be stowed on the quays, and can easily handled by the cranes which run on rails. Despatcher's office on quay.

Large Air Raid shelter serving all these berths.

The Chief Despatcher's Office for the Port of Murmansk is situated close to the entrance to the Timber Quay.

It is believed that a connection for an oil pipleine is in existence at the shore end of the this quay. A pipeline runs from underground storage tanks situated on the shore road from Murmansk to Rosta, and appears to terminate at the shore end of the Timber Quay. There have been no signs to date of the coastal tankers UKAGIR and JELIABOV either discharging or loading at this quay.

Rosta

Comprised of the following, Bunkering quays, Berth 15, Artillery Quay, Oil Jetty, Dry-docks and Repair Shops.

All this area is controlled by the Northern Fleet, with the exception of Berth 15 which is under the jurisdiction of Murmansk Port Authority.

Bunkering Quays

Capable of taking two vessels at one time for bunkering viz, FORT VERCHERES and EMPIRE PROWESS. Several small electrically driven conveyer belts are available. The quay side is not served by railway lines. Ample storage accommodation for coal available. No cranes on quay.

Fresh water is not available at this quay, but if necessary can be obtained by water boat.

Signal tower at south end of quay.

Coal is conveyed to this area by a single track line from the Marshalling Yards at Murmansk, and then to the ships' side by conveyer belting or small tubs running on rails.

Berth 15

Used originally for discharging ammunition and explosives from merchant ships, prior to them proceeding to Murmansk to discharge remainder of cargo. It was also used for loading Apatite. Offers berthage for one vessel. Fresh water is not available from quay. Quay is served by two railway lines.

Last season a shed existed at this quay for storage of Apatite, but this has now been removed and workmen have been busy in this area, but purpose of work is unknown.

During the 1943/44 Convoy Season, this quay was used for ballasting with sand.

Artillery Quay, Rosta

A small jetty used exclusively by the Red Army for loading small vessels with ammunition etc, for transfer to the Mishukov shore en route for the Northern Front. Does not offer suitable berthage for a merchant ship. No cranes on quay when last visited (1943) and no opportunity has occurred this season to note if any changes have taken place.

Field guns in considerable numbers are often stored in the area adjacent to this jetty which is patrolled by Red Army sentries and not by the usual Frontier Guard.

Oil Jetty, Rosta

Used solely for discharging Fuel Oil. (No 'spirit' tanker has used the quay since 1942.) Offers berthage for one 10,000 ton tanker. Fresh water is laid on at quay.

Dry docks and Repair Shops, Rosta

A map of this area and detailed report of all machinery installed in the shops, sizes of dry docks etc, was forwarded to MWT in 1943, a copy of which was made available for NID at the same time.

Section B

The Inlet has 45 numbered anchor berths, and though the great depths found in it preclude many more from being used, 121 ships were berthed between the arrival of JW.57 and the departure of RA.59. Thirteen destroyers were berthed alongside at Polyarnoe and Vaenga, 12 dry cargo ships were berthed at Murmansk, 28 laden and 40 light fry cargo ships and two light and 3 laden tankers were in anchor berths with the rest of the escorting war-vessels, mostly in Vaenga Bay, though a few of these similar craft were secured alongside cruisers and escort carriers.

During the Convoy Season 4 signal stations alongside the Inlet are manned by our signalmen, at Polyarnoe, Vaenga, Manukov Point and Murmansk. Communication with merchant ships at anchor is not rapid but can be effected in course of time. In the 6 winter months navigation into and within the inlet is frequently handicapped by a local and low lying fog. Severe gales are not too frequent, only two of sufficient severity to cause ships to drag their anchors being recalled in the winter of 1943–44.

APPENDIX 5: FLEET AIR ARM AND ROYAL AIR FORCE ATTACKS ON TIRPITZ IN NORTH NORWAY, JANUARY 1942–NOVEMBER 1944.

Date	Force	Aircraft	Location	Results	A/C lost
28/29 Jan 42	RAF	9 Halifax + 7 Stirling	Aasfjord	Nil	0
9 Mar 42	FAA[1]	12 Albacore	At sea	Nil	2
30/31 Mar 42	RAF	33 Halifax	Fottenfjord	Nil	5
27/28 Apr 42	RAF	31 Halifax + 12 Lancaster	Fottenfjord	Nil	5
28/29 Apr 42	RAF	23 Halifax	Fottenfjord	Nil	2
3 Apr 44	FAA[2]	40 Barracuda + 21 Corsair + 20 Hellcat + 40 Wildcat	Altenfjord	14 hits, 1 near-miss	4
24 Apr 44	FAA[3]	Cancelled owing to bad weather			
15 May 44	FAA[4]	Abandoned owing to dense low cloud over coast			
28 May 44	FAA[5]	Cancelled owing to bad weather			
17 Jul 44	FAA[6]	44 Barracuda + 18 Corsair + 12 Firefly + 18 Hellcat	Altenfjord	Nil	2
22 Aug 44 (a.m.)	FAA[7]	31 Barracuda + 10 Hellcat + 11 Firefly + 24 Corsair + 8 Seafire	Altenfjord	Nil	3
24 Aug 44 (p.m.)	FAA[8]	6 Hellcat	Altenfjord	Nil	0
24 Aug 44	FAA[9]	33 Barracuda + 10 Hellcat + 24 Corsair + 10 Firefly	Altenfjord	2 hits	6
29 Aug 44	FAA[10]	26 Barracuda + 17 Corsair + 7 Hellcat + 10 Firefly + 7 Seafire	Altenfjord	Nil	2
15 Sep 44	RAF	28 Lancaster	Altenfjord	1 hit[11]	0
29 Oct 44	RAF	38 Lancaster	Tromsø	Nil	1
12 Nov 44	RAF	32 Lancaster	Tromsø	3 hits, 2 near-misses[12]	0

[1]*Victorious*
[2]*Victorious, Furious, Searcher, Emperor, Pursuer, Fencer*
[3]*Victorious, Furious, Searcher, Emperor, Pursuer, Striker*
[4]*Victorious, Furious*
[5]*Victorious, Furious*
[6]*Formidable, Furious, Indefatigable*

[7]*Formidable, Furious, Indefatigable. Nabob. Trumpeter*
[8]*Indefatigable*
[9]*Indefatigable, Furious, Formidable*
[10]*Indefatigable, Formidable*
[11]12,000lb bomb
[12]*Tirpitz* was sunk as a result of this attack

Bibliography

Admiralty: 'Battle Summary No 22: Arctic Convoys 1941–45 (1954)
————: 'Battle Summary No 29: The Attack on the Tirpitz by Midget Submarines
 (Operation Source), 22 September 1943 (1948)
Barnett, C., *Engage the Enemy More Closely*, Hodder and Stoughton (London, 1992).
Bassett, Roland, *HMS Sheffield: The Life and Times of 'Old Shiny'*, Arms & Armour Press
 (London 1988)
Beaumont, Joan, *Comrades in Arms: British Aid to Russia 1941–45*, Davis Poynter (London,
 1988)
Broome, Capt J., *Convoy is to Scatter*, William Kimber (London, 1972)
Calder, Angus, *The Peoples' War*, Panther Books (1971)
Campbell, Vice-Admiral Sir Ian, and MacIntyre, Capt Donald, *The Kola Run: A Record of
 the Arctic Convoys 1941–45*, Frederick Muller (1958)
Churchill, Winston, *The Second World War*, Cassell & Co (1948–53)
Compton-Hall, Cdr Richard, *The Underwater War*, Blandford Books (1982)
Connell, G. G., *Arctic Destroyers: The 17th Flotilla*, William Kimber (1982)
Coulter, Surgeon Capt J. L. S., *The Royal Naval Medical Service. Vol 2: Operations*, HMSO
 (London, 1956)
Dönitz, Karl, *Ten Years and Twenty Days*, Greenhill Books (London, 1990)
Gilbert, Martin, *Road to Victory: Winston Churchill 1941–45*, Heinemann (London, 1986)
————, *Churchill: A Life*, Heinemann (London, 1991)
Hague, A., and Ruegg, B., *Convoys to Russia 1941–45*, World Ship Society (1992)
Herman, Fred, *Dynamite Cargo: Convoy to Russia*, Cassell & Co (London,1943)
Hinsley F., *British Intelligence in the Second World War*, HMSO (London, 1981)
Holman Gordon, *The King's Cruisers*, Hodder & Stoughton (London, 1947)
Humble, Richard, *Fraser of North Cape: The Life of Admiral of the Fleet Lord Fraser
 (1888–1981)*, Routledge & Kegan Paul (1983)
Jones, Robert Huhn, *The Roads to Russia: United States Lend-Lease to the Soviet Union*,
 University of Oklahoma (1969)
Irving, D., *The Destruction of Convoy PQ.17*, William Kimber (London, 1980)
Lewis, Michael, *The History of the British Navy*, George Allen & Unwin (1957)
Ludlam, Harry, and Lund, Paul, *PQ.17 Convoy to Hell: The Survivors' Story*, W. Foulsham
 & Co (London, 1968)
Morrison, John and Annie, *Lewis and Harris Seamen 1939–45*, Stornoway Gazette
 Publications (1993)
Ogden, Graeme, *My Sea Lady*, Hutchinson (1963)
Padfield, Peter, *Dönitz: The Last Führer*, Gollancz (London, 1984)
Pawlowicz, B., *ORP Garland in Convoy to Russia*, Surrey Press (1943)
Solzhenitsen, Alexander, *The First Circle*, Collins/Fontana Books (1970)
Taylor, A. J. P., *Europe: Grandeur and Decline*, Penguin Books (London, 1974)

Vian, Admiral of the Fleet Sir Philip, *Action this Day*, Frederick Muller (London, 1960)
Werth, Alexander, *The Year of Stalingrad*, Hamish Hamilton (1946)
Winton, John, *Death of the Scharnhorst*, Anthony Bird Publications (1983)

Index